Seventh Edition

Red, White, and Black

The Peoples of Early North America

Gary B. Nash

University of California, Los Angeles

Boston Columbus Indianapolis New York San Francisco Upper Saddle River
Amsterdam Cape Town Dubai London Madrid Milan Munich Paris Montréal Toronto
Delhi Mexico City São Paulo Sydney Hong Kong Seoul Singapore Taipei Tokyo

Editor in Chief: Ashley Dodge
Editorial Assistant: Stephanie Ruland
Marketing Coordinator: Jessica Warren
Managing Editor: Denise Forlow
Program Manager: Carly Czech
Project Manager: Bonnie Boehme, Cenveo
  Publisher Services
Senior Operations Supervisor: Mary Fischer
Operations Specialist: Mary Ann Gloriande
Art Director: Maria Lange

Cover Designer: PreMediaGlobal, Inc.
Cover Image: Library of Congress Prints and Photographs
  Division [LC-USZ62-104]
Digital Media Project Manager: Tina Gagliostro
**Full-Service Project Management and
  Composition:** Raghavi Khullar, Cenveo
  Publisher Services
Printer/Binder: RR Donnelley / STP Harrisonburg N
Cover Printer: RR Donnelley / STP Harrisonburg N
Text Font: Sabon LT Std

Credits and acknowledgments borrowed from other sources and reproduced, with permission, in this textbook appear on appropriate page within text.

Many of the designations by manufacturers and seller to distinguish their products are claimed as trademarks. Where those designations appear in this book, and the publisher was aware of a trademark claim, the designations have been printed in initial caps or all caps.

Library of Congress Cataloging-in-Publication Data
Nash, Gary B.
  Red, white, and black : the peoples of early North America / Gary B.
Nash, University of California, Los Angeles. —Seventh edition.
    pages cm
  Includes bibliographical references and index.
  ISBN 978-0-205-88759-0 — ISBN 0-205-88759-7 1. United
States—History—Colonial period, ca. 1600-1775. 2.
America—Discovery and exploration. 3. United States—Race relations.
I. Title.
  E188.N37 2014
  973.2—dc23

                                    2014009616

10 9 8 7 6 5 4 3 2 1

ISBN 10:   0-205-88759-7
ISBN 13:   978-0-205-88759-0

CONTENTS

PREFACE

The pages that follow began to take form in my mind several decades ago when I participated in redesigning the introductory course in American history at the University of California, Los Angeles. This effort was directed at making American history more understandable to an ethnically, a socially, and an intellectually diverse undergraduate audience by studying it as the process of change that occurred when people of widely varying cultural backgrounds interacted over a period of four centuries. Although this does not sound like a startling innovation, I discovered that it required me to read broadly in areas that had largely escaped my notice during fifteen years of studying and teaching colonial American history—anthropology, ethnohistory, African history, and Latin American history. To say that they "escaped my notice" is to put the point obliquely, for one of the thrusts of this book is that we read, think, and write selectively and in ways that reflect our cultural biases. Nothing more than changing my "angle of vision" was required to make it apparent that early American history and the early history of the American peoples were two different subjects and that the latter was comprehensible only by vastly widening the scope of my reading and thinking about the subject.

In revising *Red, White, and Black* for this seventh edition, I am indebted to reviewers of the sixth edition, whose comments and suggestions have helped me make important changes, I gratefully acknowledge. The explosion of scholarly work in early American history, especially on the roles and experiences of Native Americans and African Americans, has required me to rethink and rewrite many passages in the chapters that follow. One could not have imagined a few decades ago how much it has been possible to learn about the interaction of the diverse peoples who encountered each other in North America in the sixteenth, seventeenth, and eighteenth centuries. History is a never-ending search for a durable rendition of the past, and this edition owes a debt especially to the young historians who are contributing so much to the vibrancy of the colonial and revolutionary eras of the American past. This continuing quest for a more inclusive and nuanced history is reflected in the revisions to the chapters and in the Further Reading at the end of each chapter.

What's New in This edition?

In this edition of *Red, White, and Black*, I have made many changes to keep abreast of the latest scholarship on African American and Native American history. The extraordinary interest in these two subfields of early American history continues to flourish, adding richness and subtlety to what was known only sketchily not so many years ago.

- New archaeological studies, combined with DNA analysis, continue to refine what we know about the timing and sources of the first migration of people from Asia to the Americas thousands of years ago, helping me bring Chapter 1 up to date on this fascinating case of humans in search of new lands.
- In Chapters 1 and 2 I have also fleshed out how climate change, from about 900 A.D. through the late 1400s when Europeans first reached the Americas, helps us

understand the rise and collapse of some early indigenous societies in North America while facilitating the advent of the agricultural revolution that swept over most parts of the Americas.

- Likewise, in these first two chapters, readers will learn more than in previous editions about how European pandemic diseases staggered Native societies while paving the way for European colonization. How the vectors of disease affected Native peoples in their engagement with European colonizers also figures in revisions in later chapters.

- Recent studies of almost every Indian society in North America has added immensely to our understanding of the complex interactions—economic, political, and cultural—between Native peoples and colonizing Europeans from the late sixteenth to early nineteenth centuries. This has allowed me to add new information and refine the analyses in Chapters 3, 4, 5, 9, and 10. Many of these new studies are included in Further Reading at the end of each chapter.

- Of great importance in revising Chapters 6 and 7 is the publication of the *Atlas of the Transatlantic Slave Trade* (2010). In essays that capture a wealth of new scholarship and in a magnificent array of maps and charts that graphically display the analysis of some 27,000 slave voyages, we now have at hand important new information on every aspect of the slave trade, from the changing participation of various European maritime nations to the ages and gender of people captured in different parts of West and Central Africa, to their destinations in the Americas, to mutinies on slave ships, and much more. Especially of note is how this astounding bank of data puts the relatively small flow of captive Africans to the British American colonies in an Atlantic-wide context. New scholarship in African history has also allowed me to give greater texture to the experience of enslaved Africans in the Americas and also their cultural contributions to the lifeways of the European colonizers.

- Women's history is another sector of abundant new scholarship, and here too I have stitched new insights and research results into the narrative, as well as adding important new works of scholarship to the Further Reading section.

- In Chapter 11 readers will find a considerable expansion of how African Americans and Native Americans figured in the epochal upheaval, as it related both to the war for independence with England and to the internal struggle to revitalize and reform the old colonial order. I hope students will find much to ponder in the enlarged discussion of how revolutionary agendas for change necessarily broached the abolition of slavery in a new nation dedicated to "unalienable rights" and grappled with the fraught question of how Native people would be included in, or excluded from, the democratically conceived new republic.

- In Chapter 12 I have drawn upon a ballooning number of DNA analyses that show a degree of racial boundary crossing never imagined by historians and other social science scholars. It is becoming clear through this probing of the human genome that many decades of denying racial intermingling and even erasing examples of it from the historical record have stood in the way of appreciating how the strenuous efforts of white legislators and cultural leaders were never able to patrol the racial boundaries as effectively as they wished.

- A final new feature of this edition is the addition to each chapter of Learning Objectives, Summary, and Critical Thinking Questions.

INTRODUCTION

"God is English." Thus John Aylmer, a pious English clergyman, exhorted his parishioners in 1558, attempting to fill them with piety and patriotism.[1] That thought, though never stated so directly, has echoed ever since through our history books. As school children, as college students, and as presumably informed citizens, most of us have been brought up on what has passed for the greatest success story of human history, the epic tale of how a proud, brave offshoot of the English-speaking people tried to reverse the laws of history by demonstrating what the human spirit, liberated from the shackles of tradition, myth, and oppressive authority, could do in a newly discovered corner of the earth. For most Americans, colonial history begins with Sir Walter Ralegh and John Smith, and proceeds through William Bradford and John Winthrop to Jonathan Edwards and Benjamin Franklin. It ends with the Revolution, during which wilderness-conquering settlers pitted themselves against a mother country that had grown tyrannical and won their independence against the odds.

This is ethnocentric history, as has been charged frequently and vociferously in recent decades, both by revisionist white historians and by those whose citizenship is American but whose ancestral roots are in Africa, Asia, Mexico, or the native cultures of North America. Just as Eurocentrism made it difficult for the early colonizers and explorers to believe that a continental land mass as large as North America could exist in the oceans between Europe and Asia, historians in this country have found it difficult to understand that the colonial period of our history is the story of a minority of English colonizers interacting with a majority of Iroquois, Delawares, Narragansetts, Pequots, Mahicans, Catawbas, Tuscaroras, Creeks, Cherokees, Choctaws, Ibos, Mandingos, Fulas, Yorubas, Ashantis, Germans, French, Spaniards, Swedes, Welsh, and Scots-Irish, to mention only some of the cultural strains present on the continent.

In recent years, American historians have provided correctives to white-oriented, male-dominated, hero-worshipping history. At first, they devoted their efforts to restocking the pantheon of national heroes with new figures whose skin is not so pale. Pedestals, for example, were erected for Crispus Attucks, the half-Wampanoag, half-black fisherman of Boston who fell first at the Boston massacre; for Ely Parker, the Seneca general who helped the North win the Civil War and later served his friend, Ulysses Grant, when the latter attained the presidency; and for Cesar Chávez, the leader of the United Farm Workers, who brought major wage benefits and working conditions to the agricultural workers in this country.

Historical revisionism often begins in this tentative way, turning a monochromatic cast of characters into a polychromatic one with the story line unchanged. More than forty years ago, Vine Deloria, Jr., an outspoken Indian leader, charged that much of the "new" history "takes a basic 'manifest destiny' white interpretation of history and lovingly plugs a few feathers, woolly heads, and sombreros into the famous events of American history."[2] But historians have moved beyond this crude form of multicultural history.

---

[1]Quoted in Carl Bridenbaugh, *Vexed and Troubled Englishmen, 1590–1642* (New York, 1968), p. 13.
[2]Vine Deloria, Jr., *We Talk, You Listen: New Tribes, New Turf* (New York, 1970), p. 39.

When first drafting this book in 1972, I took Deloria's criticism to heart, believing that a fuller and deeper understanding of the colonial underpinnings of American history must examine the interaction of many peoples, at all levels of society, from a wide range of cultural backgrounds over a period of several centuries. For the colonial and Revolutionary period, this means exploring not only how the English and other Europeans "discovered" North America and transplanted their cultures there, but also how societies that had been in North America and Africa for thousands of years were actively and intimately involved in the process of forging a new, multistranded culture in what would become the United States. Africans were not merely enslaved. Native Americans were not merely driven from the land. As Ralph Ellison, the African American writer, has reasoned: "Can a people . . . live and develop for over three hundred years by simply *reacting*? Are American Negroes simply the creation of white men, or have they at least helped to create themselves out of what they found around them?"[3] To include Africans and Indians in our history in this way, simply as victims of the more powerful Europeans, is hardly better than excluding them altogether. Rather, it renders voiceless, nameless, and faceless people who powerfully affected the course of our historical development as a society and as a nation.

Breaking through the notion of Indians and Africans being kneaded like dough according to the whims of the invading Europeans was one of the main goals of this book from the start. During the last four decades, as I have revised this book for new editions, a host of resourceful and talented archaeologists, anthropologists, climatologists, evolutionary biologists, linguists, and historians have provided rich studies that add depth and complexity to this initial formulation. A body of historical literature now shows irrefutably how Africans and Native Americans were critically important participants in the making of American history. Wherever has fallen the focus of these scholarly inquiries—the French penetration of the Great Lakes region, the Spanish occupation of Florida and New Mexico, the English interaction with the Iroquois or Catawba, the English enslavement of Africans in South Carolina, Virginia, Barbados, and Jamaica—a consistent picture has emerged of the complex, intercultural birthing of the "New World." It was a new world for conquerors and conquered alike. It is the story of transformation for all involved, regardless of enormous inequalities in status and power, where European and Native worlds blurred at the edges of contact and merged at the heart of colonial existence, where Africans and Europeans made a new world together.

Every historian and anthropologist engaged in breaking old molds in the service of a more faithful recounting of how North American societies emerged has had to abandon the old master narrative of "primitive" and "civilized" peoples careening toward each other after 1492 on a collision course, surely one of the greatest cultural engagements of human history. Much utility still remains in pointing out differences in technological levels—for example, the Europeans' ability to navigate across the Atlantic and to process iron and thereby to manufacture guns and sharp-edged tools. But placing too much emphasis on technological advancement creates a mental trap in which Europeans are imagined as the principal agents of history, the African and Native peoples as the passive victims, and the outcomes as seemingly inevitable. Inevitability is a

---

[3]Ralph Ellison, *Shadow and Act* (New York, 1964), p. 301.

victor's story, one that robs history of its contingency and unexpected outcomes. This book presents historical outcomes as part of a tangled and an unpredictable human process where little is inexorable or foreordained.

Africans, Indians, and Europeans all developed various societies that functioned, for better or worse, in their respective environments. None thought of themselves as inferior people. "Savages we call them," wrote Benjamin Franklin more than two centuries ago, "because their manners differ from ours, which we think the perfection of civility; they think the same of theirs."[4] To imagine Indians simply as victims of European aggression is to bury from sight the rich and instructive story of how people who came to be known as Narragansetts, Iroquois, Choctaws, Cherokees, Creeks, and many others, which had been forming and changing for centuries before Europeans touched foot on the continent, responded creatively and powerfully to the newcomers from across the ocean. In this way, the Native people reshaped themselves while reshaping the course of European settlement.

This book adopts a cultural approach to our early history. It looks at the landmass we know as "North America" as a place where a number of different societies converged during a particular period of history—between about 1550 and 1790, to use the European system of measuring time. In the most general terms, we can define these cultural groups as Indian, African, and European, though, as we will see, this oversimplification is itself a Eurocentric device for classifying cultures. In other words, this book is not about early American history as usually defined—as the English colonization of thirteen colonies along the continent's eastern seaboard—but about the history of the *peoples* of North America during the two centuries leading toward the American Revolution.

Each of these three cultural groups was exceedingly diverse. In their cultural characteristics, Iroquois were as different from Natchez as English from Egyptians; Hausas and Yorubas were as distinct as Pequots and Creeks. Nor did the subgroups in each of these cultural blocs act in concert. The French, English, Dutch, and Spanish fought wars with each other, contending for power and advantage in the seventeenth and eighteenth centuries, just as Hurons and Iroquois or Creeks and Cherokees sought the upper hand in their respective regions. Our task is to discover what happened when peoples from different continents, diverse among themselves, came into contact with each other at particular points in history. Social and cultural *process* and *change* are of primary concern: how societies were affected and how their destinies changed by the experience of engagement with other societies. Anthropologists call this process "transculturation"; historians call it "social change." Whatever the terms, this book explores a dynamic process of interaction that shaped the history of American Indians, Europeans, and Africans in North America in the seventeenth and eighteenth centuries.

It is important to consider that when scholars speak of "cultural groups" or "societies," they are referring to abstractions. A *society* is a group of people organized together so that their needs—the sustaining of life at the most basic level—can be met. *Culture* is a broad term that embraces all the specific characteristics of a society as they are functionally related to each other—technology; modes of dress and diet; economic, social, and political organization; religion; language; art; values; methods of child-rearing; and so forth. Simply stated, "culture" means a way of life, the framework

---

[4]"Remarks Concerning the Savages of North America" (1784), in Albert H. Smyth, ed., *The Writings of Benjamin Franklin* (New York, 1907), X: 97.

within which any group of people—a society—comprehends the world around it. But "culture" and "society" are also terms that imply standards or norms of behavior. This is what is meant by "cultural traits" or "group behavior."

Employing such terms runs the danger of losing sight of the individual human beings, none of them exactly alike, who make up a society. Culture is a mental construct that scholars employ for the sake of convenience, so that highly varied and complex individual behavior can be broadly classified and compared. Because we are Americans, belonging to the same nation, speaking (or learning to speak) the same language, living under the same laws, participating in the same economic and political system, does not mean that we are all alike. Otherwise there would be no generation gap, no differences in aesthetic taste, no gendered values, no racial tension, and no political conflict. Nonetheless, taken collectively, Americans typically organize their lives differently than do people in other parts of the world. Although we must be aware of the problems of a cultural approach to history, it at least provides a way of understanding the interaction of the great mass of individuals of widely varying backgrounds who found themselves cohabiting one part of the "New World" several centuries ago.

One other cautionary note is necessary. Though I often speak of racial groups and racial interaction, these terms do not refer to genetically different groups of people. For more than a century, anthropologists poured their intellect and energy into attempts to classify all the peoples of the world, from the pygmies of Borneo to the Aleuts in Alaska, according to genetic differences. Noses were measured, cranial cavities examined, body hair noted, lips described, and hair and eye color classified in an attempt to define scientifically the various physiological types of humankind. Much was at stake in this effort. If physiological characteristics, with skin color prominent among them, could be "scientifically" determined, it would be possible to rank degrees of "cultural development" or achievement on a scale reaching from "savagery" to "civilization." It comes as no surprise that this massive effort of Western white anthropologists resulted in the conclusion that the superiority of the Caucasian peoples of the world could be "scientifically" proven.

Today, genetic sciences, and particularly the DNA breakthroughs from molecular biologists, have wiped away this long effort to establish a hierarchy of human types. Modern science finds that race is not biologically determined. Rather, it is socially and historically constructed. No objective foundation exists for the idea that a person belongs to one biological "race" or another or that a particular number of distinct races exist. It is now apparent that Europeans in the Americas fashioned different codes of race relations based on their own needs and attitudes concerning how people should be classified, treated, and separated. "Negro" in Brazil and in the United States, for example, came to have different meanings that reflected conditions and values, as well as degrees of social mingling, not genetic differences. As Sidney Mintz wisely reminds us, "The 'reality' of race is thus as much a social as a biological reality, the inheritance of physical traits serving as the raw material for social sorting devices, by which both stigmata and privileges may be systematically allocated."[5] This social sorting is highly arbitrary—down to the present day

---

[5]Sidney Mintz, "Toward an Afro-American History," *Journal of World History* (published in Switzerland), 13 (1971): 318.

when, for example, the U.S. Census Bureau for many decades obliged every resident to choose one racial category as if no people whatsoever existed with mixed genetic and cultural inheritances.

Thus, we gain little insight into the historical process by distinguishing cultural groups at the biological or physiological level. In this book, we are not considering genetically different groups but human populations from different parts of the world, groups of people with cultural differences. Most of all, we will be inquiring into the way these peoples, brought into contact with each other, changed over the course of several centuries—and changed in a manner that would shape the course of American history for generations to come.

A Word about Words

Readers of this book should understand that our choice of words—all language—is tied up with cultural attitudes and ideological stances. That Columbus "discovered America" in 1492 is a bold example of compromised language and yet what young students learned for many generations. Of course, Columbus *reached* the Americas in 1492, but he didn't discover what millions of humans already knew about because they had lived for many millennia on the western side of the Atlantic. That is an easy phrase of eurocentric phrasing to fix. But the problem runs deeper. As James Merrell, a historian of Native American history has recently argued, a tainted terminology, a "pervasive, pernicious language problem," chains us "to a lexicon crafted by the victors in the contest for America."[6] In the way an author chooses words, he chides us, he or she, even if unconsciously, privileges the history of Europeans to the detriment of Native Americans (and Africans). Merrell wants all textbooks cleansed of such words as "frontier," "backcountry," "hinterland," the "New World," the "Old World," "pre-contact," "postcontact," and even "settlers" and "settlements" because all such words, he argues, refer to the perspectives of European newcomers to the Americas and the way they occupied the land on which Native people had lived for countless generations. The "hinterland," for example, was the region west of colonial settlement in eastern North America, but it was not a "hinterland" for Native people but rather their homeland and then a zone of contact where they traded, negotiated, warred, allied, and—occasionally—intermarried with European colonists.

In this seventh edition, I have tried to avoid such linguistic traps. However, having cautioned the reader, I continue to use such words as "settler" or "settlement," while understanding that Native people were settlers and had settlements as well. Similarly a "frontier" for Europeans was on the edge of their settlements, usually westwardly. For Native people the frontier was usually eastward. And sometimes the "frontier" was a zone of contact where Native people and colonizing Europeans were co-occupying the land.

Also, though it privileges the colonizers, it is nearly impossible to purge all place names that Europeans put on the maps and used in their discourse. It is true that "the Great Lakes" was not the name used by the Huron and other Native peoples who lived on its shores, but it is the name that is familiar to students and still serviceable

[6]James Merrell, "Second Thoughts on Colonial Historians and American Indians," *William and Mary Quarterly*, 3rd Ser., 69 (2012): 451–512. The phrase is from pp. 458–459.

in a book of this kind. Likewise, when I write of "Pennsylvania's Susquehanna Valley" the reader can keep in mind that the Lenape called this ancient homeland differently. It makes sense to say that, in the wake of the American Revolution, the Iroquois ceded parts of *Iroquoia* to the victorious Americans rather than ceding parts of New York and Pennsylvania. But using every term and geographical designator so that the reader understands it as it was termed by both Europeans and Natives (or differently by the French, English, and Spanish) would make for cumbersome reading. Some historians prefer La Florida to Florida in writing about the pre-Revolutionary period because it was claimed and partially occupied by the Spanish, not the English. Similarly, Nuevo México, rather than New Mexico is the preferred term for some historians. But in the pages that follow, I have used the place names familiar today, asking the reader to understand the complexity of word choice and how the terms have changed as the process of occupying the land of North America has evolved over four centuries.

Similarly, I have used the tribal names that were used in the discourse and documents of European colonizers. The Iroquois people called their league the Haudenosaunee, but for ease of reading I have employed the term known in history books for many generations. Likewise, the Creeks, Cherokees, and Choctaws, had different names for themselves, and readers will find these terms in specialized studies by ethnohistorians and anthropologists. Having alerted readers to these linguistic tangles, it is best to proceed in a way that makes this book accessible.

A Word about Maps

Readers will find a number of maps in the pages that follow. In many cases they portray land on the eastern seaboard of North America colonized by Europeans, such as Southern New England (p. 76) or Pennsylvania (p. 107). In each case, they show the *claims* and *boundaries* of different English colonies but not land actually populated and controlled by English and other European colonizers. Those living on the ground, particularly more than about fifty to one hundred miles from the Atlantic coast, were Native people whose presence is difficult to map. Similarly, European claims of possession and dominion of the vast territories extending from the Atlantic Ocean far into the interior are mapped in most textbooks. This mapping of space was an essential part of the struggle among emergent European empires in the Americas because the planting of the king's arms established a claim to be used as European monarchies struggled for ascendancy in the Americas. This was "cartographic fiction," as one historian has put it, since territories claimed by England, France, or Spain were for the most part not occupied or controlled by them. But they could act as if they did when wars of empire ended with peace treaty negotiation. In faraway European capitals, diplomats made decisions about territorial claims that were then transferred from the vanquished European power to the victor nation. On p. 205, readers will see a map representing "European Rivalry in the Americas in 1750." No Native peoples appear on this map, and if they were to be portrayed the map would be unduly complicated and would not serve its purpose. But readers are reminded that maps do not represent the reality of human occupation and control of land; rather they are representations of the partial occupation and the imagined possession and dominion of land.

Seventh Edition

Red, White, and Black

The Peoples of Early North America

Gary B. Nash

University of California, Los Angeles

CHAPTER 1

Before Columbus

LEARNING OBJECTIVES

- Describe the origins, population, and diversity of Native societies in Ancient America, including language, social structure, and lifeways, and explain how the agricultural revolution played a role in this diversity.

- Compare the various regional societies in terms of population, agricultural production, housing, and culture and arts.

- Explain the matrilineal structure of the Iroquois people and the various roles assumed by women in this society.

- Compare and contrast the worldviews of the early Native Americans and the European colonists.

The history of the American peoples begins not in 1492 but hundreds of centuries before the birth of Christ. It was then, according to archaeologists and geologists, that humans first discovered what much later would be called North America. Thus, American history can begin with some basic questions: Who were the first inhabitants of the "New World"? Where did they come from? What were they like? How had their societies changed over the millennia that preceded the arrival of Europeans? Can their history be reconstructed from the mists of prehistoric time?

Almost all the material evidence suggesting answers to these questions comes from ancient sites of early life in the Americas. By unearthing pots, tools, seeds, ornaments, and other objects, and by establishing the age of skeletal remains of the "first Americans"

through radiocarbon dating, archaeologists, linguists, geneticists, and physical anthropologists have posited the arrival of humans in America to about 15,000 years ago. Our knowledge of this is still very tentative and hotly debated as researchers uncover new early human living sites. What is certain is that the date for the first human presence in the Americas has been pushed back farther and farther through sophisticated research.

Most Native American peoples have their own creation stories about their origins in North America itself. However, paleoanthropologists and molecular biologists studying mitochondrial DNA (mtDNA inherited through the female line of descent) generally agree that these first inhabitants of the continent were men and women from Asia (though recent discoveries suggest seaborne migrations

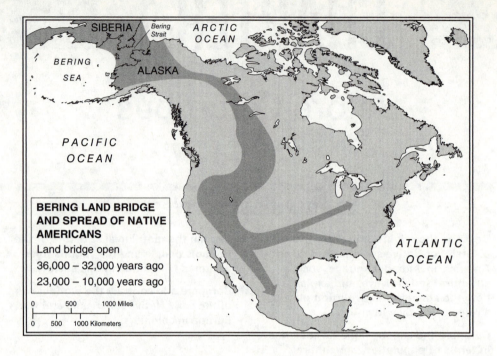

BERING LAND BRIDGE AND SPREAD OF NATIVE AMERICANS
Land bridge open
36,000 – 32,000 years ago
23,000 – 10,000 years ago

across the Pacific from Polynesia, Japan, and other parts of eastern Asia).[1] Game-hunting nomadic peoples from the inhospitable environment of Siberia, they migrated across the Bering Strait to Alaska in search of more reliable sources of food. Geologists have determined that Siberia and Alaska were connected by a land bridge only during the two long periods when massive glaciers covered the northern latitudes, locking up most of the world's moisture and leaving the floor of the Bering Sea exposed. These two long periods were from roughly 36,000 to 32,000 years ago and again from 23,000 to 10,000 years ago. At other times, the melting glaciers raised the level of water in the Bering Strait, inundating the land bridge and blocking foot traffic to North America. So when Europeans found a way to reach North America in ships 500 years ago, they encountered people whose ancestors had come on foot many thousands of years before.

Although most anthropologists agree that the migration was of Asian peoples, particularly those of Mongoloid stock from northeast Asia, the skeletal remains of these migrants also reveal non-Asian characteristics. It is probable that they represent a potpourri of different populations in Asia, Africa, and Europe, which had been mixing for thousands of years. But whatever the prior infusion of genes from peoples of other areas, these first Americans were Asiatic in geographical origin. From the vast steppes of Siberia they began trekking eastward toward a continent where no human had ever set foot. They lived in what geologists and archaeologists call the Pleistocene or Ice Age.

Cultural Evolution

Once on the North American continent, these early wanderers began trekking southward and then eastward, following vegetation and game.

---

[1]For general agreement among geneticists that present-day's five mtDNA haplogroups and Y-chromosome groups trace back to humans who crossed the Bering Land Bridge, see Brian Fagan, *The First North Americans: An Archaeological Journey* (London: Thames & Hudson, 2011), pp.16–17.

Scores of generations passed before these nomads reached the Pacific Northwest. The migratory movement ultimately brought them to the tip of South America within about 1,000 years and to the east coast of North America much later. American history traditionally emphasizes the "westward movement," but for hundreds of generations in North America, the frontier moved southward and eastward. The distances were immense—15,000 miles from the Asian homeland to Tierra del Fuego, the southernmost limit of South America, and 6,000 miles from Siberia to the eastern edge of North America. By roughly 9000 B.C, the first Americans were widely dispersed across the Western Hemisphere.

During the centuries spanned by these long migrations, one band in search of new food sources would split off from another. This process, repeated many times in many areas, marked the emergence of separate societies, numbering in the hundreds on the continent by the time the Europeans arrived. Cultural differences over thousands of years became more distinct as people in widely different ecological regions organized their lives and related to the land in ways dictated by their natural habitats. Much later, Europeans would indiscriminately lump together a wide variety of native cultures under a single rubric "Indian." But in reality, myriad ways of life had developed by the time Europeans found their way to the very old "New World." If Europeans had been able to drop down on native villages from the Atlantic to the Pacific coasts and from Alaska to the Gulf of Mexico in 1492, they would have found "Indians" living in Kwakiutl rectangular plank houses on the northwest coast, in Gothic domed thatched houses in Wichita grasslands, in earth lodges in Pawnee prairie country, and in barrel-roofed rectangular houses in Algonquian villages in the northeast woodlands. Different societies had developed a great variety of techniques for providing basic shelter because they lived in areas where building materials and weather conditions varied widely. The same diversity marked the ornaments and clothes they fashioned, the tools they employed, and the natural foods they gathered.

This diversity of Native culture in Ancient America is also evident in the languages they spoke. Linguistic scholars divide Native languages, at the point when Europeans first arrived in North America, into twelve linguistic stocks, each as distinct from the others as Semitic languages are from Indo-European languages. Within each of these twelve linguistic stocks, a great many separate languages and dialects were spoken, each as different as English from Russian. In all, about 2,000 languages were spoken by the Native Americans—a greater linguistic diversity than in any other part of the world.

How can we account for this striking diversity of Indian cultures? The explanation lies in an understanding of environmental conditions and the way in which bands of people lived in relatively self-contained communities for centuries, adapting to their natural surroundings and molding their culture in ways that allowed for survival in their region. As elsewhere in the prehistoric world, human beings were basically seed gatherers and game hunters. They were dependent for life on a food supply over which they had little control. They struggled to master their environment but were frequently at its mercy. Thus, to give a single example, as great geologic changes occurred in North America about 8000 B.C., vast areas from Utah to the highlands of Middle America were turned from grasslands into desert. Big game and plants requiring plentiful water could not survive these changes, and Native societies in these areas either had to move on to find new sources of food or to modify their cultures to the new conditions.

Another way of understanding the process of cultural change and the proliferation of culture groups is to focus on agriculture—the domestication of plant life. Like all other living organisms, human beings depend ultimately on plants to survive. For both humans and animals, plants are the source of life-sustaining fuel. The ultimate source of this energy is the sun. But in tapping this solar energy, humans and animals had to rely on plants because they are the only organisms capable of producing significant amounts of organic material through the photosynthetic process. Plant food was—and still is—the strategic element in the chain of life. It nurtured humans, and it sustained the animals that provided them with their second source of food.

When humans learned to control the life of plants—*agriculture* is the term we give to the process—they took a revolutionary step toward controlling their environment. The domestication of plants began to emancipate human beings from oppression by the physical world. To learn how to harvest, plant, and nurture a seed was to assume some of nature's functions and to gain partial control over what had been uncontrollable. In the wake of this acquisition of partial control over nature's forces, came vast cultural changes.

Dating the advent of agriculture in the Americas is difficult, but archaeologists date it at least as far back as 5000 B.C. Agriculture had already developed in southwestern Asia and Africa, and it spread to Europe at about the time peoples in the Tehuacán Valley of central Mexico were first planting maize, beans, and squash. Where agriculture occurred first, a much debated subject, is not as important as the fact that the "agricultural revolution" began independently in several widely separated parts of the world, all of which were later subordinated by European colonizers.

When the production of domesticated plant food replaced the gathering of wild plant food, dramatic changes occurred in the life of societies. First, plant domestication gradually allowed settled village life to replace nomadic existence. Second, the spread of maize, beans, and squash, which together provide a well-balanced diet, spurred population growth, for even putting as little as 1 percent of the land under cultivation produced enormous increases in the food supply. This outcome in turn caused large groups to split off to form separate societies. Third, the cultivation of plants reduced the amount of time and energy needed to obtain a food supply and thus created more favorable conditions for social, political, and religious development; aesthetic expression; and technological innovation. Last, it led in most areas to a sexual division of labor, with men clearing the land and engaging in the hunt for game while women planted, cultivated, and harvested crops.

Thus, the agricultural revolution began to reshape the cultural outlines of native societies. Population growth and the beginnings of sedentary village life were accompanied by more complex social and political organization. Bands evolved into tribes, and tribes evolved into larger political entities. Tasks became more specialized, and a more complex social structure took form. In some societies, the religious specialist became the dominant figure, just as in other parts of the world where the agricultural revolution had occurred. The religious figure organized the common followers, directed their work, and exacted tribute as well as worship from them; in return, this figure was counted on to protect the community from hostile forces.

Regional Cultures

When Europeans first reached what they came to term "the New World," Native Americans were in widely different phases of this agricultural revolution, and therefore, their cultures were marked by striking differences. A glimpse at several of the societies with which Europeans first came into contact in the early sixteenth century will illustrate the point.

In the southwest of North America, Hohokam and Anasazi societies had been engaged in agricultural production with ditch irrigation and a sedentary village life for at least two millennia before the Spanish arrived in the 1540s. By about 700 to 900 A.D., descendants of these people began to abandon the ancient pit houses dug in cliffs and to construct rectangular rooms arranged in apartment-like structures. By 1050 A.D., "Pueblo" people, as the Spanish called them, had developed planned villages composed of large terraced buildings, each with many rooms. These apartment-house villages were often constructed on defensive sites—on ledges of massive rock, on flat summits, or on steep-sided mesas—locations that would afford the Anasazi protection from their northern enemies. The largest of these villages, at Pueblo Bonito, in Chaco Canyon (in today's Four Corners region of New Mexico), contained about 700 rooms in five stories and may have housed as many as 1,000 persons.

Pueblo Bonito.

(Courtesy Josemaria Toscano/Shutterstock)

No larger apartment-house-type construction would be seen on the continent until the late nineteenth century in New York City. The roofing and flooring of the Chaco Canyon villages required cutting several hundred thousand juniper and pinyon trees with stone axes and dragging them many miles from their source north of the village complex. Within a 60-mile radius, hundreds of villages dotted the landscape, all linked together by about 250 miles of roads.

Then, around 1150 A.D., Chaco Anasazi society began to unravel. After six centuries of population growth and agricultural development, the Anasazi had apparently reached the carrying limits of a fragile and unpredictable environment. Deforesting the region led to soil erosion, and crop production was crippled by a 50-year drought. On the edge of collapse, the Natives starved or abandoned the region in search of a more hospitable environment.

Long before the Spanish arrival, descendants of the Anasazi were using irrigation canals, check-dams, and hillside terracing as techniques for bringing water to what had for centuries been an arid, agriculturally marginal area. At the same time, the ceramic industry became more elaborate, cotton replaced yucca fiber as the main clothing material, and basket weaving became more artistic. In its technological solution to the water management, its artistic efforts, its agricultural practices, and its village life, the highly stratified Pueblo society, on the eve of the Spanish arrival, was not radically different from peasant communities ruled by the nobility in most of the Euro-Asian world. Don Juan de Oñate reported home in 1599 after reaching the Pueblo villages on the Rio Grande River that the Native people "live very much the same as we do, in houses with two and three terraces."[2]

Far to the north, on the Pacific coast of the Northwest, native people organized their societies around cedar and salmon. Tlingit, Haida, Kwakiutl, and Salish people lived in villages of several hundred, drawing their sustenance from salmon and other spawning fish. Their plank houses of red cedar displayed elaborately carved pillars and were guarded by gigantic totem poles that depicted animals with supernatural power such as the bear, sea otter, bald eagle, raven, killer whale, frog, and wolf. Early European explorers, who reached this region much later than most

[2]Quoted in Thomas D. Matijasic, "Reflected Values: Sixteenth-Century Europeans View the Indians of North America," *American Indian Culture and Research Journal*, 11 (1987): 45.

other parts of the hemisphere, were amazed at the architectural and artistic skills of the Northwest Indians. "What must astonish most," wrote one French explorer in the late eighteenth century, "is to see painting everywhere, everywhere sculpture, among a nation of hunters."[3]

Carving and painting softwood from deep cedar forests surrounding their villages, native people of the Northwest defined their place in the cosmos with ceremonial face masks. Often the masks represented animals, birds, and fish—reminders of magical ancestral spirits that inhabited the four interconnected zones of their cosmos: the Sky World, the Undersea World, the Mortal World, and the Spirit World.

Ceremonial masks had a pivotal place in the potlatch, a great winter gathering where through song, dance, and ritual, Northwest Indian peoples sought to give meaning to their existence and to reaffirm their goal of achieving balance and harmony in their world. In the potlatch ceremonial dances, native leaders expressed their family lineage and their chiefly authority in the tribe. By giving away many of their possessions, chiefs satisfied tribe members and thus maintained their legitimacy. Such largesse mystified and often disturbed Europeans. Attempts by American and Canadian authorities to suppress potlatch ceremonies in the late nineteenth century never succeeded.

Far to the east, other Indian cultures evolved over thousands of years. From the great plains of the midcontinent to the Atlantic tidewater region, a variety of tribes belonging to four main language groups—Algonquian, Iroquoian, Muskogean, and Siouan—grew in strength. Their existence in eastern North America, which has been traced as far back as about 9000 B.C., was based on a mixture of agriculture, food gathering, game hunting, and fishing. Like other tribal groups that had been touched by the agricultural revolution, they gradually adopted semifixed settlements and developed a trading network linking together a vast region.

Among the most impressive of these societies were the so-called Hopewell mound-building people of the Ohio River valley, who constructed gigantic sculptured earthworks in geometric designs, sometimes in the shapes of huge humans, birds, or writhing serpents. When colonial settlers first crossed the Appalachians, after almost a century and a half in North America, they were astounded at these monumental constructions, some reaching as high as seventy feet. Their stereotype of eastern Indians as forest primitives did not allow them to believe that these were built by primitive native peoples, so they postulated that survivors of the sunken islands of Atlantis or descendants of the Egyptians and Phoenicians had wandered far from their homelands, built these mysterious monuments, and then disappeared.

Archaeologists and anthropologists now conclude that the Mound Builders were the ancestors of the Creeks, Choctaws, and Natchez. Their societies evolved slowly over the centuries, hastened by population increase associated with a warming period from about 900 to 1300 that lengthened growing seasons and allowed for the spread of the maize-bean-squash dietary trilogy north of the Rio Grande. By the advent of Christianity, Mound Builders had developed considerable complexity. In southern Ohio alone, archaeologists have pinpointed about 10,000 mounds used as burial sites and have excavated another 1,000 earth-walled enclosures, including one enormous fortification with a circumference of about three and one-half miles, enclosing about one hundred acres, or the equivalent of fifty modern city blocks. We now know from a great variety of items found in the mound tombs—large ceremonial blades chipped from obsidian rock formations in what is now Yellowstone National Park; embossed breastplates, ornaments, and weapons fashioned from copper nuggets from the Great Lakes region; decorative objects cut from sheets of mica from the southern Appalachians; conch shells from the Atlantic seaboard; and ornaments made from shark and alligator teeth and shells from the Gulf of Mexico—that the Mound Builders participated in a vast trading network that linked together hundreds of Indian villages across the continent.

---

[3]Quoted in Paul S. Boyer et al., *The Enduring Vision: A History of the American People* (Lexington, MA, 1993), p. 6.

Artist's conceptualization of Cahokia Monk Mound and satellite mounds.

(Courtesy Cahokia Mounds Historic Site, painting by William R. Iseminger)

By about 500 A.D., the Mound Builder culture was declining, perhaps because of attacks from other tribes or because severe climatic changes undermined agriculture. To the west, another culture, based on intensive agriculture, was beginning to flourish. Its center, now called Cahokia, was beneath present-day East St. Louis at the confluence of the Illinois, Missouri, and Mississippi rivers. It radiated out to encompass most of the Mississippi watershed from Wisconsin to Louisiana and from Oklahoma to Tennessee. Hundreds of villages were included in its orbit. By about 700 A.D., this Mississippian culture, as it is known to archaeologists, began to send its influence eastward to transform the life of most of the less technologically advanced woodland tribes. Like the Mound Builders of the Ohio region, these people built gigantic mounds as burial and ceremonial places. The largest of them, called Monk's Mound, rises in four terraces to a height of one hundred feet with a rectangular base covering nearly fifteen acres and containing 22 million cubic feet of earth, carried basket by basket to the site—an immense marshaling of human labor. It is larger at its base than the Great Pyramid of Egypt. Built around 1050 A.D., this huge earthwork faced the site of a palisaded Indian city that contained more than one hundred small artificial mounds marking burial sites. Spread among them was a dense settlement, called "America's first metropolis" by one archaeologist. This Mississippi valley city of Cahokia is estimated to have had a population of about 16,000 to 20,000, the most concentrated population north of the Rio Grande until the late eighteenth century.[4] Radiating out

---

[4]Biloine W. Young and Melvin L. Fowler, *Cahokia: The Great Native American Metropolis* (Urbana, IL, 2000), pp. 310-311.

from Cahokia for many miles were tilled fields that supplied the maize for the urban dwellers.

The finely crafted ornaments and tools recovered by archaeologists at Cahokia include elaborate ceramics, finely sculptured stonework, carefully embossed and engraved copper and mica sheets, and one funeral blanket for an important chief fashioned from 20,000 shell beads. These artifacts indicate that Cahokia was truly an urban center, with clustered housing, markets, and specialists in toolmaking, hide dressing, potting, jewelry making, shell engraving, weaving, and salt making.

By about 1300, 200 years before Europeans arrived on the Atlantic seaboard, the mound-building Mississippian societies had passed their prime and were dying out. Though the reasons are not yet clear, a severe earthquake that damaged Monk's Mound may have challenged the supernatural power claimed by Cahokia's chiefs. The Cahokians may also have outstripped their water supply, perhaps partly caused by the relentless cutting of nearby forests. Perhaps more important was a long period of global cooling, called "the Little Ice Age" by today's scientists. According to paleoclimatologists, from about 1300 and continuing into the mid-nineteenth century, a cooling period afflicted much of the northern hemisphere, bringing colder and more extended winters and shorter summer growing periods. This affected farmers and food production on both sides of the Atlantic, even to the extent of causing recurrent famines and, in Europe, the reduction of cattle herds deprived of adequate forage.

Whatever the reasons for Cahokia's decline, its influence had already passed eastward to transform the woodlands societies along the Atlantic coastal plain. Although the widely scattered and relatively fragmented tribes that were settled from Nova Scotia to Florida never matched the earlier societies of the midcontinent in architectural design, earthwork sculpturing, or artistic expression, they were far from the forest primitives that Europeans pictured. Changed by contact with the Hopewell and Mississippi cultures of the Ohio and Mississippi river valleys,

they added agriculture to the skills they had already acquired in exploiting a wide variety of natural plants for food, medicine, dyes, flavoring, and smoking. In the mixed natural economies that resulted, they utilized all the resources around them—open land, forests, streams, shore, and ocean.

For the most part, these people of the Northeast woodlands, on whose lands European fishermen began camping to dry their codfish in the early sixteenth century, lived in villages, especially after they had been influenced by the agricultural traditions of the Ohio and Mississippi valley societies. Locating their cornfields near fishing grounds and learning to fertilize the young plants with the heads of fish, they settled into a more sedentary pattern of life. Domed wigwams of birch and elm, copied in the early years by Europeans, were clustered together in villages that were often palisaded. The birch-bark canoes, light enough to be carried by a single adult from stream to stream, gave them a means of trading and communicating over a vast territory. The extent of development among these Eastern woodlands societies on the eve of European contact is indicated by the archaeological evidence of a Huron town in the Great Lakes region that contained more than one hundred large structures housing a total population of between 4,000 and 6,000. Settlements of this size were larger than the average European village of the sixteenth century and larger than all but a handful of European colonial towns in the Americas a century and a half after the colonizing immigrants from Europe arrived.

Along the Atlantic seaboard, from the St. Lawrence Bay to Florida, Europeans encountered scores of local tribes of the Eastern woodlands that had been cultivating native plants for more than 2,000 years. Each tribe maintained cultural elements peculiar to its people, although each shared in common many things such as agricultural techniques, the sexual division of labor, pottery design, social organization, and toolmaking. But the most important common denominator among them was that each had mastered the local habitat in a way that sustained life and ensured the perpetuation of their people. In the far north were Abenakis, Penobscots, Passamaquoddys, and others, who lived by the products of the sea and supplemented their diet with maple sugar and a few foodstuffs. Farther south, in what was to become New England, were village-based people forming into tribes that in time took the name of Massachusetts, Wampanoags, Pequots, Narragansetts, Niantics, Mahicans, and others—all occupying fairly local areas and joined together only by occasional trade. South of them, in the mid-Atlantic area, were Lenape, Susquehannock, Nanticoke, Pamunkey, Shawnee, Tuscarora, Catawba, and other peoples, who subsisted on a mixture of agriculture, shellfish, game, and wild foods. They, too, were settled in villages, where they lived a semisedentary life and where lineage and clan were more important than tribal identity.

One of the most heavily populated regions of the Atlantic coast was the Southeast, where rich and complex cultures, some of them joined in loose chiefdoms, were located. Belonging to several language groups, these peoples traced their ancestry back at least 8,000 years. Some of the most elaborate pottery making in the eastern half of the continent occurred in the Southeast, beginning about 2000 B.C. Hopewell and Cahokian burial mound techniques also influenced these cultures, and a few 100 years before Hernando de Soto marched through the area in the 1540s, grandiose ceremonial centers, such as Etowah in northwestern Georgia, whose construction involved earthmoving on a vast scale, had become a distinct feature of this area. In touch with Mississippian culture, the tribes of the Southeast evolved elaborate ceramic and basket-weaving techniques, long-distance trade, and in some cases, as with the Natchez, hierarchical and authoritarian social and political organizations.

Like Cahokia, the southeastern mound-building societies suffered a collapse as the Little Ice Age began in the 1300s, ushering in a more unpredictable and drought-prone environment. In time, smaller chiefdoms arose, including what would become the powerful Creeks and Yamasees in the Georgia and Alabama regions;

the Apalachees in Florida and along the Gulf of Mexico; the Choctaws, Chickasaws, and Natchez of the lower Mississippi valley; the Cherokees of the southern Appalachians; and several dozen smaller tribes scattered along the southeast coast. None of them built the immense ritual sites or grew into major population centers that had flourished in the tenth to thirteenth centuries in the continent's deep interior.

The Iroquois

Among the Eastern woodlands societies, the one that was to loom largest in European-Indian encounters in North America was the Iroquois. Their territory stretched from the Adirondack Mountains to the Great Lakes and from what is now northern New York to Pennsylvania. Five tribes—the Mohawks ("People of the Flint"), Oneidas ("People of the Stone"), Onondagas ("People of the Mountain"), Cayugas ("People at the Landing"), and Senecas ("Great Hill People")—composed what Europeans later called the League of the Iroquois. The Iroquois confederation was a vast extension of the kinship group that characterized the Northeastern woodlands pattern of family settlement and embraced perhaps 10,000 people at the beginning of the seventeenth century. Situated athwart major Indian trade routes in the Northeast and positioned between French and English zones of settlement, the Iroquois were intensely caught up with the onrush of Europeans, which is also to say that the settlers, whether Dutch, French, or English, were caught up with the Iroquois as well.

Not long before the arrival of Europeans, the loosely organized and strife-ridden Iroquois strengthened themselves by creating a more cohesive political confederacy. By learning to suppress intra-Iroquois blood feuds, villages gained stability, population increased, and the Iroquois developed political mechanisms for solving their internal problems and for presenting a more unified front in negotiating with their Algonquian neighbors for the use of hunting territories to the north or in admitting dependent tribes to settle

INDIAN TRIBES OF THE CARIBBEAN AND NORTH AMERICA ON THE EVE OF EUROPEAN CONTACT

on their territory. This organization facilitated the development of a coordinated Iroquois policy for dealing with the European newcomers.

Work in the palisaded villages of Iroquoia, some of which bustled with more than a thousand people, was performed communally, and land was owned not by individuals but by all in common. An individual family might till their own patch of land, but it was understood that this usage of land in no way implied private ownership. Likewise, hunting was a communal enterprise. Though individual hunters differed in their ability to stalk and kill deer (the Iroquois's most important source of meat), the collective bounty of the hunting party was brought back to the village and divided among all. Similarly, several

families occupied a longhouse, but the house itself, like all else in the community, was regarded as common property. For the Iroquois the concept of private ownership of property—the idea that each person should own his or her own land or house—would have struck at the heart of the most important theme in their value system—the reciprocal and communal principle. "No hospitals (poorhouses) are needed among them," wrote a French Jesuit in 1657, "because there are neither mendicants nor paupers as long as there are any rich people among them. Their kindness, humanity and courtesy not only makes them liberal with what they have, but causes them to possess hardly anything except in common. A whole village must be without corn, before any individual can be obliged to endure privation."[5] One Iroquois scholar has called this "upside-down capitalism," whereby the goal was "not to accumulate goods but to be in a position to provide them to others."[6]

Village settlement was organized by extended kinship groups. Contrary to European practice, the Iroquois family was matrilineal, with family membership determined through the female rather than the male line. Thus, a typical family was composed of an old woman, her daughters with their husbands and children, and her unmarried granddaughters and grandsons. Sons and grandsons remained with their kinship group until they married; then they joined the family of their wife or the family of their mother's brother. If this arrangement puzzled Europeans, so did the Iroquois woman's prerogative of divorce; if she desired it, she merely set her husband's possessions outside the longhouse door. Thus, Iroquois society was organized around the matrilineal "fireside." In turn, several matrilineal kinship groups, related by a blood connection on the mother's side, as between sisters, formed an *ohwachira*, or a group of related families. These ohwachiras were grouped together in clans. A village might be made up of a dozen or more clans. Villages or clans combined to create a nation (or "kinship state," as it has been called) of Senecas or Mohawks.[7]

Not only was Iroquois society matrilineal in social organization, but also it invested the women of the community with a share of the political power unmatched in European societies. Political authority in the villages derived from the ohwachiras, headed by the "matrons"—the senior women of the community. These clan mothers named the men representing the clans at village and tribal councils and appointed the forty-nine sachems, or chiefs, who met periodically at Onondaga as the ruling council for the confederated Five Nations. These civil chiefs were generally middle-aged or elderly men who had earlier gained fame as warriors but now "forsook the warpath for the council fire."[8]

The political power of the women extended beyond the appointment of male representatives to the various ruling councils. When individual clans met, in a manner resembling the later New England town meeting, the senior women were fully in attendance, caucusing behind the circle of men who did the public speaking and lobbying with them. An outsider might think that the men ruled, because it was they who did the public speaking and formally reached decisions. But they shared power with the women. If the men of the village or tribal council moved too far from the will of the women who had appointed them, they could be removed, or "dehorned." Only so long as the men could achieve a consensus with the women who had placed them in office were they secure in their positions.

The division of power between male and female was further extended by the role of the women in the tribal economy. Whereas men were responsible for hunting and fishing, the women were the primary agriculturists of the village. In tending the crops, the women became equally important in sustaining the community. Moreover, when the men were away on hunting expeditions, often for a period of weeks, women were left entirely in charge of the daily life of the community. To a large extent, the village "was the woman's domain," whereas "the forest belonged to the men."[9]

Even in military affairs women played an important role, for they supplied the moccasins and food for warring expeditions. A decision to

[5]Reuben Gold Thwaites, ed., *The Jesuit Relations and Allied Documents: Travels and Explorations of the Jesuit Missionaries in New France, 1610–1791* (Cleveland, OH, 1899), XLIII: 271.
[6]Daniel K. Richter, *The Ordeal of the Longhouse: The Peoples of the Iroquois League in the Era of European Colonization* (Chapel Hill, NC, 1992), p. 22.
[7]William N. Fenton, "The Iroquois in History," in Eleanor Burke Leacock and Nancy Oestreich Lurie, eds., *North American Indians in Historical Perspective* (New York, 1971), p. 139.
[8]Ibid., p. 138.
[9]Richter, *Ordeal of the Longhouse...*, p. 23.

withhold these supplies was tantamount to vetoing a military foray. Clan matrons often initiated war by calling on the Iroquois warriors to bring them enemy captives to replace fallen clan members. Thus, power was shared between the sexes, and the European idea of male dominance and female subordination in all things was conspicuously absent in Iroquois society.

In raising children, Iroquois parents emphasized character formation. That was also true of Europeans, but the Iroquois went about it differently. Iroquois parents were more permissive than their European counterparts. They did not believe in harsh physical punishment. They encouraged their young to imitate adult behavior and were tolerant of fumbling early attempts. In the first months of a baby's life, the mother nursed and protected the child and at the same time hardened it by baths in cold water. Weaning was not ordinarily begun until the age of three or four. Rather than beginning strict regimens of toilet training at an early age, Iroquois parents allowed the child to proceed at its own pace in achieving control over natural functions. Early interest in the anatomy of the body and in sexual experimentation was accepted as normal. All this was in sharp contrast to European child-rearing techniques, which stressed the importance of accustoming the child to authority from an early age and backed this up by taking the child from the breast at about two years; by toilet training at an early age; by making frequent use of physical punishment; by condemning early sexual curiosity; and by emphasizing obedience and respect for authority as central virtues. Iroquois parents would have regarded as misguided the advice of John Robinson, the Pilgrims' pastor, to the parents of his congregation: "Surely there is in all children a stubbornness, and stoutness of mind arising from natural pride, which must, in the first place, be broken and beaten down; that so the foundation of their education being laid in humility and tractableness, other virtues may, in their time, be built thereon. For the beating, and keeping down of this stubbornness, parents must provide carefully that the children's ills and willfulness be restrained and repressed. Children should not know, if it could be kept from them, that they have a will of their own, but in their parents' keeping."[10]

The approach to authority also differed for adult members of the society. Iroquois society, like most other Indian societies of North America, had little of the complicated machinery that Europeans developed to direct the lives of its members. No laws and ordinances, sheriffs and constables, judges and juries, or courts or jails—the apparatus of authority in European societies—were to be found in the Northeast woodlands prior to European arrival. Yet boundaries of acceptable behavior were firmly set. Though priding themselves on the autonomous individual, the Iroquois maintained a strict sense of right and wrong. Rather than relying on formal instruments of authority, however, they governed behavior by inculcating a strong sense of tradition and attachment to the group through communally performed rituals. It was this sense of duty, bolstered by a fear of gossip and a strongly held belief in the power of evil spirits to punish wrongdoers, that curbed antisocial behavior and produced a general domestic peacefulness among the Iroquois. In European society a crime or an unethical act might be dealt with by investigation, arrest, prosecution, sentencing, and imprisonment, involving at various steps along the way the authority of a number of people and institutional devices. In Indian society, a simpler system operated to transform the aberrant individual. He or she who stole another's food or showed cowardice in war was "shamed" and ostracized until the culprit had atoned for his or her actions and had demonstrated that he or she had morally purified himself or herself.

It is a mistake to romanticize Iroquois culture or to judge it superior to the culture of the European invader. To do so is only to invoke the same categories of "superior" and "inferior" that Europeans used to justify the violence they unleashed when they arrived in the Americas and to

---

[10]Quoted in John Demos, *A Little Commonwealth: Family Life in Plymouth Colony* (New York, 1970), pp. 134-135.

forget that exercises in ranking cultures depend almost entirely on the criteria employed. Instead of grading cultures, almost always an exercise of expansionist societies attempting to subjugate other people, we best understand Iroquois society, like English or French society, as a total social system that had evolved over many generations before Europeans arrived. In dynamic relationship with their environment and with neighboring peoples, the Iroquois had become more populous, more sedentary in their mode of settlement, more skilled in agricultural techniques, and more elaborate in their art forms. They had also emerged as one of the strongest, most politically unified, and most aggressive societies in the Northeast woodlands. Even after the formation of the League of the Iroquois, which had as one of its objectives the abatement of intertribal warfare, a staggering amount of fighting seems to have occurred between the Five Nations and surrounding Algonquian peoples. Many of these conflicts involved a quest for glory; others a quest to replace tribal members who succumbed to disease or war. Some of them may have been initiated to test the newly forged alliance of the five tribes against lesser tribes that could be brought under Iroquoian domination. Whatever the reasons, the Iroquois on the eve of European arrival were feared and sometimes hated by their neighbors for their skill and cruelty in warfare.

Pre-Columbian Population

How many Native Americans inhabited North America on the eve of European contact? For generations, anthropologists and historians have argued about preconquest population levels and have searched for methods that can provide reliable estimates. But only in recent decades have scholars conceded that most estimates made in the past have been affected by the estimator's conception of Native American societies. When Indian culture is viewed as "savage," characterized by nomadic hunters and gatherers, it is difficult to think in terms of large populations in North America. But if these societies are seen as sedentary, agriculturist, and complex in their

social organization, then larger numbers seem possible.

For many years, the accepted population of Native Americans north of Mexico in the immediate precontact period was about 1 million, with about 10 million in the Americas as a whole. This estimate, made in 1910 by the noted anthropologist James Mooney, has no credibility today, because Mooney based his estimates on rough tabulations of Indians made in various areas several decades or more after initial contact with Europeans. This method failed to recognize the precipitous population decline, approaching 90 percent in many regions, that occurred very rapidly when pathogens carried by Europeans infected Native Americans and spread like wildfire through their villages after first contacts. Today's scholars believe that the precontact population north of Mexico was at least 3 million, and some estimates run as high as 10 million. For the Western Hemisphere, the population may have been 60 to 70 million when Columbus reached it in 1492. Perhaps 700,000 lived along the Atlantic coastal plain and in the piedmont region accessible to the early European colonizers. Historical demographers will debate native population levels for many decades, but regardless of the twists and turns of this fascinating debate, we are left with the startling realization that Europeans were not coming to a "virgin wilderness," as some called it, but were invading a land that in some areas was more densely populated than their own homelands. Central Mexico, for example, probably had twice as many people per square mile as in India and China in the late fifteenth century.

The Native American Worldview

Although Native American and European cultures were not nearly so different as the concepts of "savagery" and "civilization" imply, societies on the eastern and western sides of the Atlantic had developed distinct—and sometimes radically different—systems of values in the centuries that preceded contact. Lurking behind the physical confrontations that would take place when European and Native American met were vastly different ways of looking at the world. These latent conflicts can be seen in contrasting European and Indian views of humankind's relationship to its environment, the concept of property, and personal identity.

In the European view the natural world was filled with resources for humans to use. "Subdue the earth," Christians read in the book of Genesis, "and have dominion over every living thing that moves on the earth." God still ruled the cosmos, of course, and humans could not control supernatural forces, manifesting themselves in earthquakes, hurricanes, drought, and flood. But a scientific revolution was underway in the early modern period, giving humans more confidence that they could comprehend the natural world—and thus eventually control it. For Europeans, the secular and the sacred were distinct, and the human relationship to the natural environment fell mostly into the secular sphere.

Native Americans recognized no such separation of secular and sacred. To them every part of the natural world was sacred, and the world was inhabited by a great variety of "beings," each pulsating with spiritual power and all linked together to form a sacred whole. "Plants, animals, rocks, and stars," explains Murray Wax, "are thus seen not as objects governed by laws of nature but as 'fellows' with whom the individual or band may have a more or less advantageous relationship."[11] Consequently, if one offended the land by stripping it of its cover, the spiritual power in the land—called "manitou" by some woodlands tribes—would strike back. If one overfished or destroyed game beyond one's needs, the spiritual power inherent in fish and animals would take revenge because humans had broken the mutual trust and reciprocity that governed relations between all beings—human and nonhuman. To exploit the land or to treat with

disrespect any part of the natural world was to cut oneself off from the spiritual power dwelling in all things and "was thus equivalent to repudiating the vital force in Nature."[12] To neglect reciprocal obligations in Nature's domain was to court sickness, hunger, injury, or even death.

Europeans had no qualms about treating land as a commodity to be privately held because they regarded the land as a resource to be exploited for humans' gain. Private ownership of property was one of the fundamental bases upon which European culture rested. Fences were the symbols of exclusively held property, inheritance became the mechanism for transmitting these "assets" from one generation to another within the same family, and courts provided the institutional apparatus for settling property disputes. In a largely agricultural society, property was the basis of political power. In fact, political rights in England derived from the ownership of a specified quantity of land. In addition, the social structure was largely defined by the distribution of property, with those people possessing great quantities of it standing at the apex of the social pyramid and the mass of propertyless individuals forming the broad base.

For Native Americans this view of land as a privately held asset was incomprehensible. Tribes recognized territorial boundaries, but within these limits the land was held in common. Land was not a commodity but a part of Nature that the Creator entrusted to the living. John Heckewelder, a Moravian missionary who lived with the Delawares in the eighteenth century, explained their belief that the Creator "made the Earth and all that it contains for the common good of mankind; when he stocked the country that he gave them with plenty of game, it was not for the benefit of a few, but of all; every thing was given in common to the sons of men. Whatever liveth on the land, whatsoever groweth out of the Earth, and all that is in the rivers and waters was given jointly to all and every one is entitled to

[11]James A. Clifton, ed., "Religion and Magic," in *Introduction to Cultural Anthropology: Essays in the Scope and Method of the Science of Man*, (Boston, MA, 1968), p. 235.
[12]Calvin Martin, *Keepers of the Game: Indian-Animal Relationships and the Fur Trade* (Berkeley and Los Angeles, CA, 1978), p. 34.

his share. From this principle hospitality flows as from its source."[13]

In personal identity, Indian and European values also differed sharply. Europeans were acquisitive and competitive, and over a long period of time, they had been enhancing the role of the individual. Most Europeans celebrated the wider choices and greater opportunities for the individual to improve his or her status—by industriousness, valor, or even personal sacrifice leading to martyrdom. Personal ambition, in fact, played a large role in the migration of Europeans across the Atlantic in the sixteenth and seventeenth centuries. In contrast, the cultural traditions of Native Americans emphasized the collectivity—the band, lineage, or village—rather than the individual. Because they held land and other natural resources in common and their society was less stratified than in Europe, Indians looked askance at the accumulative spirit and personal ambition of the newcomers. "In contrast to the exalted position of man in Judeo-Christian tradition," writes Calvin Martin, "the Native American cosmology conferred upon the Indian a rather humble stature."[14] Hence, in Native society the ideal of the autonomous individual was carefully restrained by the overriding commitment to clan and tribe. Rivalry flourished in Iroquois society as much as in Europe, but the tribal ethos channeled rivalries into conferring benefits upon the longhouse or the entire village.

Despite these differences, Native people and the European intruders had much in common—so much so that the time-worn European habit of seeing only "savages" and "civilized" peoples has to be recognized as a self-justified way of trying to shape the story to be passed on to future generations. At the most fundamental level, most of the societies that Europeans encountered as they colonized North America were farmers, inheritors of the agricultural revolution that transformed most of North America since the tenth century. Noteworthy as well is that European farmers coming to the Americas, though they had advantages in manuring their fields as a by-product of cattle, sheep, and pig raising, their grains—wheat, rye, and barley—were far inferior to Indian maize in terms of its life-sustaining value. Yet the vast majority of both peoples from opposite sides of the Atlantic were farmers all.

To put it squarely, it was not inevitable that the confrontation of European colonizers and Native Americans should lead to mortal combat. Inevitability is not a satisfactory explanation for any human event because it implies that human destiny is beyond human control and thus relieves individuals and societies of responsibility for their actions. As old as the tales told by conquerors, the narrative structure of inevitability is a winner's rationalization for historical clashes, a mode of explanation rarely advanced by the losing side. We shall see that the clash of cultures took many forms in the New World, with nothing predetermined but with everything dependent on the complex interweaving of many factors in particular places and at specific times.

Summary

The history of the American peoples begins hundreds of centuries before the birth of Christ. The first migrations over what is today the Bering Sea occurred during the Pleistocene Age, consisting of Asians from environmentally harsh Siberia. This migratory movement took about 1,000 years to reach the tip of South America and much longer to extend to the east coast of North America. The Native cultures that developed along the way were markedly diverse in language, clothing, tools, ornamentation,

---

[13]John Heckewelder, *Account of the History, Manners, and Customs of the Indian Nations* (Philadelphia, PA, 1819), p. 85, reprinted in Wilcomb Washburn, *The Indian and the White Man* (Garden City, NY, 1964), p. 63. In quoting material from primary sources, I have modernized spelling, punctuation, and capitalization.
[14]Martin, *Keepers of the Game...*, p. 74.

habitations, and food. This diversity likely arose from the changes in agriculture and hugely varied environmental conditions.

This agricultural revolution and long-term climate changes shaped the various regional cultures, including those of the Southwest, the Pacific coast of the Northwest, the Great Plains of the midcontinent, the Atlantic tidewater region, and the woodlands along the Eastern seaboard from the St. Lawrence to Florida. Of all the Indian societies, the Iroquois proved the most prominent in interactions with the Dutch, French, and English colonizers. With its matrilineal social organization and the prominent role given to women, the Iroquois were culturally very different from the Europeans. Indeed, a comparison of Native American and European worldviews reveals a great gulf between the European and Indian perspectives on the relationship of people to their environment, the concept of property, and personal identity.

Critical Thinking Questions

1. Native culture in Ancient America was striking in its diversity. What factors brought about such diversity?
2. Among the diverse Native groups were the Mound Builders. What are some characteristics of these people, and why might these civilizations have died out?
3. The Iroquois people were to figure most prominently in European-Indian encounters in North America. How did the Iroquois and Europeans differ in terms of the structure and operation of their culture and society?
4. Native peoples and Europeans had sharply contrasting views of the world. How did their worldviews differ, and was conflict inevitable between these two groups?

Further Reading

Colin G. Calloway, *One Vast Winter Count: The Native American West before Lewis and Clark* (Lincoln: University of Nebraska Press, 2003).

Sally A. Chappell, *Cahokia: Mirror of the Cosmos* (Chicago: University of Chicago Press, 2002).

Jared Diamond, *Collapse: How Societies Choose to Fail or Succeed* (New York: Viking, 2005)

William Engelbrecht, *Iroquoia: The Development of a Native World* (Syracuse: Syracuse University Press, 2003).

Brian M. Fagan, *Ancient North America: The Archaeology of a Continent*, 4th ed. (New York: Thames and Hudson, 2005).

Brian M. Fagan, *The Little Ice Age: How Climate Made History, 1300–1850* (New York: Basic Books, 2000).

Adam King, *Etowah: The Political History of a Chiefdom Capital* (Tuscaloosa: University of Alabama Press, 2003).

Shepard Krech III, *The Ecological Indian: Myth and History* (New York: W. W. Norton, 1999).

Charles C. Mann, *1491: New Revelations of the Americas before Columbus* (New York: Alfred K. Knopf, 2005).

David J. Meltzer, *First People in a New World: Colonizing Ice Age America* (Berkeley: University of California Press, 2009).

Ann F. Ramenofsky, *Vectors of Death: The Archaeology of European Contact* (Albuquerque: University of New Mexico Press, 1987).

Daniel K. Richter, *Before the Revolution: America's Ancient Pasts* (Cambridge: Harvard University Press, 2011).

John Thornton, *Africa and Africans in the Making of the Atlantic World, 1400–1680*, 2nd ed. (Cambridge: Cambridge University Press, 1998).

Richard F. Townsend and Robert V. Sharp, eds., *Hero, Hawk, and Open Hand: American Indian Art of the Ancient Midwest and South* (New Haven: Art Institute of Chicago and Yale University Press, 2004).

Biloine W. Young and Melvin L. Fowler, *Cahokia: The Great Native American Metropolis* (Urbana: University of Illinois Press, 2000).

CHAPTER 2

Europeans Reach North America

LEARNING OBJECTIVES

- Analyze the seafaring accomplishments of Christopher Columbus and the geographic significance of his voyages; state how he represented the time in which he lived.

- Name the biological "secret advantage" of the Europeans who came to conquer and colonize the Americas and describe its wide-ranging effects.

- Discuss the role of England in the colonization of the Americas and point out some of the challenges faced by England in this endeavor.

- Characterize the objectives and organization of French colonization in comparison with that of the Spanish, Portuguese, and English, as well as the nature of the relationship between French settlers and Native Americans.

- Describe how Europeans viewed or imagined Native Americans, in both positive and negative ways, and offer possible explanations for how these views came about.

From the fifteenth to the twentieth centuries, one of the dominant themes of history has been the militant expansion of European peoples into other continents. Only in the last 70 years has this process been reversed, as colonized people regained their independence through wars of national and cultural liberation. For Western historians, this global expansion has been closely equated with the spread of "civilization," the carrying of an allegedly superior European culture to the so-called backward areas of the world. As indigenous cultures were engulfed by colonizing Europeans, the notion grew in the Western mind that the growing outreach of European civilization put "progress" at the disposal of "primitive" peoples.

The cultural superiority of Europeans at the time they reached the Western Hemisphere is a highly loaded notion. For centuries, the categorizing of "superior" and "inferior" cultures has been the work of the conquering nations, with great emphasis placed on technological advances, such as metalworking, and on literacy. These have been promoted as benchmarks for describing and ranking cultures. Certainly literacy was an important element in the growth of European economies, the spread of urbanization, and the rise of technological and scientific innovations in Europe in the early modern period. But the contrast in economic growth and technological development between Europe, on the one hand, and Africa and the Americas, on the other, is explained by a wide range of factors. Literacy, in fact, was more widespread in the Middle East and North Africa in the fifteenth and sixteenth centuries than in Europe, yet Europe underwent more rapid economic development in the sixteenth century.

In exploring converging people in the Americas, it is best to leave aside crude comparisons, for example, between a literate Europe and a nonliterate Africa or pre-Columbian America. This kind of mind-set, leading toward claims of cultural superiority, masks the complex interaction of peoples from different parts of the world whose lives converged in the Americas.

What is important to know about European achievements in the age of Columbus is that, after a long period of recovery from the bubonic plague known as the Black Death that devastated Western Europe and parts of Africa from the 1340s to 1370s, monarchs began to assert their political authority over feudal lords and to unify their realms. This creation of power at the center of European societies placed the normal powers of the state—to tax, wage war, and administer the law—far more in the hands of ambitious monarchs. This new concentration of power was essential to the European expansionist impulse that was ripening in the second half of the fifteenth century. Also feeding this impulse was a mighty cultural revival known as the Renaissance. Beginning in Italy and spreading northward following revived commerce through Europe, the Renaissance ushered in a new, more secular age, encouraged freedom of thought, and emphasized human abilities. It reached its peak in the late fifteenth century when a dramatic series of European oceanic explorations began. Since the seventh century, Islamic culture had been the most dynamic and expansionist force in the Afro-Eurasian world, penetrating Africa deeply and extending into Europe as far

west as Cordoba, Spain. But now Christian and Jewish Europeans began to assume center stage in an epoch of transoceanic expansion.

Spanish and Portuguese Expansion into the Americas

When he made landfall on the tiny island of San Salvador in the Bahamas in 1492, Columbus thought he had reached the East Indies. This was precisely his quest—to find an all-water route to the Orient so that European traders, who trafficked in the precious spices that made European food palatable, could avoid paying tribute to the Middle Eastern middlemen who skimmed the profits off overland trading ventures. Burning with desire to liberate Jerusalem from Muslim rule and believing he had reached Old Testament lands, Columbus sent ashore for reconnaissance Luis de Torres, a converted Jew who knew Hebrew, Arabic, and Chaldaic—the biblical languages necessary for communication among Old Testament people.

In attempting to find a water route to the oldest parts of the "Old World," Columbus had stumbled upon what was a new world only in the European mind. But this fortuitous error sparked the imagination of the Europeans—one of their most valuable qualities—and fueled a revival of enterprise and overseas expansion that lasted for more than 400 years. Moreover, Columbus's four voyages set in motion a gigantic mixing of populations from different parts of the world, shifted Europe's commercial center of gravity from the Mediterranean to the Atlantic, and planted the seeds of the first global empires that would span entire oceans.

It is customary to focus on the nautical achievements and geographical importance of Columbus's voyages, and this should not be minimized because he had mastered for the first time the navigation of the last extensive body of water—the Atlantic basic—as yet unconquered. Yet his sea wanderings would have been written off as an expensive failure, once it was realized that he had not found the illusive water route to India, had it not been for the discovery of gold on Hispaniola in 1493. Without the gold and other precious metals, the newfound lands would have been only an obstacle on the water road to the Far East. Although his discovery was accidental, Columbus was still an archetypical figure of European expansion. Thoroughly medieval in his patterns of thought, he was also ambitious; adventuresome; full of practical knowledge; ready to translate an idea, however ridiculed, into action; and audacious enough to maintain his course even when his sailors were ready to mutiny in despair of ever seeing dry land again. Capitalizing on advances in marine and mapmaking technology and on earlier Portuguese oceanic explorations into the Atlantic "sea of darkness," as they called it, and down the west coast of Africa all the way to the southern tip, Columbus, like the Vikings 500 years before him, discovered that the ocean west of Europe had its limits. Columbus had at last discovered how to negotiate the circular currents and winds of the North Atlantic Ocean that, once understood, united Europe, Africa, and the Americas.

Once the Spanish found gold and silver, a wholesale rush of enterprising young men from the lesser nobility in Spain began the transatlantic adventure. By the 1550s, they had explored, and claimed, if not always conquered, the Isthmus of Panama, Mexico, most of South America except Brazil and the far southern plains, and the southerly reaches of North America from California to "La Florida." Led by military figures such as Cortés, Pizarro, Ponce de León, de Soto, and Coronado, they established the authority of Spain and the Catholic Church over an area that dwarfed their homeland in size and population. By the end of the sixteenth century, the Spanish had conquered the major centers of native population and had established a thriving transatlantic trade; and they were carrying African slaves by the thousands to their colonies and supervising the extraction of gold and silver in fabulous quantities from the lands under their domination.

From the 1490s to the 1590s, the colonization of the Americas was dominated by Spain. Its only rival was Portugal, whose energies had been absorbed in colonizing the Atlantic islands—Azores, Madeira, and Canary—that lay off the coast of Portugal and northwest Africa, and in establishing centers of trade on the east and west African coasts. Not until the 1550s did Portugal stake out a claim in Brazil, destined to become the center of its New World activities. By the end of the century, sugar production claimed the labor of most of some 25,000 Portuguese colonists and perhaps an equal number of African slaves in Brazil.

Closely tied to the economic strivings of Europe's emerging nation-states were the religious goals of colonization. Both Catholics and Protestants looked upon the occupation of the New World as a religious crusade. Indeed, Christian kings and knights, it was believed, were obligated to seek far-off lands and bring the pagan people there into due submission and godliness. Thus, Spain had been involved for centuries in conflict with the "infidel" Muslims; in fact, not until the year Columbus reached Hispaniola did Christian Spain complete the expulsion of the Moors. Conquest of the New World not only fulfilled national dreams of glory but also offered the challenge of converting to Christianity a continent filled with "heathen" people who had been seduced by Satan.

The religious motive was complicated by the Catholic-Protestant division within Christianity. For Europeans, heathens were heathens, but whether their conversion would be to Catholicism or to Protestantism depended on which European nation achieved domination over them. That Christians could be so bitterly divided, engaging in religious wars for several centuries and inflicting mass destruction in the name of God, may seem puzzling to those raised in a secular society. But the intensity of this conflict within Christian Europe becomes more understandable when we remember that for men and women of this age, as in the centuries before, religion was the organizing principle of life. Because science and technology had not yet advanced far enough to control natural forces, human mastery of the environment was slight, and people attributed what could not be understood or governed to supernatural forces, especially the intervening hand of God. With faith, not reason, dominating life, people of different religious commitments defended their ideology passionately and attacked those with variant views.

These "isms"—Protestantism and Catholicism—can be understood as prescribed codes of living, as ways of ordering and imparting meaning to one's world and one's place in it. Such ideological commitments did not differ markedly from the "isms" of today—socialism, communism, capitalism—in terms of their power to compel allegiance. These, too, are systems of values and beliefs, ways of organizing societies. Also, they give meaning to what people do and provide them with a sense of identity. Twentieth-century wars, fought with far greater ferocity and technological ruthlessness than the religious wars of the early modern era, provide a way of understanding why Christians and Muslims or Catholics and Protestants fought so relentlessly to spread their particular faith to the native inhabitants of the lands they were invading. Moreover, the religious bitterness and wars that continue today—from Ireland to the Middle East to Sri Lanka to Bosnia—remind us that religion still inspires deadly conflict.

The Spanish Conquest and the Atlantic Exchange

For a quarter century after Columbus's first voyage in 1492, the Spanish confined their colonizing efforts in the Western Hemisphere to occupying the Caribbean islands of Cuba, Puerto Rico, and Hispaniola. Then, in two bold and bloody strokes, beginning in 1519, the Spanish overwhelmed the ancient civilizations of the Aztecs and Incas. Hernán Cortés's march from

Tenochtitlan by Van Beecq, titled *La Ville de Mexique* in *Histoire de la conquete de Mexique ou de la Nouvelle Espagna.*
(Courtesy Classic Image/Alamy)

This engraving shows a merciless attack of the Spaniards on native people. From Theodore deBry, *America*—available at Columbia, NYU, NYHS. This image from among the DeBry plates that were based on Benzoni's version published in *La Historia del Mondo Nuovo* (1565).

Source: bpk, Berlin/Kunstbibliothek, Staatliche Museen, Berlin, Germany/Knud Petersen/Art Resource, NY.

coastal Veracruz over rugged mountains brought 600 soldiers into the Valley of Mexico, where for two years they fenced with Montezuma's people. Then in 1521, Cortés attacked the huge Aztec capital—Tenochtitlán (modern-day Mexico City).

The Spanish soldiers were astounded to find themselves confronting an urban population of 100,000 or more contained within a city replete with floating gardens, elaborate causeways and aqueducts, and monumental temples. The Aztecs were equally astounded at the intruders with much hair on their faces and accompanied by huge animals—large, ferocious dogs and huge "deer" more powerful than any animal the Aztecs had seen that carried metal-clad warriors on their backs and traveled faster than the fleetest

Aztec. Aided by dissident natives oppressed by Montezuma's tyranny, the Spanish brought the great Aztec ruler to his knees after a siege of seventy-five days. Over the next several decades, they extended their dominion over the Mayan people of the Yucatán and Guatemala.

In a second conquest, in 1531 to 1532, Francisco Pizarro marched from Panama through the jungles of Ecuador and into the towering mountains of Peru with a mere 168 men to overwhelm the densely settled Incas, who had built the world's greatest empire. Like the Aztecs, the Incas suffered from internal divisions. Capitalizing on this, Pizarro toppled the gold- and silver-rich Inca Empire with a momentous victory at Cajamarca, near the capital city of Cuzco, staggering

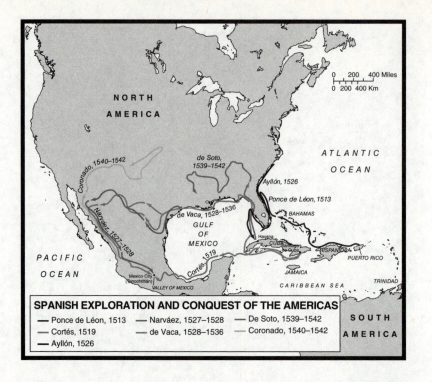

the Incas with cannon and horse-borne armored soldiers. From there, Spanish soldiers marched farther afield, plundering Inca cities and establishing their authority over native peoples in Bolivia, Chile, New Grenada (Colombia), and Argentina. By 1550, with only a few thousand soldiers, the Spanish had overwhelmed the major centers of native population throughout the Caribbean, Mexico, Central America, and the west coast of South America, creating an empire larger than any in the Western world since the fall of Rome 1,000 years before.

Spanish victories were accomplished in part by enlisting the support of subject peoples who resented Aztec and Inca overlordship. The astounding military conquest was also facilitated by bringing across the ocean two animals unknown in the Americas—mastiffs and horses—and an arsenal derived from metalworking capabilities—body armor and muskets. Yet the deadliest of all European weapons and the Spaniards' greatest ally was disease. Nearly every intruder from across the Atlantic, whether two- or four-legged, brought ashore pathogens that tore through the native peoples with a rapidity that was as gratifying to the Spanish as it was demoralizing to the indigenous people. This was part of an Atlantic exchange of people, animals, plants, and germs that would transform nearly every society on both sides of the Atlantic, though with very different results.

The secret advantage to Europeans, unbeknownst to them, was that the millions of Native peoples in the Americas had lived for many millennia isolated from epidemic diseases known in other regions of the world. The closing of the Bering land bridge thousands of years before had provided a "cold filter" through which no raging diseases could penetrate. Nor did Native peoples have herd animals, which in Eurasia and Africa lived in close contact with humans, where they acted as hosts and conduits of infectious diseases. If Native peoples did not quite live in a disease-free paradise, they were spared the killer pestilences that had severely punished Africans, Europeans, and Asians for centuries. These bacteriological infections—especially smallpox but also diphtheria, measles, cholera, whooping cough, scarlet fever, and others—were steady killers in most parts of the world, especially in densely populated regions. The Black Death alone reduced the population of Western Europe by a third, leaving hundreds of villages entirely abandoned.

Yet infected populations had gradually built up immunities against them that enabled many to survive virulent infections. Indian peoples of the Americas had no such immunities. Defenseless once they were exposed to the killer pathogens and parasites, they fell like wheat before a scythe. Whole tribes could be nearly wiped out in a few decades, leaving vast areas depopulated. On the island of Hispaniola, where an estimated 1 million Tainos were present in 1492 to witness Columbus's arrival, smallpox arrived in 1518. In what amounted to a biological holocaust, only about 1,000 Tainos were left a few decades later.

Cortés's victory in 1521 was hugely aided by a terrible onslaught of smallpox in 1520 to 1521 that may have halved the Aztec population just before the Spanish attack on Tenochtitlán. "Smallpox was the captain of the men of death in the war, typhus fever the first lieutenant, and measles the second lieutenant," writes the first historian to appreciate the role played by disease in the Spanish conquest and colonization of the Southern Hemisphere. "More terrible than the conquistadors on horseback, more deadly than sword and gunpowder, they made the conquest . . . a walkover compared with what it would have been without their aid." The killer diseases "were the forerunners of civilization, the companions of Christianity, the friends of the invader."[1] A murderous outbreak of smallpox in the 1520s, tearing at the sinews that held society together and paving the way for Spanish conquest of the Inca.

The hammer blows unleashed by infectious diseases were so catastrophic for Native people that they could hardly comprehend how their gods had failed them. Rampant disease caused mass agony, paralyzed community life, shattered leadership elites, and terrorized survivors. One of the first chroniclers of the Spanish conquest of Mexico described how smallpox, covering the bodies of horrified Aztecs, caused "great havoc." "They could not walk," wrote Fray Bernardino de Sahagún; "they only lay in their resting places and beds. They could not move; they could not stir; they could not change position, not lie on one side; nor face down, nor on their backs. And if they stirred, much did they cry out. Great was its destruction."[2]

Much more than microbes crossed the Atlantic with European explorers, conquerors, and settlers. With them came animal and plant life that transformed the landscape and altered ecosystems. Back across the Atlantic, more slowly, went plant and animal species that were equally transformative in Europe. Westward-bound ships brought wheat, barley, rye, and other grains; fruits such as peaches, pears, oranges, lemons, melons, and grapes; and vegetables such as radishes, onions, and salad greens. All of these, unknown in the Americas, perpetuated European cuisine and gradually changed Indian diets. But much more important were the herd animals of the Europeans: burros, cattle, goats, horses, pigs, and sheep. The burro pulling a wheeled cart could move ten times as much corn or cordwood as a human beast of burden. The horse could carry a messenger twice the speed of the fleetest runner. Still more transformative was livestock. Cattle, sheep, and pigs flourished, grazing in the vast grasslands of the Americas and safe from the large carnivores that attacked them in their Old World. They reproduced so rapidly that feral livestock swarmed across the countryside, often increasing tenfold in three or four years. Indeed, they flourished so well that in time they ate themselves out of their favorable environment,

[1]P. M. Ashburn, *The Ranks of Death: A Medical History of the Conquest of America* (New York, 1947), p. 98.
[2]Bernardino de Sahagún, *General History of the Things of New Spain,* trans. and edited by Arthur J. O. Anderson and Charles E. Dibble, quoted in Alfred W. Crosby, "Metamorphosis of the Americas," in Herman J. Viola and Carolyn Margolis, eds., *Seeds of Change* (Washington, DC, 1991), p. 73.

stripping away plant life and leading to topsoil erosion and desertification.

Pigs were even harder on the environment. Reproducing at staggering rates, they tore into the manioc tubers and sweet potatoes in the Caribbean islands where Columbus first introduced eight of them in 1493, devoured guavas and pineapples, ravaged lizards and baby birds—in short, stripped the land clean. Similar swine explosions occurred on the mainland of Mexico and Central America, where along with cattle they omnivorously devastated the grasslands. Meat was never lacking for European intruders (nor was leather or milk); all were there for the taking because hoofed animals from Europe took to the savannas and meadows of the Americas, as Alfred Crosby puts it, "like Adam and Eve returning to Eden."[3]

Spaniards—and later, other Europeans—naturally brought the flora and fauna that they prized most to the Americas. But also traveling with them were flora and fauna that the newcomers would gladly have left behind. Weed seeds could never be strained out of bags of fruit and vegetable seed, and once planted they proved hard to control. Hence, the Americas acquired invasive weeds, including clover, that crowded out native flora. Rats were pesky stowaways impossible to keep off ships bound across the Atlantic. Notorious carriers of disease deadly to humans, rats did their part in punishing the European colonizers, though native people bore the brunt of their vicious bites. Reproducing nearly as fast as pigs, they decimated native small animals and added a new dimension to the human struggle for life.

Whereas westbound ships transiting the Atlantic brought more misery than munificence to Native Americans—death-dealing epidemic diseases greatly outweighing the acquisition of horses and certain new foods—eastbound ships crossing the Atlantic mainly brought benefits to Europeans. Yaws and syphilis, apparently not known in Europe until about 1500, were afflictions from the Americas that created misery in the European homelands of the newcomers, but never remotely on the scale of the scathing smallpox epidemics. Table foods such as peanuts, pumpkins, pineapples, squash, and beans enriched the European diet. So did turkeys and guinea pigs. Llamas and alpacas produced wool for warmth. But by far the most important was the spread in Europe of Indian maize and potatoes. The spread was gradual because it took generations to understand the fundamental advantage the potato had over European grains. For example, across the north European plain, from the North Sea to the Ural Mountains, farmers slowly learned that by substituting potatoes for rye—the only grain that would thrive in the short and often rainy summers—they could quadruple their yield in calories per acre. Columbus had been dead for several hundred years before potato and corn production took hold in Europe. But when this phenomenon occurred, the change allowed for population growth and strengthened the sinew of Europe's diet. The same phenomenon occurred with the introduction of corn in southern Europe and Africa and later in China.

England Enters the Colonial Race

By the time England awoke to the promise of the Americas, the two Iberian powers were firmly entrenched there. England was the most backward of the European nations facing the Atlantic in exploring and colonizing the Americas. Only the voyages of John Cabot (who was in reality the Genoa-born Giovanni Caboto) gave England any title to a place in the "New World" sweepstakes. Moreover, Cabot's voyages in the 1490s were never followed up. Even the buccaneering expeditions of John Hawkins in the 1560s must be dismissed as unimportant in the expansion of Europe into America, because Hawkins was primarily involved in piracy—raiding Spanish trade in the Caribbean with the backing of Catholic-hating English merchants, who hoped to induce their government to sponsor their occasional attempts to challenge the hemispheric monopoly of Spain

---

[3]Alfred Crosby, "Metamorphosis of the Americas," in Viola and Margolis, eds., *Seeds of Change*.

and Portugal. England's only significant contact with North America had been with the Newfoundland fisheries, where English fishing fleets since the 1520s had competed with the French, Portuguese, and Spanish for the valuable cod—a vital protein source in the diet of most Europeans.

But England too sought colonies in the Americas, for colonies provided new markets and new sources of raw materials, and, if they contained gold and silver, added to the total supply of specie by which the strength of a nation was measured. By the end of the sixteenth century, England was eager to establish a foothold on the North American coast, for Spain and Portugal already dominated the South American continent and parts of the Caribbean and had claimed the southern portions of the North American landmass as well. If the English did not move soon, it would be too late. By the same token, Spain intended to resist English incursions into its sphere of influence by attacking any English settlement that dared to exist on the Atlantic coast of North America. The first known map of the tiny English settlement of Jamestown, Virginia, drawn by an Irish Catholic sailor on an English ship that delivered colonists to the Chesapeake settlement, was smuggled back to Spain. It was highly prized because it provided the necessary information for a surprise attack on this first English foothold on the North American coast.

English entry into the colonial race had origins not only in the lure of New World resources but also in the ideological war that raged in Europe throughout the last half of the sixteenth century. All the western European powers facing the Atlantic, with the exception of the Scandinavian countries, were involved in this struggle between those who professed Catholicism and those who adhered to Protestantism. This national and religious conflict continued issues and interests first raised in the Reformation and Counter-Reformation.

During much of the sixteenth century England swayed back and forth between religious ideologies, living first under the Protestant regimes of Henry VIII (1509–1547) and his sickly son, Edward VI (1547–1553), and then under the Catholic reign of his daughter Mary Tudor (1553–1558), who had married Philip II of Spain—the chief pillar of Catholic power in Europe. When Mary Tudor died and Henry's second daughter, Elizabeth, took the throne in 1558, she returned England to Protestantism. Like her father, Elizabeth favored Protestantism primarily as an expression of national independence. Always, however, the religious question hung above her head. Philip II of Spain, her brother-in-law, regarded her as a Protestant heretic and plotted against her incessantly.

In 1587 the smoldering conflict between Catholic Spain and Protestant England broke into open conflict. The English braced themselves for the seaborne attack expected from the Spanish fleet, regarded as the most powerful navy in the world. The battle that ensued is known simply as the Spanish Armada. In the spring of 1588, the Spanish fleet set sail for England, reaching its destination late in July. For two weeks a battle raged at sea. To the amazement of most of Europe, the English, aided by the Dutch, prevailed. The Spanish defeat did not establish English superiority at sea or bring England any overseas territory in recognition of its victory. It did not even propel England into the overseas colonial race. But the defeat did prevent a crushing Catholic victory in Europe and temporarily ended Spanish dreams of European hegemony. The Armada brought a temporary stalemate in the wars of religion and made clear for a generation—until 1618, when the beginning of the Thirty Years' War again threw Europe into open religious conflict—that religious uniformity could not be imposed by force. England was free to pursue its own destiny, free from the domination of other European powers.

With the way clear for overseas expansion, the "westward fever" began to catch hold in England at the end of the sixteenth century. One inconsequential effort had already been made—the planting of a small settlement on Roanoke Island, off the coast of North Carolina, in the 1580s. But after the Armada, the English gentry and merchants began to sense the profits beckoning from the New World. Their capital and experience would be indispensable in the decades ahead.

Theodore DeBry, a Flemish painter, traveled to London to meet John White, who did a watercolor of this Indian village of Secotan when he was part of the Roanoke expedition in 1587. DeBry's rendition of White's watercolor is faithful in most particulars, including the depiction of corn in various stages of cultivation. When DeBry's engravings of the New World were published in the late 1580s, Europeans got their first full view (though often distorted) of what they would meet on the other side of the Atlantic. (*Grand Voyages*, published 1590.)

Source: Library of Congress Rare Book and Special Collections Division [LC-USZ62-52444]

Urging their countrymen on were two Richard Hakluyts, uncle and nephew. In the last quarter of the 1500s, they explained the advantages of settling the remote regions on the other side of the Atlantic. Glory, profit, and adventure awaited everybody. Colonization promised the nobility an empire in the New World with new baronies, fiefdoms, and feudal estates. It offered the merchant new markets and a landmass filled with exotic produce that could be marketed at home. It invited the clergymen to convert a continent filled with "savages" for the greater glory of Christ. It beckoned the commoner to fields of adventure and limitless economic opportunity. And for the impoverished laborer, there was the prospect of starting life anew amid boundless land. The Hakluyts publicized the idea that the time was ripe for planting English stock across the Atlantic. Shakespeare contributed his bit to the national excitement by writing a play, *The Tempest*, about those who crossed the ocean to further the greatness of their country.

English participation in the age of exploration and colonization began with a generation of adventurous sea dogs and gentlemen such as Walter Ralegh, Francis Drake, Humphrey Gilbert, and Richard Grenville. With limited capital and minimal support from the Crown, they attempted much and ended mostly in failure. History books give their exploits much room because they were the first to try. But England could not become a serious colonial power in the Americas until the government, as in Spain and Portugal, gave active support to colonizing schemes, and, more important, until the merchant community and the rising middle class in England began plowing capital into overseas colonizing experiments. Thus, all the early efforts came to little or nothing—the voyages of Hawkins in the 1560s on the Spanish Main; the Roanoke voyages of 1585 to 1588, which ended in failure; the Sagadahoc settlement on the coast of Maine in 1607, which lasted only a year; and even the settlement of Jamestown, Virginia, in 1607, which limped along for several decades.

In addition to the difficulties of generating adequate financial and political support was the reality that, whether they focused on the North American continent or on the Caribbean islands, English colonizers confronted claims of rival European nations—claims usually backed up by actual occupation of territory. By the early seventeenth century, Portugal and Spain already had about 150,000 colonists in their overseas colonies. Although most of them were in Peru and Mexico, where the Spanish established major population centers at Potosí, Mexico City, and Cartagena, they had also planted outposts in southwestern North America and along the Atlantic coast from Florida to the Chesapeake Bay.

The English were also approaching a continent occupied by the French. Since 1524, when Giovanni da Verrazano had explored the eastern edge of North America, the French had dreamed of finding cities of gold and the Northwest Passage to China. They could settle, however, only where the Spanish had no use for the land. Thus, after abortive attempts to plant colonies in Florida and Brazil, which the Spanish and Portuguese wiped from the map, the French contented themselves with developing the northerly expanses of Canada.

Early Spanish Incursions in North America

When the English first tried to plant themselves at Roanoke Island off the North Carolina coast in 1585, they entered a region where the Spanish had been active for three-quarters of a century. The effects of Spanish-Indian contact along the southern Atlantic coast had rippled through the region for many decades. In this zone of intercultural contact, Indians regarded the English as a new branch of arriving Europeans, rather than as the first bearers of a strange new culture.

Spanish incursions into southeastern North America differed greatly from the main areas of their colonizing zeal—silver-rich Mexico and Peru and even secondary efforts in Chile, New Granada, Cuba, and Jamaica. The Spanish came mainly as explorers, plunderers, and traders rather than settlers, and they had great difficulty in controlling this vast region. In fact, they met with a series of costly failures. Meeting many different loosely formed chiefdoms, most of them warlike, rather than a centralized empire such as the Aztecs, the Spanish never truly dominated the Southeast.

Spanish explorers had charted the southeastern and Gulf regions of North America since the early sixteenth century, beginning with Juan Ponce de León's and Francisco Hernández de Córdoba's three expeditions to Florida between 1515 and 1521. By the latter date, the Florida tribes were fully aware of the dangers inherent in contact with Europeans, for in that year Lucas Vásquez de Ayllón, a Spanish imperial officer and member of the Royal Council of Hispaniola, lured some sixty Indians aboard his ships and whisked them away into slavery in the West Indies. "By such means," wrote a contemporary writer, Peter Martyr, "they sowed hatred and warfare throughout that peaceful and friendly region, separating children from their parents and wives from their husbands."[4]

For the next half-century, Spaniards planted small, fragile settlements on the southeastern coast of the continent, engaged in minor trade with the Indians of the region, and established missions manned briefly by Jesuit and then Franciscan fathers. But many attempts to bring the entire Gulf region under their control failed. From 1539 to 1542, Hernán de Soto led a plundering, ill-fated entrada deep into the country of what later became known as the Apalachee, Creek, Choctaw, and Chickasaw peoples, several hundred miles from the coast. Hoping to find a new silver-rich Peru—where he had helped defeat the Incas a few years before—de Soto instead died miserably. Only half of his 600 soldiers and African slaves survived tenacious Indian attacks and limped back to Mexico. What they left behind were the skeletons of hundreds of mutilated and decapitated Natives, a trail of charred villages, and microbic infections that devastated a vast region far beyond the area of immediate Spanish-Native contact.

Again the Spaniards drove northward from Mexico, under Tristán de Luna y Arellano in 1559 and under Juan Pardo in 1566 to 1568, attempting to establish their authority in the Southeast. Everywhere, they enslaved Indians, used them as provisions carriers and concubines, and lived off the land. But although Spanish weaponry and man-eating mastiffs terrorized Indians and infectious diseases did their deadly work, the military expeditions never succeeded in completely pacifying the numerous chiefdoms, whose expert bowmen were more than a match for the armored Spanish horsemen.

In 1565, the Spanish made a more concerted effort to establish themselves in eastern North America. Angered by the construction of a French fort at the mouth of the St. John's River in that year, they founded San Agustín (St. Augustine), now the oldest continuously inhabited town in the continental United States. After massacring the French, the Spanish established St. Augustine as a military outpost and a mission town coordinating Spanish religious efforts on the southeastern missionary frontier. On occasion, as in 1597, the various coastal tribes attempted to wipe out the Spanish missions and trading posts along the coast and to drive the Spaniards back to Florida. But the Franciscans kept returning, as if God had meant for them to settle all the Indians of the region within the sound of the mission bell. Reaching the Indian's soul, the Spanish friar proved more effective than the Spanish soldier.

Crucifix and mission bell outperformed sword and gun among the Guale, Apalachee, and Timucua. Respecting tribal customs such as polygamy and matrilineality, the Franciscan priests converted most of the Florida Indians by the 1640s. But the Spanish black robes could stop neither smallpox nor influenza. Ghastly numbers of Indians succumbed to European diseases. This partly explains the short-lived revolts of the Apalachee in 1647 and of the Timucua in 1656. Yet, by 1650 the Spanish had established about 44 mission towns from today's Savannah to northern Florida.

Meanwhile, Nuevo Mexico became a second region of missionary activity. Francisco

---

[4]Quoted in John R. Swanton, *Early History of the Creek Indians and Their Neighbors*, Smithsonian Institution, Bureau of American Ethnology, Bulletin 73 (Washington, DC, 1922), p. 33.

Vásquez de Coronado had explored the area in 1540 to 1542, and half a century later, the Spanish mounted their first big incursion into the ancient homelands of the Pueblo people along the Rio Grande. Thrusting northward along the Rio Grande from the Spanish mining region in northern Mexico, Don Juan de Oñate's expedition, with 83 wagons and 129 men, reached the heart of the Pueblo region in 1598. There he found some 86,000 Native people, their numbers reduced by severe droughts that had imperiled agriculture in the late thirteenth century, living in about 60 villages. Santa Fe, founded only three years after Jamestown, became the administrative center of Spanish colonization.

With little gold and silver to exploit, the Spanish northern borderlands were interesting chiefly to Franciscan missionaries. The Spanish established small presidios, or garrisons, in this far-flung southwestern territory, and they commandeered the labor of some Indians while mixing with Indian women. But the primary institution of New Mexico was the Franciscan mission, which in many cases served also as presidio and administrative center. Hence, the Spanish presence in New Mexico was numerically insignificant. Even as late as 1680, probably no more than 1,500 Spaniards lived there. By 1800, the number had grown only to about 20,000 in the Southwest, and of these the vast majority were descendants of Native people who had mingled with Spanish soldiers. With no fur trade to conduct or no minerals to extract, and with no fertile lands beckoning incoming immigrant farmers, the Spanish pattern of settlement contrasted sharply with that of the English on the eastern side of the continent.

Marked differences also marked the Spanish missionaries' own methods. In early Florida, and much later in California, they tried to gather Indians within mission complexes where priests could closely supervise every aspect of life. The California missions took root in areas where

Indian peoples were widely scattered and led a seminomadic existence, so this scheme bore some of the marks of forced agricultural labor. To the Franciscan friars, supremely indifferent to physical deprivation, this semi-incarceration of Native people was essential to their goal of mingling conversion with a "full social and cultural reorientation of native life."[5] In New Mexico, however, Pueblo people had lived in settled villages along the Rio Grande for centuries, practicing agriculture extensively. Here the Franciscans made no attempt to gather native people within the mission walls, but instead built their churches on the edges of settled towns. This practice led to a division of life "between a town-oriented secular aspect and a church-oriented religious aspect."[6]

The lack of a mutually advantageous economic tie, such as that which united French and Algonkians in New France, tended to place the full emphasis in Spanish-Indian relations on religious conversion. This tendency usually led to a determined effort by the colonizers to effect a wholesale cultural change among the Native people, which produced tension from the outset. Thus, the mid-seventeenth-century outbreaks of violence against the Franciscan missionaries of Florida by Guale, Apalachee, and Timucua Indians were paralleled in New Mexico, where Pueblo people often staunchly resisted the imposition of the Spanish Catholic worldview. The Franciscans' work among the Pueblo people along the Rio Grande in New Mexico "was less an effort to transfer individuals from an Indian-type community to [a] Spanish-type community than it was to remake Indian communities into tightly knit, church-centered social units with Indian leadership still operative."[7] Under this program, the Franciscans were able to convert thousands of Pueblos in the mission churches they built on the edges of ancient native villages in the early 1600s. But they had far fewer souls to convert because the Native population, hammer struck by European diseases,

[5]Charles Gibson, *Spain in America* (New York, 1966), p. 196.
[6]Ibid., p. 197.
[7]Edward H. Spicer, *Cycles of Conquest: The Impact of Spain, Mexico and the United States on the Indians of the Southwest, 1553–1960* (Tucson, AZ, 1962), p. 287.

was plummeting rapidly—by about two-thirds from the 1590s to the 1630s.

However, in the 1670s, when the Pueblo people probably numbered no more than 17,000, Franciscans went beyond attempting to overlay Pueblo culture with a thin veneer of Catholicism. Spanish priests began to restrict traditional Pueblo religious activities—forbidding ball games and sacred kachina dances, destroying masks and prayer sticks, and imprisoning and flogging Pueblo priests and medicine men. At the same time, Spanish soldiers and ranchers offended the Pueblo people by enslaving hundreds of Natives. In every Pueblo north of El Paso, Native people answered this attempt to undermine traditional culture by attempting to drive the Franciscans and Spanish colonizers out of the region altogether.

Called Popé's Rebellion after the Pueblo medicine man who coordinated it, the revolt was a holy war to defend the Pueblo religion and way of life. In 1680, the Pueblo rebels destroyed every church in New Mexico; killed 21 of 40 priests and about 400 Spanish settlers; laid waste to Spanish ranches, fields, and government buildings; and drove the remaining Spaniards out of Pueblo country. Over the ruins of the Spanish plaza in Santa Fe they rebuilt their kiva, the deep chamber where Pueblos engaged in activities. Pueblo people of the Rio Grande willingly borrowed the material culture of the Spanish, but their well-integrated communities fought tenaciously against attempts to impose a religion and culture meant to obliterate their ancient cultural identity.

After Popé's Rebellion, the Spanish tried to reassert their control, but not until the early 1700s could they begin to establish control along the Rio Grande—and then only by declaring a cultural truce, with eased demands for Pueblo labor tribute and certain Pueblo rituals permitted in return for nominal acceptance of the Catholic faith. Spanish authority was not fully established until about 1740. By that time, the deadly work of European diseases had devastated the Native population. By 1800, only a sliver of the Native population that had met Spaniards in the late 1500s existed in New Mexico. Though faced with less resistance, Spanish missionaries found that they had fewer and fewer native people to convert to Catholicism.

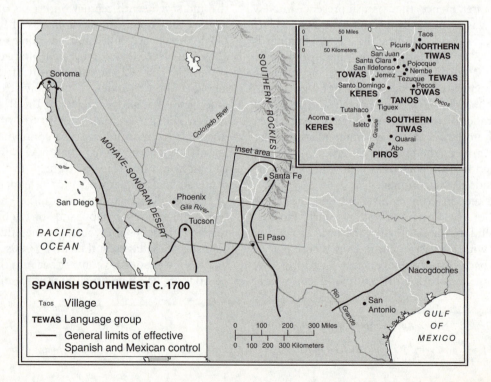

SPANISH SOUTHWEST C. 1700

Taos   Village

TEWAS   Language group

—— General limits of effective Spanish and Mexican control

In California the Spaniards made a brief and an intermittent contact with the native population beginning in 1542, but the first permanent settlements did not appear until 1769. In that year Spanish forces landed at San Diego. Promptly constructing a presidio, or fort, they founded the Mission San Diego de Alcalá, the first of twenty-one Spanish missions eventually erected in California. During the two centuries that preceded the founding of the San Diego mission, Spanish influence on Native cultures in most parts of California was negligible. The Native population at the time of contact numbered some 300,000 persons, and this number diminished slowly during the first two centuries of intermittent contact. Most Native communities were organized by lineage of clan, though the Chumash and Gabrielinos along the southern coast lived in towns with more centralized political organizations. Indian culture in these southern coastal towns may have changed during the years prior to the first Spanish settlements, but Spanish influence in other areas was negligible.

During the late 1700s, Spanish intrusion into the lands of various California Native societies disrupted community stability and drastically altered native lifestyles. The missions that dotted the coast between San Diego and San Francisco drew their recruits from small dispersed villages, not the settled villages of New Mexico. Spanish encroachment forced many Indians to abandon their hunting and gathering practices and lineage-based political systems to take their places in the rigidly hierarchical ranking system that existed within the missions. The missionaries turned many natives into sedentary horticulturists and craftspersons, although a few were recruited as vaqueros, or cowboys, to tend the large herds of cattle and horses on the outlying mission estates. During the late eighteenth and early nineteenth centuries, the Indian population within reach of the mission system declined dramatically as periodic epidemics of smallpox, measles, dysentery, pleurisy, pneumonia, and syphilis took their ghastly toll.

The French Penetration of North America

The French, like the Spanish, were a force in the Americas before the English arrived. Their activities in the late sixteenth and early seventeenth centuries were confined to harrying Spanish and Portuguese shipping, trading surreptitiously with Iberian settlers in the Caribbean and South America, and planting tiny fishing and trading settlements on the North American mainland.

French fisherman had worked along the coasts of Newfoundland and Nova Scotia since the early sixteenth century. A sporadic fur trade with the Natives of the area began in 1534 with Cartier's exploration of the Gulf of St. Lawrence. These efforts convinced the French that the St. Lawrence River corridor could be profitable, even if the climate was inhospitable. Realizing that only the St. Lawrence and Hudson rivers provided access by water into the interior of the northern parts of the continent, the French wisely chose to plant their first settlements near the mouth of the St. Lawrence in 1603. From there they pushed forward their quest for another form of New World gold—the skins of fur-bearing animals.

By the end of the sixteenth century, the French were most numerous among the hundreds of European fishing ships that came annually to Canadian waters. When the Spaniards and Portuguese wiped out the French settlements at the mouth of the Rio de Janeiro and on the southeastern coast of North America respectively in 1560 and 1565, the French decided to concentrate to the north, where their commercial activities would be free from Spanish and Portuguese molestation.

Though fishing was valuable, the fur trade turned out to be vastly more profitable. Nothing more was required than to bring trade goods desired by Indians across the Atlantic, anchor a few ships in a sheltered bay of the St. Lawrence, and wait for Native traders to arrive with pelts. Military conquest was unnecessary and in fact would only adversely affect trade with the Indians. Even large settlements were not required, for the fur trade involved a simple barter relationship. Once in place, the fur trade linked Native peoples to the developing capitalist world economy.

In time, the French decided to plant permanent settlements in North America because without a colonial population base, their trading posts were subject to the predatory raids of the Dutch, English, or any other colonizing nation. Thus, the French planted a colony in 1604 at Port Royal, Nova Scotia, and in 1608 established a second settlement at Québec. This attempt to solidify claims to the northern part of the continent was enough to induce the English, a thousand miles to the south, to mount a campaign of extermination against the French. Although England and France were not at war, the governor of Virginia, Sir Thomas Dale, commissioned a seasoned explorer and Atlantic sea dog, Samuel Argall, to attack the French settlements in 1613. Just a few months after he had abducted Mataoka (Pocahontas) in Virginia, Argall wiped out the French settlement at Port Royal.

For the next few decades, the French struggled to plant tiny settlements in the face of growing English opposition centered in New England. But France was preoccupied with the Thirty Years War in Europe and could spare neither men nor money for overseas development. By 1643, after almost half a century of colonization, fewer than 400 Frenchmen lived in New France. Most of them were Indian traders or Jesuit priests, who had come in considerable numbers to convert Native people. As one royal governor of Canada later remarked, only two kinds of business existed in New France: the conversion of souls and the conversion of beaver.

Under the leadership of Samuel de Champlain, backed by the Company of New France, New France was established on a more permanent footing. By offering free land, the company lured farmers from France to establish a permanent agricultural society. By 1660, fewer than 3,000 French people huddled in small towns along the St. Lawrence River (as compared with twenty times that number in New England).

Whereas the Dutch, English, and Spanish typically used military force or guile to wrest land and political submission from their Indian neighbors, the French in the north forged much different relations with Native societies of the St. Lawrence River valley and the upper Great Lakes region. The French were so few in number that they could not have entertained the slightest hope of survival without the friendship of the Native peoples surrounding them. A high proportion of these French settlers were male, thereby adding to their dependency on Indian neighbors. In contrast to the English and the Dutch settlements, where the sex ratio among Europeans was far more balanced, Frenchmen freely took Indian mistresses, concubines, and wives. They exhibited no embarrassment at this mixing of blood and were hard put to understand English qualms about interracial relations. Also, the French Catholic Church was more permissive in this regard. In Nova Scotia, where French women were scarce, intermarriage was so common that one authority believes that by 1676 virtually all French families had Native blood in their veins. In the more settled areas of the St. Lawrence River valley, where the Algonkian tribes were less sedentary and Jesuit priests raised some objections to racial mixing, interracial liaison rather than interracial marriage was more customary. The Jesuits frowned on church marriages between the two cultures, but they could do nothing about the sexual urges of their parishioners. "In the Night time," wrote Baron de Lahontan, "all of them, barring the Jesuits, roll from house to house to debauch the women savages." Farther west at the trading posts, "miscegenation between the *coureurs de bois* and the Indian women was the rule rather than the exception."[8]

---

[8]Alfred G. Bailey, *The Conflict of European and Eastern Algonkian Cultures, 1504–1700: A Study in Canadian Civilization* (Sackville, NB, 1937), p. 112.

DEFEAT OF IROQUOIS AT LAKE CHAMPLAIN.

CHAMPLAIN'S FIGHT WITH THE IROQUOIS

This engraving from *The Voyages of Samuel de Champlain* (1613) is often attributed to Champlain himself, but the inaccuracies in the picture suggest that the artist was not present at the battle. The depiction of this fight in 1609 between Mohawks (right) and Champlain and his Indian allies (left) contains many errors: there are no palm trees on the shores of Lake Champlain, the Indians did not use hammocks, and the boats at the water's edge do not resemble canoes. Nevertheless, the picture does convey the deadly impact of firearms on warriors accustomed to fighting in ranks, using bows and arrows, and protected by wooden or wicker shields. *(North Wind Picture Archives/Alamy)*

The practice of racial intermixture became official government policy in the 1660s when Colbert, Louis XVI's architect of imperial reorganization, called for a full-fledged integration of the races. Colbert ordered the French settlers "to civilize the Algonquins . . . and the other savages who have embraced Christianity, and dispose them to come and settle them in community with the French, live with them, and bring up their children in their manners and customs." In spite of opposition from the Catholic Church, Colbert also encouraged intermarriage and urged the governor of New France to bring about a mingling of the cultures "in order that, having but one law and one master, they may form only one people and one blood."[9] It was a policy contrived to bring the Indians under French control, not by destroying or weakening the indigenous population but by assimilating it. A half-century later, two lettered Virginians, William Byrd and Robert Beverly, pondered this "Modern Policy" adopted by France in Canada and lamented that English "false delicacy" in the early years on the Chesapeake had kept them from making a "prudent

---

[9]Quoted in ibid., p. 107.

alliance" through intermarriage, as the French had done.[10]

To be sure, racial mingling almost always linked French men and Indian women, and the offspring of these liaisons followed the mother. This trend meant that Native blood was rarely added to the French gene pool. But despite this evidence of French ethnocentrism, frequent intermixing brought contacts of the most intimate nature between the two peoples, and this intimacy could not help but bring about greater mutual understanding. For Indian leaders, marriage would seal trading networks and military alliances with the French. For the undermanned and "underwomaned" French colonists, intimate relations with native peoples of the St. Lawrence region made good sense.

Equally important in establishing relatively nonviolent relations was the fact that virtually every man in early New France was there either to trade furs or to convert the Indians. Both tasks required Native cooperation. Thus, French traders traveled hundreds of miles into the remote Great Lakes regions of the Hurons, establishing trading posts, learning the language and customs of the tribes, and finding Native consorts who would aid their access to furs, especially the beaver pelts much prized for broad-brimmed hats in Europe, and sealed the friendship of their trading partners. In the English and the Dutch settlements, the Indian trader was the exception rather than the rule, since the vast majority of European immigrants after the first few years were farmers engaging in an activity to which the Indians had nothing to offer once the colonizers understood Native techniques of cultivating indigenous crops.

Those who were not fur traders in New France were generally Jesuit priests. They established missions, martyred themselves in hostile Indian country, and worked for the greater glory of their God by converting Natives to Catholicism.

Fur trading and missionary work often went hand in hand, with missions established at important river junctions where the fur trade took place. Jesuits trekked northward to the farthest shores of the Gulf of St. Lawrence and westward as far as Lake Huron. Their main efforts were concentrated among some 15,000 to 20,000 Hurons (Wendats) who were settled in the Great Lakes region in towns of several thousand.

The Jesuits were more willing than the Puritans to accept that Native beliefs in a supreme being, in the immortality of the soul, and in supernatural forces could be revised sufficiently to find acceptance from their Christian God. Whereas most Puritans insisted that Indians of the New England area renounce their way of life and abandon their religious beliefs as a starting point in accepting Christianity, the Jesuits studied the Indian structure of belief and attempted to change it slowly. Jesuits did not contest the Native belief that the manitous—great spirits—smiled upon a successful hunt or military victory; rather, they tried to persuade Indians that thanks should go to the power of Christ. "Indians were not so much being converted to Christianity," writes one historian, "as Christ was being converted into a manitou."[11] The statement of Father Ragueneau in 1647, which the Puritan clergy would have deplored, reveals the ethnocentrism of the French—but an ethnocentrism tempered by respect and affection. "One must be very careful before condemning a thousand things among their customs, which greatly offend minds brought up and nourished in another world. It is easy to call irreligion what is merely stupidity, and to take for diabolical working something that is nothing more than human. . . ."[12]

This greater flexibility in approaching Native culture on its own terms, even while demeaning it, led to a much greater degree of cultural engagement in New France than in New England. The meager Puritan missionary activity focused

[10]William K. Boyd, ed., *William Byrd's Histories of the Dividing Line Betwixt Virginia and North Carolina* (Raleigh, NC, 1929), pp. 3–4; Robert Beverly, *The History and Present State of Virginia,* Louis B. Wright, ed. (Chapel Hill, NC, 1947), pp. 38–39.
[11]Richard White, *The Middle Ground: Indians, Empires, and Republics in the Great Lakes Region, 1650–1815* (New York, 1991), p. 26.
[12]Quoted in W. J. Eccles, *The Canadian Frontier, 1534–1760* (New York, 1969), p. 48.

on the weakest tribes, those that had lost or were losing their political autonomy and cultural self-sufficiency. Weakened by disease and warfare and demoralized by the rapid growth of the English population, small tribes abandoned some of their traditional ways and attempted to refashion themselves in the white man's image. Living in "praying villages," they conformed to English clothing styles, work habits, and forms of worship. In contrast, some of the greatest successes of the Jesuits in New France were among the most powerful Indian societies, although the priests never made much headway among the Iroquois. Like the English Protestant clergy, the Jesuit priests believed that the true conversion to Christianity ultimately required giving up "savage" ways. But the Jesuits adopted a more gradualist approach and worked within a colonizing society that did not pursue a militant policy of establishing political domination over native people.

The different nature of French-Indian relations is also evident in the Gallic attitude toward Native sovereignty. In all European-Indian contacts, the concept of sovereignty was used to connote political authority and can be regarded as a kind of litmus test of the balance of power between the two cultures. All Europeans regarded Native peoples as inferior, and all pursued sovereignty as the ultimate goal, for if Native peoples recognized European law and kingly authority, they were, in effect, surrendering their political independence.

Whenever Indians yielded sovereignty, subjugation was not far behind. For example, when the New Englanders fought the Pequots in 1637, their goal was to bring under English jurisdiction a powerful tribe that had refused to accept Puritan sway. Similarly, as soon as they were strong enough, by the late 1620s, the Chesapeake colonists forced the Indians to recognize their sovereignty. But in New France, the governing council was debating as late as 1664 whether or not an Algonkian Indian who had raped the wife of a French colonist should be prosecuted in the French court of justice—a telltale argument

revealing that French sovereignty had not yet been established. A half-century later, in 1714, when the Indians declared that the French had no right to jail or punish them for drunkenness, since they were not subject to the laws of the colony and since the liquor, not the drinker of it, was responsible for breaches of conduct, the French acquiesced because "the matter is extremely delicate." Conceding the Natives' claim of jurisdiction over wrongdoers, the French passed laws prohibiting the sale of alcohol to the Indians. When crimes were committed by Indians under the influence of alcohol, the French courts attempted to discover the illegal supplier, prosecute the supplier for violating French law, and charge the supplier with damages committed by the drunken Native. This was not the English way.

The French policy did not always reflect greater understanding of the Indians or acceptance of their culture. First and foremost, it was a policy born of weakness. "The French were unable to impose their law on the Indians, and for one good reason," writes one historian, "to have attempted to do so with any degree of vigor would have alienated the Indians, and this the French could not afford to do."[13] But from this policy founded on weakness came the most lastingly intimate, if not fully amicable, relations between Europeans and Native Americans on the continent. By regulating their own subjects in relations with Natives and by continuing to recognize the sovereignty of the Algonkians, the French coexisted fruitfully with Native societies to a degree unprecedented elsewhere in North America. That their settlements were so small and competed so little for cleared land doubtless helped this relative harmony.

In spite of the relatively pacific character of French-Algonkian relations, the Indians were not spared the ravages that beset other Native societies after European arrival. Epidemic diseases were not a matter of policy or national character, and they struck the Hurons as mortally in 1633 to 1634 and again in 1649 as they had the Natives of New England. Nor could the French,

---

[13]Ibid., pp. 78–79.

however good their intentions, avert the attacks on their Huron allies by the Iroquois after the European rivalry for the fur trade began. Once the beaver supply dwindled in their ancient hunting grounds, the Iroquois seized the role of middlemen between the European traders at Albany and the Huron and Ottawa tribes of the Great Lakes region. When this undertaking could not be accomplished through diplomacy, as in the late 1640s, the Iroquois resorted to war. Within a few years they had decimated the Hurons and other tribes living around Lake Erie. War raged intermittently thereafter with the Iroquois exploiting the remaining beaver in their newly conquered territories and hijacking fleets of fur-laden canoes from the northern Ottawa country as they headed for French markets in Montreal. Bringing home to their Iroquois villages were not only Huron-captured beaver pelts but Huron captives by the hundreds to replace Iroquois who themselves had been decimated by the 1630s smallpox onslaught. By the 1660s half or more of the Iroquois villagers were Huron captives from the beaver wars.

Although Catholicism and French values helped shape the relationship with Indian societies, economic and demographic factors sometimes counted for more. This trend is demonstrated by French relations with the Natchez of the lower Mississippi region in the early eighteenth century, which contrast starkly with the French experience in Canada. The Natchez were a highly stratified and ritualistic people, the southernmost descendants of the ancient Mound Builders. In their social hierarchy, theocratic authority, hereditary class system, and celebration of war, they more closely approximated Europeans than any other Native group in eastern North America. After de Soto had scourged the country in 1540 to 1541, they experienced little contact with Europeans until the arrival of French explorer Rene-Robert Cavalier de La Salle, who laid claim to the lower Mississippi valley for France in 1682. For another three decades, until the French established a small trading post on the Mississippi River in

1713, the Natchez, several thousand strong, had only occasional contact with French missionaries or French and English traders.

When the French planned to seize control of the interior of the continent in the second decade of the eighteenth century, they brought soldiers, women, and enslaved Africans with them. Trade with the Natchez was only incidental to French purposes. When the Natchez killed five traders in retaliation for the ill treatment they had received, the French executed several minor chiefs. When tension flared again in 1722, the French governor burned three Natchez villages to the ground and demanded that the Natchez emperor, Tattooed Serpent, send him the head of one of the minor chiefs, though this act violated tribal custom, by which all chiefs were immune from the death penalty.

The draconic policy of the French led to further hostilities. In 1729, after the French demanded land cessions without compensation, including the site of an important Native village, the Natchez mounted an offensive to drive their oppressors away. "We walk like slaves, which we shall soon be," counseled a Natchez chief calling for war. "Is not death preferable to slavery?"[14] By this time the French had no use for the Natchez in the lower Mississippi and felt no qualms about attempting to intimidate them. Though the Natchez overpowered the French at Fort Rosalie in 1729, killing several hundred of the French and taking prisoner many women, children, and absorbing several hundred enslaved Africans into their villages, they beat back the French only temporarily. Reinforcements arrived in 1731; with the aid of Choctaw allies, the French stormed the Natchez strongholds with cannon. Killing more than 1,000 Natchez, the French burned many captives at the stake and sold some 400 into slavery in St. Dominigue. The surviving Natchez, scattering into small bands, sought refuge among other southeastern tribes. By the end of the year, the Natchez nation, once nearly 6,000 strong, had ceased to exist as a sovereign people. Finding no way of utilizing the Indians to their own

---

[14]Quoted in Alan Taylor, *American Colonies* (New York: Viking, 2001), p. 390.

advantage, the French worked toward the elimination of these ancient sun-worshipping people with a thoroughness that would have aroused the envy of the English in New England, the Dutch in New Netherland, or the Spanish in Mexico.

Imagining Native Americans

The English approaching the North American coast had to reckon with Spain and France, whose established claims forced the English to look to the middle part of the Atlantic seaboard for a toehold on the continent. Well aware of the Spanish presence, the English would build their forts facing the sea, to fend off Spanish attacks, rather than facing inland where the Indian danger lay. It was the prudent work of those who knew they were intruding on territory claimed by Spain.

But it was another people, the indigenous inhabitants of the land, who most forcefully claimed English attention. What did men like Gilbert and Ralegh know about the Native occupiers of the land as they approached the forbidding coast of North America in the 1580s? How would they be received by these people whom Columbus, thinking he had reached India, mistakenly called Indians? How would the English obtain the use or possession of land that these Indians occupied? How were ideas about the nature of Native peoples influenced by the thorny question of obtaining sovereignty over the land? And how would the Indians' long experience with Spanish and French traders, missionaries, plunderers, and colonizers affect the native disposition toward the English?

The first English colonizers doubtless experienced the apprehensions that fill the minds of those who attempt to penetrate the unknown. But they were far from uninformed about the native people of the Americas. Beginning with Columbus's description of the "New World," published in several European capitals in 1493 and 1494, a mass of reports, stories, and promotional

accounts had circulated among sailors, merchants, geographers, politicians, and church people involved in the early voyages of discovery, trade, and settlement. These sources became the basis for understanding the Natives and their habitats as adventurers approached the eastern edge of land in the western Atlantic Ocean.

From this literature, the early colonists could hold a split image of the North American Natives. On the one hand, it seemed that the Indians were a gentle people who would be receptive to those who came not to harm them but to live and trade with them. Columbus had written of the "great amity towards us" that he encountered in San Salvador in 1492 and described the Arawak people there as "a loving people without covetousness," who "were greatly pleased and became so entirely our friends that it was a wonder to see." The Arawaks "brought us parrots and cotton thread in balls, and spears and many other things, and we exchanged for them other things, such as small glass beads and hawks' bells, which we gave to them."[15] Verrazano, the first European to navigate the eastern edge of the continent, wrote with similar optimism from what became known as the Bay of New York in 1524. The Natives were graceful of limb, tawny colored, with black alert eyes, and "dressed in birds' feathers of various colors, and they came toward us joyfully, uttering loud cries of wonderment, and showing us the safest place to beach the boat."[16]

From this time on, accounts of Natives of the Americas included many such enthusiastic descriptions of native people and their eagerness to receive European explorers and settlers. This positive image of the Indians not only reflected the friendly reception that Europeans apparently received in Newfoundland, parts of Florida, and elsewhere in the Caribbean and South America, but also represented an understanding of the Americas as an earthly paradise—a Garden of Eden where war-torn, impoverished Europeans could find a new life amid nature's bounty. That Columbus thought he had found the Gihon, one

[15]Quoted in Wilcomb E. Washburn, ed., *The Indian and the White Man* (Garden City, NY, 1964), p. 4.
[16]Lawrence C. Wroth, *The Voyages of Giovanni da Verrazano, 1524–1528* (New Haven, CT, 1970), p. 137.

of the biblical rivers flowing from Eden, when he reached the Orinoco River in 1498, is vivid testimony to this strain in European thinking.

Another reason existed for drawing a favorable image of the North American natives. The English, like other European colonizers, hoped that trade with Natives would yield great profits. Indeed, the early English voyages were not primarily intended for the purpose of large-scale settlement and agricultural production. Trade with the Indians, the search for gold and silver, and discovery of the Northwest Passage were the principal goals. So a special incentive existed for seeing the Natives as something more than "savages." Only a friendly Indian could be a trading Indian. If trade was the key to overseas development, then English promoters logically suggested that the Indian might be receptive and generous—a person who could be wooed and won to the advantages of trade.

However, a counterimage of the Indian also lodged itself in the minds of the English approaching North America. This negative view featured a savage, hostile, beastlike person, and even people cursed by God because they were descended from the ancient Israelites. Spanish and French literature of colonization bristled with such depictions. As early as the first decade of the sixteenth century, Sebastian Cabot had paraded in England three Eskimos taken captive on his voyage to the Arctic in 1502. A contemporary described the Natives as flesh-eating, primitive specimens, who "spoke such speech that no man could understand them, and in their demeanour like to brute beasts."[17] A flood of pamphlets in the second half of the sixteenth century described the Natives in terms that could have caused little optimism concerning the reception that Europeans would receive. These accounts portrayed the Indians as crafty, brutal, loathsome half-men whose cannibalistic instincts were revealed, as one pamphleteer wrote in 1578, by the fact that "there is no flesh

or fishe, which they finde dead, (smell it never so filthily) but they will eate it, as they finde it, without any other dressing [cooking]."[18] Other accounts depicted the Natives as bestial, living in sexual abandon, and in general moved by unbridled passion rather than reason.

The English had another reason for imagining that not all would be friendship and amiable trading when they encountered Native Americans. For years they had read accounts of the Spanish experience with Aztecs and Incans in Mexico and Peru—and the story was not a pretty one. Chief among these Spanish accounts was the work of the Dominican friar Bartholomé de Las Casas, whose *Brevissima Relación de la Destrucción de las Indias* was translated into English and published in 1583. The English could delight in Las Casas's gory descriptions of Spanish cruelty and genocide, for such stories confirmed all the worst things that the Protestant English believed about the Catholic Spaniards with whom they were about to go to war. The Hakluyts eagerly contributed to the "Black Legend" concerning the Spanish colonizers, labeling them "hellhounds and wolves."

Such accounts, useful in fueling anti-Spanish and anti-Catholic prejudices, also suggested that when Europeans met "primitive" people, slaughter was unavoidable. Moreover, Las Casas was rebutted by a host of Spanish writers who justified Spanish behavior by insisting that the Indians had precipitated bloodletting and, because of their unalterably bestial nature, could be dealt with in no other way. However useful the accounts of Spanish cruelty might have been for Protestant pamphleteers, the English embarking for the Americas must have wondered whether the same experience awaited them. The English knew from their own violent invasions of Ireland and the Netherlands in the late sixteenth century that indigenous peoples did not ordinarily welcome those who came to dominate and butcher them. However tractable

[17]Richard Hakluyt, *Divers Voyages Touching the Discoveries of America, and the Ilands Adjacent unto the Same* (1582), Hakluyt Society *Publications*, 1st Ser., 7 (London, 1850): 23.
[18]Vilhjalmur Stefansson, ed., *The Three Voyages of Martin Frobisher* (London, 1938), 2: 23.

and amenable to trade the Indians might appear in some of the English literature, the image of a hostile savage who awaited Christian adventurers could never be blotted from the English mind. Knowing that they enjoyed the same technological superiority as the Spanish, English leaders believed that if they desired, they could lay waste the country they were entering. The English experience with the Irish, in whose country military officers like Gilbert and Ralegh had gained experience in the subjugation of "lesser breeds" for several decades, suggested that the English were fully capable of every cruelty contrived by the Spanish. To imagine the Indian as a savage beast was therefore a way of predicting the future, preparing for it, and justifying what one would do, even before one caused it to happen.

Another factor nourishing negative images of the Indian related directly to the Native possession of land. For the English, as for other Europeans, the Native occupation of the land presented problems of law, morality, and practicality. As early as the 1580s, George Peckham, an early Catholic promoter of colonization, had admitted that some of the English doubted their right to seize the land of others. In 1609, Robert Gray, another promoter of colonization, asked: "By what right or warrant can we enter into the land of these Savages, take away their rightful inheritance from them, and plant ourselves in their places, being unwronged or unprovoked by them?"[19] It was a weighty question, for the English, like other Europeans, had organized their society around the concept of private ownership of land and regarded this concept as important evidence of their superior culture.

The land problem could be partially resolved by arguing that the English did not intend to take the Natives' land but wanted only to share with them what seemed a superabundance of territory. In return, they would extend to the Indians the advantages of a richer culture, a more advanced civilization, and, of most importance, the Christian religion. This was the argument used by the governing council in Virginia in 1610 when it advertised in England that the settlers "by way of merchandizing and trade, do buy of them [the Indians] the pearls of earth, and sell to them the pearls of heaven."[20] It did not matter that the Chesapeake tribes had indicated no desire to exchange their land for such Christian instruction as a ragged band of the English could provide.

Another, more portentous way of answering the question of English rights to the land was to deny the humanity of the Indians. Were the English entitled to "plant ourselves in their places?" asked Robert Gray. Yes, if the Indians' inhumanity disqualified them from the right to possess land. "Although the Lord hath given the earth to children of men," he wrote, "the greater part of it [is] possessed and wrongfully usurped by wild beasts, and unreasonable creatures, or by brutish savages, which by reason of their godless ignorance, and blasphemous idolatry, are worse than those beasts which are of most wild and savage nature."[21] This line of reasoning was filled with danger for the Indian. Although many leaders of colonization would avow that "every foot of land which we shall take unto our use, we will bargain and buy of them," others conveniently suggested that Indians, merely by being "Godless" and "savage," as defined by English invaders, had disqualified themselves from rightful ownership of the land.[22] In this sense, much was to be gained by projecting deeply negative images of native peoples. The darker the

[19]*A Good Speed to Virginia* (1609), quoted in Wesley Frank Craven, "Indian Policy in Early Virginia," *William and Mary Quarterly*, 3rd Ser., 1 (1944): 65.
[20]*A True Declaration of the Estate of the Colonie in Virginia . . .* (1610), in *Tracts and Other Papers, Relating Principally to the Origin, Settlement, and Progress of the Colonies in North America . . .*, Peter Force, comp. (Washington, DC, 1884), 3, No. 1: 6.
[21]*A Good Speed to Virginia* (1609), quoted in Gary B. Nash, "The Image of the Indian in the Southern Colonial Mind," *William and Mary Quarterly*, 3rd Ser., 29 (1972): 210.
[22]William Strachey, *The Historie of Travell into Virginia Britania* (1612), Louis B. Wright and Virginia Freund, eds., Hakluyt Society *Publications*, 2nd Ser., 103 (London, 1953): 26.

image—the more it defined aboriginal peoples in nonhuman terms—the stronger was the European claim to the land of the New World. Defining the Indian as a "savage" or "brutish beast" or "tawny serpent" did not give Europeans the power to dispossess Natives of their land. But it gave them the moral sanction to do so if and when physical force became available. The Spanish, Portuguese, Dutch, French, and English differed little in this regard.

A pamphlet published in London as the first English expedition was preparing to embark for Roanoke Island illustrates the tension between the positive and the negative English images of the Indians. Written by George Peckham, who had accompanied Humphrey Gilbert on a voyage to Newfoundland in 1583, *A True Report, of the late discoveries, . . . of the Newfound Landes* clearly expressed the emerging formula for English colonization: formal expressions of goodwill, explanations of mutual benefits to be derived from contact between English and Native peoples, and yet, lurking beneath the surface, dark images and the anticipation of violence. Peckham began with an elaborate defense of the rights of maritime nations to "trade and traffic" with "savage" nations and assured the English that this would be "profitable to the adventurers in particular, beneficial to the Savages, and a matter to be attained without any great danger or difficulty." Some of the natives, he allowed, would be "fearful by nature" and disquieted by the "straunge apparrel, armor, and weapons" of the English, but "courtesy and mildness," along with a generous bounty of

"pretty merchandises and trifles [such] as looking glasses, bells, beads, bracelets, chains, or collars" would soon win them over and "induce their barbarous natures to a liking and mutual society with us."[23]

Following this explanation of how he hoped the English might act and how the Natives might respond, Peckham revealed what he believed the more likely course of events:

> But if after these good and fair means [are] used, the savages nevertheless will not be herewithal satisfied, but barbarously will go about to practice violence either in repelling the Christians from their ports and safe landinges or in withstanding them afterwards to enjoy the rights for which both painfully and lawfully they have adventured themselves thither. Then in such a case I hold it no breach of equity for the Christians to defend themselves, to pursue revenge with force, and to do whatsoever is necessary for attaining of their safety, for it is allowable by all laws . . . to resist violence with violence.[24]

Thus, two conflicting images of Native peoples wrestled for ascendance in the English mind as the first attempts to challenge the Spanish and French in North America began. At times the English imagined the Native as a backward but receptive person with whom amicable and profitable relations might be established. But the negative image, filled with visions of violence and bloodshed, swirled in the minds of those who were sailing toward land already occupied by people of a different culture.

Summary

From the fifteenth to the twentieth centuries, a dominant theme of history has been the militant expansion of European peoples into other continents. The expansionist impulse arose in the fifteenth century through a variety of factors, including the new concentration of power in the hands of monarchs and the rich cultural awakening of the Renaissance.

---

[23]David Beers Quinn, ed., *The Voyages and Colonizing Enterprises of Sir Humphrey Gilbert*, Hakluyt Society *Publications*, 2nd Ser., 84 (London, 1940): 450–452.
[24]Ibid., p. 453.

The exploits of Columbus in crossing the Atlantic and the conquests by Cortés, Pizarro, Ponce de Léon, de Soto, and Coronado opened the door for the exploration and colonization of the Americas in the sixteenth and seventeenth centuries by Spanish, Portuguese, French, and English settlers. Along with these colonizers, however, came unwelcome microbes, against which the Native peoples had little or no immune defense and so were devastated by diseases like smallpox. The exchange of flora and fauna that took place in both directions across the Atlantic triggered dietary and environmental changes, enhancing the European diet with corn, beans, squash, and other staples while bringing domestic animals to the Americas with negative ecological results. Underlying the European approach to and interaction with the indigenous peoples was an imagined characterization of the Native American as both a "backward" but receptive person with whom a relationship might be established and a person bent on great violence and bloodshed who would rise up as an enemy.

Critical Thinking Questions

1. A predominant theme of history from the fifteenth to the twentieth centuries has been the invasion of continents by Europeans intent on conquering and settling. What motivated such expansion, and how did the Spanish and Portuguese carry out their plans in the Americas?
2. Native peoples in the Americas had been isolated from many serious and lethal diseases for thousands of years. How did this change when the Europeans entered the picture? How, if at all, might history have changed if the tables had been turned, that is, if Natives had infected the Europeans with deadly microbes?
3. When England finally entered the race to the Americas, other European powers—the French, Spanish, and Portuguese—were already there. What factors impelled the English to set their sights on colonizing the Americas?
4. The early English colonists likely had a divided view of Native North Americans. How could this view be described, and what experiences and information might have shaped such a view?

Further Reading

Ida Altman, *Emigrants and Society: Extremadura and Spanish America in the Sixteenth Century* (Berkeley: University of California Press, 1989).

Daniela Bleichmar and Pater C. Mancall, eds., *Collecting Across Cultures: Material Exchanges in the Atlantic World* (Philadelphia: University of Pennsylvania Press, 2011).

Philip Boucher, *Les Nouvelles Frances: France in America, 1500–1815* (Providence: Brown University Press, 1989).

James F. Brooks, *Captives and Cousins: Slavery, Kinship, and Community in the Southwest Borderlands* (Chapel Hill: University of North Carolina Press, 2002).

Paul Butel, *The Atlantic* (London: Routledge, 1999).

Alfred W. Crosby, *The Columbian Exchange: Biological and Cultural Consequences of 1492* (Westport: Greenwood, 1972).

Alfred W. Crosby, *Germs, Seeds, and Animals: Studies in Ecological History* (Armonk: M. E. Sharpe, 1994).

J. H. Elliott, *Empires of the Atlantic World: Britain and Spain in America, 1492–1830* (New Haven: Yale University Press, 2006).

Pieter Emmer, *The Dutch in the Atlantic Economy, 1580–1880: Trade, Slavery, and Emancipation* (Aldershot, England: Ashgate, 1998).

Alison Games, *Migration and the Origin of the English Atlantic World* (Cambridge: Harvard University Press, 1999).

Allan Greer, *The People of New France* (Toronto: University of Toronto Press, 1997).

Ramon A. Guitérrez, *When Jesus Came, the Corn Mothers Went Away: Sexuality, Love, and Conquest in New Mexico, 1500–1846* (Stanford: Stanford University Press, 1991).

Henry Kamen, *Spain's Road to Empire: The Making of a World Power, 1492–1763* (London: Allen Lane, 2002).

Andrew L. Knaut, *The Pueblo Revolt of 1680: Conquest and Resistance in Seventeenth-Century New Mexico* (Norman: University of Oklahoma Press, 1995).

Jane Landers, *Black Society in Spanish Florida* (Urbana: University of Illinois Press, 1999).

Peter C. Mancall, *Fatal Journey: The Final Expedition of Henry Hudson; A Tale of Mutiny and Murder in the Arctic* (New York: Basic Books, 2009).

Ian K. Steele, *Warpaths: Invasions of North America* (New York: Oxford University Press, 1994).

David I. Weber. *Bárbaros: Spaniards and Their Savages in the Age of Enlightenment* (New Haven: Yale University Press, 2005).

Michael Witgen, *An Infinity of Nations: How the Native New World Shaped Early North America* (Philadelphia: University of Pennsylvania Press, 2012).

CHAPTER 3

Cultures Meet on the Chesapeake

LEARNING OBJECTIVES

- Compare and contrast the two English colonies of Roanoke and Jamestown from the standpoint of purpose, organization, and outcome.

- Explain the importance of tobacco to the English colony in Virginia; examine the role of indentured servants in its production, focusing on the type of life they led.

- Trace the relationship between the English colonists and Native Americans in the Chesapeake region; evaluate the roles played by Captain John Smith, Powhatan, and Pocahontas.

- Discuss the causes, main events, and results of the war of 1622, as well as the aftermath of the war of 1644.

The first encounters between English settlers and the Native peoples of North America occurred in the temperate zone of the Chesapeake Bay and the lands just south of this vast waterway. For a third of a century, from 1585 to 1620, this was the only region in which the adventuring English intruded on ancient homelands of American Indians. Though the number of settlers involved was small, only a few thousand, the impact was great—both on the English and on the Algonquian peoples of this region. The latter had already met and repulsed Europeans who had made brief incursions into the Chesapeake area in the 1560s. But the Spaniards (who soon departed) proved much easier to deal with than the English, who were determined to maintain a foothold on the continent once they arrived. The course of Anglo-Indian relations on the Chesapeake shaped English sensibilities and strategies for many decades and in faraway regions. As for the Native people, trade with the English intruders tapped them into the emerging global economy stretched over four continents.

The Failed Colony at Roanoke

England's first real attempt to establish colonies in the Americas came in 1585, when Walter Ralegh, a favorite at the court of Queen Elizabeth, organized a major expedition of ships and men. A year before, Ralegh had led a reconnaissance voyage along the North

43

American coast from Florida to the Carolinas, for the English at this time still knew little about the climate and natural resources of the area between French-claimed territory in the St. Lawrence region and Spanish-held Florida. Relying on a Portuguese pilot who had accompanied an earlier Spanish voyage along the coast, Ralegh's men made landfall on the Carolina Outer Banks and established contacts with the local Natives on Roanoke Island. Two Indians, Manteo and Wanchese, were induced to return to England. Displayed in London, they were invaluable in the publicity campaign that Ralegh launched for a large expedition in 1585.

The second Roanoke voyage marked the first extended encounter between Indians and the English-speaking, Protestant variety of Europeans. Some 600 men in seven ships sailed from England in April 1585 and reached the Outer Banks that summer. Of these, 107 were left on Roanoke Island the next summer, with promises that a relief expedition would return the following spring. Natives of the Chesapeake region then learned who these English people were and what they intended. Likewise, the accounts of the Roanoke experience by Thomas Harriot, later published in London as *Brief and True Report of the New Found Land of Virginia*, helped plant ideas in the minds of other English coming to the Americas of the people they were likely to encounter.

Though differing in detail, all accounts agree that the Natives of the Carolina coast were receptive to the English in 1585. Arthur Barrow, a member of the 1584 expedition, wrote that "we were entertained with all love, and kindness, and with as much bounties after their manner, as they could possibly devise. We found the people most gentle, loving and faithful, void of all guile, and treason." Barrow remarked that the Indians were "much grieved" when their hospitality was shunned by the suspicious English.[1] Other accounts, although less complimentary to the Indians, also claimed that the indigenous people were eager to learn about the artifacts of English

culture. Though wary, they extended their hospitality. Since the English came in small numbers, the Natives probably did not regard them as much of a threat. No conflict occurred until the English discovered a silver cup missing and promptly dispatched a punitive expedition to a nearby Native village. When the Indians denied taking the cup, the English, deciding to make a show of force, burned the village to the ground and destroyed the Indians' supply of corn. After that event, relations deteriorated.

Aware of their numerical disadvantage and convinced that the local Indian leader was organizing mainland tribes against them, the English employed force in large doses to convince the local Natives, who were in fact divided over how to cope with the English intrusion, of the invulnerability of the English. As one member of the expedition admitted, "Some of our company towards the end of the year, showed themselves too fierce, in slaying some of the people, in some towns, upon causes that on our part, might easily enough have been born withal."[2] Given this course of events, the coastal tribes must have concluded that the English were untrustworthy, quick to resort to arms, and dangerously unpredictable.

The 1585 Roanoke adventurers scanned the horizon for sight of the relief expedition in the early summer of 1586. But the ships that finally appeared belonged to Sir Francis Drake, who had been conducting piratical raids on Spanish St. Augustine and only incidentally dropped in on the Roanoke colony. Discouraged at the failure of the relief expedition to appear and being short of food, the colonizers clambered aboard Drake's ships for a ride home. About six weeks later the relief expedition arrived, only to find the colony abandoned. From the relief ship, about fifteen men were left to guard the fort that had been erected on Roanoke Island, but they were nowhere to be found when another relief expedition arrived in July 1587 with 110 adventurers, led by John White. These adventurers were to become the famous "Lost Colonists," for when White's

---

[1]David Beers Quinn, ed., *The Roanoke Voyages, 1584–1590*, Hakluyt Society *Publications*, 104 (London, 1955), p. 108.
[2]Ibid., pp. 381–382.

next relief expedition finally reached Roanoke in 1590 (earlier attempts at sending out ships having been thwarted by the Spanish Armada), no trace could be found of the colonists. Given the previous hostility between settlers and Indians, it is likely that they had succumbed to local tribes bent on avenging their losses.

The Roanoke voyages were never large nor fully capitalized enough to have planted permanent, self-sustaining colonies. They served only as token English challenges to Spain in North America, but were useful in accumulating knowledge about the region that was soon to become the focus of English overseas colonization. As the first sustained contact between English and Native American cultures, the voyages were a resounding failure. "What was lost in this famous lost colony," writes one historian, "was more than the band of colonists who have never been traced. What was also lost and never quite recovered in subsequent ventures was the dream of Englishmen and Indian living side by side in peace and liberty."[3]

For two decades after the Roanoke experiment, the English launched no new colonial adventures. A few English sea captains, representing merchants who dabbled in the West Indies trade, looked in on the coast of North America and attempted to barter with the Natives. They reported that their relations were generally friendly. But no further English attempts at colonization came until after the death in 1603 of Queen Elizabeth. Though much had been done during her reign to propagandize overseas colonizing and to obtain for it the backing of the Crown and the mercantile wealth of the nation, North America, so far as it was an arena of European colonization, still belonged to the Spanish and the French.

Reestablishing Virginia

The English founded their first permanent settlement in the Americas at Jamestown, Virginia, in 1607. But it was not a colony at all, at least not in the sense of being a political unit governed by the mother country. Rather, it was a business enterprise, the property of the Virginia Company of London, made up of stockholders and a governing board of directors that answered directly to King James I. Its primary purpose was to return a profit to its shareholders—merchants, political figures at the royal court, and others who had invested capital in the hope that the English could duplicate the remarkable success of the Spanish and the Portuguese in Mexico, Peru, and Brazil.

The king's charter to the Virginia Company of London began with the suggestion that the company concern itself with bringing the Christian religion to such people "as yet live in darkness and miserable ignorance of the true knowledge and worship of God." Christianizing the Indians of the Chesapeake area concerned many of the English engaged in a rivalry with Spain for the uncommitted peoples of the earth. (A recent analogy is the ideological struggle for the uncommitted people of the Third World by communist and capitalist countries after World War II.) But far more important to those who subscribed to shares in the Virginia Company was a return on their investment. Captain John Smith, who was to become a central figure in the drama unfolding in Virginia, later wrote: "We did admire how it was possible such wise men could so torment themselves and us with such strange absurdities and impossibilities: making Religion their colour, when all their aime was nothing but present profit. . . . For I am not so simple to think that any other motive than wealth will ever erect in Virginia a Commonweale."[4]

How would the Virginia Company enrich its stockholders? Nobody was quite sure, but it was assumed that profits in the New World would come in a variety of ways: through the discovery of gold and other minerals; by trade with the Indians; by production of pitch, tar, potash, and other products of the forest needed by the English navy; through the development of a fishing industry; and, best of all, by discovering the

[3]Edmund S. Morgan, "Slavery and Freedom: The American Paradox," *Journal of American History,* 59 (1972–1973): 16.
[4]Edward Arber and A. G. Bradley, eds., *Travels and Works of Captain John Smith* (Edinburgh, 1910), 2: 928.

illusive passage through the North American continent to Cathay. Some of these objectives had been realized in other English joint-stock ventures in Russia, in the Middle East, and in the Far East. Why not in North America?

Once sufficient capital was obtained, the principal problems were to recruit laborers who would go to the colony as employees of the Virginia Company and to establish the kind of administration and authority that would channel their energies toward the desired goals. Both these problems proved thorny in the early years. And nobody knew that they were attempting to plant an agricultural colony in a region that had experienced the worst drought in 800 years.

The tiny fleet that set sail for Virginia in December 1606 carried about 120 colonists under the command of Captain Christopher Newport. Sixteen weeks later, after stopping in the West Indies for water and provisions, they made landfall on the Chesapeake Bay. The English went ashore with provisions, and a few weeks later the ships disappeared over the horizon, leaving the small band of English alone in a land entirely unknown to them.

What followed in the next nine months, before Captain Newport returned with supplies and additional immigrants, is a dismal tale of human weakness and misfortune. The sea-weary colonists explored the area, built a fort and shelters within it, planted crops, and organized a bit of fishing. But the colonists spent much of their time dividing into factions and organizing plots against each other. The supplies quickly dwindled, and the colonists were soon on starvation rations. Some deserted to the Native villages where food, they assumed, could be found. Dysentery, caused by the brackish water of the drought-stricken Jamestown area, plagued the settlement. One of the members of the resident council of governors was expelled by his exasperated colleagues. A second was sentenced to execution as a spy for the Spanish, who were thought to be planning the elimination of the colony. A

third was saved from hanging only by the arrival of the reprovisioning ships from England. When Newport returned in January 1608, only thirty-eight of the original settlers were still alive. Three days later fire destroyed most of the crude buildings in Jamestown and most of the freshly unloaded supplies.

Twice in 1608 and once in 1609 the Virginia Company of London sent out ships with new colonists and supplies. But the "starving time" continued, and, as one of the leaders later wrote, "dissentions and jars were daily sown amongst them [the colonists], so that they choaked the seed and blasted the fruits of all men's labors."[5] Although the Virginia Company sent more than 900 colonists to the colony in the first three years, by the winter of 1609 to 1610 only sixty survived. In London, while the directors of the Virginia Company circulated promotional pamphlets such as *Good Speed to Virginia* and *Virginia Richly Valued*, street talk rumored that the colony was a dismal failure. Investors glumly counted the money they had wasted on this ill-starred enterprise, and people asked what had gone wrong with the plan to establish an English foothold in North America.

One of the flaws in the plans of English promoters of colonization was miscalculating the resources of the North American coast. Most investors and adventurers in the colony hoped to duplicate the Spanish experience in Mexico and Peru, dreaming of finding precious minerals that would make them wealthy. They hoped to utilize a native labor force or at least to profit from trade with the Indians. But Virginia was not Mexico or Peru. Its earth contained neither gold nor silver, and thus all the frantic digging that was done in the early months and all the loading of ships with mica-speckled dirt (which the colonists thought must contain gold) brought only a depletion of energy and shattered dreams. "Our gilded refiners, with their golden promises," wrote John Smith, "made all men their slaves in hope of recompence. There was no talk, no hope,

---

[5]John Rolfe, *A Relation of the State of Virginia* (1616), quoted in Perry Miller, "Religion and Society in the Early Literature: The Religious Impulse in the Founding of Virginia," *William and Mary Quarterly*, 3rd Ser., 6 (1949): 29.

nor work, but dig gold, wash gold, refine gold, load gold [in order to load] a drunken ship with so much gilded [mica-filled] dirt."[6]

Doubling the disappointment was their inability to commandeer the labor of the region's Indians, who they believed could be easily exploited. Upon Indian backs the English would build a prosperous society. Cortés had conquered the mighty Aztec empire with a few hundred men and then turned the labor of thousands of Indians to Spanish advantage. Pizarro had done the same in Peru. Why not so in Virginia?

But in the Chesapeake region the English found that the indigenous people were not so densely settled and could not be easily subjugated. Smith later wrote that the Spaniards were fortunate to colonize "in those parts where there were infinite numbers of people who had manured the ground so that food was provided at all times."[7] Moreover, the Spanish got the "spoil and pillage" of the well-developed regions they colonized because they brought with them a military force capable of overpowering the native society. But the English settled in Virginia where no wealthy Indian empire awaited their conquest. Nor could some 20,000 Natives of the Chesapeake region, living in about 169 villages, be molded into a labor force at the Europeans' command, for the English brought with them neither an army of *conquistadores* nor an army of priests to convert Indians to the European religion. Unable to exploit or utilize the Native population, the Virginia settlers found the hoped-for New World paradise far from utopian.

A third flaw in the English plan of settlement was the composition of the early Jamestown settlers. Of those who arrived, many were gentlemen-adventurers ill-equipped to undertake the rugged work of colony building—men who became only a drain on the tiny settlement's resources. By the same token, there were far too

few laborers and farmers—men who could cut trees, build houses, and till the soil. John Smith complained that a small number of adventure-seeking gentlemen would have been well enough, but "to have more to wait and play than work, or more commanders and officers than industrious labourers" was foolishness, "for in Virginia a plain soldier that can use a pickax and spade, is better than five knights."[8] Those who had been bred to a life of labor were not much better. "A more damned crew hell never vomited," growled the president of the company. His opinion was echoed by one of Virginia's first historians, who described the original colonizers as "unruly sparks, packed off by their friends, to escape worse destinies at home . . . , poor gentlemen, broken tradesmen, rakes and libertines, footmen, and such others, as were much fitter to spoil or run a Commonwealth, than to help to raise or maintain one."[9] This bizarre selection of colonists created manpower problems and led to chronic social tension. Men of high social standing were regarded in England as essential to the strength and stability of society. But in a settlement on the edge of a vast, heavily peopled continent, they created only resentment, unwilling to work themselves and unable to command the respect of those under them.

The most revealing example of the chronic tension in early Virginia is the case of Captain John Smith. Son of a poor West Country tenant farmer, Smith at age 16 embarked on war as a career. Before reaching his mid-twenties, he had traveled and fought his way across Europe and back as a professional mercenary in the employ of various local warlords. He fought duels in Transylvania, he claimed, battled the Turks on the plains of western Hungary, was captured and enslaved for several years in Istanbul, escaped into Russia, and worked his way back to England by way of North Africa. His military experience, his skill as a

[6]Arber and Bradley, eds., *Works of Smith . . .* , 1: 104.
[7]Quoted in Sigmund Diamond, "From Organization to Society: Virginia in the Seventeenth Century," *American Journal of Sociology*, 63 (1958): 460.
[8]Ibid., p. 461.
[9]George Sandys to John Ferrar, 1623, in Susan M. Kingsbury, ed., *The Records of the Virginia Company of London* (Washington, DC, 1906–1935), 4: 23; William Stith, *The History of the First Discovery and Settlement of Virginia* (New York, 1865), p. 103.

mapmaker, and his toughness suggested to Virginia's organizers that Smith would be a good man to have along when the going got rough.

Even on the ocean voyage, Smith fell out with some of the leaders of the expedition, and they clapped him in irons on the *Susan Constant*. When they opened secret orders upon arrival on the Chesapeake, the gentlemen leaders discovered that Smith had been named a member of the Virginia governing council. This change aroused further resentment. Smith had little patience with men who claimed that their social origins excused them from manual labor, and he said so bluntly. As it happened, he was one of the few who possessed the courage and ability to explore and map the region around Jamestown, establish contact with the Natives, negotiate with them, and attempt to organize the colony's slender human resources. His exertions, however, alienated the gentlemen councilors around him. They saw his disdain for their social rank as a calculated attempt to gain control of the colony and to depose them in the process. But by September 1608, Smith had outlasted most of his enemies. For a year he ruled the colony as president of the council.

Reorganization and Tobacco

After three years of failure, the Virginia Company directors in London recruited ordinary farmers instead of soldiers of fortune. Under a new system of recruitment, about 1,200 new immigrants came to Virginia in 1610 and 1611 with promises of free land at the end of seven years' labor for the company. But even with new manpower, the Virginia Company could not develop staple crops or find a way of returning a profit to its investors. By 1616, death and reimmigration to England had reduced the population to 351. Again the company raised the ante. This time they offered one hundred acres of land outright to anyone who would journey to the colony. Instead of pledging limited servitude for the chance to become sole possessor of land, an English citizen trapped at the lower rungs of society at home could now become an independent landowner in no more time than it took to clamber aboard a ship bound for the Chesapeake. Now the company operated to promote and sell land, aiming to encourage settlers to come to Virginia to pursue their fortunes independently. In time, if the colony proved itself valuable, the Virginia Company could sell profitably the land they hoped to rid of Native people. Other concessions were made. In 1619, the company allowed the election of a representative assembly, which would participate in governing the colony and thus bind the colonists emotionally to the land. In the same year, the company shipped a boatload of unmarried women to the colony in order to improve morale and touch off a small population explosion.

Responding to these concessions, more than 4,500 colonists flocked to Virginia between 1619 and 1624. They no longer came as employees of the Virginia Company of London or as individuals to be governed entirely at the discretion of the resident council and the governing council in London. Through its failures, the company had learned that only by promising immediate ownership of land and by allowing a degree of local government could it hope to keep the colony alive and growing. After almost two decades, London entrepreneurs adjusted their original plans to match the realities of North America.

The new inducements to settlement helped rescue the colony from social disorder and unprofitability. But crucial to Virginia's revival was the discovery that tobacco grew exceptionally well in the bottomlands of the Chesapeake region. Widely used in the seventeenth century as a mild narcotic, tobacco had first been brought to Portugal from Florida in the 1560s, a dubious gift of the New World to the Old. But it was Francis Drake's boatload of the "jovial weed," procured in the West Indies in 1586 and then popularized among the English upper class by Ralegh, that converted the plant from medicinal purposes to a social addiction. By the early seventeenth century, the smoking craze swept England. Youngbloods developed various tricks and affectations as a part of the smoking cult: the "Ring," the "Whiffle," the "Gulp," and the

"Retention" became a part of a new social habit. Even the opposition of King James I could not arrest the popularity of smoking. Sounding like a modern physician, James anonymously published *Counterblast to Tobacco* (1609), in which he described smoking as "a custom loathsome to the eye, hateful to the nose, harmful to the brain, dangerous to the lungs, and in the black stinking fumes thereof, nearest resembling the horrible stygian smoke of the pit that is bottomless."

This was to no avail. English society, as well as Europeans everywhere, cried for more New World tobacco leaf, oblivious to the dangers lurking in its delights. At first, the West Indies supplied the bulk of the crop, but experiments with tobacco culture in Virginia proved phenomenally successful. Virginia shipped its first crop to England in 1617; seven years later, it exported 200,000 pounds of leaf, and by 1638, the crop exceeded 3 million pounds. Tobacco became to the Chesapeake region what sugar was to the West Indies and silver to Mexico and Peru.

Tobacco, of course, would not grow by itself, and as the demand grew, English planters on the Chesapeake sought a source of cheap labor. Spanish and Portuguese colonizers had incorporated the Native populations into a forced labor system that approximated slavery. But the English lacked the power in the early years to enslave the local tribes. So the tobacco planters looked to England for their labor supply— and particularly to the most depressed segment of the population, made up of young men and women willing to sell their labor for four to seven years in exchange for passage across the Atlantic and a chance, after they had served their time, to become independent landowners and tobacco planters. England was full of such people, for population growth and the enclosure of land had created an army of unemployed. "Our country [is] overspread," wrote a magistrate in Kent, "not only with unpunished swarms of idle rogues and counterfeit soldiers but also with

numbers of poor and weak but unpitied servitors [debtors]."[10]

Such impoverished immigrants were called *indentured servants* because they committed themselves to serve a master for a specific period of time. They differed from the earlier employees of the Virginia Company only in that they had contracted their labor to an individual rather than to a company. Put to work in the tobacco fields, an indentured servant could tend about 1,000 to 2,000 tobacco plants, which could be expected to yield tobacco worth about £100 to £150 a year. Few people in England could generate an equivalent income for a year's labor; in fact, a family farm might yield only twenty pounds a year.

After tobacco proved successful, Virginia landowners clamored for indentured servants in order to bring more land under cultivation. Some were Africans, beginning with several dozen Angolans from West Central Africa captured from a Portuguese slaver by a Dutch privateer and brought to the Chesapeake Bay for sale in 1619. Brought by the shipload, these servants were auctioned at the dock to the highest bidder. The more servants a landowner could purchase, the greater the crop the landowner could produce; larger crops brought more capital with which to purchase more land and additional servants. Thus, Edmund Morgan writes, "Virginia differed from later American boom areas in that success depended not on acquiring the right piece of land but on acquiring men. . . . Men rushed to stake out claims to men, stole them, lured them, fought over them—and bought and sold them, bidding up the prices to four, five, and six times the initial cost."[11]

Life for these indentured servants was often nightmarish. If malarial fevers of the swampy Chesapeake area and malnutrition did not kill them within a few years, then the work routine imposed by masters, who treated them like cattle, usually did. What might happen to a man

[10]Quoted in Peter Clark, "The Migrant in Kentish Towns, 1580–1640," in Peter Clark and Paul Slack, eds., *Crisis and Order in English Towns, 1500–1700* (Toronto, 1972), p. 117.
[11]Edmund S. Morgan, *American Slavery, American Freedom: The Ordeal of Colonial Virginia* (New York, 1975), pp. 114–115.

[1]

A

COUNTERBLAST

TO

TOBACCO.

Hat the manifold abuſes of this vile cuſtome of Tobacco-taking, may the better be eſpied ; It is fit, That firſt you enter into Conſideration both of the firſt Original thereof, and likewiſe of the Reaſons of the firſt entry thereof into this Countrey ; for certainly as ſuch Cuſtoms that have their firſt Inſtitution, either from a godly, neceſſary, or honourable ground, and are firſt brought in by the means of ſome worthy, vertuous, and great Perſonage ; are ever, and moſt juſtly holden in great and reverent eſtimation and account by all wiſe, vertuous and temperate Spirits : So ſhould it by the contrary, juſtly bring a great Diſgrace into that ſort of Cuſtoms, which having their Original from baſe Corruption and Barbarity, do, in like ſort, make their firſt entry into a Country, by an inconſiderate and childiſh affectation of Novelty, as is the true caſe of the firſt Invention of Tobacco-taking, and of the firſt entry thereof amongſt us. For Tobacco being a common Herb, which (though under divers Names) grows

B   almoſt

Title page of James I, *Counterblast to Tobacco* (c. 1608).

(Courtesy A Counterblast to Tobacco, a treatise written by James I of England (1566-1625) published in an anti-smoking pamphlet, 1672 (b/w photo), English School, (17th century)/Private Collection/The Bridgeman Art Library)

who challenged this system befell an ordinary immigrant named Richard Barnes in 1624. His tongue loosened by alcohol in a local tavern, Barnes uttered some "base and detracting" words against the resident governor. For this offense it was ordered that he "be disarmed [and] have his arms broken and his tongue bored through with an awl [and] shall pass through a guard of 40 men and shall be butted [with muskets] by every one of them and at the head of the troop kicked down and footed out of the fort; that he shall be banished out of James City and the Island, that he shall not be capable of any privilege of freedom of the country . . . [hereafter]."[12]

Barnes was not an indentured servant but a freeman; indentured servants who defied the will of the ruling group of tobacco planters found life even more hazardous. Servitude in early Virginia was different from early chattel slavery only in degree. Unrestrained by the courts, which in the mother country protected the rights of servants against unduly oppressive masters, servant owners treated their bondsmen as pieces of property. John Rolfe, one of the leading figures of the colony, reported in 1619 that the "buying of men and boys" and even the gambling at cards for servants in Virginia "was held in England a thing most intolerable." Six years later, an English merchant refused to take a shipload of indentured servants to Virginia because, as he explained, "servants were sold here up and down like horses." What occurred in "boomtime Virginia" was "not only the fleeting ugliness of private enterprise operating temporarily without check, not only greed magnified by opportunity, producing fortunes for a few and misery for many," but also the beginning of "a system of labor that treated men as things."[13] No wonder, then, that of some 10,000 persons transported to Virginia between 1607 and 1622, only about 2,000 were still alive at the end of that period. "Instead of a plantation," wrote one English critic, Virginia "will shortly get the name of a slaughter house."[14]

English-Indian Relations

Historians do not know exactly what the English expected of the Algonquian occupiers of the land as they approached the Chesapeake Bay in the spring of 1607. Nor is it possible to be certain whether the Native destruction of a Spanish Jesuit mission on the York River in 1571 bespoke a generalized hostility toward Europeans. But it is likely, given the English belief that the Roanoke colony had been reduced to a pile of bones by the Natives a generation earlier, and given the Indians' sporadic experience with Europeans as militaristic people, that neither side was very optimistic about encountering each other. English pessimism must have intensified when Indians attacked the Jamestown expedition near Cape Henry, the most seaward point of land in the Chesapeake Bay region, where the first landfall was made. From this event on, the English proceeded with extreme caution, expecting violence and treachery from the Natives, even when they approached in outwardly friendly ways. When the one-armed Captain Newport led the first exploratory trip up the newly named James River, just weeks after a tiny settlement had been planted at Jamestown, he was confused by the friendly greeting. The Indians, a member of his group wrote, "are naturally given to trechery, howbeit we could not find it in our travell up the river, but rather a most kind and loving people."[15] This account describes how the Algonquians wined and dined the English, explaining that they were "at odds" with other tribes, including the Chesapeake tribe that had attacked the English at Cape Henry.

We now know that the Natives of the region—some 20,000—were accurately describing their situation when they said they were

---

[12]Ibid., p. 124.
[13]Ibid., p. 129.
[14]Francis Jennings, *The Invasion of America: Indians, Colonialism and the Cant of Conquest* (Chapel Hill, NC, 1975), p. 79.
[15]Philip L. Barbour, ed., *The Jamestown Voyages Under the First Charter, 1606–1609*, Hakluyt Society *Publications*, 2nd Ser., 136 (London, 1969): 103–104.

"at oddes" with other tribes. Some forty small chiefdoms lived in the Chesapeake Bay region. Wahunsunacock, known to the English as Powhatan, was the paramount chief of about thirty of these, and in fact he had forged the most centralized Algonquian polity in the southeastern region. For years before the English arrived, he had been consolidating his hold on the lesser tribes of the area, while warding off inland tribes of the Piedmont. In this situation Powhatan probably saw an alliance with the English as a means of extending his power in the tidewater area while simultaneously neutralizing the power of his western enemies. At the same time, his unpleasant experience with Europeans, including a clash just three years before with a passing English ship, whose crew had been hospitably entertained but then had killed a local chief and kidnapped several Indians, no doubt made Powhatan wary of these newcomers. From the Powhatan viewpoint, the newcomers "were potentially useful and potentially dangerous."[16] Among the smaller chiefdoms he had dominated, many local leaders saw an alliance with the English as a way to escape Powhatan's clutches.

John Smith and others quickly perceived the intertribal tensions as well as the linguistic differences among the Natives. But they convinced themselves that no tribal leader could find potential advantage in the arrival of the English. Perhaps because their position was so precarious, with dysentery, hunger, drought, and internal strife debilitating their tiny settlement, the English could afford only to regard all Indians as threatening. Hence, hostile and friendly Indians were seen as different only in their outward behavior. Inwardly they were identical—"savage," treacherous people who waited only for a chance to drive the English back into the sea from which they had come.

During the first months of contact, the confusion in the English mind surfaced again and again. In the autumn of 1607, during the "starving time," when food supplies were running perilously low and all but a handful of the Jamestown settlers had fallen too ill to work, the colony was saved by Powhatan. His men brought food to keep the struggling settlement alive until the sick recovered and the relief ship arrived. Many saw this gesture as an example of Powhatan's covert hostility rather than as an attempt of the chief to serve his own interests through an alliance with the English. "It pleased God (in our extremity)," wrote John Smith, "to move the Indians to bring us Corne, ere it was halfe ripe, to refresh us, when we rather expected . . . they would destroy us."[17] As a man of military experience among "barbarian" people in other parts of the world, Smith was not willing to believe that the Natives, in aiding the colony, might have found the survival of the English in their own interest. Another leader of the colony could attribute the Indians' generous behavior only to the intervention of the white people's God. "If it had not pleased God to have put a terrour in the Savages heart," he wrote, "we had all perished by those wild and cruell Pagans, being in that weake estate as we were."[18]

In December 1607, Smith was captured during one of his exploratory incursions into Powhatan's country and marched to Werowocomoco, the seat of Powhatan's confederacy. Powhatan seems to have wanted to employ this opportunity to impress the English with his power and thus arranged a mock execution ceremony for Smith. At the critical moment, as the executioners prepared to deliver the death blows, the chief's favorite daughter, Pocahontas, threw herself on Smith to save him. About twelve years old, Pocahontas had been a frequent visitor to Jamestown, undoubtedly as an emissary of her father, and was well-known to Smith. But rather than understanding the rescue in symbolic terms, as Powhatan's way of indicating his strength but also

[16]Helen C. Rountree, "The Powhatans and the English: A Case of Multiple Conflicting Agendas," in Rountree, ed., *Powhatan Foreign Relations, 1500–1722* (Charlottesville, VA, 1993), p. 178.
[17]Arber and Bradley, eds., *Works of Smith* . . . , 1: 8–9.
[18]Barbour, ed., *Jamestown Voyages* . . . , pp. 144–145.

THE EARLY CHESAPEAKE

- Chickahominy tribe
- Powhatan Confederacy
- - - - Powhatan's Crescent

MONACAN TERRITORY

CHESAPEAKE BAY

ATLANTIC OCEAN

Potomac River

Rappahannock River

Chickahominy River

Powhatan

Henrico

Paspahegh

Jamestown

Werowocomoco

York River

Cape Charles

Cape Henry

James River

Kecoughtan

Nansemond

Approximate boundary of Powhatan Confederacy

his desire to forge a bond with the newcomers, Smith and other Virginians took Pocahontas's gesture as a spontaneous outburst of love for the English—an un-Indian-like act attributable to English superiority or perhaps to God's intervening hand. Hostility was on the English mind, sporadic hostility had already occurred, and Powhatan's deliverance of the English leader, at a time when the colony was almost defenseless, was thus not conceived as a conciliatory act.

In the aftermath of the incident, Pocahontas became a kind of ambassador from Powhatan to the struggling Jamestown colony, an agent who became fluent in the English language and kept her father informed on the state of the internally divided English. By late 1608, more colonists had arrived in Jamestown, and Smith, as the new president of council, adopted an aggressive stance, burning Indian canoes, fields, and villages in order to extort desperately needed Indian maize and to

John Rolfe Baptism of Pocahontas by John Gadsby Chapman (1840).

(Courtesy Architect of the Capitol)

cow Powhatan and his lesser chiefs into submission. Aware that Virginia could not be resupplied from England every few months and that the colonists were unable to sustain themselves in their new drought-struck environment, Smith sought a forced trade with Powhatan. But by now, Powhatan had determined to let the English starve, a policy made clear not only by his refusal to trade corn but also by his withdrawal of Pocahontas. On penalty of death, Powhatan forbade his young daughter to enter the English settlement. "Captain Smith," warned Powhatan at a confrontation of the two leaders in January 1609, "some doubt I have of your coming hither, that makes me not so kindly seek to receive you as I would [like]. For many do inform me your coming is not for trade, but to invade my people and possess my country."[19]

Leading a colony where some men were deserting to Native villages while others starved, Smith raided Indian villages for provisions and slaughtered Native people of both sexes and all ages. Meanwhile, colonists began to occupy Indian land in the James River valley. Powhatan retaliated by attacking the English wherever he could. Even the arrival of fresh supplies and several hundred new colonists in the summer of 1609 did not help, for the provisions were quickly exhausted, the colonists ravenously consuming more than they produced. When the relief ships departed in October 1609, with John Smith aboard one of them, Virginia embarked upon a winter of despair. Under the surveillance of Powhatan, who ambushed foraging colonists whenever he could, the death toll mounted.

---

[19]Quoted in Philip L. Barbour, *Pocahontas and Her World* (Boston, MA, 1970), p. 46.

George Percy, Smith's successor, wrote that after the horses had been eaten, the dysentery-racked Virginians "were glad to make shift with [such] vermin as dogs, cats, rats, and mice." When these were exhausted, men resorted to "things which seem incredible, as to dig up corpses out of graves and to eat them—and some have licked up the blood which hath fallen from their weak fellows. And amongst the rest, this was most lamentable, that one of our colony murdered his wife, ripped the child out of her womb and threw it into the river, and after chopped the mother in pieces and salted her for his food, the same not being discovered before he had eaten part thereof."[20]

Powhatan's policy of withdrawing from trade with the encroachers had succeeded. By the spring of 1610, the Spanish ambassador to England, Alonso de Velasco, reported home that "the Indians hold the English surrounded in the strong place which they had erected there, having killed the larger part of them, and the others were left, so entirely without provisions that they thought it impossible to escape." Virginia could be easily erased from the map; Velasco counseled his government, "by sending out a few ships to finish what might be left in that place."[21] What the Spanish ambassador did not know was that two relief ships had reached Jamestown in May 1610 and found the situation so dismal that Sir Thomas Gates, arriving to assume the governorship of the colony, decided to embark the remaining sixty survivors, set sail for England, and admit that the English had failed on the Chesapeake. On June 7, 1610, Gates ordered the forlorn settlement stripped of its meager possessions, loaded the handful of survivors aboard, and set sail down the James River for the open sea. The ships dropped anchor for the night after reaching the Chesapeake Capes and planned to start the return ocean voyage on the following day.

On the next morning, three ships hove into sight. They carried 150 new recruits sent out by the Virginia Company and a new governor, Sir Thomas West, Lord De La Warr. Jamestown, a death trap at its moment of extinction, was reborn.

Newly armed and provisioned, the revitalized Jamestown colonists revived their militaristic Indian policy in what amounted to an on-again, off-again war between 1610 and 1613. The new attitude toward the Powhatan Confederacy was apparent in the orders issued in 1609 for governing the colony. Earlier, the Virginia Company had instructed, "In all your passages you must have great care not to offend the naturals, if you can eschew it."[22] Now the governor was ordered to launch a military occupation of the region between the James and the York rivers; to make all tribes tributary to him rather than to Powhatan; to extract corn, furs, dyes, and labor from each tribe; and, if possible, to mold the natives into an agricultural labor force as the Spanish had done in their colonies. As the English settlement gained in strength, Smith's successors continued his policy of military foraging and intimidation. From 1610 to 1613, Powhatan attacked the colonists whenever opportunities presented themselves, and the English mounted fierce attacks that decimated three small tribes and destroyed two Native villages. Much of the corn that sustained the colony in these years seems to have been extracted by force from Powhatan's villages, although chiefdoms on the fringe of Powhatan's rule gladly traded maize for English shovels, hatchets, scissors, glass beads, and bells.

In 1613, the English kidnapped Pocahontas in a move designed to obtain a return of English prisoners and a quantity of weapons that the Indians had acquired over the years and, as Pocahontas's abductor, Captain Samuel Argall put it, to force payment of "a great quantitie of Corne."[23] Understanding that his daughter was

---

[20]Quoted in ibid., pp. 64–65.
[21]Quoted in Grace Steele Woodward, *Pocahontas* (Norman, OK, 1969), p. 120.
[22]E. G. R. Taylor, ed., *The Original Writing of Correspondence of the Two Richard Hakluyts*, Hakluyt Society *Publications*, 2nd Ser., 77 (London, 1935): 494.
[23]Quoted in Woodward, *Pocahontas*, p. 156.

not in harm's way, Powhatan made limited concessions to the English but refused to satisfy all the ransom conditions. In the following year, when the 28-year old widower John Rolfe vowed to marry Pocahontas, Powhatan reluctantly assented to the first Anglo-Indian marriage in Virginia's history and signed a humiliating peace treaty, where Powhatan recognized the overlordship of the English king. Pocahontas became the instrument of an uneasy truce between the two societies and returned to England with Rolfe and other members of Powhatan's Confederacy in 1616 in order to promote further colonization of the Chesapeake. She died at age 21 on the eve of her return to Virginia in 1617, after giving birth to a son and helping to raise the money that pumped new lifeblood into the Virginia Company and consequently sent hundreds of new fortune-seekers to the Chesapeake as part of the population buildup that would lead to a renewal of hostilities five years after her death.

Notwithstanding misconceptions, suspicion, and violence on both sides, the English and the Powhatans lived in close contact during the first decade of English settlement, and cultural interchange and trade occurred on a broad scale. Although it has been a commonplace in the popular mind that the Europeans were "advanced" and the Indians were "primitive," the technological differences between the two cultures were

When John Smith published his *Generall Historie of Virginia* in 1624, London's Robert Vaughan provided sometimes fanciful illustrations of Smith's heroism. Here, in 1608, Smith seizes the gigantic Powhatan, chief of the Chesapeake Bay tribes, by the scalplock. In the background, English soldiers match firearms against Indian bows and arrows. Smith never bested Powhatan, but this early confrontation is accurate. (*John Smith, Generall Historie of Virginia, London, 1624.*)

Source: Library of Congress Prints and Photographs Division [LC-USZ62-51971].

equaled or outweighed by the similarities between these two agricultural societies. The main technological advantages of the English were their ability to traverse large bodies of water in wooden ships and their superiority in fashioning iron implements and weapons. But the Indians quickly incorporated such iron-age items as kettles, fishhooks, traps, needles, knives, and guns into their material culture. In return, they provided the English with an understanding of how to use nets and weirs to catch the abundant fish and shellfish of the Chesapeake waters, and introduced the intruders to a wide range of agricultural products unknown in Europe before 1492. The English in Virginia learned from the Natives how to cultivate tobacco, corn, beans, squash, pumpkins, and other food products. Algonquians also introduced the English to a wide range of medicinal herbs, dyes, and such important devices as the canoe.

Such cultural interaction proceeded even while hostility and sporadic violence was occurring in the early years. It was facilitated by Indians living among the English as day laborers, while a number of settlers fled to Native villages rather than endure the autocratic English rulers and oppressive tobacco planters. This sojourning brought an understanding of the other's culture. Thus, even while the English pursued a policy of intimidation in the early years, they recognized the resilience and strength of the Algonquians' culture. Smith marveled at the strength and agility of the Chesapeake tribespeople, at their talent for hunting and fishing, and admired their music and entertainment. He noted that they practiced civil government, that they adhered to religious traditions, and that many of their customs and institutions were not unlike those of the Europeans. "Although the countrie people be very barbarous," he wrote, "yet have they amongst them such government, as that their Magistrats for good commanding, and their people for due subjections, and obeying, excell many places that would be counted very civill." Other English,

such as the Anglican minister Alexander Whitaker, who proselytized among the Indians, wrote that it was a mistake to suppose that the Indians were merely savage people, "for they are of body lustie, strong, and very nimble: they are a very understanding generation, quicke of apprehension, suddaine in their dispatches, subtile in their dealings, exquisite in their inventions, and industrious in their labour."[24] So, while both sides adjusted uneasily to the presence of the other, both were involved in cultural engagement and borrowing.

The War of 1622 and its Aftermath

After the increase of population that accompanied the rapid growth of tobacco production, relations between the two peoples underwent a fundamental alteration. While giving Virginia an important money crop, the cultivation of tobacco created an enormous new demand for land. As more and more colonists pushed up the rivers that flowed into the Chesapeake Bay to carve out tobacco plantations, the Natives of the region perceived that what had previously been an abrasive and sometimes violent relationship might now become a disastrous one. Powhatan had retired in 1617, just as tobacco cultivation began to expand rapidly. His younger brother, Opechancanough, who assumed leadership of the tidewater tribes, concluded that he must embark upon a program of military renaissance and spiritual revitalization.

Opechancanough was battling not only against the land-encroaching English but also against the diseases they were spreading among the Native population. The deadliest of all European weapons were the microorganisms brought ashore in nearly every immigrant. In the Chesapeake region minor epidemics had taken their toll in the 1580s and again in 1608. Between 1617 and 1619, another epidemic decimated the Powhatan tribes.

---

[24]Arber and Bradley, eds., *Works of Smith . . .* , 1: 43–84; Whitaker, *Good News from Virginia* (1613), quoted in Roy H. Pearce, *The Savages of America: A Study of the Indian and the Idea of Civilization* (Baltimore, MD, 1953), p. 13.

In leading a reorganization of his people, Opechancanough relied heavily on Nemattanew, a war captain and charismatic religious prophet whom the English called "Jack of the Feather." Nemattanew led warriors into battle "covered with feathers and swans wings fastened onto his shoulders . . . as though he meant to flye."[25] A shadowy figure who came often to the English settlements, Nemattanew had convinced his tribe that he was immortal and that they would be immune to musket fire if they rubbed their bodies with a special ointment. In March 1622, as Opechancanough was piecing together plans for a unified attack on the Virginia settlements, a colonist murdered Nemattanew in retaliation for another colonist's death. Nemattanew's death triggered the famous Indian assault two weeks later that dealt the colony a staggering blow; but the highly combustible atmosphere, generated by a half-dozen years of white expansion and pressure on Native hunting lands, was the fundamental cause of the attack.

Although it did not achieve its goal of ending English presence in the Chesapeake area, the carefully planned Indian attack of 1622 and the famine that followed it wiped out about one-quarter of the white population. Included among the victims was Opechancanough's nephew by marriage, John Rolfe. It was the final straw for the Virginia Company of London, which declared bankruptcy and left the colony to the governance of the Crown.

The more important result was that those who survived the attack now felt free to pursue a ruthless new Indian policy. Even though several leaders in the colony confided to men in England that the real cause of the Indian attack was "our owne perfidious dealing with them," it was generally agreed that henceforward the colonists would be free to hunt down the Indians wherever they could be found. Abandoning an obligation to "civilize" and Christianize the Natives, the Virginians adopted a no-holds-barred approach to "the Indian problem." With never a nod to all the pre-1622 bloodshed, one Virginian wrote:

> Our hands which before were tied with gentleness and fair usage, are now set at liberty by the treacherous violence of the Savages . . . so that we, who hitherto have had possession of no more ground than their waste and our purchase at a valuable consideration to their own contentment gained, may now by right of war, and law of nations, invade the country, and destroy them who sought to destroy us; whereby we shall enjoy their cultivated places, turning the laborious mattock into the victorious sword, . . . and possessing the fruits of others labours. Now their cleared grounds in all their villages (which are situated in the fruitfullest places of the land) shall be inhabited by us, whereas heretofore the grubbing of woods was the greatest labor.[26]

In these sentences one detects a note of grim satisfaction that the Indians had succeeded in wiping out one-quarter of the colonists. John Smith, writing from England two years after the attack, noted that some men held that the attack "will be good for the Plantation, because now we have just cause to destroy them by all means possible." Another writer expressed the prevalent genocidal urge by reasoning that the Natives had done the colonists a favor by sweeping away the previous English reluctance to annihilate them. "Victory," he wrote, "may be gained many ways; by force, by surprize, by famine in burning their corn, by destroying and burning their boats, canoes, and houses, by breaking their fishing weirs, by assailing them in their huntings, whereby they got the greatest part of their sustenance in winter, by pursuing and chasing them with our horses and blood-hounds to draw after them, and mastiffs to tear them."[27]

---

[25]Quoted in James Horn, *A Land as God Made It: Jamestown and the Birth of America* (New York, 2005), p. 206.
[26]Edward Waterhouse, "A Declaration of the State of the Colony and Affaires in Virginia . . . " (1662), in Kingsbury, ed., *Records of Virginia Company*, 3: 556–557.
[27]*Travels and Works of Smith*, 2: 578–579; Waterhouse, "State of the Colony," in Kingsbury, ed., *Records of Virginia Company*, 3: 557.

Once the Virginians slaked their thirst for revenge, the only debatable point was whether the extermination of the tidewater Indian tribes would work to the benefit or disadvantage of the colony. One prominent planter offered "reasons why it is not fitting utterlye to make an exterpation of the Savages yett" and then assured his neighbors that he was not against genocide per se but opposed the destruction of a people who, if properly subjugated, could enrich all Virginians through their labor. But both subjugation and assimilation required more time and trouble than the Virginians were willing to spend. The simpler course, consistent with instructions from London to "root out [the Indians] from being any longer a people," was to follow a scorched-earth policy, sending military expeditions each summer to destroy villages and crops.[28] In 1629, the council negotiated a peace treaty but then rejected it because a state of "perpetual enmity" would serve the colony better.

For a number of years after the 1622 attack, the Virginians were not strong enough to carry out their genocidal policy on Native peoples. But by 1640, Virginia had grown to about 8,000 settlers. By 1662, the population had swelled to 25,000, and the colony was shipping 7 million pounds of tobacco a year to England. Although the Crown appointed a royal governor to rule in conjunction with an appointed council and an elected House of Burgesses, the real power in the colony lay at the local level, where each tobacco planter operated with little regard for centralized authority. Men like Governor John Harvey, appointed in 1626, could complain that the planters acted "rather for their owne endes than either seekinge the generall good or doinge right to particular men."[29] But he could do little to curb the appetites of the land-hungry, profit-conscious tobacco planters. When he proposed a lasting peace with the Indians and a promise to leave the Chesapeake tribes unmolested on the land they were occupying, the planters refused to cooperate. Having clawed their way to the top of the rough-hewn planter society, they eagerly conducted a fur trade with more distant tribes but had no intention of allowing the governor to interfere with their takeover of large tracts of land or their continuation of an aggressive Indian policy in the tidewater region. When Harvey tried again in 1635 to impose his will, Virginia's leaders plotted against him, provoked violence, and evicted him from the colony while sending petitions back to the mother country complaining of his arbitrary and unreasonable policies.

It was such tough, self-made, ambitious people as these, unhindered by religious or humanitarian concern for the Natives and unrestrained by government, that the Chesapeake tribes had to confront after 1630. They also had to face the rapidly shifting population balance—the drastic decline of their numbers by disease and war during the first quarter century of English presence and the rapid increase of English colonists after 1624. Even so, the Natives continued to follow their traditional way of life. Years of contact with Europeans had done little to convince them that they should remodel their religion, social and political organization, or values and beliefs on English patterns. Powhatan's people eagerly incorporated technological innovations and material objects of the newcomers into their culture, but they resisted or rejected the other aspects of European life.

Though greatly weakened by disease and war, many Algonquians were still determined to drive out the English intruders, rather than adapt to an alien culture. Though far fewer in number than in 1622, Powhatan Confederacy tribesmen attacked in April 1644 under the leadership of the aged, crippled, and nearly blind Opechancanough. His warriors carried him into battle on a litter. That the young warriors were willing to risk an all-out attack, knowing the grim reprisals

---

[28]John Martin, "The Manner Howe to Bringe the Indians into Subjection," in Kingsbury, ed., *Records of Virginia Company*, 3: 705–707.

[29]Quoted in Bernard Bailyn, "Politics and Social Structure in Virginia," in James Smith, ed., *Seventeenth-Century America: Essays in Colonial History* (Chapel Hill, NC, 1959), p. 97.

that would rain down on them if they failed, indicates "the stubborn resistance of the Indians to cultural annihilation."[30]

The Powhatan tribes were again the losers in the war of 1644, although they killed hundreds of colonists, about one-twelfth of the white population. They lost partially because the aid they expected from white Marylanders, whose relations with Virginia had always been abrasive, did not materialize. Yet their determination apparently convinced the Virginians that Indians could rarely be cowed into submissiveness. Rather than risk future wars, the colonists altered the policy of the 1620s by signing a formal treaty in 1646 with the survivors of the Powhatan Confederacy. It drew a line between red and white territories and promised the Natives safety in their territory north of the York River. In return, the Powhatan tribes agreed to render military assistance in the event of an attack by tribes outside the Chesapeake area and promised a yearly tribute of beaver skins to the Virginia colony in acknowledgment of their subject status. Powhatan's Confederacy died with this peace treaty.

When Virginians took a census in 1669, only 11 of the 28 tribes described by John Smith in 1608 and only about 2,900 of the 20,000 Indians present when the English arrived remained in the colony. The English victory in the clash of the two societies was mostly due to the continued immigration of new settlers to the colony during an era when disease drastically thinned the Natives ranks. Also important to the Indians' decline was their inability to unite against the incoming Europeans. They outnumbered the English during the first two decades of settlement and might have expected to be further aided by the fierce internal divisions that gripped the Virginia colony for years. But in times of military crisis, the colonists were better able to unite, if only momentarily, than were the tribes of the Chesapeake region.

A more indirect factor in the decay of Indian strength was the growing functionlessness of the Chesapeake tribes after the English no longer depended on the maize trade. This can be best understood by looking comparatively at the English and the Spanish systems of colonization. In the Spanish colonies, the densely settled Indians had been utilized effectively as a subjugated labor force, both in the silver mines and in agriculture. The Spanish had unerringly located the Native population centers in Mexico and Peru and had made them the focal points of their colonizing efforts. The Indians supplied the bulk of the labor for Spanish extractive and productive enterprises in the early decades; hence it was not only desirable but also necessary to assimilate them into the European culture. Moreover, the Spanish church had a vested interest in the Indians. It sent hundreds of missionaries to New Spain to obtain as many conversions as possible for the greater glory of the church. Also, because the Spanish immigrants were disproportionately male, Indian women served the function of mistress, concubine, and wife. Though regarded as inferior to Spanish women, thousands of Native women became the sexual partners, inside and outside marriage, of Spanish men, and in this way were of the utmost importance to the colonizers. Of course, none of these roles could be fulfilled until the Native societies had been subordinated to Spanish authority. And the Spanish employed mass killing and terrorization to ensure their ascendancy in the first period of contact. Thereafter, Spanish colonizers regarded Native peoples not primarily as a threat, though the possibility of Native uprisings was always present, but as a population that could answer the economic, religious, and biological needs of the colonizers. In spite of the catastrophic spread of European diseases, which reduced the Indian population by as much as 75 percent in the first century of contact, an impressive degree of acculturation and assimilation took place in the Spanish colonies.

In English Virginia, none of these factors pertained except in the most limited way. The English brought no military force comparable to the conquistadores to subjugate the Chesapeake tribes

---

[30]Nancy Lurie, "Indian Cultural Adjustment to European Civilization," in Smith, ed., *Seventeenth Century America*, pp. 51–52.

and drive them into agricultural labor. The Anglican Church sent only a handful of clergy to the colony, and they made only token efforts to mount a missionary campaign. Their power over local settlers, so far as relations with the Indians were concerned, was minimal. Nor was there any significant sexual conjoining of English males and Native women, partly because of English squeamishness about women of another culture, but probably even more because Indian women, living in tribes not subjugated by the English, had no inclination to consort with men of the intruding society. Interracial marriages were almost unknown in Virginia, except in frontier areas where trappers and traders often made liaisons with Native women.

Only in the maize and fur trade, where the Indian was food producer, trapper, and skin dresser, did the Natives serve the needs of the white colonists. But the trade for corn lasted only until the colonists became self-sufficient by about 1616, and the fur trade was of negligible importance in the early Virginia settlements. What the colonists primarily wanted from the Indian was cleared land. Within the first generation of European settlement, neither side possessed the military capacity to best the other. But for the English, subjugation was unnecessary. With little to contribute to the goals of English colonization, Native people were regarded mostly as an obstacle. In an almost perfect reversal of Spanish Indian policy, the English in Virginia after 1622 worked to keep the two cultures apart. Like the Spanish policy, this plan was based on calculations of self-interest. Differences in the exploitable resources of the Spanish and the English colonies, in the density of Indian population, in the demographic composition of the colonizing and colonized societies, and in the social backgrounds of the colonists, rather than differences in national character, in attitudes toward the indigenous people, or in national policy, were chiefly responsible for the pursuit of assimilation in Spanish America and the goal of racial separation in Virginia.

Summary

The first encounters between English invaders and the Native peoples of North America occurred in the Chesapeake Bay region and lands just south of it. After the failed attempt at a Roanoke colony, the English established their first permanent outpost in the Americas at Jamestown, Virginia, in 1607. Colonizing Virginia, however, was fraught with difficulties, including severe drought and an inappropriate mix of settlers. Encouraging English colonization was the rising demand for tobacco, which grew extremely well in this area. Out of the need for cheap labor to increase tobacco production, the indentured servant system came about, with its harsh practices and largely empty promises to those who offered their labor in exchange for passage across the Atlantic.

Indian-English relations, as illustrated by those between Powhatan, Pocahontas, and Captain John Smith, were marked by misconceptions, suspicion, and violence on both sides. Even so, during the first decade of English settlement, the English and the Powhatans lived in close contact with much cultural interchange and trade taking place. However, after the increase of population that accompanied the rapid growth of tobacco production, relations between the two peoples deteriorated and resulted in the wars of 1622 and 1644, with the Powhatans losing in both clashes.

Critical Thinking Questions

1. Of the English Chesapeake colonies, Roanoke failed and Jamestown met with greater success. What explanation can be offered for the difference?
2. Francis Drake's boatload of the "jovial weed" in 1586 altered the view of tobacco: from medicinal aid to object of personal pleasure. How were the English planters in Virginia able to meet the increased demands for more tobacco?

3. Pocahontas not only was an authentic figure of history but also has been the subject of various artistic imaginings. On the basis of what is actually known about her, what importance might history attach to her?
4. The wars of 1622 and 1644 took tolls on both Natives and white settlers, with the Natives ultimately becoming the greater losers. What factors played into the decline of the Chesapeake tribes?

Further Reading

Kathleen M. Brown, *Good Wives, Nasty Wenches, and Anxious Patriarchs: Gender, Race and Power in Colonial Virginia* (Chapel Hill: University of North Carolina Press, 1996).

Frederic W. Gleach, *Powhatan's World and Colonial Virginia: A Conflict of Cultures* (Lincoln: University of Nebraska Press, 1997).

April Lee Hatfield, *Atlantic Virginia: Intercolonial Relations in the Seventeenth Century* (Philadelphia: University of Pennsylvania Press, 2004).

James Horn, *A Land as God Made It: Jamestown and the Birth of America* (New York: Basic Books, 2005).

Karen Kupperman, *Roanoke: The Abandoned Colony* (Totowa: Rowman and Allanheld, 1984).

Karen Kupperman, *Settling with the Indians: The Meeting of English and Indian Cultures in America, 1580–1640* (Totowa: Rowman and Littlefield, 1980).

Edmund S. Morgan, *American Slavery, American Freedom: The Ordeal of Colonial Virginia* (New York: W.W. Norton, 1975).

Michael Leroy Oberg, *The Head in Edward Nugent's Hand: Roanoke's Forgotten Indians* (Philadelphia: University of Pennsylvania Press, 2008).

Helen C. Rountree, *Pocahontas's People: The Powhatan Indians of Virginia through Four Centuries* (Norman: University of Oklahoma Press, 1990).

Helen C. Rountree, *Pocahontas, Powhatan, Opechancanough: Three Indian Lives Changed by Jamestown* (Charlottesville: University Press of Virginia, 2005).

Alden T. Vaughan, *American Genesis: John Smith and the Founding of Virginia* (Lincoln: University of Nebraska Press, 2003).

Margaret Holmes Williamson, *Powhatan Lords of Life and Death: Command and Consent in Seventeenth-Century Virginia* (Lincoln: University of Nebraska Press, 2003).

Peter H. Wood, Gregory Waselkov, and M. Thomas Hatley, eds., *Powhatan's Mantle: Indians in the Colonial Southeast* (Lincoln: University of Nebraska Press, 1989).

CHAPTER 4

Cultures Meet in the Northeast

LEARNING OBJECTIVES

- Discuss the Dutch presence in North America—the motivations of this group of settlers, the success of the Dutch West India Company, and the relations between the Dutch and the Algonquians and Iroquois.

- Characterize Puritanism: its beginnings, its vision, its purpose in leaving England for the "New World," and the features of its Massachusetts colony.

- Describe relations between the Pilgrims and the Native peoples of the Massachusetts coast. Discuss what factors created distrust and enmity and on how the Puritan theory of land possession contributed to discord.

- Explain the origins and outcome of the Pequot War in the 1630s and its significance for Native peoples in southern New England.

While Indians of the Powhatan Confederacy were planning their attack on the white settlements of Virginia in 1622, Dutch and English colonizers were entering Native territory hundreds of miles to the north. The commerce-minded Dutch established the first European foothold in the northeastern Atlantic seaboard. Therefore, the religion-minded Pilgrims and Puritans who followed would have to reckon carefully with the Dutch presence and their trading relationships with Native peoples.

Whether they were Dutch or English, the European newcomers came face-to-face with diverse Algonquian peoples, some of them composing largely autonomous small tribes and others, such as the Iroquois, that were populous, powerful, and organized into confederacies. Relationships among all these Indian societies, sometimes amicable and often hostile, went back hundreds of years. Into this maze of Indian relations, contending Europeans made their way filled with ambition and uncertainties.

The Dutch in the Northeast

The Hollanders had achieved independence from their own colonial masters, the Spanish, only in 1609. But even by then, they had become the principal carriers of seaborne commerce in Western Europe and had begun interloping in the Spanish and Portuguese trade to the Americas. Colonists, glad to get more favorable prices from the Dutch in the cloth and slave commerce, traded illegally with them. Then, in a burst of spectacular achievement, the Dutch leaped to the front of the race for wealth in the Americas. In 1621, Dutch merchants and investors launched the Dutch West India Company, impressively capitalized and fully supported by the government. Its goals were commerce and conquest—to gain control of as much of the European-African-New World trade as possible and to plant colonies wherever the opportunity arose.

Success came quickly. In 1628, the Dutch West India Company fleet intercepted and captured the entire annual Spanish flotilla, homeward bound from the Caribbean. The Dutch scooped up enough gold in this single exploit—about 15 million guilders—to pay a 50 percent dividend to the company's shareholders with enough left over to finance a military campaign against the Portuguese settlements in northeastern Brazil. For the next half-century, the Dutch controlled shipping to the Americas, reducing Spanish and Portuguese trade to insignificance.

At the same time, the Dutch began to take over the African slave trade. By 1637, when they captured Elmina Castle, the center of Portuguese slaving activities on the Gold Coast (now Ghana), they had all but driven the Portuguese from the Atlantic slave trade. Soon they seized Spanish bases—Curaçao, Saba, St. Martin, and St. Eustatius. This undertaking was accompanied by assaults on Portuguese Brazil, culminating in 1630, when the Dutch overwhelmed the Portuguese and took control of their profitable sugar plantations on the northeast coast, the most important source of sugar for the kitchens of Europe. Other arms of the vast Dutch trading empire reached the East Indies, India, Ceylon, and Formosa.

The mighty Dutch also made their distinctive imprint on the North American mainland. Henry Hudson, sailing as an employee of the Dutch East India Company, initiated a trade in furs with the Indians in 1609. Five years later, the Dutch established a trading post high on the Hudson River near Albany. Shortly after the chartering of the Dutch West India Company in 1621, they planted New Amsterdam on the present site of New York City. This became the center of Dutch colonization in North America for the next half-century. By the 1620s, the small Dutch settlement was sending home 10,000 furs a year, linking their economy closely to their Indian neighbors.

The Natives engaging in trade with the Dutch were the descendants of nomadic hunters who had come to the region some 8,000 years before. Living on the margin of the agricultural zone, they combined hunting and fishing with agriculture, though the latter, by the time the Dutch arrived, was their primary subsistence activity. Utilizing their environment seasonally, they engaged in winter hunting, spring stream fishing, and autumn harvesting and hunting.

The Algonquian tribes divided labor by gender. Men hunted and fished, whereas women were responsible for all phases of agriculture—planting, maintaining, and harvesting crops—as well as for fishing and gathering wild plants. These distinct roles were not accompanied, as in the case of the Iroquois, by the adoption of a matrilineal kinship system or the conferring of a degree of political power upon women. In most of the Northeast, kinship remained patrilineal, and men continued to dominate political and religious life.

Political leadership of Algonquian tribes in the Northeast was held by single individuals, who were called "sachems" or "sagamores." The sachem's role was to coordinate village activities that concerned the group as a whole—hunting, trade, the administration of justice, and diplomacy. The sachem's authority depended on maintaining the consent of his people. This, in turn, depended on the sachem's ability to communicate with the spiritual forces thought to control the fate of the tribe. "Their authority is most precarious," wrote one Frenchman among the Abenaki, "if indeed, that may be called authority to which obedience is in no wise obligatory."[1]

---

[1] Reuben Gold Thwaites, ed., *The Jesuit Relations and Allied Documents, 1610–1791* (Cleveland, OH, 1896), II: 73.

Sachems and sagamores were not chiefs or lords whose title was inherited and authority unquestioned but were "coordinators and ceremonial representatives for their people."[2]

On the eve of European intrusion the Algonquian-speaking people of the Northeast were more densely settled than in the Chesapeake region, probably numbering as many as 200,000 between Maine and New York. Among them, the most numerous were the Abenaki, Pawtucket, Massachusett, Narragansett, Pequot, Wampanoag, Mahican, and Mohawk. All these village-based and loosely connected groups had been in contact with Europeans for many generations. Fishermen who dried their catches on shore and engaged in minor trade had provided the northerly tribes with knowledge of European culture since the first quarter of the sixteenth century, and short-lived French and English attempts at settlement in the first decade of the seventeenth century gave them further understanding of the people from across the sea.

The Dutch radiated out in small numbers from New Amsterdam. They planted settlements to the north in the Connecticut River valley, to the south in the Delaware River valley, and to the east on Long Island. Their numbers were small, and in time they would be overwhelmed by the more numerous English. But their power at sea was never to be underestimated, as Virginians found out as late as 1667, when Dutch raiders captured twenty tobacco ships in the James River, and in 1672, when they repeated this success. Although the Dutch never settled more than 10,000 people in their mid-Atlantic colonies, they exerted a strong influence on English affairs. When three Anglo-Dutch wars erupted in Europe between 1650 and 1675, the colony at New Netherland became a target of English attack. It was captured by the English in 1664, recaptured by the Dutch in 1673, and then almost immediately retaken by the English. This event marked the end of Dutch political authority in North America.

Unlike the Virginians on the Chesapeake or the Puritans in New England, the Dutch immigrated in small numbers, and their principal goal was not farming but the profitable bartering of European trade goods for the skins of the beaver, otter, and deer, especially the beaver that one historian calls "arguably the most famous commodity in North America."[3] The Dutch did their utmost to preserve the Indians' goodwill because they were vastly outnumbered and dependent on the Indian trade for profit.

From the Native point of view, there was little to fear from the Dutch presence, for these bearded Europeans were few in number, showed no voracious appetite for land, and eagerly traded commodities that Indians wanted and could obtain by trapping animals that existed abundantly in their territory. Yet trading with Europeans contained a hidden danger. Prior to the arrival of Europeans, Indians had hunted for subsistence, their modest needs ensuring the conservation of game. But once the pelts of fur-bearing animals entered the international Atlantic market, Indians began hunting relentlessly to satisfy their trading partners. Under such conditions, Native hunters quickly exhausted the beaver supply in particular areas. When this outcome occurred, as it did to Mahican suppliers of the Dutch during the first quarter of the seventeenth century, the fur merchants of the Dutch West India Company began to cultivate their enemies, the Mohawks, the easternmost of the Iroquois tribes whose territories stretched westward to the Great Lakes. Eclipsing the Mahicans, the Mohawks became the major supplier of pelts to the Dutch and in this way became a formidable power in the Northeast.

The tendency of the Dutch fur trade to trigger or intensify intertribal hostilities became more pronounced in the second quarter of the seventeenth century. To the north of the Dutch settlements, the French were also building a fur trade with the powerful Hurons, who commanded the territories north of the Great Lakes.

---

[2]Neal Salisbury, *Manitou and Providence: Indians, Europeans, and the Making of New England, 1500–1643* (New York, 1982), p. 42.

[3]Shepard Krech III, *The Ecological Indian: Myth and History* (New York, 1999), p. 173.

In time, the depletion of furs in the region under Iroquois control enticed them into attacking the Hurons. If successful, the Iroquois could divert the vast fur resources of the Canadian north from Montreal, the center of French trading activities, to Albany, the main Dutch trading post, and thus make Amsterdam rather than Paris the major recipient of North American beaver skins. To this end, the Dutch cultivated ties with the Iroquois and supplied the firearms necessary to destroy the Hurons. This maneuver turned an ancient smoldering Iroquois-Huron hostility into all-out war.

In the second quarter of the seventeenth century, the great Huron nation, comprising 30,000 people or more, and already severely weakened by a ferocious outbreak of smallpox in the 1630s, was nearly destroyed by Iroquois enemies seeking control of the Hurons' beaver supply. The victorious Iroquois used the Dutch trade connection to increase their power. All this was triggered by tiny Dutch and French settlements and trading posts scattered along the waterways of the St. Lawrence and Hudson River valleys whose population, even after almost a half-century of settlement, totaled no more than 3,000.

Smaller Indian tribes in the vicinity of New Amsterdam that had neither the strength nor the geographical advantage to play a role in the fur trade suffered greatly in the 1640s. A few years before, the Dutch West India Company had recruited more settlers to build up an agricultural base of society. This effort required land purchases from local Indian bands such as the Rockaways and Carnasees. Having sold their land, however, the Indians saw no reason to leave it until Dutch farmers took it up. Now agriculturists from both societies lived side by side in areas such as Long Island, Rockaway, and Staten Island. When Dutch cattle trampled Indian fields or the Indian dogs attacked Dutch cattle, tempers flared. The governor of the Dutch West India Company, Willem Kieft, added to the tension by taxing all local Natives to repair the sagging finances of the colony. The Indians resisted this attempt to exact tribute, venturing the opinion that Kieft "must be a very mean fellow to come and live in this country without being invited . . . and now wish to compel them to give them their corn for nothing."[4]

Dutch expansion and sharp trading with Indian bands in the region soon produced sporadic violence. When this involved loss of life among the Dutch, the Dutch demanded the surrender of the responsible Indians to their system of justice. As permanent settlers and agriculturists, the Dutch wanted unqualified recognition of their sovereignty. By 1643, when local tribal chiefs refused to buckle under, the Dutch unleashed military force. Eighty Dutch soldiers fell upon two encampments of Wequasesgeeks, who had been granted refuge from their Indian enemies by the Dutch. The Dutch soldiers butchered women and children as well as men. Through this genocidal attack, Governor Kieft made clear to all tribes within New Amsterdam's orbit that they must accept Dutch trading terms, pay tribute when required, and recognize Dutch authority.

Dutch-Indian relations in the New Amsterdam region did not differ much from English contacts with Native Americans on the Chesapeake. After the first few decades, the Dutch had little to gain from trade, since the beaver in the area had been exhausted. Nor were the local Natives useful as potential converts to the Dutch form of Christianity because the Dutch West India Company sent few missionaries to convert the local Indians. Moreover, the Dutch did not require Indian wives, for they were plentifully supplied with women from their homeland.

In this situation, with land settlement replacing trade as the main economic activity, the local tribes became obstacles to Dutch expansion and Dutch authority. With the Native people composed of separate small bands, it was all the easier for the Dutch to fix on a military solution

---

[4]Quoted in Allen W. Trelease, *Indian Affairs in Colonial New York: The Seventeenth Century* (Ithaca, NY, 1960), p. 66.

to the "Indian problem." Many Indians resisted Dutch authority, but their strength was ebbing after decades of killer diseases and attritional warfare. When the English overpowered the Dutch in New Netherland in 1664, they encountered only demoralized remnants of an earlier Indian population.

By contrast, Dutch-Indian relations at Albany were peaceful and profitable. Probably not more than one hundred Dutch resided there in the 1640s, but they neither attacked nor were attacked by the powerful Mohawks, for both peoples admirably served each other's needs. Though greatly outnumbered, the Albany settlers did not hesitate to sell arms and ammunition to the Mohawks, knowing that they would be used to gain control over Huron tribespeople aligned with the French. Every gun in Indian hands contributed to the profitable flow of beaver skins to Amsterdam by way of the Hudson River rather than to Paris by way of the St. Lawrence River. In New Amsterdam, where the colonists were far more numerous than the Indians and the Indians far more divided, the Dutch enforced strict regulations against the sale of firearms.

The Dutch fur empire in North America came to a crashing halt when England, after a generation of civil war culminating in the restoration of Charles II in 1660, decided to make a second great effort in colonizing the West Indies and the North American mainland. Now, the Dutch colony of New Netherland became a prime English objective. To take it would remove the Hollanders entirely from the eastern seaboard and consolidate the English empire in North America.

To this end, an English military expedition seized New Netherland in 1664. Dutch New Netherland became the English royal colony New York, New Amsterdam became New York City, and its Dutch inhabitants were obliged to incorporate themselves into the English colonial system. Though several generations would pass before the English made up even half the population of New York, political authority, trade, and military affairs were now securely lodged within the British imperial system.

For the Natives of the New York City region, the change of political authority meant little, for the Dutch and the English were hardly distinguishable to them. The English takeover could not change the fact that disease and war had already decimated the small Algonquian tribes on the lower Hudson. In the last third of the seventeenth century, the small tribes of Manhattan, Long Island, and the lower Hudson River valley declined further, as the Natives struggled for existence through a mixture of hunting, fishing, farming, and day labor in white settlements. Their relationship to the Europeans became almost entirely servile. A Long Islander summed it up in 1670: "There is now but a few upon the Island, and those few no ways hurtful but rather serviceable to the English, and it is to be admired, how strangely they have decreast by the Hand of God, since the English first setling of those parts."[5]

Hostile Indians had become friendly Indians, but the friendliness was only the outward expression of internal social and political disorganization and the cultural dependency that accompanied it. In this state of demoralization, alcohol contributed further to the Indians' demise. Dutch authorities had prohibited selling alcohol to Indians, "yet every one does it," remarked one observer in 1679.[6] Two years later, a Minisink sachem bitterly remonstrated that alcohol had caused the death of sixty of his people in three years. English authorities affirmed in the next decade that Indians in the colony "are free and not slaves" and should not be made lifetime servants against their will, but this order did little to stop the dwindling Indian population from losing not only its cultural autonomy but its physical freedom as well.

---

[5]Daniel Denton, *A Brief Description of New York* (1670), quoted in ibid., p. 179.
[6]Bartlett B. James and J. Franklin Jameson, eds., *Journal of Jaspar Danckaerts, 1679–1680,* (New York, 1913), p. 79.

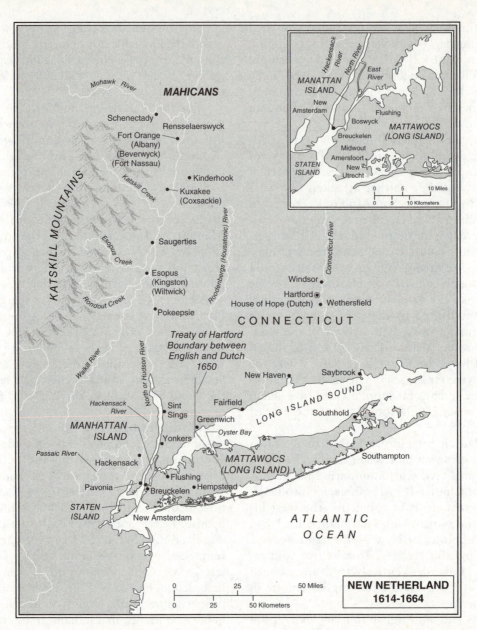

Mohawk River

MAHICANS

Schenectady
Rensselaerswyck
Fort Orange
(Albany)
(Beverwyck)
(Fort Nassau)

KATSKILL MOUNTAINS

Katskill Creek

Kinderhook
Kuxakee
(Coxsackie)

Esopus Creek

Saugerties

Roodenbergs (Housatonic) River

Esopus
(Kingston)
(Wiltwick)

Rondout Creek

Pokeepsie

CONNECTICUT

Windsor
Hartford
House of Hope (Dutch)   Wethersfield

Treaty of Hartford
Boundary between
English and Dutch
1650

New Haven   Saybrook

Walkil River

North or Hudson River

Hackensack
River   Sint
Sings   Fairfield
Greenwich   Southhold

MANHATTAN
ISLAND   Yonkers   Oyster Bay

LONG ISLAND SOUND

Passaic River   Hackensack

**MATTAWOCS
(LONG ISLAND)**   Southampton

Flushing
Pavonia   Breuckelen   Hempstead

STATEN
ISLAND   New Amsterdam

ATLANTIC
OCEAN

0   25   50 Miles
0   25   50 Kilometers

**NEW NETHERLAND
1614-1664**

Hackensack River   North River

MANATTAN
ISLAND   East
River

New
Amsterdam   Flushing
Boswyck

Breuckelen   **MATTAWOCS
(LONG ISLAND)**

STATEN
ISLAND   Midwout
Amersfoort
New
Utrecht

0   5   10 Miles
0   5   10 Kilometers

At Albany, the advent of the English brought no significant change in Indian relations. The Iroquois continued to deal with merchants who were primarily Dutch, to negotiate through interpreters who were Dutch, and to receive European goods in return for their furs. The furs, however, after passing through New York City, traveled to English rather than Dutch markets, and the trade goods that the Indian fur suppliers received came from England rather than Holland. This alteration mattered little to the Iroquois trappers. Far more important than the substitution of English for Dutch political administration was the fact that the fur trade itself had been in a state of long-term decline since about 1660. Nothing in the English conquest of the colony could reverse this trend because the decline was caused by the exhaustion of the beaver east of the Great Lakes and the difficulties of outwitting the French for control of the western beaver sources.

Puritanism

If the Algonquian Indians of the Northeast were learning about the dangers of trade with small numbers of Dutch traders and settlers, they would realize by the 1630s that a different breed of Europeans, intensely religious, was swarming to their ancient homelands. The most numerous of these English, they would learn, called themselves Protestants.

Puritanism was, among other things, a religious reform movement. Since the reign of Henry VIII, when England had turned toward Protestantism, Catholic-Protestant tensions had racked the country. When Elizabeth ascended the throne in 1558, she attempted to forge a religious compromise. But avowed anti-Catholics regarded the Church of England that flourished under her reign as at best a halfway house between a corrupt and a pure church and at worst barely distinguishable from the Church of Rome with its liturgy, vestments, rituals, and oppressive bureaucracy. Some of them wanted a more radical cleansing of Catholic elements in order to gain greater purity in their church. Thus, they became known as purifying radicals, or Puritans.

Puritanism was also a political and social response to long-range changes that had been occurring in English society. Men and women of this era lived at a time when traditional feudal society was giving way to what we now think of as a more modern social order. This brought the overturning of the traditional church, the growth of cities, the enclosure of land (for pasturing sheep and thus pulling land from food production), an increase in trade, and the rise of a capitalistic society in which the individual had far more freedom to move and make economic decisions. The most visible social effects of these long-term trends were uprooted peasants cast off the land, an increase in vagabondage and poverty, and frightening increases in urban crime as people swarmed into the pestilential cities, particularly into London, which grew from about 75,000 in 1550 to 200,000 in 1600 and to 350,000 in 1635.

The changes overtaking the English pleased many but unsettled others. In the older medieval ethos, people lived within a fixed system of hierarchies in church, government, economic organizations, and family. Life in an English rural village reflected this emphasis on rank and order. Every individual was contained within a web of relationships that conferred both rights and responsibilities. There was the manorial hierarchy with lord, steward, and tenants; the parish hierarchy with vicar, church wardens, and overseers of the poor; the hierarchy of the established church with archbishop, bishops, deans, canons, and visitors; and the hierarchy of economic enterprise with corporations, guilds, masters, journeymen, and apprentices.

But in modernizing England, individuals gradually worked themselves free of the authority of corporate groups. Little by little, they made inroads on the religious authority, which dictated individual belief; on the political authority, which strictly governed civil behavior and defined political rights in a limited way; and on the economic authority, by which guilds and monopolies granted by the Crown closely regulated prices, wages, and conditions of work. Thus "protesters," or Protestants, began challenging the authority of the Church of Rome; individual entrepreneurs challenged the right of the guilds to regulate work; individual enterprises challenged monopolies that excluded outsiders from areas of economic activity; and agricultural operators began buying small farmsteads and consolidating them into larger agricultural units, dislocating tenant farmers in the process.

To Puritans, the sight of individuals breaking free of traditional restraints was fearsome. In religion, they applauded this because it involved placing the individual in a more direct relationship with God by removing the traditional intermediaries—especially the Catholic Church. But Puritans deplored individualism in other areas of life because it left people to their own devices, whereby they acted out the worst fantasies of social anarchy. Social order, respect for authority, morality—all seemed to be crumbling amid the new social and economic order. Everywhere "idle and masterless men," as one social critic phrased it, roamed the land.

The concept of "every man alone," the individual operating freely in time and space, is at the core of our modern system of values and behavior. But to intellectuals, social critics, and religious leaders of the late sixteenth century, this concept conjured up frightening visions of chaos. Individualism as a mode of behavior threatened the concept of community—of people bound together by obligations and responsibilities. Now, under a newer ethic, the individual rather than the group became the conceptual unit of thinking. To Puritans this was the enemy of a tight-knit community.

Puritans addressed this problem of the individual versus the community through a new discipline intended to create a regenerated social order. At its core was an ethic that stressed work or industriousness as a primary way of serving God. One did not have to occupy a high station or follow a profession but only to work hard in whatever station one found oneself, be that lawyer, blacksmith, or common laborer. Each "calling" was equally worthy in God's sight and, if followed conscientiously, would lead the individual toward spiritual grace. One of the Puritan leaders wrote: "If thou beest a man that lives without a calling, though thou has two thousands to spend, yet if thou has no calling, tending to public good, thou art an unclean beast. God sent you unto this world as unto a workhouse, not a playhouse."[7]

Puritans organized themselves into religious congregations where men and women labored together, disciplined themselves, and worked for mutual salvation. Each member not only worked for his or her own perfection but also scrutinized the behavior of others for signs of waywardness. Furthermore, to reform their society at large, the Puritans believed they must assume responsibility—moral stewardship—over all those around them. In a chaotic and criminal world, God's "elect" must not only save themselves but also assume the burdens of civil government in order to reform society at large. Others who could

not find Christian truth in their hearts might have to be coerced and controlled, directed and dominated. Thus, all would be bound together in covenant to do God's work. Puritanism was, thus, a radical plan to bring about the conversion of the whole society. A mass movement with an ideological vision would rule the land—a radical departure from traditional thought, which held that kings ruled by divine right and delegated their authority to those below them.

The rise of Puritanism during Queen Elizabeth's reign (1558–1603), and the subsequent persecution of Puritans by her successor, James I, is a familiar story. Here it is enough to understand that despite their initial successes, Puritans were increasingly harassed under King James. By the 1620s, many were convinced that to reform English society, they would first have to carry out their crusade in another part of the world. Economic opportunity also beckoned abroad, at a time when many Puritans were feeling the effects of economic depression in England, where population growth ran up against the same Little Ice Age phenomena of frequent droughts and crop failures that had beset Native Americans in the era of European conquest. But ideological commitment marked them off from the Virginia colonizers. Fired by a vision of building a Protestant utopia, they arrived in New England far differently disposed than English settlers to the south. In Virginia, by contrast, the spirit of community well-being and an ideological vision were conspicuously absent. Economic ambitions, rather than being contained and limited within a set of moral prescriptions, were pursued in and of themselves.

The Puritans were by no means the first Europeans to reach the shores of what they called New England. Fishermen of various European nationalities had been working at the Newfoundland Banks and drying their catches on Cape Cod and the coast of Maine since the early sixteenth century. Hundreds of fishing ships had visited the New England coast and made contact with local Natives before 1607, when the English first attempted colonization in the region. The small

---

[7]Quoted in Perry Miller and Thomas H. Johnson, *The Puritans* (New York, 1938), pp. 325–26.

number of men alighting on the coast of present-day Maine, beset with food shortages, fire, and inhospitable winds, lasted only briefly. Not until 1620 did a permanent settlement take root at Plymouth, Massachusetts, this time planted by several hundred English Pilgrims who had earlier fled to Holland. Slowly, in the 1620s, other fur-trading and fish-drying settlements took root along the coast. But none of these compared with the great Puritan migration that began in 1630 when 11 ships and some 700 passengers set out from England. They were the vanguard of a swarming movement that by 1660 had brought about 20,000 people to New England's shores.

The Elusive Utopia

Led by John Winthrop, a member of the English gentry, the Puritans set about building their "City on the Hill." They hoped to establish communities of pure Christians who collectively swore a covenant with God that they would work for his ends, knowing that in return, he would watch over them. Puritan immigrants would bring individualistic impulses that had flowered in England under control as all worked for the common good. To accomplish this undertaking, they agreed to employ what today we might regard as authoritarian means. No diversity of opinion concerning religious beliefs could be tolerated. Government would be limited to those visibly filled with God's grace as determined by Puritans already in the church. Offenders, both civil and religious, would be rooted out and punished severely. Every aspect of life would be integrated in the quest for utopia. Participants in the experiment, at least initially, agreed to give up some of their freedoms in order to accomplish greater goals. They sought homogeneity, not diversity, and believed that the good of the community outweighed protecting the rights of its individual members. The Puritans in England had formulated an ideology of rebellion, but now it would be employed as an ideology of control.

John Winthrop.
(Courtesy Classic Image/Alamy)

As in Virginia, the early months were difficult. More than 200 of the first 700 immigrants perished, and a hundred more, chronically depressed by their first winter in the forbidding New England climate, returned to England the next spring. But Puritans kept coming. They began "hiving out" along the shores of Boston's Back Bay, along the rivers that emptied into it, south into what was to become Connecticut, and north along the rocky Massachusetts coast. Massachusetts quickly achieved a diversified, viable economic base, which had been so sorely lacking in early Virginia. A militant work ethic and self-discipline explain this success, but the quality of leadership exercised by such men as Winthrop, John Cotton, John Eliot, Richard Mather, and Thomas Shepard, who were experienced in local government, law, and the uses of exhortation, gets some of the credit. The typical early leader in Virginia was a soldier of fortune or a roughneck adventurer whose instincts were mostly predatory. Massachusetts was led in the early years by university-trained ministers, experienced members of the English lesser gentry, and men compulsively determined to fulfill what they regarded as God's prophecy for New England.

Nevertheless, Massachusetts experienced dissension and conflict in the early decades, both within its communities and in contact with the Natives of the region. Even on the voyage across the Atlantic, some inkling appeared that the sun would not always shine on the Puritan experiment. In midvoyage Winthrop felt compelled to lecture the expedition that respect for authority was essential to this new venture. Once on firm ground, and surrounded by boundless land, it proved difficult to squelch acquisitive instincts or to keep people closely bound in covenanted communities. Restless souls began moving away from the center of authority. Others, remaining at the center, agitated for a broader-based political system and a decentralization of authority that would give the individual towns the right to manage their own affairs. After only two years,

Winthrop wondered whether the Puritans had not gone "from the snare to the pit." Thirteen years later, he was still struggling to convince those around him that "if you stand for your natural corrupt liberties, and will do what is good in your own eyes, you will not endure the least weight of authority, but will murmur and oppose, and be always striving to shake off that yoke."[8]

Winthrop's troubles multiplied. In 1631, when Roger Williams arrived in New England, the established leaders faced a contentious and visionary man who defied religious orthodoxy as they defined it. Williams preached that the Puritans were not truly pure because they would not separate completely from the Church of England. He argued that they interpreted the Bible incorrectly. Perhaps most alarming, he charged that the colonists were intruding on Indian soil and illegally depriving the Natives of their rights. By 1635, Williams was defying the civil magistrates who tried to punish him for his teachings. Convinced that Williams would split the colony into competing religious groups and destabilize authority through his religious perfectionism, the Massachusetts magistrates banished him from the colony and planned to ship him back to England. But Williams escaped and trekked southward, where he started a small settlement of his followers—the seed of the colony of Rhode Island.

Even as the magistrates banished Williams, they faced another preacher of unorthodoxy—Anne Hutchinson. Brilliant and charismatic, she had proven her value to the community as a midwife, healer, and spiritual counselor after arriving in 1634 with her husband and eleven children. But in the next two years she emerged as more than a counselor. She gathered many in Boston for religious discussions and then began to dissect the previous Sunday's sermons, raising points of criticism concerning the theological interpretations of John Wilson, the city's minister. Soon she was the center of a movement called Antinomianism—a variant interpretation of

---

[8]Quoted in Richard S. Dunn, *Puritans and Yankees: The Winthrop Dynasty of New England, 1630–1717* (Princeton, NJ, 1962), p. 24.

Puritan doctrine that stressed the mystical elements of God's grace and the futility of applying rules and regulations to govern the process by which each individual came to terms with his or her God. By 1636, Boston was divided into two camps, and Hutchinson was drawing to her circle not only those who believed in her theological views but also most of the discontented in the community—merchants who were disgruntled with the government's price controls, young people who disliked the rigid rule of their elders in church and government, women chafing under male authority, and artisans who resented wage controls imposed to arrest the inflationary trend that had begun.

Determined to rid themselves of this second thorn, the clergy and the magistrates tried Anne Hutchinson in 1636. After two long interrogations, the Puritan leaders excommunicated her from the Boston church and banished her from the colony for preaching eighty-two erroneous theological opinions. The sentence read to her at the trial's end conveys the fear aroused in Boston and the determination of the magistrates to squelch further division within the community. "Forasmuch as you, Mrs. Hutchinson, have highly transgressed . . . and offended and troubled the Church with your errors," intoned the judge, "and have drawn away many a poor soul, and have upheld your revelations; and forasmuch as you have made a lie. . . . Therefore in the name of our Lord Jesus Christ . . . I do cast you out . . . and deliver you up to Satan . . . and account you from this time forth to be a heathen and a publican . . . and I command you in the name of Jesus Christ and of this Church as a leper to withdraw yourself out of the congregation."[9] With a number of her followers, Hutchinson followed the route of Roger Williams to Rhode Island. The colony's leaders had demonstrated the lengths to which they were prepared to go to ensure homogeneity.

New England could not really remain homogeneous, no matter how many nonconformists were banished from its midst. Nor could the acquisitive instincts that ate at the concept of community be forever dampened. The work ethic brought material gains, and with worldly success individuals developed the ambition to reach still higher—precisely what the Puritan leaders feared would destroy the stable harmonious system they were trying to build. Population increase, geographical expansion, and trade with the outside world all worked against the idea of a closed corporate community suffused with religiosity. In spite of the leaders' admonitions that "the care of the public must oversway all private respects," Massachusetts, even in the early years, demonstrated the difficulty of setting down land-hungry immigrants in the North America and expecting them to restrain their appetites and individualistic urges. The centrifugal forces of the environment were more than a match for the centripetal forces of religious ideology.

Puritans and Indians

Given the Puritan ideal of community and the centrality of the idea of reforming the world in their image, it might be thought that the conflict and limited acculturation that characterized Anglo-Indian contacts on the Chesapeake would have been replaced in New England by less hostility and greater interaction. But this was not the case.

English exploratory incursions and small-scale attempts at settlement in the early seventeenth century had to contend with the fact that the French and Dutch had already established permanent settlements and a trading network that extended from Nova Scotia to New Amsterdam. The French and the Dutch had built the trade on a system of reciprocal relations with the Natives of the region. None of the first English attempts at settlement fared well because the English adopted the more militaristic stance toward the Indians recommended by John Smith, following his voyage to the New England coast

---

[9]Quoted in Emery Battis, *Saints and Sectaries: Anne Hutchinson and the Antinomian Controversy in the Massachusetts Bay Colony* (Chapel Hill, NC, 1962), p. 246.

Trial of Mrs. Hutchinson.

Anne Hutchinson.

(Courtesy North Wind Picture Archives/Alamy)

in 1614. English expeditions attacked and kid-napped coastal Natives on several occasions. In 1614, one of Smith's captains captured more than twenty Indians and sold them into slavery in Malaga, Spain. Such a brass-knuckles approach guaranteed that the English, when they began to arrive in the 1620s, would not be welcomed as people with whom amicable relations could be expected.

It was not brute force or superior numbers, however, that paved the way for a permanent English presence in New England. Rather, it was disease. In 1616, English fishermen stopped on the coast and triggered a "virgin soil epidemic"— the implantation of viruses into a population with no immunological defense. Tens of thousands of Natives died within a single year, especially in the region from Massachusetts Bay to Plymouth Bay, where entire villages were swept away or abandoned. Five years later, an English-man moving through the area wrote that the Indians had "died on heaps, as they lay in their houses, and the living that were able to shift for themselves would run away and let them die, and let their carcasses lie above the ground without burial. . . . And the bones and skulls upon the several places of their habitations, made such a spectacle . . . that as I traveled in that forest near the Massachusetts [tribe], it seemed to me a new-found Golgotha."[10] Three-quarters or more of the Native inhabitants of southern New England probably succumbed to the disease. Such carnage forced a reshuffling of Algonquian-speaking people. Remnants of villages and fragments of families had to resettle and re-form into viable groups that could feed and defend themselves.

When the Pilgrims arrived at Plymouth in 1620, they disembarked in the area where Natives had recently suffered catastrophic population losses from smallpox. This not only opened up the land for the Pilgrims but also greatly weakened the Indians' ability to resist them. The English had the further good fortune of encountering Tisquantum, known to the English as Squanto. A Wampanoag whom an English ship captain had kidnapped in 1614 and then sold him as a slave in Spain, Squanto had been smuggled to England, where he joined an English captain on several trips to the New England coast. On the second of these trips, Squanto found that most of his tribe had been killed by the plague, but he remained in the present-day Cape Cod area and was there when the Pilgrims landed. Through Squanto's friendship, the Pilgrims received important assistance in the early years.

Relations between the Pilgrims and the Native people of the Massachusetts coast were relatively friendly until after the newcomers discovered the Natives' underground cold-storage cellars and stole as much of the corn, placed there for winter use, as they could carry off. Even then the Indians chose to minimize contact with the settlers, though after death had reduced the Plymouth colony to about fifty persons in the spring of 1621, the vulnerability of the English invited Indian attack.

The need of the local Wampanoags for a military ally to aid them in their struggle with the neighboring Narragansetts probably explains why they tolerated English abuses and even signed a treaty in 1621 that formed the basis for trade and mutual assistance. The logic of the Wampanoag diplomacy became clear when Miles Standish and other Pilgrims aided them in a dispute with their enemies in 1621. The Wampanoags considered the treaty as an alliance of equals, but the English, regarding themselves as culturally superior, saw it as submission by the Indians to English domination.

This surface amity lasted only a year, however. In 1622, about sixty non-Pilgrim newcomers to the colony created serious friction. The new colonists settled themselves at Wessagusset, some distance from the Pilgrim colony, stole corn from the neighboring Massachusetts tribe, and planned attacks on the Indians when they refused to trade with the needy, but arrogant, newcomers. Under cover of a story that the Indians

---

[10]Thomas Morton, "New English Canaan," in *Tracts and Other Papers Relating Principally to the Origin, Settlement and Progress of the Colonies in North America*, Peter Force, comp. (Washington, DC, 1836), II, No. 5: 19.

Source: The Huntington Library, Art Collections, and Botanical Gardens.

were conspiring against both white communities, Standish, who had long harbored grudges against several insulting Massachusetts, led an offensive against the friendly Indians, killing eight of them and impaling the head of the sachem Wituwamet on top of the fort at Plymouth as an emblem of white power. Hearing of the deteriorating relations, John Robinson, formerly the Pilgrims' minister in Holland, wrote Governor Bradford in dismay, asking why the English indulged in needless violence. Were "civilized" men in the wilderness, asked Robinson, beginning to act like "savages," forgetting that they were supposed to represent order and piety? Singling out Miles Standish, the militia captain of Plymouth,

Robinson wrote: "It is . . . a thing more glorious, in men's eyes, than pleasing in God's, or convenient for Christians, to be a terror to poor barbarous people. And indeed I am afraid lest, by these occasions, others should be drawn to affect [this kind of behavior] in the world."[11] As for the Indians, they "could not imagine, from whence these men should come," wrote Thomas Morton, a friend of the Indians, "or to what end, seeing them perform such unexpected actions." From that time on, the English colonists were called "Wotowquenange, which in their language signifieth stabbers or cutthroats."[12]

When the Puritan migration began in 1630, Natives of the New England coast had more than

---

[11]William Bradford, *Of Plymouth Plantation, 1620–1647*, Samuel Eliot Morison, ed. (New York, 1966), p. 375.
[12]Morton, p. 76, quoted in Salisbury, *Manitou and Providence. . .* , p. 133.

a generation of experience with English ways. Little that they had encountered made them optimistic about future relations, although their own intercultural hostilities continued to make the newcomers potentially valuable allies, and their desire for trade goods persisted. As for the Puritans, they were publicly committed to interracial harmony but privately preparing for the worst. The charter of the Massachusetts Bay Company claimed that the "principal end of this plantation" was to "win and incite the natives of [the] country, to the knowledge and obedience of the only true God and Savior of mankind, and the Christian faith."[13] But the instructions of the company to John Winthrop reveal what was anticipated: all men were to be trained in the use of firearms; Indians were to be prohibited from entering the Puritan towns; and any colonists so reckless as to sell arms to the Indians or instruct them in their use were to be deported to England where they would be severely punished. While ordering that Indians must be fairly treated, the company reflected the garrison mentality that settlers, once landed and settled, displayed. The Puritans would initiate no missionary activity for thirteen years.

In the first few years of settlement, the Indians did little to arouse Puritan anger. Their sachems made overtures of friendship, supplied the colonists with corn during the difficult first winter, and eagerly engaged in a minor trade. One Puritan leader recounted his surprise that during the first winter, when the Puritans "had scarce houses to shelter themselves, and no doors to hinder the Indians' access to all they had in them, . . . where their whole substance, weak wives and little ones lay open to their plunder; . . . yet had they no food or stuff diminished, neither children nor wives hurt in the least measure, although the Indians came commonly to them at those times, much hungry belly (as they used to say) and were then in number and strength beyond the English by far."[14]

This state of coexistence lasted only a few years. Smallpox struck the eastern Massachusetts bands in 1633 and 1634, killing thousands as far north as Maine and as far south as the Connecticut River valley, where in one village all but 50 of nearly 1,000 inhabitants died in one devastating blow. The colonists believed that this was proof that God had intervened on their behalf at a time when their land hunger was causing friction over rights to land. The town records of Charlestown, for example, state that "without this remarkable and terrible stroke of God upon the natives, [we] would with much more difficulty have found room, and at far greater charge have obtained and purchased land."[15] As in Virginia, the need for land provided the incentive for steering away from rather than toward equitable relations between the two societies. That the population buildup came so quickly in Puritan New England only hastened the impulse to regard Indians as objects to be removed rather than subjects to be assimilated.

The Question of Land

Puritan theories of land possession clarify this tendency to classify Indians in ways that privileged violence over assimilation or coexistence. Like other Europeans, Puritans claimed the land they were invading by right of discovery. This theory derived from the ancient claim that Christians were everywhere entitled to dispossess non-Christians of their land. A second European legal theory, called *vacuum domicilium*, bolstered Puritan claims that land not "occupied" or "settled" went by forfeit to those who attached themselves to it in a "civilized" manner. Before he set foot

---

[13]Nathaniel B. Shurtleff, *Records of the Governor and Company of the Massachusetts Bay in New England*, 5 vols. (Boston, MA, 1853–54), I: 17.
[14]Edward Johnson, "Wonder-Working Providence," quoted in Salisbury, "Conquest of the 'Savage': Puritans, Puritan Missionaries, and Indians, 1620–1680" (Ph.D. dissertation, University of California, Los Angeles, CA, 1972), pp. 63–64.
[15]Quoted in Alden T. Vaughan, *New England Frontier: Puritans and Indians, 1620–1675* (Boston, MA, 1965), p. 104.

in North America, John Winthrop wrote the following:

> As for the Natives in New England, they inclose no land, neither have any settled habitation, nor any tame cattle to improve the land by, and so have no other but a natural right to those countries, so as if we leave them sufficient for their use, we may lawfully take the rest, there being more than enough for them and us.[16]

By this logic, entitlement to land in "New England" required only the assertion that because their way of life did not conform to European norms, the Natives had forfeited the land that they "roamed" rather than "settled." By European definition the land was *vacuum domicilium*—a "vast and empty chaos," as one early colonist described New England.[17]

The slender power of the disease-ravaged coastal tribes of the Massachusetts Bay region and the legal principles invoked under the concept of *vacuum domicilium* positioned the Puritans favorably to establish their beachhead in North America. The remnants of the formerly populous Massachusett and Pawtucket peoples were in no position to resist and, in fact, willingly consented to the occupation of their lands by the Puritan vanguard that inhabited Naumkeag (renamed Salem) in 1629 and the 3,000 newcomers who came in the next four years. In return for land, of which they now had a surplus, the Natives gained the protection of the English against their Micmac enemies to the north. Hence the Puritans adopted the position that the local Indians were domesticated subjects, living in separate villages but answering to Puritan government and law.

Still in a very fluid stage, Puritan-Indian relations, by about 1634, began to revolve around the land question. As pressure on available land resources mounted rapidly, another epidemic in 1633 struck down many Native people throughout a wide swath from the St. Lawrence River to Long Island. The English again saw the divine hand intervening on their behalf, paving the way for settlements as the Indians fell before the power of the English God. Yet the radical separatist Roger Williams of Salem disputed the claim of the Massachusetts Bay leaders that their royal patent entitled them to occupy Native land without first purchasing it from the Natives. Williams had immersed himself in Indian culture shortly after his arrival in 1631—one of the few English to do so—and by the next year was learning their language. Williams contended that the Puritans were illegally and sinfully grabbing Indian land and would have to answer for this before God and authorities in England. Arguing that the Natives of the region used the land in rational and systematic ways, he directly challenged the Puritan claim that the Indians' random use of land had left a *vacuum domicilium*.

The Massachusetts magistrates indignantly dismissed these ideas, burned the pamphlet in which Williams advanced his arguments, and banished him from the colony. Traveling to Rhode Island with some of his followers, Williams was offered land by a Narragansett sachem and found "among the savages," as he wrote, a place where he and his followers could peaceably worship God according to their consciences. Winthrop responded to Williams's argument that "if we had no right to this land, yet our God hath right to it, and if he be pleased to give it us (taking it from a people who had so long usurped upon him and abused his creatures) who shall control him or his terms?"[18] Claiming that God directed all Puritan policy, Winthrop charged that anyone opposing Puritan policy was challenging God himself.

Understanding that seizing Indian land by right could be reckless, Puritans continued to

---

[16] "General Considerations for the Plantation in New England . . . " (1629), in Allyn B. Forbes, ed., *Winthrop Papers*, 5 vols. (Boston, MA, 1929–1947), 2: 118.

[17] Robert Cushman, "Reasons and Considerations Touching the Lawfulness of Removing out of England . . . ," in John Demos, ed., *Remarkable Providences: Readings on Early American History*, 2nd ed. (Boston, MA, 1991), p. 7.

[18] Quoted in "Generall Considerations for the Plantation in New England . . . " (1629), in Allyn B. Forbes, ed., *Winthrop Papers*, 5 vols. (Boston, MA, 1929–1947), 2: 534n.

purchase land from local tribes. But the purchases were often made to obtain a favorable legal settlement where rival groups of colonists claimed the same tract of land. In such cases, a deed to the land in dispute from a Native seller was the best way to convince a court of one's claim. Even in cases in which intra-European rivalry favored the purchase of Indian land, the sale could be accomplished through a variety of stratagems designed to reduce the cost to the white settler. Turning livestock into cultivated Indian fields over a period of time often convinced a tribe that their land was losing its value. Alcohol was sometimes used to reduce the negotiating skill of the Indian seller. Another method was to buy the land at a rock-bottom price from an Indian sachem who falsely claimed title to it and then take to court any disputing sachem who claimed ownership. Before an English court, with its white lawyers, judges, and juries, the Indian claimant rarely won his or her case. Perhaps most effective of all was fining an Indian for minor offenses of English law—walking on the Sabbath or illegally entering a town, for example—and then "rescuing" the Indian from the debt he or she was unable to pay by discharging the fine in return for a tract of his or her land. None of these tactics worked in areas where Indian tribes were strong and unified. But they were effective among the decimated and divided tribes of southern New England.

The Pequot War

All the factors that operated in Virginia to produce friction between the two societies—English land hunger, a negative view of Native culture, and intertribal Indian hostility—were present in New England. They were vastly augmented by another factor unknown on the Chesapeake—the Puritan sense of mission. For people of such high moral purpose, who lived daily with the anxiety that they might fail in what they saw as the last chance to save corrupt European Protestantism, the Indian stood as a direct challenge to their "errand into the wilderness." The Puritans' mission was to tame and civilize their new environment, to convert "wilderness" into sacred space, and to build a pious commonwealth that would "shine like a beacon" back to decadent England. But how could order and discipline in holy communities be brought to the new environment unless its roaming original inhabitants were tamed and "civilized"? Governor William Bradford of Plymouth tellingly described the land he was entering as "a hideous and desolate wilderness full of wild beasts and wild men."[19] Land, beast, and human must all be brought under control. To do less was to allow chaos to reign when God's will was that Christian order be imposed. As one historian has explained, the Indian reminded the English of what they must not become. The Native was the counterimage of the civilized human, lacking in what was most valued by the Puritans—civility, Christian piety, purposefulness, and the work ethic. If such people could not be reconstructed as red Puritans, then white Puritans would have failed in regulating the land to which God had directed them. God would surely answer such a failure with his wrath.[20]

In this providential view of history, many Puritan leaders, if not ordinary settlers, felt an urgent need to master the "savagism" they encountered. However, mastering "savagism" did not require eliminating the "savages." From their writings it appears that Puritans would have preferred to convert the "heathen" to Christianity. But this could be accomplished only through great expenditure of time and effort. The Spanish and the Portuguese had sent hundreds of missionaries along with the conquistadores and settlers. But the Puritans came with only their own ministers, and these ministers had more than enough to do to maintain piety, unity, and moral standards within the white communities. Proselytizing the Natives of New England never received a high priority. Much was written about foiling Satan, who had "decoyed those miserable savages hither, in hopes

[19]William Bradford, *Plymouth Plantation*, p. 62.
[20]Roy H. Pearce, *The Savages of America: A Study of the Indian and the Idea of Civilization* (Baltimore, MD, 1953), pp. 3–24.

that the gospel of the Lord Jesus Christ would never come here to destroy or disturb his absolute empire over them," but little was done to save the Native Americans from Satan.[21]

Rather than convert the "savages" of New England, the Puritans attempted to bring them under civil government, making them strictly accountable to the ordinances that governed white behavior in Massachusetts. Insofar as Indians were willing to subject themselves to the new white code of behavior, usually out of fear, the Puritans prevailed. They could keep a close eye on all Natives within the areas of white settlement and bring them to court for any offenses against white law. Many of the smaller bands of eastern Massachusetts, severely weakened by European diseases or living in fear of strong and hostile neighbors, bent to the newcomers. But the question of control became a military problem when the Puritans encountered a tribe that was sufficiently strong to resist the loss of its cultural identity and political sovereignty.

Such were the Pequots—a strong and numerous people. By the 1630s, they had built a trading network of tributary groups and viewed the Narragansetts as their main rival in southern New England. The Pequots worked hard to convince the neighboring Narragansetts that only by uniting against the English could either tribe survive. But their arguments went unheard. Following the advice of Roger Williams, the Narragansetts agreed to ally themselves with Massachusetts Bay, leaving the Pequots virtually alone in their determination to resist the English.

Hostilities between the Pequots and the English were ostensibly triggered by the murder of two white ship captains and their crews. One of the mariners, John Stone, was hated among the English, for he had attempted to murder Governor Prence of Plymouth and had later been banished from Massachusetts for other misdeeds. Two years after Stone's death in 1634, John Oldham was found murdered on his ship off present-day Block Island. Using these incidents as justification for a punitive expedition against the unsubmissive Pequots, a joint

Connecticut-Massachusetts force marched into Pequot country and demanded the murderers (who, as it turned out, were not Pequots) as well as a thousand fathoms of wampum, an accepted unit of exchange, and some Pequot children as hostages.

The Pequots understood that the issue, ostensibly about the death of several English mariners, was much broader, involving an interlocking set of disputes over land, trade, competition for food during several years of crop failures, and political control of the region. These were the real causes of the war that broke out shortly. At the center of the tensions were the English-Dutch trade rivalry and intertribal Indian hostilities. Since 1622, the Dutch in New Amsterdam had controlled the Indian trade of the region through their connections to both the Pequot and the Narragansett, the area's two strongest tribes. Watching the rapid expansion of the English in the early 1630s, the Dutch purchased land on the lower Connecticut River—an area on which several English groups had their eyes—and built a trading post there to defend their regional trading monopoly. Some of the Pequots' discontented client tribes, however, were already breaking away, signing separate trade agreements with and ceding land to the English. Amid such fragmentation, expansionist New England was ready, with the aid of its Narragansett allies, to drive the Dutch traders from southern New England and to subdue the Pequots who occupied some of the area's most fertile soil. The Pequots first tried to placate the English, though they were not prepared to subject themselves to English authority, by making a huge wampum tribute. When Pequot attempts to negotiate the dispute failed, they chose to resist.

In the ensuing war, the English found the Pequots more than a match until they were able to surround a secondary Pequot village on the Mystic River in May 1637. The English and their Narragansett allies attacked before dawn, infiltrated the town, and set fire to the Pequot wigwams before beating a fast retreat. In the meleé, about twenty Narragansetts suffered wounds at the hands of the English, who found it difficult to distinguish

[21]Cotton Mather, *Magnalia Christi Americana: or, The Ecclesiastic History of New England* (New York, 1967), II: 556.

between Indian enemies and allies. Retreating from the flame-engulfed village, the English regrouped and waited for fleeing survivors. Most of the victims were noncombatants, since most of the Pequot warriors were gathered at a nearby village. Before the day was over, the English slaughtered a large part of the Pequot tribe. Rounding up Pequots who escaped or were not at the fort, the English sold them to other tribes, shipped them to the West Indies for sale as slaves, and distributed about 250 captured women and children to serve as lifelong household servants in the towns of Massachusetts and Connecticut. Thus began what one historian calls the Americans' "first way of war"—the conquest of an enemy population through the complete destruction of villages and fields and the killing of noncombatant women and children as well as male warriors.[22]

In their accounts of the war, Massachusetts and Connecticut leaders exuded religious zeal. One of New England's first historians, William Hubbard, wrote that dozens of captured Pequots were put on board the ship of Captain John Gallup, "which proved [to be] Charon's ferry-boat unto them, for it was found the quickest was to feed the fishes with 'em."[23] One of the militia captains wrote that at Mystic Fort, "God . . . laughed [at] his enemies and the enemies of his people to scorn, making them as a fiery oven . . . [and] filling the place with dead bodies." Governor William

One year after the ferocious Pequot War of 1637, Londoners heard about it from the English point of view in John Underhill's *Newes from America*. Underhill was one of the Puritan military leaders who led the attack on the Pequots at their Mystic River palisaded fort. This schematic drawing depicts the attack on the fort. *(Library of Congress Rare Book and Special Collections Division Washington, D.C [LC-USZ62-32055])*

---

[22]John Grenier, *The First Way of War: American War Making on the Frontier, 1607–1814* (Cambridge, MA, 2005).
[23]William Hubbard, *A Narrative of the Troubles with the Indians in New England* (1677), quoted in Carolyn T. Foreman, *Indians Abroad, 1493–1938* (Norman, OK, 1943), p. 29. In Greek mythology, Charon ferried the recently deceased across the river Styx to their place in Hades.

Bradford of Plymouth wrote that "it was a fearful sight to see them thus frying in the fire and the streams of blood quenching the same, and horrible was the stink and scent thereof; but the victory seemed a sweet sacrifice, and they gave the praise thereof to God, who had wrought so wonderfully for them, thus to enclose their enemies in their hands and given them so speedy a victory over so proud and insulting an enemy."[24] In 1638, at the Treaty of Hartford, the Pequot nation was declared dissolved.

The genocidal behavior of the "civilized" Puritans demonstrated at Mystic Fort shocked the Narragansett "savages" who fought with the Puritans. According to one English officer, they came after the victory and "much rejoiced at our victories, and greatly admired the manner of Englishmen's fight . . . it is naught [bad or wicked] because it is too furious and slays too many men."[25] It was a poignant comment on the different conduct and function of warfare in the two societies. Indian war had traditionally been limited and sporadic—"far less bloody and devouring than the cruel wars of Europe," as Roger Williams put it. Whereas the Indians "might fight seven years and not kill seven men," the English were schooled in terror tactics from their invasion of Ireland a generation before.[26]

By exterminating or enslaving the Pequots, Puritans proved their political and military ascendancy while setting a precedent for extirpative warfare that would become common on the settlers' frontier. Their victory also allayed the anxiety and disunity that had overtaken the colony. Coming on the heels of three years of intense internal discord centered on the challenges to the power of the magistrates by Roger Williams and Anne Hutchinson, the war refocused the attention of the elders and common people alike.

Victory over the Pequots decisively established English sovereignty over all the Native peoples of southeastern New England except the Narragansetts and removed the one remaining obstacle to expansion into the Connecticut River valley. The tribes of southern New England, reduced to less than one-quarter of their former population, adjusted as best they could to the realities of Puritan power. The fur trade kept the two societies in touch and provided the means by which English iron goods became incorporated into the material culture of the Indians. But the flourishing trade of the 1630s petered out by midcentury as the beaver supply in New England dwindled.

In spite of these trade contacts, most of the postwar remnant groups struggled to maintain their Native way of life. Some of the weaker and more demoralized bands followed the handful of missionaries, finally spurred to action in 1643 by English critics who charged that religious conversion had long been ignored. Now missionaries found that some Natives were drawn to the Christian God in the hope for protection against epidemic diseases. After ten years of effort, about 1000 Natives were settled in four villages of "praying Indians," though most had still not declared their conversion to Puritan Christianity. Even among these, defections were numerous in the 1670s when war broke out again in Massachusetts. As in the case of Virginia, the Natives incorporated certain iron implements and articles of clothing obtained in the European trade into their culture, but overwhelmingly, even after major military defeats, they preferred to resist acculturation if it meant adopting English religion, forms of government, styles of life, or methods of social and economic organization.

For Puritans and non-Puritans migrating to New England in increasing numbers after midcentury, the Indians' usefulness was dwindling. Hundreds of enslaved Natives still toiled

---

[24]John Mason, "A Brief History of the Pequot War," Massachusetts Historical Society *Collections*, 2nd Ser., 8 (Boston, MA, 1826): 140–141. Bradford, *Plymouth Plantation*, p. 296.
[25]John Underhill, "News from America," quoted in Salisbury, *Manitou and Providence*, p. 222.
[26]Williams's description of English and Indian war is quoted in Colin Calloway, *New Worlds for All: Indians, Europeans and the Remaking of Eastern America* (Baltimore, MD, 1997), p. 97.

in Puritan households; in coastal towns Indian men served on fishing boats, and many Indian women performed domestic labor. But the Indian population collapsed in the seventeenth century. The church took only a minor interest in Native Americans, who in any event could rarely satisfy the qualifications that Puritans placed on their own people for church membership. The Indian trade withered, as fishing, lumbering, shipbuilding, and agriculture became the mainstays of the colonizers' economy. This loss of Indian utility within English society, combined with the special tendency of Puritans to doubt the Indians' capacity for meeting the cultural and religious standards required in their New Jerusalem, made close and reciprocal contacts between the two societies increasingly tenuous.

Summary

The Dutch were the first to establish a European presence in the northeastern region of North America, in the early 1620s, followed later by the English Puritans. These groups settled in New Netherland, Massachusetts, Rhode Island, and the Connecticut River Valley. In so doing, they came in close contact with the diverse Algonquian peoples, who had to contend with the newcomers as well as the enmity that frequently existed between various Native societies.

The Dutch were motivated by commerce, particularly the fur trade, which, as it grew, triggered or intensified intertribal hostilities among Native people. After being seized by the English in 1664, New Netherland became the royal colony of New York, but the Natives in New York City, already greatly diminished by disease and war, could barely distinguish between the Dutch and the English. When the Pilgrims came to New England in 1620, and later the Puritans flocked there in great numbers in 1630, however, the Natives met a type of European they had not yet experienced. This brand of Protestantism brought religious zeal, a worldview, and a perspective on land possession—and, most especially, deadly disease—that spelled doom for a large number of Natives to the region. Resisting the English agenda on land, trade, and political control of the region, the strong Pequot tribe went to war against the English settlers in 1637; the subsequent English victory would ensure English sovereignty over all the Native peoples of southeastern New England except the Narragansetts. Throughout the seventeenth century, contacts between the Puritans and Native tribes grew increasingly tenuous.

Critical Thinking Questions

1. Motivated largely by commerce, the Dutch established a presence in, among other areas, the northeastern Atlantic seaboard. How did their drive for trade, particularly the fur trade, influence their relationship with the Algonquian and other Native tribes?
2. The English Puritans, who were flocking to the New England coast after 1630, came armed with a vision of a "city on a hill" in which settlers, as pure Christians, would work to bring about God's purpose. In what ways did this idealistic vision falter within their own communities and vis-à-vis the Native people of the region?
3. Although the Pequot War of 1637 erupted over the murder of two white ship captains and their crew, what were the "real" underlying reasons for the war?

Further Reading

Virginia DeJohn Anderson, *New England's Generation: The Great Migration and the Formation of Society and Culture in the Seventeenth Century* (New York: Cambridge University Press, 1991).

Richard Archer, *Fissures in the Rock: New England in the Seventeenth Century* (Hanover: N.H. University Press of New England, 2001).

William Cronon, *Changes in the Land: Indians, Colonists, and the Ecology of New England* (New York: Hill & Wang, 1983).

Francis Jennings, *The Invasion of America: Indians, Colonialism, and the Cant of Conquest* (Chapel Hill: University of North Carolina Press, 1975).

Shepard Krech III, ed., *Indians, Animals, and the Fur Trade: A Critique of "Keepers of the Game"* (Athens: University of Georgia Press, 1981).

Eva LaPlante, *American Jezebel: The Uncommon Life of Anne Hutchinson* (San Francisco: Harper, 2004).

Ann M. Little, *Abraham in Arms: War and Gender in Colonial New England* (Philadelphia: University of Pennsylvania Press, 2007).

Gloria L. Main, *Peoples of a Spacious Land: Families and Cultures in Colonial New England* (Cambridge: Harvard University Press, 2001).

Jenny Hale Pulsipher, *Subjects unto the Same King: Indians, English, and the Contest for Authority in Colonial New England* (Philadelphia: University of Pennsylvania Press, 2005).

Daniel K. Richter, *Facing East from Indian Country: A Native History of Early America* (Cambridge: Harvard University Press, 2001).

Neal Salisbury, *Manitou and Providence: Indians, Europeans, and the Making of New England, 1500–1643* (New York: Oxford University Press, 1982).

David J. Silverman, *Faith and Boundaries: Colonists, Christianity, and Community among the Wampanoag Indians of Martha's Vineyard* (Cambridge: Cambridge University Press, 2005)

CHAPTER 5

The Coastal Societies: Resistance, Accommodation, and Defeat

LEARNING OBJECTIVES

- Explain the origins and outcome of Metacom's War and what it represented to white settlers and the Natives of coastal New England.

- Describe the factors that brought about Bacon's Rebellion in the Chesapeake region; indicate what this rebellion showed about the attitudes and internal disputes of White colonists.

- Characterize the relations between Indians and settlers in South Carolina; point out how intertribal rivalry

affected these relations and discuss the rise of the Indian slave trade.

- Evaluate the motivations and strategies of the Tuscaroras and Yamasees in their wars with European settlers in the Carolinas.

- Compare the early Indian-White relations of William Penn's "Holy Experiment" in Pennsylvania with those in late seventeenth-century New England, Virginia, and South Carolina and give possible reasons for differences.

The Native American was rarely a passive agent in the first century of engagement with European intruders, as was dramatically apparent in the last quarter of the seventeenth century in Massachusetts and the first quarter of the eighteenth century in South Carolina. Indian tribes in both regions rose up to avoid becoming subjugated people. In other areas, such as Virginia and Pennsylvania, small tribes resisted encroachment by Europeans but, bereft of Indian allies and weakened by population decline, moved out of the path of European colonial expansion or yielded to confinement on reserved parcels of land.

Faced with the growing power of the Europeans, Native societies improvised a variety of responses, ranging from resistance to accommodation to withdrawal. Each of these was an attempt to preserve tribal unity and hold to traditional lifeways, albeit modified by incorporation of European material goods and, sometimes, spiritual ideas. Rather than conceiving of these coastal Native societies as brittle and static, and thus unable to adapt to the arrival of dynamic European culture, we better perceive them as equally dynamic and malleable societies with which the colonists wished to mix, but only on certain terms.

The period from 1675 to 1725 was one of great stress for the coastal tribes but did not cause wholesale cultural disintegration as some historians have claimed. What is most remarkable is that so many of the coastal Native societies that experienced the brunt of European population buildup and maiming pandemics fought with a determination that far exceeded their declining numbers. This can be seen by exploring the time of troubles for Native peoples of the coastal plain in New England, in the new Quaker colony of Pennsylvania, in the Chesapeake Bay region, and in what became the Carolinas.

Metacom's War

Following the Pequot War of 1637 in New England, the Narragansetts, who had joined the English against the Pequots, maintained as much of their autonomy as possible by keeping their distance from the English colonists. But the Narragansetts occupied precisely the territory toward which Puritan expansion into the Connecticut River valley was moving. In 1643, the colonies of Massachusetts, Connecticut, and Plymouth, eager to forge an offensive league against the powerful Narragansetts (and also against the pestiferously deviant colony of Rhode Island), formed the New England Confederation. Military preparedness was the purported goal of the Confederation; military conquest was its true purpose. By allying with the Mohegans, enemies of the Narragansetts, the Puritans strengthened themselves. In 1643, when the Narragansett sachem Miantonomo

sold a large tract of valuable land on Narragansett Bay to the arch-heretic Samuel Gorton, hated throughout Puritan New England for his outspoken criticism of Massachusetts Indian policy, the New England Confederation arranged the murder of Miantonomo by his Mohegan enemies.

Threatened by the Puritans' growing power, the Narragansetts maneuvered for protection. In 1644, they decided "freely . . . and most humbly to submit, subject, and give ourselves, peoples, lands, rights, inheritances, and possessions . . . unto the protection, care, and government" of King Charles I "upon condition of His Majesty's royal protection." This was no admission of subjection to the Puritan colonists. Rather, the Narragansetts gained royal protection from "any of the natives in these parts" and pointedly declared that they could not "yield over ourselves unto any [in New England] that are subjects themselves in any case."[1] One year later, the Puritans mobilized for war against the Narragansetts. Calculating the odds, the Narragansetts submitted to a treaty that saddled them with the cost of the mobilization and required a large cession of land. By such tactics the Puritans gradually eroded the land base of the Narragansetts, who, along with the Wampanoags, were the chief obstacle to territorial expansion.

While land-hungry Puritans pushed southward and westward and their population grew to 25,000 by 1650 and 60,000 by 1675, a few men attempted to Christianize the remaining fragments of the eastern New England tribes. Led by John Eliot, Thomas Mayhew, and Daniel Gookin, the missionaries concentrated their efforts among Native peoples whose numbers had been deeply diminished by epidemics and war, who had already lost much of their land, and who had already become economically dependent upon the colonizers. "The Algonquians who converted," one historian tells us, "were those whose communal integrity had been compromised step-by-step—from

[1]John R. Bartlett, ed. *Records of the Colony of Rhode Island . . .*, 10 vols. (Providence, RI, 1856–65), I: 134–35.

the plague of 1616 to the treaties of political submission—and whose sources of collective identity and individual social stature had been destroyed."[2] Several thousand "praying Indians" gathered in fourteen villages, where they adopted English methods of agriculture, prayed to the English God and adopted English hairstyles, dress, and customs.

Yet the praying Indians did not abandon completely their old religious beliefs; rather they wove together elements of the old and the new, stitching customary Native spiritual beliefs with Christian doctrine. Thus, they provided for their survival within the expanding realm of Puritan settlers. One key advantage of the praying towns was greater power than that possessed by non-missionized Indians in protecting their land from neighboring whites who hungrily eyed fertile Native tracts. Although the praying villages appeared to be halfway houses on the road to full assimilation into white society, the Puritans rarely acted as if accepting made-over Indians was part of their overall plan. This attitude must have been apparent to acculturated Indians like the Christianized John Neesnummin, who was denied lodging in Boston when he visited there in 1708.

Other New England tribes, in which stronger leaders and greater numbers prevailed, fended off the missionaries. "Each of the great sachems of the mid-seventeenth century—Massasoit, Metacom, Ninigret, Uncas—resisted the missionaries as threats to his tribe's survival."[3] Metacom, sachem of the Wampanoags, is said to have told John Eliot "that he cared no more for the white man's gospel than he did for the button on Eliot's coat."[4] But even the more cohesive tribes, which had maintained a degree of independence from the sprawling Puritans, were aware by the early 1670s that their position was worsening steadily. Their options were limited. They could submit to the English colonies by selling their land, thus putting themselves fully under Puritan government and performing day labor within the white people's settlements. Or they could sell their land for whatever they could get and migrate westward, placing themselves under the protection of the stronger Iroquois tribes at their backs. Or they could attempt what had never been successfully undertaken before anywhere on the continent—a pan-Indian offensive against people who greatly outnumbered them and possessed a far greater military capability.

The Wampanoags chose the third alternative. In part, this choice pivoted on the leadership of Metacom, or King Philip, as the English called him. Metacom was a son of Massasoit, the Wampanoag leader who had allied himself with the Plymouth settlers when they first arrived in 1620 and had fought with them against other tribes throughout his life. Massasoit had died in 1661, and Metacom had watched his older brother, Wamsutta, preside over the deteriorating position of the Wampanoags. In 1662, Wamsutta died mysteriously after the Plymouth officials had interrogated him about rumors concerning an Indian conspiracy. For the next decade, Metacom brooded over the position of his people and was forced to accept one humiliating blow after another. The worst came in 1671 when he was compelled to surrender a large stock of guns and accept a treaty of submission in which he agreed not to sell any land without permission of the Plymouth colony government. From that time on, he began building a league of Native resistance, convinced that only Indian initiatives could reverse the steady loss of Wampanoag land and arms. Still valuing their ancient cultural traditions, the Wampanoags sought new alliances with nearby tribes and embarked on a war to revitalize their culture, which they came to believe had been polluted by close engagement with the colonizers in their midst.

[2]Neal Salisbury, "Red Puritans: The 'Praying Indians' of Massachusetts Bay and John Eliot," *William and Mary Quarterly*, 31 (1974): 50.
[3]Ibid., p. 38.
[4]G. E. Thomas, "Puritans, Indians, and the Concept of Race," *New England Quarterly*, 48 (1975): 6.

"Philip, King of Mount Hope."

(Courtesy Library of Congress Prints and Photographs Division Washington, D.C [LC-USZ62-96234])

The triggering incident of Metacom's War was the trial of three Wampanoags hauled before the Puritan courts for an act of tribal vengeance against a Christianized, Harvard-educated Indian, John Sassamon, who had served for a time as Metacom's assistant. Sassamon was a man caught between two cultures. Though he had fled white society some time after his Harvard experience, Sassamon informed the government at Plymouth in the spring of 1675 that the Wampanoags were preparing for a general attack on the English settlements. When he was found murdered shortly afterward, the Plymouth officials listened to an Indian who claimed he had witnessed the murder and could identify the felons. Three Wampanoags swung at the end of English ropes in June 1675.

War did not break out immediately. In fact, the haphazard and sporadic burning and looting that occurred during the next few weeks suggests that Metacom was attempting to restrain the more fiery young men of his tribe who were pushing hard for a war that would restore the honor that their fathers had compromised over the years. But the war came in full force on June 25, 1675—the day of a total lunar eclipse, which the Indians may have interpreted as a spiritual invitation to violence. Rankling at the thought of how much had been sacrificed to accommodate the white invaders, the young Wampanoag males girded themselves for battle. Revitalization of their culture through war was probably as important a goal as the defeat of the white encroachers.

In the first months of the war, Metacom's followers conducted daring hit-and-run attacks on the Plymouth colony villages. These were launched without the assistance of the other tribes in New England—the Narragansetts, Nipmucs, and Mohegans. But when the English colonists failed to unify militarily to assault the Wampanoags and when Native warriors easily evaded their pursuers, many other Indians decided that this was the opportunity they had long awaited. With tribe after tribe joining Metacom, towns all along the edge of Puritan settlement felt the sting of Indian raids by late summer in 1675. Although the English retained the allegiance of the Niantics and Mohegans, many of whom

fought side by side with the white New Englanders, most of the Pocomtucks and Pocassets—the latter inspired by the female leader Weetamoo, the widow of Wamsutta—joined Metacom's cause. Of most importance, the Narragansetts, who had stayed officially neutral while apparently offering clandestine aid to the Wampanoags, were driven into the war in December 1675 when a Puritan army massacred hundreds of their women and children in a half-built Indian fort. Even the Nipmucs, a tribe of local Indians near present-day Springfield, who had silently nursed grievances for years but were thought by the colonists to be faithful allies, joined the offensive by late summer. A few months later, the River Indians of the upper Hudson River mobilized for an attack on the New Englanders. Their plans were aborted only when the governor of New York convinced the Mohawks to attack the River Indians.

By the first November snowfall, Native forays conducted by highly mobile Indian warriors had laid waste the entire upper Connecticut valley and New England's frontier villages. Fighting with smoothbore muskets, they proved to be much better marksmen than colonial militiamen. By March 1676, Metacom's forces were attacking Medfield and Weymouth, less than twenty miles from Boston and Providence. Thoughts of English superiority began to fade as Indian ambushes punished the colonial forces. Resistance to the military draft of eligible men increased by the spring of 1676, while eastern communities grumbled at the influx of refugees from the frontier towns. Food scarcities in the towns, providing opportunities for profiteering among merchants who controlled supplies, added to white fear and discouragement. Even in times of military crisis, it seemed, Puritan community cohesiveness had frayed badly.

However, in the spring of 1676, the Indian offensive waned, not as the result of colonial military victories but because of food shortages and disease among the Natives. In what became a war of attrition, they had more and more difficulty obtaining food supplies and weapons to replenish their depleted stores. At first, Metacom's warriors obtained guns and ammunition from the Mohawks near Albany; but when the New York authorities cut this vital supply line and convinced the Mohawks to attack the Wampanoag winter encampment, Metacom's forces suffered a mortal blow.

Slowly, in the summer of 1676, groups of Natives began to head west to seek shelter among tribes there or to lay down their arms. Puritan leaders executed most of the leaders who surrendered or were captured. But to pay for the costs of the war, the New Englanders sold hundreds of other Indians into slavery, including Metacom's wife and son. One Massachusetts leader surrounded about 200 Indians in Maine after inviting them to parley under a flag of truce and then sold all but eight of them into slavery. New England ships carried the enslaved Indians to Bermuda and Jamaica and even to Cádiz, Spain, where they were auctioned to buyers as if they were Africans.

Puritan forces vanquished Metacom in a battle near the Wampanoag village where the war had begun, with an Indian warrior shooting Metacom in the back. Regarded by the Puritans as an agent of Satan—"a hellhound, fiend, serpent, caitiff and dog," as one leader put it—soldiers carried his head triumphantly back to the English settlements.[5] By the end of autumn, the war was over, although "hunting redskins became for the time being a popular sport in New England, especially since prisoners were worth good money, and the personal danger to the hunters was now very slight."[6]

At the end of the war, about a thousand English and perhaps five thousand Indians lay dead, a casualty rate probably unequaled in any later American war. About another thousand Natives were enslaved and shipped to the English West Indies. Of some ninety Puritan towns, fifty-two had been attacked and thirteen destroyed by the "tawny serpents," as Cotton Mather called them. Not for forty years would white settlements advance again westward to the point where they had been on the eve of the war. Native villages were devastated even more completely.

For the Natives of coastal New England, it was nearly the last gasp. Had they been able to secure the aid of the Abenakis, a powerful tribe on the northern frontier that had strong connections with the French, or with the Mohawks, the easternmost Iroquois nation, the outcome might have been different. But the enemy that never let up on the Native people was ancient intertribal hostility. Equally important, the stronger interior tribes cared more about their trading partnership with the English than the fate of the coastal Indians. The survivors now faced the bitter fact that the English had prevailed and must now be recognized as their "protectors." In the aftermath of the war, the New England Confederation imposed harsher regulation even on the tribes that had remained neutral or rendered military assistance. By a law passed in 1677, most remaining Indians, regardless of their religious preferences, were confined in one of the four surviving praying villages controlled by English supervisors. Hundreds of others became tenant farmers and servants-for-hire in the English villages.

In spite of the English victory, accomplished as much by the exhaustion of the Indian effort as through English military superiority, Metacom's War demonstrated that some of the coastal tribes were prepared to risk extinction rather than become a colonized and culturally imperialized people. The Puritans never worked for a truly assimilationist policy because they were not prepared to accept the Indians except as unresisting subjects controlled by, but not included within, English society. The weakest of the coastal tribes succumbed to this policy, but the stronger chose to resist, even at the risk of annihilation.

Bacon's Rebellion

While New Englanders fought for their lives during 1675 to 1676, the Chesapeake colonists were also locked in a struggle that involved not only conflict between Natives and newcomer

---

[5]Quoted in Alvin M. Josephy, Jr., *The Patriot Chiefs: A Chronicle of American Indian Resistance* (New York, 1958), p. 35.
[6]Douglas Edward Leach, *Flintlock and Tomahawk: New England in King Philip's War* (New York, 1966), p. 237.

settlements but also war within White society. By the time Metacom's War was over in New England, several hundred colonists and a larger number of Natives lay dead in Virginia and Maryland, the capital city of Jamestown was smoldering in ashes, and a thousand English troops were on their way across the Atlantic to suppress what the king took to be an outright rejection of his authority in Virginia. This deeply tangled conflict, called Bacon's Rebellion, took its name from the 29-year-old planter Nathaniel Bacon, who had come to the Chesapeake only two years before.

Bacon's Rebellion seemed to come almost without warning. Virginia had grown rapidly since midcentury, achieving a population of about 40,000 by 1670. Sir William Berkeley presided over the colony as royal governor, an office he had held intermittently for more than twenty years. Pitted against both the Indians and the royal governor was Bacon, a Cambridge-educated and scandal-ridden newcomer who enjoyed status as the governor's second cousin and a member of his council. Bacon had arrived in Virginia with enough wealth to purchase an already established tobacco plantation, complete with a number of enslaved Africans.

Bacon emerged as the spokesman of many who scrambled for economic gain in Virginia and were deeply troubled by declining opportunity, which they associated with Berkeley's Indian policy. In 1646, at the end of the second Indian uprising against the Virginians, the Powhatan tribes were guaranteed by treaty the territory north of the York River, which ran northwest from the Chesapeake Bay into the interior of Virginia. Both the Native and European leaders had agreed that granting each society exclusive land rights in specified regions might keep the peace.

For almost three decades after 1646, no major conflict had occurred. In fact, a profitable trade for furs with several tribes developed, although some in Virginia grumbled that the trade was monopolized by the governor and his

circle of favorites. This stabilization of Indian relations, however, became increasingly odious to the wave of new immigrants who arrived in Virginia in the 1650s and 1660s, and especially to the hundreds of White indentured servants who had served their time only to find that in an era of depressed tobacco prices, they could not compete with established planters. As their numbers grew, the new settlers and indentured servants put more and more pressure on the government to open up for settlement the lands north of the York River. Why should this region be reserved forever for a handful of Indians, they argued, when the Virginia charter ran all the way to the "South Sea," leaving plenty of room to the west for the local tribes? Governor Berkeley wrote home on several occasions that one of every three or four people was landless or impoverished and that all of them "we may reasonably expect, upon any small advantage the enemy may gaine upon us, would revolt . . . in hopes of bettering their condition by sharing the plunder of the country with them."[7]

Land hunger and constriction of opportunity mixed with Indian disgruntlement to turn a small incident of frontier Indian-White tension into a galloping war. In July 1675, a group of Doegs, affronted by the failure of a planter to pay them for goods they had traded, attempted to confiscate his hogs. The planter's overseer killed one Doeg. The Doegs then took revenge, killing the overseer. Thirty of the neighboring planters launched a retaliatory assault, not only killing ten Doegs but also slaughtering fourteen friendly Susquehannocks, who had been allied to the Virginians for many years. When the Virginia government did nothing to make reparations for the deaths of the friendly Susquehannocks, the Indians sought revenge through attacks on outlying settlements along the Maryland and Virginia frontier.

The spiraling violence, as White Virginians later admitted, stemmed from the land fever and hatred of Indians that led to "taking up the very towns or lands they [the Indians] are seated upon, turning their cattle and hogg on them, and

[7]Edmund S. Morgan, "Slavery and Freedom: The American Paradox," *Journal of American History*, 59 (1972–73): 21–22.

if by vermin or otherwise any be lost, then they exclaim against the Indians, beat and abuse them (notwithstanding the Governor's endeavor to the contrary)."[8] Contributing to the frontiersmen's attacks was the fact that the Virginia Indians had been drastically reduced in number and power in the previous decades so as to offer only weak resistance to the "land lopers," as they were later dubbed. Fewer than 1,000 Indian males remained in the Virginia region by this time, and these, as Berkeley had written in 1671, "are absolutely subjected, so that there is no fear of them."[9]

Such weakness invited White violence. Marylanders and Virginians could put 1000 armed men in the field, and just this event occurred in September 1675. Chesapeake planters and militiamen marched against an abandoned stockade on the Potomac River, which had been assigned to the Susquehannocks by the Maryland government. Surrounding a village containing about one hundred adult males with their families, they demanded that the chiefs come out to parley. When the Susquehannocks denied any responsibility for the frontier attacks, White militiamen led their chiefs away from the village and murdered them.

Though the militia officers involved in this crime were tried, the local courts fined them only lightly or cleared them of the charges. Appalled by this English "savagery," Berkeley denounced the attack and the legal proceedings. But he found scanty support in the colony. Heavily outmatched, the Indians served only as an obstacle to further expansion. Hence, few Virginians would speak on their behalf or act against those who precipitated hostilities with them. With the Susquehannocks now fully committed to war, despite overwhelming odds against them, Virginians prepared for what they had already heard was happening to the north under the leadership of Metacom. Rumors swept through the colony that the Susquehannocks were offering vast sums to western Indian nations to join in attacking the Europeans and even that a confederacy linking Metacom's followers and the southern Indians had been formed.

Bent on revenge, the Susquehannocks attacked during the winter of 1675 to 1676, killing thirty-six colonists. Angered and apprehensive, the frontiersmen turned on the Natives closest at hand, the settled Appomattox and Pamunkeys, who lived within the White area of settlement on reservations that a postwar writer admitted "had long been coveted by neighboring Virginians."[10] In what has been labeled a "blood sacrifice," Nathaniel Bacon assumed the leadership of a frontier movement and began annihilating friendly Indians in the region.[11] Arguing that the subject Indians "have been so cunningly mixed among the several nations of families of Indians that it hath been very difficult for us, to distinguish how, or from which of those said nations, the said wrongs did proceed," Bacon asked Governor Berkeley for a commission to lead his volunteers against any Indians he could find.[12] When Berkeley refused to sanction indiscriminate attacks, the fiery Bacon announced he would proceed with or without the governor's approval. Berkeley declared Bacon a rebel, stripped him of his councilor's seat, and led an expedition of 300 Virginia planters to capture the frontier leader. Bacon, in turn, gathered his forces around him and headed for the wilderness and "a more agreeable destiny than you are pleased to design me," as he defiantly informed the governor.[13]

Attempting to salvage the deteriorating situation, Berkeley dispatched punitive expeditions to chastise any Indians who had attacked the white settlers, while also pursuing peace negotiations. Meanwhile, he planned a string of forts along the frontier to keep peace between the two

[8]"Virginia's Deploured Condition" (1676), Massachusetts Historical Society *Collections*, 4th Ser., 9 (Boston, MA, 1869): 164.
[9]Quoted in Wilcomb E. Washburn, *The Governor and the Rebel: A History of Bacon's Rebellion in Virginia* (Chapel Hill, NC, 1957), p. 20.
[10]"Virginia's Deploured Condition," p. 166.
[11]Washburn, *The Governor and the Rebel . . .*, p. 35.
[12]Quoted in ibid., p. 37.
[13]Ibid., p. 41.

peoples. It was a defensive—and an expensive—policy. The money to build and garrison the forts could come from only one source—the pocketbooks of the planters, who would have to pay increased taxes.

Berkeley misjudged both the White settlers and the Indians. The Susquehannock sachems could not control their own warriors, who were launching attacks even as their chiefs negotiated with the governor. As for the White Virginians, they wanted no part of the governor's expensive containment policy. The tobacco market had slipped badly in recent years, an epidemic had carried off half the colony's cattle the previous summer, a drought had cut deeply into the 1675 harvest, and now, they argued, the governor proposed a weak and expensive solution to the biggest Indian crisis in three decades. In their minds, the problem could be more easily and less expensively solved.

By May 1676, Bacon had declared himself the leader of the rebellious frontiersmen, determined to pursue their own Indian policy. Their first objective was a fortified settlement of Occaneechee Indians, who had been regarded as friendly and had recently destroyed a band of Susquehannocks encamped near them as evidence of their fidelity to the Virginians. Attacking the unsuspecting Occaneechees at midnight, Bacon's men annihilated the band. Later critics claimed that £1,000 in beaver skins inside the Occaneechee fort had whetted the appetites of Bacon's men.

With his supporters growing at every new attack on the Natives, Bacon marched to Jamestown to confront the governor, who had charged him with treason for defying the royal government. Bacon demanded a commission to legitimize his attacks on the Indians; under great pressure the governor acceded. But when Bacon left with his Indian fighters, Berkeley again declared him in rebellion, gathered his own supporters, and pursued Bacon's force. For the rest of the summer, Bacon's and Berkeley's forces maneuvered around each other, recruiting additional support, sniping at each other's heels in quasi-military forays,

and puzzling over how to stop the chain of events that had started with a disagreement over Indian policy. Time was on the side of Berkeley because once the Natives had been crushed, the Virginia rebels were anxious to return to their homes. Moreover, Berkeley's reports of the rebellion in England had brought the dispatch of a thousand royal troops. By the time they arrived with a royal investigating commission in January 1677, Nathaniel Bacon was dead of swamp fever, and his followers had melted back into the edges of settlement, though twenty three were captured and delivered to the hangman.

Although Bacon's followers fumed at high taxes, favoritism in government, and the tight grip on power and profit exercised by Berkeley and his friends, it was the governor's protective Indian policy before the first bloodshed and his unaggressive policy thereafter that provided the strongest impetus for insurrection. No longer fearing an Indian population shrunken by decades of disease and sporadic fighting, the Virginians demanded a war of extermination. Peace had been useful for many years because the Treaty of 1646 left plenty of room for expansion. But the population of Virginians had quadrupled in the intervening thirty years while the Indians had grown only weaker. It was not peace that frontier Virginians now wanted, but war.

The royal investigators perceived this genocidal urge shortly after arriving in Virginia in 1677. In a message to the House of Burgesses, which was debating a peace treaty with the remaining Natives, the commissioners denounced the "inconsiderate sort of men who soe rashly and causelessly cry up a war and seem to wish and aim at an utter extirpation of the Indians." When a peace treaty was signed in May 1677, one of its articles referred specifically to the "violent intrusions of divers English into their [the Indians'] lands, forcing the Indians by way of revenge, to kill the cattle and hogs of the English."[14] Thus, Virginians recognized that settlers had purposely goaded Indians into

[14]Ibid., p. 161.

retaliatory attacks, which were then used to justify a war of extermination.

Bacon's Rebellion proved that, even if dedicated to preserving peace between the two societies, the highest authorities in an English colony could not prevent genocidal attacks by white colonists. Though he represented the authority of the king, Berkeley could not control Virginians who saw the Indians as an impediment to acquiring new land on the frontier. After 1675, the House of Burgesses, reflecting the interests of local planters, withdrew the governor's power to disallow individual land grants, an authority that the governor had exercised since 1666 to prevent new immigrants from taking up land too close to Indian settlements. Thereafter, Virginians easily intimidated Indians into selling their land in areas adjacent to white settlement. As the Secretary of Virginia wrote in 1678, "The English would ordinarily either frighten or delude them into a bargain and for a trifle get away the ground . . . , then he comes and settles himself there and with his cattle and hogs [and] destroys all the corn of the other Indians of the town. . . . This was a great cause of this last war, and most of those who had thus intruded and were consequently the principal cause of it were notwithstanding amongst the forwardest in the rebellion and complained most of grievances."[15]

For the Susquehannocks and other tribes of the coastal region, the lesson must have been painfully clear. Even when they recognized the authority of the Europeans, declared themselves subject to English law, abided by that law, and even fought against the Indian enemies of the White government, they could not expect to live in peace. The same authority that bound them to treaties of amity and mutual defense with the colony of Virginia was the authority that was unable to control its own White subjects. They also learned that even when European society was divided against itself, as in Virginia in 1676, they could be outmatched by the more populous and better-armed colonists. Scattered in small villages,

each representing a fragment of a tribe that had once been larger and more powerful, the coastal Indians were doomed whether they chose war or peace. The price of survival in Virginia, as in New England, was the sacrifice of an independent tribal authority. What remained was submission to White rulers and life as tenant farmers, day laborers, and domestic servants.

Colonizing South Carolina

As some of the English spilled blood in Bacon's Rebellion, others mounted a colonizing effort to the south of the Chesapeake in what was to become South Carolina. This vast, fertile region later became the center of the plantation slave system in North America; but in the 1660s, when English settlement began, it was in the eyes of the colonizers no more than another wilderness frontier, though in fact it was heavily populated by Native people.

South Carolina was one of the Restoration colonies, founded in the aftermath of a long period of English civil war and the reinstallation of the English monarchy in 1660. Strategic considerations dictated that England cement its claims on the North American coast by removing the Dutch in the Middle Atlantic area and establishing a presence between the Chesapeake and Spanish Florida. With this in mind, Charles II issued charters for a cluster of colonies in the mid-Atlantic region—New York, New Jersey, Pennsylvania, and Delaware—and for the colony of Carolina on the lower Atlantic coast. All these charters, specifying title to vast tracts of land and conferring rights of government, were granted to favorites and creditors of the king, men who had stood by Charles II when he was in exile during the republican regime of Oliver Cromwell in the 1650s. In the case of Carolina, the recipients of the king's favor were the Duke of Albemarle, who had been a leading officer in the royalist army; the Earl of Clarendon, the king's chief minister; the Earl of Craven, a prominent royalist during

---

[15]Quoted in ibid., p. 161.

the years of the English civil war; Sir William Berkeley, the governor of Virginia; and Sir John Colleton, a prominent Barbados planter and supporter of the monarchy during its years of eclipse. All these men had claims on the king; all had political power that the restored king was eager to keep on his side; and all saw the opportunity to extend their wealth and power by planting a colony in Carolina.

After Charles II granted a proprietary charter to these men in 1663, they devised a framework of government that they hoped would entice a large number of settlers to Carolina and avoid the instability that had beset earlier English colonies. The main work of drafting a blueprint for the Carolinas fell to Anthony Ashley Cooper, an expert in colonial affairs who had served Cromwell while still maintaining friendly connections with the exiled king. In 1669, working with his friend and protégé John Locke, the tutor of Cooper's children and secretary to the Council for Trade and Plantations, Cooper devised a bizarre combination of the modern and the feudal. In order to attract colonists, land was offered not at a bargain price but for nothing. At first, each adult male immigrant could claim 80 acres; later the proprietors upped the ante to 150 acres. But this liberal land system was grafted onto a semi-medieval system of hereditary government, which provided the eight Carolina proprietors, their deputies, and a limited number of quasi-noblemen with a monopoly of legislative, administrative, and judicial power. They would hold undisputed reign through an elaborate system of courts, committees, and councils—all tied to the wisdom and authority of eight proprietors in London.

The reality of settlement in Carolina bore little correspondence to this plan. Nobody who came to the colony took the distant London proprietors very seriously, least of all the tough, unsentimental planters who streamed in from Barbados and Virginia, where depressed economic conditions had made a new start in the Carolina wilderness seem attractive. They came to take up 150 acres of free land and quickly laid claim to the best land they could find without respect for proprietary plans for settling in compact, rectangular patterns. The land they occupied first lay along the rivers, the arteries of transportation by which they could transport their crops to market.

In government, as in land affairs, they did what they pleased. The London proprietors appointed a governor to take command, but he quickly found that without the cooperation of the local planters, he could do nothing. Viewing the London proprietors as self-interested aristocrats who knew nothing about the rigors and problems of frontier life, the planters set about shaping their own institutions of government.

Carolina-Indian Relations

For the scattered and politically separate tribes of the Carolina country—Guales, Yamasees, Apalachees, Tuskegees, Hitchitis, Westos, Kukssoes, Catawbas, and many others—the arrival of the English provided both opportunities and dangers, depending on their previous position. The missionized Indians of Spanish Florida probably feared the English, believing correctly that they would now be subject to English attacks and the onslaught of other tribes drawn into the English orbit. For the coastal Indians of the region around the mouth of the Ashley River, site of the maritime center of Charleston, the English may have appeared as saviors, for these tribes had been under heavy attack from their western neighbors for a number of years. "We have them in a pound," exclaimed one of the first English colonists in a letter to London, "for to the southward they will not go, fearing the Yamasee. . . . The Westoes are behind them a mortal enemy of theirs, whom they say are the man eaters. Of them they are more afraid than the little children are of the bull beggers in England. To the northward they will not go for there they cry that is Hiddeskeh, that is to say sickly, so that they reckon themselves safe when they have us amongst them."[16] To the west of the Westos, the

---

[16]Quoted in Verner W. Crane, *The Southern Frontier, 1670–1732* (Ann Arbor, MI, 1956), p. 67.

Creeks—a loose amalgam of mostly Muskogee-speakers—may also have looked favorably upon the English arrival because an alliance with the newcomers promised an opportunity to gain indisputable control of the Carolina interior.

Prior to English arrival, the inland Westos had gained an edge in the regional internecine hostility largely because they had been able to build a trade connection with traders in Virginia, who provided them with guns. Now the Westos found that they would have to use their English weapons against the incoming English who had allied with their coastal enemies. Within months of their arrival, the English had secured the friendship of local tribes along the Atlantic shore. Creek villagers, several hundred miles to the west, soon sent emissaries to the coast, professing their friendship and suggesting a military alliance.

For the English colonists, the intricacies of intertribal rivalry, once unraveled, offered rich opportunities. The southeastern part of the continent, it was apparent, was more densely populated than the Northeast. If the major clusters of peoples still forming into self-identified Cherokee, Creek, and Choctaw nations could be drawn into trade, the settlers might reap vast wealth from contact with the Native peoples. The Spanish had done little to exploit this potential, for their main goal had been to stake out a claim to the territory and protect it by establishing missions that gathered local Indians into a sedentary, agricultural, Christian life.

One of the first Englishmen in South Carolina, Henry Woodward, quickly perceived the trade potential of the area. He had come to Carolina on a scouting expedition in 1666, remained for two years with the coastal Cusasitas, and became the first Englishman to penetrate the interior—"a country so delicious, pleasant and fruitful," he reported, "that were it cultivated doubtless it would prove a second paradise."[17] Woodward and the other leaders also knew that Virginians had already opened a profitable trade with the Catawbas and Westos to the west and northwest.

It was not beaver that beckoned in the Carolina-Indian trade, for this valuable animal that had enriched so many traders to the north was available only in small numbers in the warmer climate of South Carolina. Instead it was deerskin, also highly marketable in Europe and available in the Carolina country in great profusion. "There is such infinite herds," wrote one of the Carolina leaders in 1682, "that the whole country seems but one continued [deer] park."[18] From 1699 to 1715, South Carolina exported an average of 54,000 deerskins a year, and thereafter, the trade increased, reaching more than 150,000 skins in some years. Even at great distances from the English coastal beachheads, Native villagers had become part of the supply chain that reached deep into Europe and even beyond.

Most of the original settlers came from the sugar island of Barbados. They had anticipated using African slave labor to carve out plantations, just as they had done in the Caribbean. But soon after arriving, they perceived a faster way to wealth. The trade for deerskins almost immediately became a trade for Indians. This outcome was not anticipated by the early Carolina settlers, and in fact the rapid growth of the Indian slave trade caused consternation in London, where the proprietors had no desire to mimic Spanish enslavement of Native peoples and also feared all-out war. To be sure, African slavery was already a familiar part of colonizing in the Americas, and Indians defeated in war had been enslaved in other colonies. Columbus had initiated this practice by sending about 1,400 Indians home to Spanish slave markets in the 1490s. Virginians were buying enslaved Indians, usually children, by the 1670s. But nowhere in English North America had colonists instigated a systematic Indian slave trade based on predatory raids. Yet this quickly became the cornerstone of commerce

---

[17]Ibid., p. 13.
[18]Quoted in ibid., p. 111.

for the Charleston merchants in the era before rice became the backbone of the economy. Inured to the use of slave labor from their experience in Barbados, the early Carolinians embraced the enslavement of Indians without qualms. For Native peoples of the Southeast it was a double disaster: thousands were caught in the spider web of Atlantic-wide commerce, while thousands more died as European diseases became all the more virulent as a result of the movement and confinement of Native Americans.

In many respects, the Indian slave trade resembled the African slave trade. The Carolinians did not penetrate the interior themselves but formed alliances with coastal Native groups, whom they armed, rewarded with European trade goods, and encouraged to make war on weaker tribes, some of whom were ancient enemies. By the early 1670s, slave coffles marched through the Carolina backcountry to the coast in much the same fashion as they filed through the African interior to the coastal trading forts. Once in Charleston, the captives were transferred by

slave traders to ships for the "Middle Passage" to other colonies, much as Africans crossed the Atlantic during the process of forced relocation. Most of Carolina's enslaved Indians were destined for the West Indies, although a sizable number remained in the colony, and several thousand were shipped northward to New York and New England. In 1708, the population of the White settlements in Carolina included about 5,300 whites, 2,900 enslaved Africans, and 1,400 enslaved Indians. Among those consigned to perpetual bondage a telling difference emerged: predominately male Africans worked alongside predominately female Indians.

As the Carolina proprietors feared, the Indian slave trade plunged the colony into a series of Indian wars. Through their agents in the colony, the proprietors forged a trade agreement with the inland Westos. But independent planters, resentful of the Indian trade monopoly claimed by the London proprietors, thwarted this policy by eliminating the Westo tribe. Unwilling to risk their own lives against the Westos, the

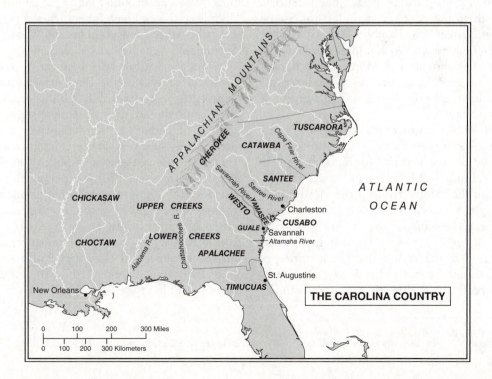

Carolina planters armed the Shawnees, who had migrated across the Appalachian Mountains, and offered them lavish gifts to defeat and enslave the proprietary-linked Westos. In early 1680, the subcontracted war against the Westos began. Three years later, the Carolina proprietors in London learned that not more than fifty of their former allies and trading partners were still alive. The rest had been killed or sold into slavery. Destroyed with the Westos was the proprietary Indian trade monopoly.

For the next few decades, the private traders who had now grasped control of the provincial government armed the coastal Savannahs and engaged in an orgy of slave trading. Typically, the price for an Indian slave was an English gun along with ammunition and perhaps a hatchet. The search for more and more slaves took the Savannahs farther and farther afield until they were conducting slave operations deep into the interior and far southward into Spanish Florida. Indian slave trading reached its peak in 1704, when South Carolina's governor, James Moore, led about 1,000 Creek warriors and 50 of his countrymen into Florida's Apalachee territory. Other raids in the next six years left the Spanish mission system in a shambles. At least 15,000 Timucuas, Guales, and Apalachees were caught in the net of English slavery. Marched to Charleston, they were sold to the slave dealers and shipped out to all points in England's growing hemispheric empire.

The London proprietors were helpless to stop these perversions of their Indian policy. When they denounced the Indian slave trade as immoral and reckless, the colonists replied that the public safety required the elimination of some of the lesser tribes and maintained that transporting them out of the colonies or using them as slaves kept them "from being put to cruel deaths" by the Savannahs. The proprietors were not fooled by this twisted logic. They understood perfectly, as they informed the colonial government, that the colonists were exploiting the Savannahs'

> covetousness of your guns, powder, and shot and other European commodities . . . to destroy the habitations of these poor people into whose country we were chearfully received by them, cherished and supplied when we are weak, or at least never have done us hurt.[19]

As some had predicted, abuses of the Indian trade and encroachments on their land finally led the Savannahs to end their alliance with the Carolinians. Understanding that the wheel might turn against them, most of the Savannahs in 1707 migrated northward into the backcountry of Maryland and Pennsylvania. But rather than letting the Savannahs extricate themselves from the trade dependency, the Carolinians offered huge bounties to about 450 Catawba Indians to attack and extirpate them. Small numbers of Carolinians joined the Catawbas in attacking the Savannahs. Governor John Archdale justified the policy by writing that "thinning the barbarous Indian natives" had seemed necessary. The "thinning" was so thorough that by the end of the first decade of the eighteenth century, the two principal tribes of the coastal plain, the Westos and the Savannahs, were virtually extinct.[20]

For the Indian tribes of the Carolina region, the arrival of the English was disastrous. Many of the coastal tribes had been incorporated into the Spanish mission system. Though this arrangement had rendered them dependent and altered their way of life, it had not destroyed them. But the settlement of South Carolina had catastrophic effects, for it introduced a trade in European cloth, guns, and other goods that pitted one tribe against another and greatly intensified Indian warfare. Even the stronger tribes of the area with whom the English forged trade alliances found that after they had used English guns to enslave weaker tribes, they themselves were scheduled for elimination.

---

[19]Quoted in ibid., pp. 139–140.
[20]John Archdale, "A New Description of Carolina" (1707), in Alexander A. Salley, *Narratives of Early Carolina, 1650–1708* (New York, 1911), p. 285.

Yet the Indian desire for trade goods was so strong that nothing could deter new tribes from forging alliances with the colonizers while others were being destroyed. The Creeks, the strongest of the interior tribes (though still in the process of coalescing as a political entity), abandoned their ancient villages on the Chattahoochie River in the late seventeenth century and migrated eastward to the Altamaha in order to be closer to the English. Even a terrible smallpox epidemic that spread through their villages in 1697 did not convince the Creeks that the European connection might better be spurned. Vast quantities of deerskins, carried on the backs of Native burdeners, moved eastward along the Indian trail that led from more than 500 miles deep in the interior to the coastal trading center of Savannah. Supplied with English weapons, the Creeks also served the English by making war on the Spanish and their client tribes and on the Choctaws of the Alabama and Mississippi region. "Through the media of intensified warfare, hunting and trading," a historian of the Creeks has written, "the Creeks became, comparatively speaking, a fiercely acquisitive and affluent Indian society," and yet "abjectly dependent upon the English trading system."[21] In effect, by 1715, "virtually all Indian societies in the American South," one historian concludes, "were ensnared in an economic matrix of debt, slaving, militarization, and warfare."[22]

The Tuscarora and Yamasee Wars

In the early eighteenth century, the depopulation of the region south of Virginia continued. Disease took a terrible toll in Indian villages, with major epidemics striking the region in 1696, 1718, and 1738. This depopulation led to the formation of polyglot villages as disease-ravaged Native people struggled to blend dialects, traditions,

and lineages. War added to the woes of southern indigenous peoples. The Tuscaroras were the first to be drawn into the ghastly cycle of trade, war, and elimination coordinated by the South Carolina colonizers from the small beachheads they had established along the coast.

The Tuscaroras, the southernmost Iroquoians, were a numerous people living in North Carolina in about fifteen large villages, where they gathered hemp, grew crops, and tended orchards on tidewater plantations they had cultivated for generations. For years, neighboring tribes, allied with Virginia and South Carolina traders, had raided their villages, stealing their children and selling them to the White slave traders. In 1709, they had watched a swarm of Germans and Swiss, led by Baron de Graffenried, invade their lands with the tacit consent of the provincial government. In local trade, they also found they could expect little from the Europeans' system of justice. They recognized, however, the difficulties of forging a pan-Indian alliance and were aware of what had happened to those who resorted to force against the colonial settlers. Better than taking this step, they decided, they would migrate northward to Pennsylvania, where they might obtain refuge in the Quaker colony. In 1710, their leaders met with representatives of the Pennsylvania government and the Iroquois League under whose protection they wished to place themselves. Their hopes were shattered, however, for the Pennsylvania government backed away from promising refuge.

Finding withdrawal impossible, the Tuscaroras gathered many local tribes with similar grievances and fell on the European encroachers in 1711. They killed about 140 English, Germans, and enslaved Africans. Boiling with internal dissension and as yet thinly populated, North Carolinians turned to neighboring colonies for help since it had only a ragtag militia to send against the Tuscaroras. Virginia's government promised clothing and money but no soldiers, for the

---

[21]David H. Corkran, *The Creek Frontier, 1540–1783* (Norman, OK, 1967), p. 53.
[22]Robbie Ethridge, *From Chicaza to Chickasaw: The European Invasion and the Transformation of the Mississippi World, 1540–1715* (Chapel Hill, NC, 2010), p. 232.

Virginians were unwilling to sacrifice their lives to defend the North Carolinians, with whom they were engaged in a bitter boundary dispute.

In South Carolina, the embattled North Carolinians found the assistance they needed. Historians have sung the praises of the South Carolina government for altruistically coming to the rescue of its northern neighbors and for assuming "the financial and military burdens" of the war.[23] In truth, the Indian slave traders of South Carolina gladly entered the fray because they sniffed profit in the breeze. Colonel John Barnwell, a fiery Irish immigrant and an important South Carolina Indian trader, led an army of some 700 soldiers into Tuscarora country. But the army included only thirty-three whites, for the South Carolinians intended their Indian allies, especially the Yamasees, to do most of the fighting for them. Behind the offer of assistance to the beleaguered North Carolinians stood the chance to defeat the Tuscaroras and enslave large numbers of them for sale on the West Indian market. Before Barnwell reached the Tuscarora forts in January 1712, many of the Indians in his army had deserted. But the remainder of the force defeated one group of Tuscaroras and took thirty slaves. To Barnwell's dismay, however, his Yamasee allies deserted with their prizes.

Barnwell moved on to destroy hundreds of Tuscarora houses and take several prisoners whom, as recorded in his journal, he "ordered immediately to be burned alive."[24] He then stormed another Tuscarora fort; but finding his own forces weak and badly supplied, he arranged a truce. Faced with returning to South Carolina with only a handful of slaves, Barnwell broke the truce and scoured the countryside for additional prisoners on his way back to South Carolina. Responding to this truce violation, the Tuscaroras renewed their attacks, and the South Carolinians were again invited to enrich themselves by helping their neighbors. A special representative

of the North Carolina government, urging a second expedition, advertised the "great advantage [that] may be made of slaves there," with 3,000 or 4,000 Tuscaroras ready for plucking.[25]

James Moore, a veteran of slaving expeditions in Spanish Florida, led the second expedition. Recruiting an army of 33 White colonists and nearly 900 Cherokees, Yamasees, Creeks, and Catawbas, he stormed the Tuscarora fort at Neoheroka in March 1713 and soundly defeated the North Carolina tribe. Moore's army burned alive several hundred of the enemy in the fort; slaughtered 166 male captives regarded as unsuitable for slavery; and led back to the Charleston slave market 392 Tuscaroras, mostly women and children. The South Carolina attackers suffered fifty-seven casualties—twenty-two whites and thirty-five Indians. In the course of the war, the Tuscaroras lost nearly 600, while as many as 400 may have been enslaved.[26] The scattered remnants of the tribe drifted northward in the aftermath of war, seeking shelter under the wing of the Iroquois and contributing to the Iroquois's distrust of English settlers.

In 1715, two years after the Yamasees had participated in the defeat and enslavement of the whites' enemies in North Carolina, they provided the leadership for the largest and most successful anti-European resistance movement in the eighteenth-century South. Spearheading a pan-Indian uprising that encompassed many of the fragmented remains of the coastal societies as well as the powerful and populous interior tribes—Creeks, Choctaws, and Cherokees—the Yamasees came as close to wiping out the European colonists as ever Native Americans came in the eighteenth century. Only the last-minute success of the Carolinians in winning the Cherokees to their side saved the colony from an Indian revolt that, according to the South Carolina Assembly, included fifteen Indian nations with a total population of more than 30,000.

[23]For example, M. Eugene Sirmans, *Colonial South Carolina: A Political History* (Chapel Hill, NC, 1966), p. 111.
[24]Quoted in Chapman J. Milling, *Red Carolinians* (Chapel Hill, NC, 1940), p. 120.
[25]Ibid., p. 128.
[26]Crane, *Southern Frontier . . .*, p. 161.

The Yamasees, like almost every other Southern tribe, had eagerly sought trade connections with the English and then lived to regret the dependency fostered by the trade. Even while the Yamasees were attacking weaker tribes in order to supply the Charleston slave traders and were helping the Carolinians subdue the Tuscaroras, they were reaching the desperation point in their relations with the English settlers. Cattle raisers in the coastal area south of Charleston expanded so rapidly in the first decade of the eighteenth century that the Carolina government passed an act in 1707 "to limit the bounds of the Yamasee settlement, to prevent persons from disturbing them with their stocks." Despite the argument that the act was designed to help the Yamasees, the real intention, as its title indicated, was to restrict the Indians to reservations in order to open up the rest of the land to white settlers. Three years later, the Carolina authorities were struggling with encroachers who were taking up land within the territory reserved for the Yamasees.

Even more oppressive were the Indian traders upon whom the Yamasee people had come to depend. The Indian commissioners established in 1709 listened repeatedly to reports "of the callous brutality of some of the traders, of petty thieving, of illegal enslavement of free Indians, of the abuse of rum to facilitate sharp dealing, of the use of cheating weights," and, as a Virginia Indian trader informed his London agent in 1715, of the debauching of Indian women when their men were on deer-hunting and slave-raiding expeditions.[27] Gradually the English reduced the Yamasees to peonage. A report to the Indian commissioners in 1711 detailed that the Yamasees were in debt to the amount of 100,000 skins—the equivalent of four or five years of hunting. When Charleston traders began seizing Yamasee women and children to be sold as slaves in partial payment of these debts, the Yamasees revolted, as much against the slave trade itself as against particularly barbarous traders.

Attacking on Good Friday, April 15, 1715, the Yamasee had carefully coordinated with the interior Apalachees, Euchees, Creeks, and others who had been equally exploited in the trade. The powerful Creeks were spurred on by the French, who had been building forts and trading posts in the lower Mississippi valley since 1701 and trying to woo the Creeks away from the English. Both the English and French believed the emerging Creek leader, Emperor Brims of Coweta, who planned the attacks in a general strategy to drive the Europeans out of the Southeast. All along the border settlements and wherever traders resided, the Creeks and Yamasees struck, aided by lesser tribes of the coastal plain. Refugees poured into Charleston during the summer of 1715, as the Carolina government frantically patched together a military force of planters, indentured servants, slaves, and mercenaries from Virginia and North Carolina. Supplies arrived even from far-off New England, as the authorities in Charleston issued gloomy predictions that if the Carolinians succumbed, Indian tribes all over the continent would be inspired to hurl themselves at white settlements.

At first, the Yamasee guerilla tactics worked. Striking English settlements at will, the Yamasee had Carolinians despairing at Indians "skulking in the bushes and swamps that we know not where to find them nor could follow them if we did so that we may as well go to war with the wolfs and bears."[28] In the fall of 1715, the Carolinians mounted effective counterattacks on the Yamasee, but the more numerous Creeks were still carrying the torch to every settlement they could reach. More dangerous, they were negotiating with the Cherokees, the largest Indian nation neighboring the Southern colonies. Residing in the mountainous southern Appalachia area, the Cherokees, according to an estimate in 1715, could muster nearly 4,000 warriors and boasted a total population four times as large. During the first half-year of the war, the Cherokees had

[27]Ibid., pp. 165–166.
[28]Quoted in Colin Calloway, *New Worlds for All: Indians, Europeans and the Remaking of Early America* (Baltimore, MD, 1997), p. 103.

remained neutral, but the chances of the hard-pressed Carolinians seemed to rest on obtaining their support or at least preventing a Creek-Cherokee alliance. In an evenly matched struggle, both sides made frantic attempts to secure their pledge of allegiance.

Recognizing the momentous importance of their decision, the Cherokees wavered back and forth, first agreeing to an alliance with the English in August 1715, but then failing to appear for a scheduled November offensive against the Creeks. Desperate for decisive action, the Carolina government sent a military expedition of 300 soldiers, including one company of enslaved Africans, deep into the mountainous Cherokee country to galvanize the wavering Indian nation. While the expedition leaders promised a shower of trade goods and pressed the Cherokees for a commitment, a dozen Creek headmen also harangued the Cherokee chiefs and argued for a joint attack on the White army encamped in the woods nearby. The Cherokees were split between a war party and a peace party. When the war party prevailed, they fell on the Creek emissaries and killed them. It was the Cherokees' dependence on the English trade goods that finally swung them against the Creeks. As they told the Carolinians, unless they were at war with the Creeks "they should have no way in getting of Slaves to buy ammunition and Clothing from the White traders."[29]

With the Cherokees arrayed against them, the Creeks abandoned the towns they had settled in eastern Carolina and migrated back to their old town sites on the Chattahoochee River to be nearer the source of English trade goods. To replace their trading and military connections with the English, they sought new links to the French on the Alabama River and the Spanish in Florida. The remaining Yamasees fled south to join the Spanish in Florida.

For white Carolinians, the flight of the Creeks and the Yamasees left new lands open for the taking. But their thirst for revenge in a war that had cost them more than 400 lives and £400,000 was nearly unquenchable. Many of the Yamasee and the Creek Indians, wrote an Anglican clergyman in the colony, "were against the war all along; but our military men are so bent upon revenge, and so desirous to enrich themselves, by making all the Indians slaves that fall into their hands, but such as they kill (without making the least distinction between the guilty and the innocent, and without considering the barbarous usage these poor savages met with from our villainous traders) that it is in vain to represent to them the cruelty and injustice of such a procedure."[30]

The Yamasee War defined both the limits of White economic exploitation and the limit of Indian resistance. Nowhere in colonial America was exploitation of the indigenous people less restrained by church, government, or the attitudes of the people than in South Carolina. By 1717, a White population of only about 1,500 males had succeeded in employing the larger tribes to enslave and shatter nearly a dozen coastal tribes and then had driven a wedge between the Creeks and the Cherokees at the moment when an alliance between them might have ended English presence in the region. Throughout this process, covering almost a half-century, the primary weapon of the English had been trade goods. Despite callow abuses in the Indian trade and the devastating toll that slave raiding took on tribes as far west as the Mississippi, it was only with great reluctance, usually accompanied by internal division, that tribes of the Carolina region turned on those who supplied them with European goods. One Indian delegation put it bluntly during the Yamasee War: Their people "cannot live without the assistance of the English."[31] They had been fatally implicated in an Atlantic commercial system and in English attempts to drive the Spanish from the lower South.

[29]Crane, *Southern Frontier . . .* , p. 182.
[30]Ibid., p. 179n.
[31]Quoted in James H. Merrell, "The Indian's New World: The Catawba Experience," *William and Mary Quarterly*, 41 (1984): 553.

As in other parts of the continent, the key to English success in an area where they were greatly outnumbered was the promotion of intertribal hostility. This was not only instrumental in procuring slaves who were profitably sold in New England and the West Indies, but also was a major factor in depopulating tribes whose land then became accessible to the settlers.

This doubly baneful effect of the English connection—always outweighed by the powerful Indian hunger for English trade goods—became the basis of French attempts to win the Creeks to their side. Since the late seventeenth century, the French had been building forts and establishing contacts with the interior tribes. As early as 1702, Pierre Le Moyne Iberville, the architect of the French empire in Louisiana, parleyed with chiefs from the warring Choctaw and Chickasaw nations, attempting to convince them of the destructive nature of the English connection. For almost a decade, he pointed out, the Chickasaws had allied themselves with the Charleston traders, using English guns to raid the Choctaws and selling the captives they took in order to procure still more guns and ammunition. In the course of taking about 500 slaves, the Chickasaws had killed more than 1,800 Choctaws and lost some 800 of their own warriors. The English delighted in this arrangement, he explained, for they built their fortunes on the trade in slaves and guns while watching the Choctaws and Chickasaws decimate each other. When the two tribes had sufficiently weakened each other, they would no longer be able to protect their land from the English settlers, whose strength grew with the death of every Indian, whether friend or enemy. Iberville offered peaceful trade with both nations, not for slaves but for deerskins.

For the land-hungry English cattle raisers and rice growers of eastern Carolina, who were importing slaves from Africa in ever-growing numbers by the early eighteenth century, the Indian slave trade had no direct benefits because the profits accumulated in the hands of the Charleston merchants. But the secondary advantages were invaluable, for the Indian population of the lower South followed a downward trajectory as a result of the slave trade, thus facilitating expansion southward and westward from the initial settlements around Charleston. A recent analysis of the Indian slave trade estimates that between 1670 and 1715, the number of enslaved, most of them shipped to distant points, reached 25,000 to 50,000.[32] The most recent estimate pegs the decline of the Indian population due to disease, warfare, and enslavement during the first half-century of English settlement at about 80 percent.

Penn's "Holy Experiment" and Quaker-Indian Relations

For several hundred years, historians have explained the history of Indian-White relations as an inevitable clash between "savage" and "civilized" people. Told from the victor's point of view, the outcome of the contest was predetermined. The irresistible rhythms of human life, we are told, the unswervable forces beyond control of puny individuals, and the "laws of history" and "manifest destiny" determined the contest between two cultures. As one wise philosopher has explained, such arguments about inevitable historical outcomes shift the weight of responsibility from particular individuals and groups to "vast impersonal forces . . . better made to bear such burdens than a feeble thinking reed-like man."[33]

The notion that Indian-White relations were inevitably violent and inexorably resolved in the Europeans' favor is refuted by the arrival of a band of ideologically fired English settlers who reached North America only a few years after the Indian wars of the 1670s. William Penn and his Quaker followers, who streamed into

---

[32]Alan Galley, *The Indian Slave Trade: The Rise of the English Empire in the American South, 1670–1717* (New Haven, CT, 2002), pp. 298–299.
[33]Isaiah Berlin, *Historical Inevitability* (London, 1954), p. 20.

New Jersey and Pennsylvania in the 1680s, were entering a maelstrom of bloody racial conflict that had reached a peak in Metacom's War in New England, in the Indian war ignited by Nathaniel Bacon in Virginia, and in the fierce Indian wars touched off by early colonizers in South Carolina. But unlike other colonists, Quakers came with peace on their minds. In fact, as pacifists, they categorically forswore violence. Along with Penn's pledge not to allow one acre of land to be settled until he had purchased it fairly from the local Lenape, a conglomeration of Unami- and Munsee-speaking bands that would gradually coalesce into what became known as Delawares, pacifism made the crucial difference.

A mere handful of colonizers had settled in the fertile region between the Hudson River and the Chesapeake Bay before the 1660s, most of them Swedes, Dutch, and Finns under the control of the Dutch West India Company. Then, in the 1670s and 1680s, a wave of English settlers came to the Delaware River valley, which comprised what would become the colonies of East and West Jersey, Pennsylvania, and Delaware. These were the tribal homelands of a loose collection of small tribes, of which the Lenape was the largest.

Among all the tribes of the coastal plain, the Lenape had retained their land and way of life the longest, primarily because only a small number of Europeans settled in their region during the half-century when the populations of Massachusetts, Connecticut, Maryland, and Virginia grew rapidly. When Europeans did arrive in large numbers, most of them came as devotees of the Society of Friends—a radical Protestant sect born in the heat of the English Civil War of the 1650s. Pledged to the principle of nonviolence and just relations among people of all religions and races, the Society of Friends, or Quakers, maintained peaceful interracial relations in the Delaware River valley that sharply contrasted with the relations in other parts of North America.

The Quaker immigration focused first, in the 1670s, on East and West Jersey, formerly part of New Netherland. Then in the 1680s, it shifted to Pennsylvania, which became the center of the Quakers' hopes for a utopia on the western shore of the Atlantic. Like the Puritans, Quakers burned with the bright heat of religious conviction. Like the Puritans, they regarded the English Protestant Church as corrupt and renounced its formalistic elements. But they carried the Puritan revolt against Anglicanism to its extreme, decrying all institutions standing between the individual believer and God. The Quaker was persuaded that every believer might find God's grace within one's heart unaided by priests, ministers, liturgy, or other devices.

Quakers had suffered severe persecution in England after the rise of their movement in the 1650s and therefore began to formulate plans for founding overseas colonies of their own. They sent their advance agents, seen as God's shock troops, to many of England's colonies, where they were often reviled, mutilated, deported, and even hanged for practicing their faith. Then in 1681, glad to be rid of the pesky Quakers, Charles II granted an immense territory to William Penn, an important English Quaker. Penn vowed to make it a refuge for the persecuted of the world, where people of all colors, religions, and national backgrounds could live together in peace. Whereas others regarded war and violence as unavoidable when the English settled among Indians, Penn prepared for peace and interracial harmony in Pennsylvania.

Quakers arriving in the Delaware River valley, therefore, threatened no violence to the Indians. However, the Natives of the area had little reason to believe that these Europeans would be different from others they had known for three-quarters of a century. From exposure to Dutch, Swedes, Finns, and scattered English, the local tribes had learned of European technology, disease, material culture, and values. By the time the Quakers arrived, the Lenape had extensive experience with European firearms and alcohol, two key commodities in the trade that they conducted in beaver, otter, and deerskins. Like almost every other tribe that came in contact with the Europeans, they had suffered a major population decline. On the eve of the Quaker arrival, the Lenape warrior strength was about 1,000, less than half of what it had been before three smallpox epidemics hammered the tribe between 1620 and 1670.

The Quakers who clambered ashore in Penn's new colony, recruited in England from the rising middle ranks, were primarily farmers. Like other colonists, they hungered for land. Nor did they differ from other English immigrants in seeking better material lives. But offsetting these built-in potentialities for friction was the Quakers' belief that despite a historical record that seemed to prove otherwise, people of different cultures and values could live together in friendship and peace. Their optimism was not the product of ignorance, for they knew of the two bloody conflicts in New England and Virginia that occurred just a few years before Penn received his grant for Pennsylvania. Yet they were committed to pacifism and were convinced that what others had not achieved could be accomplished in the Quaker "Holy Experiment."

Even before he set foot in Pennsylvania, Penn laid the groundwork for peaceful relations. In a letter transmitted by his commissioners who preceded him to Pennsylvania, he wrote to the Delawares: "The king of the country where I live, hath given unto me a great Province therein, but I desire to enjoy it with your love and consent, that we may always live together as neighbors and friends . . ."[34] In this single statement, Penn recognized the Indians as the rightful owners of the territory and gave notice that only with their consent would he allow settlers to establish their farms within the bounds of his charter. Colonists must purchase land from him. But he in turn would sell no land until he had first purchased it himself from the local chiefs. Penn strengthened his commitment by pledging that the injustices suffered previously by the Indians would no longer be tolerated. He promised strict regulation of the Indian trade and a ban on the sale of alcohol. Voltaire was later moved to write (though not with strict accuracy) that this was "the only

league between those nations [Indian] and the Christians that was never sworn to, and never broken."[35]

When the first Quaker settlers arrived, they immediately began land negotiations with the Lenape. The Indians may have been suspicious of Penn's promises, which must have sounded like other European expressions of goodwill that had quickly evaporated. But the Lenape were no doubt impressed with the lavish supply of trade goods offered for the land along the Delaware River north of the site of what became the capital city of Philadelphia. Included were quantities of wampum, blankets, duffels, kettles, hoes, axes, knives, mirrors, saws, scissors, awls, and items of clothing. Also included were rum, powder, shot, and twenty guns, indicating that even those who professed nonviolence and wished to ban the sale of alcohol as a way of stabilizing relations could not deny Indians the trade goods they most desired.

Another factor conducive to peaceful relations was the absence of an extensive Indian trade. The fur trade flourished north of Pennsylvania, and though Penn made efforts to divert the interior trade so that it would pass through Philadelphia rather than Albany and New York, he was unsuccessful. This failure was disappointing to Penn and his merchant friends, but in the long run it minimized the chances for misunderstanding and hostility between Pennsylvania and the small tribal communities of eastern Pennsylvania.

So long as Penn's influence was strong, Indian relations remained generally harmonious, though the buildup of the mostly Quaker population, about 18,000 by 1700, caused various groups of Lenape to retreat to the interior. However, Penn resided only briefly in his colony, and after 1712, when he suffered several disabling strokes, he played almost no role in its affairs. Coinciding with the end of his influence was a development that soured Indian relations in Pennsylvania: the arrival of waves of land-hungry and

---

[34]C. A. Weslager, *The Delaware Indians: A History* (New Brunswick, NJ, 1972), p. 156.
[35]Quoted in Thomas E. Drake, "William Penn's Experiment in Race Relations," *Pennsylvania Magazine of History and Biography*, 68 (1944): 372.

Benjamin West, *William Penn's Treaty with the Indians.*

(Courtesy Library of Congress Prints and Photographs Division [LC-USZ62-133865])

PENNSYLVANIA AND THE
LOWER COUNTIES OF DELAWARE
1681–1740

0   25   50 Miles
0   25   50 Kilometers

PENNSYLVANIA

The Walking Purchase 1737

Delaware River

Shamokin

APPALACHIAN MOUNTAINS

Lehigh River

Schuylkill River

NEW

Harris Ferry

Ephrata

Lancaster

Newtown
Log College   Trenton
Wrightstown   Pennsbury
Bristol
Burlington

Wright's
Ferry

Susquehanna River

Germantown
Shackamaxon
Philadelphia
Chester   Tinicum
Marcus Hook

JERSEY

MARYLAND

Wilmington (Fort Christina)
New Castle
Salem

Joppa

Bohemia
Manor

Bridgeton

Baltimore

Potomac River

Dover

DELAWARE
BAY

Arundelton
(Annapolis)

LOWER
COUNTIES
OF
DELAWARE   Lewes

CHESAPEAKE BAY

VIRGINIA

ATLANTIC
OCEAN

St. Marys

nonpacifist European settlers. When migrants who were not Quaker flooded the colony, the Friends' commitment to pacifism wavered. And when Quakers lost political control of the area, the last chance of an unsubjugated Indian society along the coastal plain of North America quietly disappeared. The limitations of the Quakers' Indian policies became clear. Penn's successors—first his wife and then his sons—never considered limiting the influx of non-Quaker settlers for the sake of the Native peoples whom the massive immigration threatened.

Thus, the Quaker policy of toleration for all religious and ethnic groups attracted the very European groups whose land hunger and disdain for the Indians undermined the Quaker attitude of trust and love. In 1710 and 1711 came the first of these, a group of Swiss Mennonites who settled sixty miles inland from Philadelphia. In 1717, a much larger group of German Protestants arrived, the vanguard of an influx of German immigrants who by mid-eighteenth century constituted about 40 percent of the colony's population. In the following year, another wave of immigrants poured in—this time Scots-Irish, who began to locate in the area around present-day Harrisburg. None of these groups shared Quaker idealism about interracial harmony. They had been driven from their homelands by chronic economic depression and were concerned only about building a new life, centered around tilling the soil. To obtain land cheaply and live in a colony where they were free to practice their religion was all they asked. But they were not prepared in return to accommodate themselves to the local tribes, particularly if land speculators and government officials in Philadelphia cooperated with them in defrauding the Natives of their land.

Ironically, many of the Indians whom these refugees from European oppression confronted were also recent refugees. In the late seventeenth and early eighteenth centuries, Pennsylvania's Susquehanna River valley became a sanctuary for a number of tribes that had heard of the benevolent Quaker-Indian policy. From Maryland came the Nanticokes and Conoys to escape war and enslavement that had decimated their tribes for several decades. "The people of Maryland," the Pennsylvania government was told by one Indian spokesman, "do not treat the Indians as you and others do, for they make slaves of them and sell their children for money."[36] From Virginia and North Carolina came the Tuscaroras and Tutelos for similar reasons. From the southwest came the Miamis and Shawnees, who had formerly lived in the Ohio River valley and traded with the French. Europeans who arrived later in the eighteenth century reaped benefits from these Indian refugees, who had cleared the land for crops, settled village sites near water transportation, and established trails for hunting. When Germans and Scots-Irish immigrants pushed into the interior, they used Indian routes to advance west, occupied Indian town sites, and took over the cleared fields.

The Lenape and other refugee tribes watched their situation deteriorate even as William Penn lay dying in England in 1718. They complained bitterly in Philadelphia that new immigrants were building mill dams downstream from them, blocking the fish from coming upstream to spawn. Settlers poured in, squatting on land that had not been sold to Penn's government. But rather than fight, the tribes preferred to vacate their land, knowing what had happened in Virginia and New England when Indians resorted to violence. By 1724, the main branch of the Lenape had migrated westward, part of them to an area not far beyond the limits of white settlement but others all the way to the Ohio River. They left heavy with resentment. A generation later, when they allied with the French and attacked their former English allies, the Pennsylvanians would reap the bitter harvest they had earlier sown. A leading Pennsylvanian wrote of their displacement: "These poor people were much disturbed . . . yet finding they could no longer raise corn there for their bread they quietly removed up the river

---

[36]Quoted in Weslager, *Delaware Indians . . .* , p. 182.

Susquehannah, though not without repining at their hard usage. . . . 'Tis certain they have the same reason to resent this as all those other Indians on this continent have had for the foundation of their wars that in some places they have carried on so terribly to the destruction of the European inhabitants."[37] It was at this point that the Lenape people began to call themselves Delawares.

Eastern Pennsylvania was emptied of its Native population in the second quarter of the eighteenth century. Pennsylvanians gained some Delaware land by assigning settler rights in the proximity of Indian villages—a tactic that usually drove Indians away. Settlers acquired other Delaware land by conniving with other tribes. Particularly, the Pennsylvanians turned to the Iroquois for help in expelling the last of the local Lenape. The provincial government proposed an alliance with the Iroquois under which the powerful northern confederacy would assume suzerainty over all smaller tribes residing in Pennsylvania. The object of the alliance was to drive the Delawares from their homelands without resorting to force. Thus, in 1732, the Iroquois pressured one band of the Delawares to give up their lands at Tulepehocken, about sixty miles from Philadelphia, and migrate higher up the Susquehanna River to Shamokin where they were to live under the supervision of a minor Iroquois chief.

The Walking Purchase of 1737 fraudulently stripped the Delawares of their last land preserve, the area between the Lehigh and the Delaware rivers known as the Forks of the Delaware. This act ended Penn's dream of harmony between Indian and European peoples. Two years before, James Logan, Pennsylvania's largest land speculator, produced what he alleged was a copy of an old deed signed in 1686 by which the forebears of the present Delaware leaders had ceded this land to William Penn. But the inability of Logan to produce an original copy, the lack of any reference to the transaction in the land records of Philadelphia, and the rarely mistaken oral tradition of the Indians, by which land transactions were scrupulously passed from generation to generation—all point to the conclusion that by now the Pennsylvanians were confident enough of their strength to force from the Delawares what they could not get by agreement.

Though the Delaware chiefs challenged the validity of the deed, they faced the combined opposition of the Pennsylvanians and the Iroquois. Finally, they signed a confirmation of the alleged 1686 document, bowing to arguments that resistance would not halt incoming squatters from encroaching on their lands. In 1737, the Quaker government arranged to "walk off" the bounds of the Indian deed, which granted William Penn's heirs all the land from a specified point in Bucks County westward as far as a man could walk in a day and a half. Two of Penn's sons, who had recently arrived in Pennsylvania to bolster their sagging estates through the sale of land, personally participated in sending secret parties scouting through the woods to blaze a trail so that three specially trained walkers, operating as a relay team, could cover the ground as swiftly as possible. By this device the Penns extended their claim under the infamous "Walking Purchase" almost sixty miles into Delaware territory, far beyond the limits intended by the Delaware chiefs.

Nearly 1,200 square miles now became the property of the Penns. The ten square miles they set aside as an Indian reservation did not diminish the bitterness of Delaware leaders. After the Delawares refused to move off their land, Pennsylvania authorities paid the Iroquois to remove the eastern Delawares. "We now expect from you," signaled Pennsylvania's governor to the Iroquois in 1741, "that you will cause these Indians to remove from the lands in the forks of the Delaware and not give any further disturbance to the persons who are now in possession."[38]

A year later, Iroquois representatives gathered with the eastern Delaware chiefs in Philadelphia to fulfill their pledge. At a grand council the Iroquois flayed the Delawares:

---

[37]Quoted in Francis Jennings, "The Delaware Interregnum," *Pennsylvania Magazine of History and Biography*, 89 (1965): 178.
[38]Weslager, *Delaware Indians . . .* , p. 190.

Let this Belt of Wampum serve to chastise you; you ought to be taken by the hair of the head and shaked severely till you recover your senses and become sober; . . . We conquered you, we made women of you, . . . and [you] can no more sell land than women. . . . This land that you claim is gone through your guts. You have been furnished with clothes and meat and drink by the goods paid you for it, and now you want it again like children as you are. . . . For all these reasons we charge you to remove instantly.[39]

This withering blast stripped the eastern Delawares of their options. For several generations they had recognized themselves as subordinate to the Iroquois. But the tie had been reciprocal, for if the eastern Delawares recognized the authority of the Iroquois in matters of war and diplomacy, the Iroquois also counted on the Delawares as one of the southern "posts" of their league and had respected Delaware management of their own land affairs. Now the eastern Delawares left Philadelphia humiliated by their former protectors. The Iroquois, lavishly rewarded for their intercession, departed Philadelphia with wagons bulging with shoes, stockings, hats, blankets, hatchets, hoes, and other goods. The retreating Delawares would not forget, however. The taunts of the Iroquois that they were women and children still rang in their ears a dozen years later, when they were among the first of the western tribes allied to the French to deliver devastating strikes along the Pennsylvania frontier at the outset of the French and Indian War. The Indian friends of the Society of Friends had been turned into bitter enemies under the weight of population buildup, speculator greed, and the acquiescence of the second generation of Quakers.

The process of decimation, dispossession, and decline among the Indian societies of the coastal areas was thus accomplished in different ways during the first century of English colonization. In New England and on the Chesapeake, the demise was almost complete by the time

English settlement was beginning in Pennsylvania and South Carolina. It had come in the north after steady resistance from the stronger tribes, who finally succumbed in pitched battle to an enemy that sought no genuine accommodation with them and was able to keep enough tribes out of the fray to prevail in a war of attrition. In Virginia and Maryland, another course of events defeated the tidewater tribes. Here the Indians genuinely strove for accommodation following the unsuccessful resistance movements of 1622 and 1644. As in New England, even as a friendly colonized people, they were obstacles in the path of an acquisitive and expanding plantation society.

In South Carolina still another variation in the process of decline occurred. It was not dead Indians but Indians alive and in chains that benefited the white settlers. The buildup of the white population was slow enough and the desire among the Indians for trade goods intense enough that the White Carolinians could watch the coastal tribes obliterate each other in the wars for slaves, and then, when they were exhausted, employ the same strategy against the more powerful interior tribes.

The result was roughly the same in all the colonies along the seaboard. By the 1680s in the older colonies and by the 1720s in the newer ones, the coastal tribes were shattered. Devastated by disease and warfare, the surviving members of these tribes either incorporated themselves as subjects of stronger inland groups or entered the White people's world as detribalized servile dependents. The Indian's failure to survive cannot be attributed to an unwillingness or inability to intermix with the European newcomers—learning their languages, intermingling with them, adapting to their methods of trade and negotiation—as some historians have argued. The failure, rather, was to adapt too well to the material culture of the colonizers. The attachment to European trade goods and the persistence of ancient intertribal hostilities thwarted

[39]*Minutes of the Provincial Council of Pennsylvania*, 16 vols. (Philadelphia and Harrisburg, 1851–1853), 4: 578–580.

pan-tribal resistance, which alone could have ensured the survival of the coastal societies. "European trade had triumphed; European civilization had not."[40]

Too much can be made of the inability of the coastal tribes to unite in order to ensure their survival. Indian "factionalism" is the common explanation for their eventual defeat, and it carries with it the implication that Indians were incapable of political unification because of their backwardness. This viewpoint forgets, however, that "Indian" is a term invented by Europeans to describe a great variety of peoples who did not think of themselves as united in any racial, political, or even cultural sense. "European" is a similar term, used to embrace a number of people who would have shuddered at the idea that they were politically, culturally, or religiously the same. They had been fighting each other furiously in Europe for centuries. As colonizers in North America, they continued their antagonisms. Moreover, specific European groups, such as the English, were deeply factionalized. In Metacom's War, these divisions among English colonizers were so great that they were only barely able to defeat an enemy whom they greatly outmatched in men and supplies. Metacom's difficulties in obtaining the aid of neighboring tribes was real; but this fact must be considered alongside the

picture of Governor Andros of New York invading Connecticut as the war was in progress, the sight of Bostonians expelling from their town the Massachusetts refugees who streamed in from burned-out frontier villages, and the fact of Rhode Island's neutrality during the war.

Although they were defeated, the coastal societies performed a major service for tribes farther inland. Their prolonged resistance gave the interior Indian nations time to adapt to the European presence and to devise strategies of survival as the westward-moving, swarming settlers approached them. "People like the Iroquois," it has been pointed out, "owed a great deal to the resistance of the coastal Algonkians, and both peoples were well aware of this."[41] The coastal tribes provided a buffer between the Indians of the interior and the Europeans, and when the coastal tribes lost their political autonomy, their remnants were often incorporated into the larger inland tribes. These were important factors in the far stronger opposition that the Iroquois, Cherokees, and Creeks offered to European encroachment—a resistance so effective that, for the first century and a half of European colonization, the European newcomers were restricted to the coastal plain, unable to penetrate the Appalachians where the interior tribes, often allied with the French, held sway.

Summary

As European intrusion intensified in the regions inhabited by the coastal tribes, Native people reacted in different ways. Some resisted colonial expansion, as exemplified by Metacom's War in Massachusetts in 1675, which ended in an English victory and catastrophe for the Native people. Resistance also marked the conflicts between Native Americans and South Carolinians in the Tuscarora and Yamasee Wars and in the Indian slave trade that arose in this region. Other Native tribes accommodated by allying with the English or withdrawing. The latter was the case in Virginia, where Bacon's Rebellion, fueled by land hunger and hatred of Indians, had the added dimension of warring between whites. In Pennsylvania, where William Penn brought his peace-loving and justice-seeking Quakers, hopes were high for harmonious coexistence between the English and the Natives. After relatively peaceful relations

[40]James H. Merrell, *The Indians' New World: Catawbas and Their Neighbors from European Contact through the Era of Removal* (Chapel Hill, NC, 1989), p. 91.
[41]T. J. C. Brasser, "The Coastal Algonkians: People of the First Frontiers," in Eleanor Burke Leacock and Nancy Oestreich Lurie, eds., *North American Indians in Historical Perspective* (New York, 1971), p. 73.

for nearly half a century, unprecedented in North America, the situation unraveled after Penn's death. The Delawares ultimately also reacted to land fraud and violence by withdrawing westward.

By the first quarter of the eighteenth century, the coastal tribes were devastated by disease; warfare; attachment to European trade goods; and ongoing ancient intertribal enmity, which impeded united resistance. Even so, the coastal societies, in their defeat, contributed to the fate of tribes farther inland. By resisting so fiercely and persistently, they gave the interior Indian nations time to adapt to the European presence and to create survival strategies in the face of it.

Critical Thinking Questions

1. The outcome of Metacom's War was disastrous for the Native population of coastal New England. What contributed to the ultimate defeat of the Indian tribes, and how did the Indian people accommodate—or not accommodate—to this loss?
2. While Metacom's War was raging in New England, Bacon's Rebellion had erupted in the Chesapeake region. What roles did Nathaniel Bacon and Sir William Berkeley play in this rebellion?
3. Most of the original settlers of South Carolina came from the sugar island of Barbados and had made use of African slave labor there; once in Carolina, they saw a faster way to wealth. What constituted that faster way, and what effects did it have on the peoples caught up in it?
4. Unlike many other colonists, the Quakers flooding into Pennsylvania and New Jersey came with peaceful intentions. In what ways did William Penn contribute to the "Holy Experiment," and what happened to this experiment once Penn withdrew from the colony?

Further Reading

Kathryn E. Holland Braund, *Deerskins and Duffels: The Creek Indian Trade with Anglo-America, 1685–1815* (Lincoln: University of Nebraska Press, 1993).

Colin G. Calloway, *New Worlds for All: Indians, Europeans, and the Remaking of Early America* (Baltimore: Johns Hopkins University Press, 1997).

James Drake, *King Philip's War: Civil War in New England, 1675–1676* (Amherst: University of Massachusetts Press, 1999).

Alan Gallay, *The Indian Slave Trade: The Rise of the English Empire in the American South, 1670–1717* (New Haven: Yale University Press, 2002).

Patricia Galloway, *Choctaw Genesis, 1500–1700* (Lincoln: University of Nebraska Press, 1995).

Steven Hahn, *The Invention of the Creek Nation, 1670–1763* (Lincoln: University of Nebraska Press, 2003).

Paul Kelton, *Epidemics and Enslavement: Biological Catastrophe in the Native Southeast, 1492–1715* (Lincoln: University of Nebraska Press, 2007).

David LaVere, *The Tuscarora War: Indians, Settlers, and the Fight for the Carolina Colonies* (Chapel Hill: University of North Carolina Press, 2013)

James H. Merrell, *The Indians' New World: Catawbas and Their Neighbors from European Contact through the Era of Removal* (Chapel Hill: University of North Carolina Press, 1989).

William A. Pencak and Daniel K. Richter, eds., *Friends and Enemies in Penn's Woods* (University Park: Pennsylvania State University Press, 2004).

Joshua Piker, *Okfuskee: A Creek Indian Town in Colonial America* (Cambridge: Harvard University Press, 2004).

William L. Ramsey, *The Yamasee War: A Study of Culture, Economy, and Conflict in the Colonial South* (Lincoln: University of Nebraska Press, 2008).

Amy C. Schutt, *Peoples of the River Valleys: The Odyssey of the Delaware Indians* (Philadelphia: University of Pennsylvania Press, 2007).

CHAPTER 6

Europe, Africa, and the Americas

LEARNING OBJECTIVES

■ Characterize African civilization—including social organization, agricultural skills, and culture—in the late fifteenth century, when Europeans began to make extensive contact with the continent.

■ Give an overview of the 366 years of the Atlantic slave trade, incorporating the reasons it arose; the major participants, both African and European; and the estimated number of Africans removed by slave traders by the 1750s and their destinations in the Americas.

■ Describe the plight of Africans captured as slaves as they were transported from Africa to the Americas, focusing especially on shipboard conditions.

■ Explain how enslaved Africans became part of the North American colonies, including the steady stripping away of their rights, and compare their role in the Southern colonies with that in the Northern colonies.

■ Discuss how enslaved Africans fared in South America vis-à-vis North America and suggest some reasons for the difference.

The African slave trade, which began in the late fifteenth century and continued for the next 400 years, is one of the most important and tragic phenomena in the history of the modern world. Involving the largest forced migration in history, the slave trade and slavery were crucially important in building the transoceanic colonial empires of European nations and in generating the wealth that later produced the Industrial Revolution. Every maritime European power was involved: at first Portugal and Spain, then France, Holland, and England, finally Denmark, Sweden, and Norway. Operating behind the water-borne scenes were German and Italian bankers, Asian textile producers, and an array of other intermediaries. Together, these varied peoples made the gruesome slave trade truly global.

After 1492, Europe's orientation gradually shifted from the Mediterranean Sea to the Atlantic Ocean. The production locales of valuable and much desired commodities such as silver, gold, sugar, coffee, rice, and tobacco moved from the "Old World" to the Americas. In this creation of a dynamic system of trade and communication throughout the Atlantic basin, Africa became essential. For Europeans, Africa became the indispensable source of human labor that enabled them to unlock the profits buried in the productive soils of the Americas.

The economic importance of the slave trade and slavery to Europeans who were connecting different zones of the Atlantic basin can hardly be overstated. But often overlooked in the story of post-1492 European intrusions in the Americas is the cultural diffusion that took place when some 12 million Africans were brought to the Western Hemisphere. Probably four out of every five persons who crossed the Atlantic to take up life in the Americas from 1500 to 1821 were enslaved Africans. As a result, in most parts of the colonized territories, slavery "defined the context within which transferred European traditions would grow and change."[1] As slaves, Africans were Europeanized; but at the same time, they Africanized the culture of Europeans in the Americas. In addition, the slave trade created the lines of communication for the movement of crops, agricultural techniques, diseases, and medical knowledge between Africa, Europe, and the Americas.

Just as they were late in colonizing the New World, the English lagged far behind their Spanish and Portuguese competitors in reaching the west coast of Africa, in entering the Atlantic slave trade, and in establishing enslaved Africans as the backbone of the labor force in their overseas plantations. Moreover, among the English colonists in the Americas, those on the mainland of North America were a half-century or more behind those in the Caribbean in converting their plantation economies to slave labor. By 1670, for example, more than 100,000 Africans labored in Portuguese Brazil, while about 30,000 cultivated sugar in English Barbados; but in Virginia, only about 2,000 worked in the tobacco fields. Extensive cultural interaction of Europeans and Africans did not begin in North America until more than a century after it commenced in the vast South Atlantic region of the hemisphere. Much that occurred as the two cultures met in

the Iberian colonies was later repeated in the Anglo-African interaction; yet the patterns of acculturation differed markedly in North and South America in the seventeenth and eighteenth centuries.

The Atlantic Slave System

A half-century before Columbus crossed the Atlantic, a Portuguese sea captain, Antam Gonçalvez, made the first European landing on the West African coast south of the Sahara. What he might have seen, had he been able to travel the length and breadth of Africa, was a continent of extraordinary variation in geography and culture. Little he might have seen would have caused him to believe that African peoples were naturally inferior or that they had failed to develop over time as had the peoples of Europe. Europeans invented the notion of African "backwardness" and cultural impoverishment after the slave trade had deposited millions of Africans in the Americas. This myth served to justify the cruelties of the slave trade and to assuage the guilt of Europeans involved in the largest forced dislocation of people in history.

The peoples of Africa numbered about 50 million in the late fifteenth century when Europeans began making extensive contact with the continent. They lived in widely varied ecological zones—in vast deserts, in grasslands, and in great forests and woodlands. As in Europe, most people farmed the land and struggled to subdue the forces of nature in order to sustain life. That the African population had increased so rapidly in the 2,000 years before European arrival suggests the sophistication of the African agricultural methods. Part of this expertise in farming derived from skill in iron production, which had begun in present-day Nigeria about 450 B.C. This ability to fashion iron implements triggered the new farming techniques necessary to sustain larger populations. With large populations came

[1]Sidney W. Mintz, "History and Anthropology," in Stanley L. Engerman and Eugene D. Genovese, eds., *Race and Slavery in the Western Hemisphere* (Princeton, NJ, 1975), p. 483.

greater specialization of tasks and thus additional technical improvements. Small groups of related families made contact with other kinship groups and over time evolved into larger and more complicated societies. The pattern was similar to what had occurred in other parts of the world—in the Americas, Europe, the Middle East, and elsewhere—when the "agricultural revolution" occurred.

Recent studies of "precontact" African history have shown that the "culture gap" between European and African societies when the two peoples met was not as large as previously imagined. By the time Europeans reached the coast of West Africa, large trading empires had been in existence for centuries. The Kingdom of Ghana, for example, embraced the immense territory between the Sahara Desert and the Gulf of Guinea and from the Niger River to the Atlantic Ocean between the fifth and tenth centuries. Extensive urban settlement, advanced architecture, elaborate art, and a highly complex political organization evolved during this time. During Europe's Middle Ages, two-thirds of all the gold circulating in the Mediterranean region came across the Sahara Desert from the gold-bearing regions of Ghana's Niger and Senegal rivers.

Invasion from the north by Muslim warriors weakened the Kingdom of Ghana, which in time gave way to the Kingdom of Mali. At the center of the Mali Empire was the city of Timbuktu, noted for its extensive wealth and its Islamic university, where the faculty was as distinguished as any in Europe.

Lesser kingdoms such as those of Kongo, Zimbabwe, and Benin had also been in the process of growth and cultural change for centuries before Europeans reached Africa. Their inhabitants were skilled in metalworking, weaving, ceramics, architecture, and aesthetic expression. Many of their towns rivaled European cities in size. Many communities of East and West Africa had complex religious rites, well-organized regional trade, codes of law, and elaborate political organization.

Cultural development in Africa, as elsewhere in the world, proceeded at varying rates. Ecological conditions had a large effect on this development. Regions blessed by good soil, adequate rainfall, and abundance of minerals, as in coastal West Africa, underwent rapid population growth and cultural elaboration after interregional trade began. Where inhospitable desert or nearly impenetrable forest held forth, societies remained small and changed at a crawl. Contact with other cultures also brought rapid adaptations, whereas isolation impeded cultural change. The Kingdom of Ghana bloomed partly because of the trading contacts with Arabs, who had conquered the area by the eleventh century. Cultural change began to accelerate in East African Swahili societies after trading contacts began to flourish with the merchants from Arabia, India, and the East Indies in the tenth century.

The forced migration across the Atlantic began unofficially in the 1440s when Portuguese merchants began kidnapping and then trading slaves for horses on the West African coast. In 1456, when Diego Gomes, representing the Portuguese crown, negotiated treaties of commerce and peace with several African coastal rulers, the slave trade received official sanction. So far as the Africans were concerned, the trade represented no striking new economic activity, since they had long been involved in regional and long-distance trade across the continent. This was simply the opening of contacts with a new and more distant commercial partner. This event is notable because of the persistent myth that European powers raided the African coasts for slaves, marching into the interior and kidnapping hundreds of thousands of helpless and hapless victims. In actuality, the early slave trade involved a reciprocal relationship between European purchasers and African sellers, with the Portuguese monopolizing trade along the coastlands of tropical Africa for the first century after making contact there. Trading itself was confined to coastal strongholds where slaves, most of them captured in the interior by other Africans, were sold on terms agreed to by the African sellers. In return for gold, pepper, ivory, and slaves, African slave merchants received attractively priced European guns, horses, bars of iron and copper, brass pots and tankards, glass beads, rum, and, especially, textiles. These merchants occupied an economic role not unlike that of the Iroquois middlemen in the fur trade with Europeans.

Slavery was not a new social phenomenon for either Europeans or Africans. It flourished in ancient Greece and Rome, in early modern Russia and eastern Europe, in the Middle East, and in the Mediterranean world. Slavery had gradually died out in Western Europe by the fourteenth century, although the status of serf was not too different in social reality from that of the slave. But of most importance, slavery and serfdom had nothing to do with skin color in any of these regions.

Within Africa itself, slavery had also existed for centuries. Like other peoples, Africans accepted it without question as a part of human organization and an important part of accumulating wealth. However, slavery involved personal service, often for a limited period of time, rather than lifelong, degraded, agricultural labor. Slavery of a similar sort had also existed in Europe, mostly as the result of Christians enslaving Muslims and Muslims enslaving Christians during centuries of religious wars. One became a slave by being an "outsider" or an "infidel," by being captured in war, by voluntarily selling oneself into slavery to obtain money for one's family, or by committing heinous crimes. Enslavement severely restricted an individual's rights and sharply limited opportunities for upward movement, but the enslaved were regarded nevertheless as members of society who deserved protection under the law and were entitled to certain rights, including education, marriage, and parenthood. Slaves in Africa often served as soldiers, administrators, and even royal advisors. Of most importance, the status of slave was not irrevocable and did not automatically pass on to the slave's children.

For centuries, African societies had been involved in an overland slave trade that transported black slaves from West Africa across the Sahara Desert to Roman Europe and the Middle East. But this was an occasional rather than a systematic trade, and it was designed to provide the trading nations of the Mediterranean with soldiers, household servants, and artisans, rather than mass agricultural labor.

The African slave trade would never have become more than a minor commerce, as it was from the 1450s to the 1490s, without a growing labor shortage created by European overseas expansion. Between 1456 and 1505, Portugal brought about 40,000 enslaved Africans to Mediterranean Europe and the Atlantic islands—the Madeiras and Canary islands. But the need for slave labor lessened in Europe as populations there began to grow in the late fifteenth century. It is possible, therefore, that were it not for the colonization of the Americas, the early slave trade might have ceased after a century or more and be remembered simply as a short-lived incident stemming from early European contacts with Africa.

When Europeans reached the Americas, the course of history changed momentously. Once Europeans found the gold and silver mines of Mexico and Peru, and later, when they discovered a new form of gold in the production of sugar, coffee, indigo, rice, and tobacco, their hunger for human labor grew astonishingly. At first, Indians seemed to be the obvious source of labor, and in some areas, such as Mexico and Brazil, Spaniards and Portuguese were able to coerce native populations into agricultural and mining labor. But European diseases ravaged native populations, and the colonizers found that Indians, far more at home in their environment than white settlers, were difficult to subjugate. Indentured white labor from the mother country was another way of meeting the demand for labor, but this source was far too limited. It was to Africa that colonizing Europeans ultimately resorted. Formerly a new source of trade, the continent now became transformed in the European view into the repository of vast supplies of human labor—"black gold."

From the early sixteenth to the late nineteenth centuries, for 366 years, Europeans transported Africans out of their ancestral homelands to fill the labor needs in their colonies of North and South America and the Caribbean. The most recent estimates, always slippery, place the number who reached the shores of the Western Hemisphere at about 10.7 million (though another million or more never survived the Middle Passage).[2] Nearly as many, in the long period from 650 to 1900, were traded northward and eastward across the Sahara, the Red Sea, and the Indian Ocean. In addition, untold millions lost their lives while being marched from the interior to the coastal trading forts or during the "Middle Passage" across the Atlantic. Even before the English arrived in the Chesapeake Bay in 1607, the Spanish and Portuguese had carried several 100,000 enslaved Africans to their Caribbean and South American colonies. Before European nations outlawed the slave trade in the nineteenth century, far more Africans than Europeans had crossed the Atlantic Ocean and taken up life in the Americas. Black slaves, as one eighteenth-century Englishman put it, became "the strength and the sinews of this western world."[3]

Although the Spanish began to transport enslaved Africans across the Atlantic to work in the gold mines of Hispaniola in 1510, it was sugar that transformed the African slave trade. Produced in Asia and the eastern Mediterranean world since the eighth century, sugar was for centuries a costly exotic item confined to sweetening the diet of the rich. By the mid-1400s, the liking for the taste of sweetness had spread rapidly, and the center of sugar cane production had shifted to the Madeira Islands off the northwest coast of Africa. Here, for the first time, an expanding European nation, Portugal, established an overseas plantation society based on slave labor. The plantation system—composed of large landholding, forced gang labor, and production of cash crops marketed in Europe—formed the backbone of European mercantilism,

the economic system whereby Europe's colonies produced wealth for the benefit of home countries.

From the Madeira Islands, the cultivation of sugar spread to Portuguese Brazil in the 1560s and then to Barbados and other tiny specks of land dotting the Caribbean in the first half of the seventeenth century. By this time, Europeans were acquiring an almost insatiable taste for sweetness. Sugar became one of the first luxuries transformed into a necessary item in the diets of the masses of Europe. The wife of the poorest English laborer took sugar in her tea by 1750, it was said. "Together with other plantation products such as coffee, rum, and tobacco," writes one anthropologist, "sugar formed part of a complex of 'proletarian hunger-killers,' and played a crucial role in the linked contribution that Caribbean slaves, Indian peasants, and European urban proletarians were able to make to the growth of western civilization."[4]

Once established on a large scale, the Atlantic slave trade dramatically altered the pattern of slave recruitment in Africa. At first, led by economic and political elites, Africans sold to Europeans individuals captured in occasional wars or those whose criminal acts had cost them their tribal rights. But the vast new demand for a New World labor supply changed this process because criminals and "outsiders" could not be found in sufficient number to satisfy the growing European demand. Therefore, African kings, using European guns, resorted to warfare against their neighbors as a way of obtaining "black gold" with which to trade. By 1730, Europeans were providing about 180,000 weapons a year to African slave traders. The spread of kidnapping and organized violence in Africa soon became vital to commercial relations with European powers, while simultaneously muscling up the sway of the most militarily effective kingdoms. By the 1750s, slave traders were removing about 50,000 Africans each year.

[2]David Eltis and David Richardson, *Atlas of the Transatlantic Slave Trade* (New Haven, CT, 2010). http://www.slavevoyages.org.
[3]Eric Williams, *Capitalism and Slavery* (Chapel Hill, NC, 1966), p. 30.
[4]Sidney W. Mintz, "Time, Sugar, & Sweetness," *Marxist Perspectives,* No. 8 (1979), p. 60.

In the forcible recruitment of slaves, young males—most of them 10 to 24 years old—were preferred over women. Primarily, this represented the preference of New World plantation owners for male field laborers. But it also reflected the decision of vanquished African villagers to yield up more men than women to raiding parties because women were the chief agriculturists in their society and, in matrilineal and matrilocal kinship systems, were too valuable to be sacrificed.

The slave trade itself became an immensely profitable enterprise. In the several centuries of intensive slave trading that followed the establishment of New World sugar plantations, European nations warred constantly for trading advantages on the West African coast. The coastal forts, the focal points of the trade, became strategic targets in the wars of empire. The great Portuguese slaving fort at Elmina on the Gold Coast, begun in 1481, was captured a century and a half later by the Dutch. The primary fort on the Guinea coast, started by the Swedes, passed through the hands of the Danes, the English, and the Dutch between 1652 and 1664. As the demand for slaves in the Americas rose explosively after 1650, European competition for trading rights on the West African coast grew intense. By the end of the century, monopolies for supplying European plantations in the Americas with their annual quotas of slaves became a major issue of European diplomacy. The Dutch were the primary victors in the battle for the Slave Coast. Hence, for most of the century, a majority of enslaved Africans who were fed into the expanding Western Hemisphere markets crossed the Atlantic in Dutch ships.

Not until the last third of the seventeenth century were the English of any importance in the slave trade. English attempts to break into the profitable trade began only in 1663, when Charles II, recently restored to the English throne, granted a charter to the Royal Adventurers to Africa, a joint-stock company headed by the king's brother, the Duke of York. Superseded by the Royal African Company in 1672,

these companies enjoyed the exclusive right to carry slaves to England's overseas plantations. For thirty-four years after 1663, each slave they brought across the Atlantic bore the brand *DY* for the Duke of York, who himself became king in 1685. In 1698, individual merchants pressured Parliament to break the Royal African Company's monopoly. Thrown open to individual entrepreneurs, the English slave trade grew enormously. In the 1680s, the Royal African Company had transported about 5,000 to 6,000 slaves annually (though interlopers brought in thousands more). In the first decade of free trade, the annual average rose above 20,000. English involvement in the trade increased for the remainder of the eighteenth century until, by the 1790s, England had become the foremost slave-trading nation in Europe. In the 366 years of the Atlantic slave trade about one third of all captives crossing that Atlantic were on ships organized and outfitted in England, even though England withdrew from the slave trade in 1808.

Capture and Transport of Slaves

No accounts of the initial enslavement of Africans, no matter how vivid, can quite convey the pain and demoralization that must have accompanied the forced march to the west coast of Africa and the subsequent loading aboard ships of those who had fallen captive to the African suppliers of the European slave traders. One historian has called it "the most traumatizing mass human migration in modern history."[5]

As the demand for African slaves doubled and redoubled in the eighteenth century, the hinterlands of Western and Central Africa were invaded again and again by the armies and agents of both coastal and interior kings. Perhaps three-quarters of the slaves transported to English North America came from the part of Western Africa that lies between the Senegal and Niger

[5]Nathan I. Huggins, *Black Odyssey: The Afro-American Ordeal under Slavery* (New York, 1977), p. 25.

rivers and the Gulf of Biafra. Most of the others were enslaved in Angola on the west coast of Central Africa. State-sponsored slaving activities in these areas were responsible for considerably depopulating the region in the eighteenth and nineteenth centuries.

Once captured, slaves were marched to the sea in "coffles," or trains. A Scotsman, Mungo Park, described the coffle he marched with for 550 miles through Gambia at the end of the eighteenth century. It consisted of seventy-three men, women, and children tied together by the neck with leather thongs. Several captives attempted to commit suicide by eating clay; another was abandoned after being badly stung by bees; still others died of exhaustion and hunger. After two months, with many of its members physically depleted by thirst, hunger, and exposure, the coffle reached the coast. There, their captors herded them into fortified enclosures called barracoons.

The anger, bewilderment, and desolation that accompanied the forced march, the first leg of the 5,000-mile journey to the Americas, only increased with the actual transfer of slaves to European ship captains, who carried their human cargo to the Americas. "As the slaves come down to Fida from the inland country," wrote one European trader in the late seventeenth century, "they are put into a booth or prison, built for that purpose, near the beach . . . and when the Europeans are to receive them, they are brought out into a large plain, where the [ships'] surgeons examine every part of every one of them, to the smallest member, men and women being all stark naked. Such as are allowed good and sound, are set on one side, and the others by themselves; which slaves so rejected are called Mackrons, being above 35 years of age, or defective in their lips, eyes, or teeth, or grown grey; or that have the venereal disease, or any other imperfection."[6] Such dehumanizing treatment was part of the commercial process by which slave traders selected and bargained for "merchandise." But it was also part of the psychological assault meant to strip away self-respect and self-identity from the Africans.

Cruelty followed cruelty. After purchase, many slaves were branded with a hot iron signifying the company, whether Spanish, Portuguese, English, French, or Dutch, that had purchased them. Thus were members of "preliterate" societies first introduced to the alphabetic symbols of "advanced" cultures. "The branded slaves," one account related, "are returned to their former booths" where they were imprisoned until a full human cargo could be assembled.[7] Such gathering of a full cargo involved moving along the African coast from port to port. On average this coasting period lasted about three months in the early eighteenth century and doubled as the century wore on. Often within sight of the African coastline, many thousands of Africans died before the transatlantic Middle Passage began.

The next psychological wrench came with the ferrying of slaves, in large canoes, to the waiting ships at anchor in the harbor. An English captain described the desperation of slaves who were about to lose touch with their ancestral land and embark upon a vast ocean that many had never seen. "The Negroes are so willful and loathe to leave their own country, that they have often leaped out of the canoes, boat and ship, into the sea, and kept under water till they were drowned, to avoid being taken up and saved by our boats, which pursued them; they having a more dreadful apprehension of Barbados than we can have of hell."[8] Part of this fear was the common belief that on the other side of the ocean, Africans would be eaten by the white savages. "I was now persuaded that I had gotten into a world of bad spirits," wrote Olaudah Equiano, one of the few slaves to publish a firsthand account of his enslavement, "and that they were going to kill me. Their complexions, too,

---

[6]Quoted in Basil Davidson, *The African Slave Trade: Precolonial History,* 1450–1850 (Boston, MA, 1961), p. 92.
[7]Ibid.
[8]Quoted in Daniel P. Mannix and Malcom Cowley, *Black Cargoes: A History of the Atlantic Slave Trade, 1518–1856* (New York, 1962), p. 48.

"Negro's Cannoes Carrying Slaves on Board of Ships at Manfroe," in Jean Barbot, "A description of the Coasts of North and South Guinea . . . "

(Courtesy The New York Public Library/Art Resource)

differing so much from ours, their long hair, and the language they spoke . . . united to confirm me in this belief."[9] Also feeding suicidal urges was the African belief in the transmigration of the soul upon death to the homeland. Death in this sense was preferable to a life of unending misery.

The fear that inspired suicide while still on African soil intensified on the second leg of the voyage—the "Middle Passage" from the West African coast to the New World. Conditions aboard ship were horrendous, even though it was to the advantage of the ship captains to deliver

as many slaves as possible on the other side of the Atlantic. Pitiful rations led to undernourishment, limited water produced dehydration, confinement below decks in leg irons for weeks spread diseases, and the absence of basic hygiene ate at self-respect. Olaudah Equiano described how he was "put down under the decks, and there I received such a salutation in my nostrils as I had never experienced in my life: so that with the loathsomeness of the stench and crying together, I became so sick and low that I was not able to eat. . . . I now wished for the last friend, death, to relieve

[9]*The Interesting Narrative of the Life of Olaudah Equiano*, written by himself, edited by Robert J. Allison (Boston, MA, 1995), p. 53.

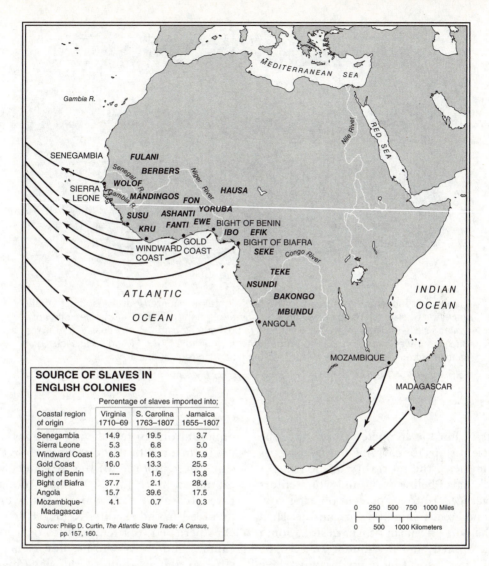

SOURCE OF SLAVES IN
ENGLISH COLONIES

Coastal region of origin	Percentage of slaves imported into;		
	Virginia 1710–69	S. Carolina 1763–1807	Jamaica 1655–1807
Senegambia	14.9	19.5	3.7
Sierra Leone	5.3	6.8	5.0
Windward Coast	6.3	16.3	5.9
Gold Coast	16.0	13.3	25.5
Bight of Benin	----	1.6	13.8
Bight of Biafra	37.7	2.1	28.4
Angola	15.7	39.6	17.5
Mozambique-Madagascar	4.1	0.7	0.3

Source: Philip D. Curtin, *The Atlantic Slave Trade: A Census,* pp. 157, 160.

me; but soon, . . . on my refusing to eat, one [sailor] held me fast . . . while the other flogged me severely."[10]

For ship captains, good profits hinged on preserving rather than destroying life. Yet brutality was endemic, both in pitching overboard any slaves who fell sick on the voyage and in punishing offenders with almost sadistic intensity as a way of creating a climate of fear that would stifle insurrectionist tendencies. John Atkins, aboard an English slaver in 1721, described how the captain "whipped and scarified" several plotters of rebellion and sentenced others "to cruel deaths, making them first eat the heart and liver of one of them killed. The woman he hoisted up by the thumbs, whipped and slashed her with knives, before the other slaves, till she died."[11] Though the naval

---

[10]Ibid., p. 54.
[11]Quoted in Davidson, *African Slave Trade . . . ,* pp. 94–95.

Pamphlets published in England in the late eighteenth century often used schematic drawings of slave ships to show the inhumanity of "tight packing." In this depiction of a 320-ton slave-trading vessel, there appears to be a human cargo of 451 enslaved Africans. Because it was expected that numerous slaves would die in the "Middle Passage," ship captains often crowded more slaves into the hold than regulations allowed.

Source: Library of Congress Rare Book and Special Collections Division Washington, D.C [LC-USZ62-44000].

architects of Europe competed to produce the most efficient ships for carrying human cargoes to the Americas, the mortality on board, for both black slaves below decks and white sailors above, averaged 10 to 20 percent on each voyage. On one French ship 408 Africans perished at sea. The port physician of Charleston, South Carolina, opined "it is a wonder any escape with life" after inspecting many arriving slave ships.[12]

That Africans sometimes attempted suicide and mutiny during the ocean crossing shows that even the heartless violence used in capturing, branding, selling, and transporting them from one continent to another was not enough to make the captives submit tamely to their fate. Recent analyses of more than 27,000 slave ship voyages show that shipboard revolts erupted

on about one of ten slaving voyages with half of the insurrections occurring while the slave ships were moored off the African coast while taking on more slaves. Women, though separated from men on slave ships, were often involved in the revolts. Nearly 100,000 Africans perished in attempting to overpower the captain and crew, who used every means possible to deliver them to the slave markets in the Americas. An eighteenth-century historian of slavery, attempting to justify the terroristic devices employed by slavers, argued that "the many acts of violence they [the enslaved] have committed by murdering whole crews and destroying ships when they had it in their power to do so have made these rigors wholly chargeable on their own bloody and malicious disposition which calls for the same confinement as

---

[12]Edmund Berkeley and Dorothy Smith Berkeley, *Dr. Alexander Garden of Charles Town* (Chapel Hill, NC, 1969), p. 124.

if they were wolves or wild boars."[13] The modern reader may suspect English self-justification in this characterization of enslaved Africans, but it also shows that submissiveness was often not a trait of those who were forcibly carried to the Americas. So great was this resistance that special techniques of torture had to be devised to cope with the thousands of slaves who were determined to starve themselves to death on the Middle Passage rather than reach the Western Hemisphere in chains. Ship captains frequently ordered brutal whippings and hot coals applied to the lips to open the mouths of recalcitrant slaves. When this did not suffice, a special instrument, the *speculum oris,* or mouth opener, was employed to wrench apart the jaws of a resistant slave.

Taking into consideration the mortality involved in the capture, the forced march to the African coast, and the Middle Passage, probably not more than one in two captured Africans lived to see the Americas or lasted there more than a few years. Many of those who did survive must have been psychologically numbed as well as physically depleted by the experience. But one further step remained in the soul-testing process of enslavement—the auctioning to a colonial master and transportation to his place of residence, where typically every fourth arriving African would die within the first four years on American soil. All in all, the relocation of any African brought westward across the Atlantic may have averaged about six months from the time of capture to the time of arrival at the plantation of a European slave master. During this protracted personal crisis, the slave was completely cut off from most that was familiar—family, wider kinship networks, community life, and other forms of social and psychological security. Still facing these victims of the European demand for cheap labor was adaptation to a new physical environment, a new language, new work routines, and, of most

importance, a life in which bondage for themselves and their offspring was unending.

Slavery in the North American Colonies

Even though they were long familiar with Spanish, Dutch, and Portuguese use of slave labor, English colonists did not turn immediately to Africa to solve the problem of cultivating labor-intensive crops. When they did, the English were merely copying their European rivals as they worked to fill the colonial labor gap. No doubt, the stereotype of Africans as uncivilized made it easier for the English to fasten chains upon them. But the fact remains that the English came to the Americas, like the Spanish, Portuguese, Dutch, and French, to make a fortune as well as to build religious and political havens. Given the long hostility they had borne toward Indians and their experience in enslaving them, any scruples the English might have had about enslaving Africans quickly disappeared.

Making it all the more natural to employ Africans as a slave labor force in the mainland colonies was the precedent that English planters set on their Caribbean sugar islands. In Barbados, Jamaica, and the Leeward Islands (Antigua, Montserrat, Nevis, and St. Christopher), the English in the second and third quarters of the seventeenth century learned to copy their European rivals in molding Africans into a sugar-field slave labor force. By 1680, when there were not more than 7,000 enslaved Africans in mainland North America and the institution of slavery was not yet unalterably fixed, upwards of 130,000 Africans had been brought to toil on sugar plantations in the English West Indies. Trade and communication were extensive between the Caribbean and mainland colonists, so settlers in North America had intimate knowledge concerning the potentiality of slave labor.

---

[13]Edward Long, *The History of Jamaica* (London, 1774), quoted in Mannix and Cowley, *Black Cargoes . . . ,* p. 111.

Not surprisingly, then, the North American colonists turned to the international slave trade to fill their labor needs. What *is* surprising is that the North American colonists did not turn to slavery more quickly than they did. For more than a half-century in Virginia and Maryland, primarily White indentured servants and not enslaved Africans labored in the tobacco fields. Moreover, those Africans who were imported before about 1660 were held in various degrees of servitude, most for limited periods and only a few for life.

The transformation of the labor force in the Southern colonies came only in the last third of the seventeenth century in Virginia and Maryland and in the first third of the eighteenth century in North and South Carolina. The reasons for this shift to a slave-based agricultural economy in the South are twofold. First, English entry into the African slave trade gave the Southern planter an opportunity to purchase slaves more readily and more cheaply than before. Cheap labor was what every tobacco or rice planter sought, and when the price of slave labor dipped below that of indentured labor, the demand for Africans increased. Second, the supply of White servants from England began to dry up in the late seventeenth century, and those who did cross the Atlantic were spread among a growing number of colonies. Thus, in the late seventeenth century, the number of Africans imported into the Chesapeake colonies began to grow, while the flow of White indentured servants diminished to a trickle. As late as 1671, the enslaved made up less than 5 percent of Virginia's population and were outnumbered at least three to one by White indentured servants. In Maryland, the situation was much the same. But within a generation, by about 1700, Africans represented one-sixth of the population and probably a majority of the labor force. A Maryland census of 1707 tabulated 3,003 White bound laborers and 4,657 black slaves. Five years later, the slave population had almost doubled. Within another generation White indentured servitude was declining rapidly, and in all the Southern colonies, enslaved Africans made up the backbone of the agricultural workforce. "These two words, *Negro* and *slave*," wrote one Virginian, had "by custom grown Homogenous and Convertible."[14] By 1750, enslaved Africans made up about 40 percent of the population in Maryland, Virginia, and South Carolina.

To the north, in Delaware, Pennsylvania, New Jersey, and New York, where English colonists had settled only in the last third of the 1600s, slavery took root on a more limited basis because cold winters did not allow the labor-intensive year-round crops that made massive slave labor profitable. New York was an exception and shows how a cultural preference could alter labor patterns usually determined by ecological factors. Before 1664, the Dutch had practiced slaveholding extensively, encouraged in part by the Dutch West India Company, one of the chief international suppliers of slaves. The population of New York remained largely Dutch for the remainder of the century, and the English who slowly filtered in saw no reason not to imitate Dutch slave owners. Thus, New York became the largest importer of slaves north of Maryland. In the mid-eighteenth century, the areas of original settlement around New York and Albany remained slaveholding societies with about 20 percent of the population composed of enslaved Africans and 30 to 40 percent of the White householders owning human property.

As the number of Africans increased, lawmakers constructed legal codes for strictly controlling their activities. Southern legislators largely borrowed these "black codes" from the law books of the English West Indies. Bit by bit the laws deprived the African immigrant—and a small number of enslaved Indians as well—of rights enjoyed by others, including indentured servants. Gradually, in the eyes of society and the law, the slave became chattel property, little different than a horse or mule. In this process of dehumanization, nothing was more important than the rule of hereditary lifetime service. Once servitude became perpetual, relieved only by death, the stripping away of all other rights followed

[14]Quoted in Winthrop D. Jordan, *White Over Black: American Attitudes toward the Negro, 1550–1812* (Chapel Hill, NC, 1968), p. 97.

ATLANTIC SLAVE TRADE
1550–1700

Source: David Eltis and David Richardson, *The Transatlantic Slave Trade*, pp. 200–203.

BRITISH NORTH AMERICA, 15,000
OLD WORLD, 25,100
SPANISH AMERICA, 350,600
BRITISH CARIBBEAN, 311,400
FRENCH CARIBBEAN, 37,900
DUTCH CARIBBEAN, 142,000
PORTUGESE BRAZIL, 813,700

ATLANTIC OCEAN
PACIFIC OCEAN

0   500   1000 Miles
0   500 1000 Kilometers

ATLANTIC SLAVE TRADE
1701–1800

Source: David Eltis and David Richardson, *The Transatlantic Slave Trade*, pp. 200–203.

BRITISH NORTH AMERICA AND USA, 298,000
SPANISH AMERICA, 146,000
BRITISH CARIBBEAN, 1,811,800
FRENCH CARIBBEAN, 1,000,400
DUTCH CARIBBEAN, 363,300
PORTUGESE BRAZIL, 1,990,799

ATLANTIC OCEAN
PACIFIC OCEAN

0   500   1000 Miles
0   500 1000 Kilometers

as a matter of course. When the condition of the slave mother was passed on to the child, then slavery had been extended to the womb.

With the passage of time, Africans in North America had to adapt to a more and more restricted world. Earlier in the seventeenth century they had been treated much as indentured servants, bound to labor for a specified period of years but thereafter free to work for themselves, hire out their labor, buy land, move as they pleased, and, if they wished, hold slaves themselves. But, by the 1640s, Virginia was forbidding blacks the use of firearms. In the 1660s, courts began describing marriages between white women and enslaved Africans as "shameful matches" and "the disgrace of our nation"; during the next few decades, interracial fornication became subject to unusually severe punishment, and interracial marriage was banned.

These discriminatory steps were slight, however, in comparison with the stripping away of rights that began toward the end of the century. In rapid succession slaves lost their right to testify before a court; to engage in any kind of commercial activity, either as buyer or seller; to hold property; to participate in the political process; to congregate in public places with more than two or three of their fellows; to travel without permission; and to engage in legal marriage or parenthood. In some colonies, legislatures even prohibited the right to education and religion, for lawmakers thought these might plant the germ of freedom in slaves. Step by step, White masters hedged their slaves within a legal system that made no allowance for their education, welfare, or future advancement. Even the restraints on the slave owner's freedom to deal with bondspeople in any way he or she saw fit came under attack. Early in the eighteenth century, many colonies passed laws forbidding the manumission of slaves by individual owners, a step designed to squelch the strivings of the enslaved for freedom and to discourage those who had been freed from helping fellow Africans to gain their liberty.

The movement to annul all the slave's rights had both pragmatic and psychological dimensions. The greater the proportion of slaves in the population, the greater the danger to white society, for every colonist knew that when he or she purchased a man or woman in chains, he or she had bought a potential insurrectionist. The larger the specter of black revolt, the greater the effort of White society to neutralize it by further restricting the rights and activities of slaves. Following a

black revolt in 1712 that took the lives of nine whites and wounded others, the New York legislature promptly passed a slave code that rivaled those of the Southern colonies. Throughout the Southern colonies, the fear of slave insurrection ushered in routinized violence as the means of ensuring social stability. Allied to this need for greater and greater control was the psychological compulsion to dehumanize slaves by taking from them the rights that connoted their humanity. It was far easier to rationalize the merciless exploitation of those who had been defined by law as something less than human. "The planters," wrote an Englishman in eighteenth-century Jamaica, "do not want to be told that their Negroes are human creatures. If they believe them to be of human kind, they cannot regard them . . . as no better than dogs or horses."[15]

Thus occurred one of the great paradoxes in American history—the building of what many thought would be a utopia in the wilderness upon the backs of black men and women wrenched from their African homeland and forced into a system of abject slavery. White colonists imagined America as a liberating and regenerating force, it has been pointed out, but it became instead the scene of a "grotesque inconsistency." In the land heralded for freedom and individual opportunity, the practice of slavery, unknown for centuries in the mother country, became as much a part of the landscape as trees and rivers. As in other parts of the Americas, North America became the scene of "a disturbing retrogression from the course of historical progress."[16]

The mass enslavement of Africans intensified White racial prejudice. Once slave codes entered the law books, slavery cast Africans into such lowly roles that the initial bias against them was confirmed and strengthened. Initially, unfavorable impressions of Africans had coincided with labor needs to bring about their mass enslavement. But it required slavery itself to crystallize the negative racial feelings into a deep and almost unshakable prejudice that grew for

[15]Long, *The History of Jamaica* (London, 1774), II, Book 2, p. 270.
[16]David Brion Davis, *The Problem of Slavery in Western Culture* (Ithaca, NY, 1966), p. 25.

centuries. Caught in the web of perpetual servitude, the slave had little opportunity to prove the White stereotype wrong. Socially and legally defined as less than human, African Americans became a truly servile, degraded people in the eyes of the Europeans. This view was used as further reason to keep them in slavery, for it was argued that they were worth nothing better and were incapable of occupying any higher role.

Slavery in North and South America

Because slavery existed in virtually every part of the Americas, the best way to discover what was unique about the system of bondage that formed in the North American colonies is to compare it with slavery in other regions of the Americas. Fewer than one in twenty-five slaves brought to the Western Hemisphere came to British North America. The 280,000 Africans who arrived there between 1619 and 1780 were dwarfed by the 2.2 million transported to Portuguese Brazil, the 2.7 million taken to British, French, and Dutch plantations in the West Indies, and the 300,000 imported into Spanish America.

How did slaves fare in different parts of the Americas, and how can we explain the differences in their treatment, their opportunities for emancipation, and their chances, once free, to carve out a worthwhile niche for themselves in society?

The first historians to study slavery comparatively in the Americas argued that crucial differences evolved between the status of slaves in the Spanish or Portuguese colonies and the English colonies. These differences, they maintained, largely account for the fact that racial mixture is much more extensive today in Latin America than in North America, that formal policies of segregation and discrimination were never embodied in Latin American law, and that the racial tension and conflict that has characterized twentieth- and twenty-first-century American life has been modulated in Latin American countries such as Brazil. Interracial marriage can be taken

as one illuminating example of these differences. "Miscegenation," a word invented in New York City in 1864 to sneer at racial intermarriage, has never been prohibited in Brazil and other parts of South and Central America, and such prohibition was thought a senseless and an artificial separation of people. In the American colonies, however, White cultural standard-bearers thought otherwise. Legal prohibitions against interracial mixing began in the mid-seventeenth century, and virtually every North American colony prohibited mixed marriages by the early eighteenth century. Modified from time to time, these laws remained in force throughout the period of slavery and in many states continued after the abolition of slavery. As late as 1948, mixed marriages were prohibited by law in twenty-nine states, including seventeen outside the South. Not until 1967 did the Supreme Court strike down state laws prohibiting interracial marriage.

Such differences as these, it has been argued, indicate that slavery in Spanish and Portuguese America was never as harsh as in British America, nor were the doors to eventual freedom so tightly closed. In Latin America, Africans mixed socially and sexually with the White population from the beginning; they were never completely stripped of political, economic, social, and religious rights; they were frequently encouraged to work for their freedom; and, when the gate to freedom was opened, they found it possible to carve a place of dignity for themselves. In the North American colonies, by contrast, slaves lost all their rights by the early eighteenth century and were thereafter treated as mere chattel property. Emancipation was rare, and several colonies nearly prohibited it in the eighteenth century. Those African Americans who did obtain their freedom, especially after the American Revolution, found themselves consigned to the lowliest positions in society. Resenting the aspirations of free blacks, White lawmakers gradually rescinded the social and political rights initially granted them as citizens. In entitling his book *Slave and Citizen,* Frank Tannenbaum, a pioneer in the comparative study of slavery, summarized his view of the differing fates of the African migrant in the two continents of the Western Hemisphere.[17]

By what series of events or historical accidents had the Africans in the Latin American colonies been placed on the road to freedom, while in English North America the road traveled by blacks always led to a dead end, even after freedom was granted? Tannenbaum and those who followed him suggested that the answer lay in the different ideological and cultural climates in which the Africans struggled in the Americas. Those enslaved by the Spanish and Portuguese entered a colonial culture that was Catholic in religion, semimedieval and authoritarian in its political institutions, conservative and paternalistic in its social relations, and Roman in its system of law. Africans brought to North America, by contrast, confronted a culture that was Protestant in religion, libertarian and "modern" in its political institutions, individualistic in its social relations, and Anglo-Saxon in its system of law. Ironically it was the "premodern" Spanish and Portuguese culture that protected slaves and eventually prepared them for something better than slavery. The Catholic Church not only sent its clergy to the New World in far greater numbers than did the Protestant churches, but also devoted itself to preserving the human rights of Africans. Affirming that no individual, no matter how lowly his or her position or corrupt his or her behavior, was unworthy in the sight of God, the Catholic clergy toiled to convert people of every color and condition, wherever and whenever they found them. Indians and Africans in the Latin American colonies therefore became fit subjects for the zeal of the Jesuit, Dominican, and Franciscan priests. The church, in viewing masses of enslaved Indians and Africans as future Christians, had a tempering effect on what slave masters might do with their slaves or what legislators, reflecting planter opinion, might legislate into law.

In a similar way the application of Roman law in the Iberian colonies served to protect the slave from becoming mere chattel property, for Roman law recognized the rights of slaves and the obligations of masters to them. The slave undeniably occupied the lowest rung on the social ladder, but he or she remained a member of the community, entitled to legal protection from a rapacious or sadistic master.

Still a third institution mediated between master and slave—the government itself. Highly centralized, the Spanish and Portuguese political systems revolved around the power of the monarch and the aristocracy, and this power was expected to radiate out from its metropolitan centers in Europe to the New World colonies. Colonies existed under strict royal governance, and since the Crown, closely tied to the Catholic Church, was dedicated to protecting the rights of slaves, slave owners in the colonies had to answer to a social policy formulated at home. In sum, a set of interconnecting institutions, derived from a conservative, paternalistic culture, worked to the advantage of enslaved Africans by standing between them and their masters. Iberian institutions, transplanted to the New World, prohibited slave owners from exercising unbridled rein over their slaves and ensured that the slave, though exploited, was also protected and eventually prepared for full membership in colonial society.

In the English North America and Caribbean colonies, it is argued, these intermediating institutions were notably absent. Slave masters were far freer to follow their impulses in their treatment of slaves and in formulating laws that undergirded slavery. In North America, government was more localized and democratic, church and state more separate, and individuals less fettered by tradition and authority. Hence slaves were unusually at the mercy of their masters. The Protestant Church had little interest in proselytizing slaves. When it did, its authority was far more locally based than in the Spanish and Portuguese colonies and therefore subject to the influence of the leading slave owners of the area.

Government too was less centralized; England allowed the colonists to formulate much of

[17]Frank Tannenbaum, *Slave and Citizen: The Negro in the Americas* (New York, 1946).

their own law and exercised only a weak regulatory power over the plantations. Anglo-Saxon law, transferred to the New World, was silent on the subject of slavery because slavery had not existed in England for centuries. This silence left colonists free to devise new law, as harsh and exploitative as they wished, to cope with the labor system they were erecting. In North America, it is maintained, slave owners molded a highly individualistic, libertarian, and acquisitive culture that brooked few checks on the right of slave owners to exploit their human property exactly as they saw fit. In the Anglo-American culture, property rights became transcendently important. With relatively few institutional restraints to inhibit slave owners, nothing stood between new African immigrants and a system of total subjugation. Consequently, Tannenbaum and others have argued, a far more closed and dehumanizing system of slavery evolved in the more "enlightened" and "modern" environment of the English colonies than in the more feudalistic and authoritarian milieu of the Spanish and Portuguese colonies.

In recent decades, historians, sociologists, and anthropologists have challenged this analysis of slavery and race relations in the Americas. By looking too intently at Spanish and Portuguese laws, traditions, and institutions in the mother countries, historians underestimated the gap that often separated legal pronouncements from social reality. Is it possible that in the Spanish and Portuguese law books, slaves were carefully protected, but in actuality their lives were as bad as or worse than in the English plantations? Laws do not always reflect actual social conditions. For example, if we had only the post–Civil War legal statutes as a guide to the status of the African Americans in the nineteenth and twentieth centuries, we might conclude that they enjoyed equality with White Americans in the modern era because the laws guarantee nothing less. But what the law specified and what actually occurred are two different things.

Looking more closely at local conditions in various New World colonies, historians have found that the alleged differences between North and South American slavery do not loom so large. Where the Catholic Church and royal authority were well established, such as in urban areas, the treatment of slaves was indeed more humane than in areas of the American colonial South, such as South Carolina, where the Protestant churches took only shallow root. But in rural areas of the Spanish and Portuguese colonies, where slavery was most extensively practiced, the church's sway was less strong and the authority of the Spanish colonial officials was more tenuous. In these areas individual slave masters dealt with their slaves as they saw fit, much as in the English colonies.

Moreover, recent studies show that wide variations in the treatment of slaves occurred *within* the colonies of each European nation. In Puritan New England and Quaker Pennsylvania, conditions were never so inhumane as in the South, partly because the Puritan and Quaker churches acted as a restraint on the behavior of slave owners and partly because slaves, always a small percentage of the population, were more frequently employed as artisans and household servants than in the South, where mass agricultural labor was the norm. Likewise, conditions were far better for slaves in the Brazilian urban center of Recife than on the frontier plantations of the remote southern province of Rio Grande do Sul.

Other factors, quite separate from the ideological or cultural climate of a given area, counted greatly. The most important element shaping a slave society was its economic base. Where Africans worked in the plantation system, producing cash crops such as sugar, coffee, tobacco, and rice, they suffered thralldom at its brutal worst. In these areas, the conditions of human life could be appalling. These included English rice plantations in the eighteenth century, Portuguese coffee plantations in the nineteenth century, and sugar plantations of all European colonizers from the seventeenth to the nineteenth centuries. Maximizing profit was the overriding goal on such plantations, and it was often achieved by literally working slaves to death and then replacing them with newly imported Africans.

When agricultural areas were enjoying boom times and rapid expansion, as in the cases of eighteenth-century South Carolina and nineteenth-century Cuba, the exploitation of slaves was usually found at its extreme limits because special incentives existed for driving bondsmen and bondswomen to the limit of human endurance. Also of great significance in the lives of slaves was the kind of crop they were employed at growing. Sugar was particularly labor intensive, its cultivation requiring the most strenuous, debilitating labor, as opposed, for example, to wheat or corn. Perhaps nowhere was the treatment of slaves so callously regarded as on the sugar plantations of the Caribbean, where the combination of absentee ownership, the work regimen, and the highly capitalized nature of the economic system made life a living hell for slaves, regardless of whether they toiled on English Barbados, Dutch Surinam, French Saint Dominigue, or Spanish Cuba.

In fringe areas, by contrast, where slaves were used for occasional labor or as domestic servants and artisans, conditions were better. In northerly areas, where only one crop a year was possible, winter brought slack times. In cities the work rhythms were not so intense, and the social climate encouraged a religious and humanitarian ideology that tempered the brutality inherent in the master-slave relationship. In Anglo-Dutch New York City and Portuguese Recife, as well as in rural New England and New France, the chance for slaves to carve out a meaningful life was much greater than on the expanding cash crop plantations.

Another factor affecting the dynamics of particular slave societies was the simple ratio of blacks to whites. Where slaves represented a small fraction of the total population, such as in New England and the mid-Atlantic English colonies, slave codes did not strip African Americans of all their rights. Religion and education were commonly believed to be beneficial to slaves, and no protests were heard when Quakers and Anglicans set up schools for Negroes in places such as Boston and Philadelphia. Marriage was customary, and black parents often baptized their children in the Protestant churches, even though death brought burial in a separate "strangers" graveyard. Slaves were freer to congregate in public places and were recognized before courts of law in these areas.

From Maryland to Georgia, however, conditions were markedly different. In the Chesapeake colonies, slaves represented about 40 percent of the population by the mid-eighteenth century, and in South Carolina they outnumbered whites at all times after 1710. In these areas, lawmakers created more repressive slave codes. The same was true in the English Caribbean islands, where whites were vastly outnumbered throughout the eighteenth century. Because they were surrounded by those whom they had enslaved, control became a crucial factor for white slave owners, who lived in perpetual fear of black insurrections. Numerically inferior, they took every precaution to ensure that their slaves would have no opportunity to organize and plot against them. Living in a kind of garrison state amid constantly circulating rumors of black revolt, White planters heaped punishment on black offenders and retaliated with ferocity against black aggression in the hope that they could cow other slaves into submissiveness. Castration for sexual offenses against whites and burning at the stake for plotting or participating in insurrection were common punishments in colonies with a high proportion of black slaves. But where slaves represented only a small fraction of the population, usually no such elaborate attempts were made to define their inferior status in precise detail or to leave them so completely at the mercy of their owners.

Two other factors affecting the lives of slaves operated independently of the national backgrounds of their owners. The first was whether or not the slave trade was still open in a particular area. When the slave trade continuously brought new supplies of Africans, the treatment of slaves was usually harsh, for a slave worked to death could easily be replaced. Where the slave trade was closed, however, masters took greater precautions to safeguard their capital investment, and that was in human property.

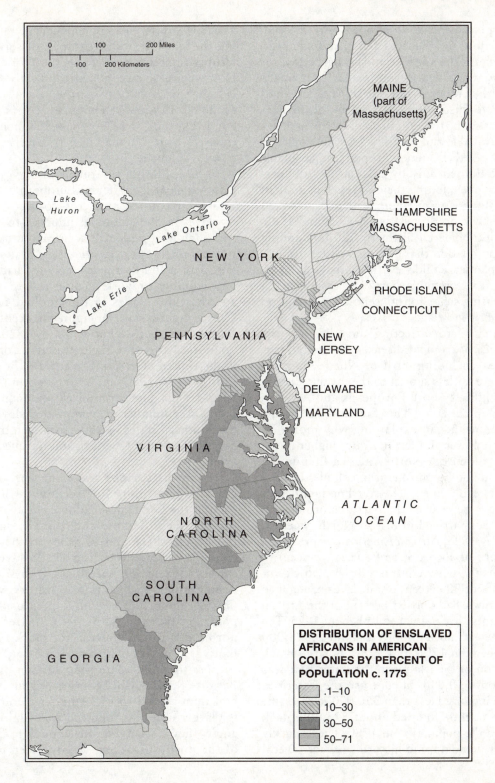

Lake Huron

Lake Ontario

Lake Erie

NEW YORK

PENNSYLVANIA

VIRGINIA

NORTH CAROLINA

SOUTH CAROLINA

GEORGIA

MAINE (part of Massachusetts)

NEW HAMPSHIRE

MASSACHUSETTS

RHODE ISLAND

CONNECTICUT

NEW JERSEY

DELAWARE

MARYLAND

ATLANTIC OCEAN

0   100   200 Miles

0   100   200 Kilometers

DISTRIBUTION OF ENSLAVED AFRICANS IN AMERICAN COLONIES BY PERCENT OF POPULATION c. 1775

.1–10

10–30

30–50

50–71

Slave replacement could happen only through reproduction, and that was a long and an uncertain process. The sugar island of Barbados, for example, was a death trap for Africans in the eighteenth century. From one-third to one-half of all slaves died within three years of their arrival. But with fresh supplies of African slaves readily available and with few restraints on their treatment of their human property, sugar planters were limited only by calculations of cost-efficiency in exploiting their slaves. This state of affairs, along with ravaging epidemics, resulted in a ghastly mortality. Between 1712 and 1762, deaths outnumbered births by 120,000 among a slave population that averaged about 50,000. English planters could view this carnage as an inevitable, if a regrettable, part of amassing wealth by producing sugar for household consumption in every British village.

A final factor affecting slave life was the prevalence of tropical diseases. In the temperate zones, including most of North America, slaves were far less subject to the ravaging fevers that swept away both Europeans and Africans in the tropical zone. This factor is of the utmost importance in explaining why mortality rates were lower and fertility rates higher in the English colonies of North America than in the Caribbean and South American colonies of various European powers. The startling fact is that less than 4 percent of the Africans brought to the Americas arrived in British North America, and yet by 1825, African Americans represented 36 percent of all peoples of African descent in the hemisphere. By contrast, Brazil, which imported about 38 percent of all slaves brought to the Americas, had only 31 percent of the African descendants alive in the hemisphere in 1825. The British West Indies imported about 1,818,000 slaves between 1700 and 1790, but the black population of the islands in the latter year was only about 350,000. In contrast, the American colonies imported less than 350,000 in the same period, but they counted about 575,000 black people in the population in 1780. These starkly different demographic histories reflect several variables—differences in male-female ratios during the slave period, treatment of slaves, and fertility rates among free Negroes, for example. However, these factors may ultimately sort out, it is clear that the Africans who were brought to the North American colonies, except those in South Carolina and Georgia, had a much better chance for survival than their counterparts in the tropical colonies.

Alongside the treatment of slaves on the plantations of the different European colonizers, we need to consider the access to freedom found by slaves in one colony as opposed to another. Although historians still argue about comparative treatment, they largely agree that slaves in the Spanish and Portuguese colonies had greater opportunities to work themselves free of bondage than did slaves in the English colonies. Census figures for the eighteenth century are fragmentary, but we know that by 1820, the ratio of free Negroes to slaves was about one to six in the United States, one to three in Brazil, one to four in Mexico, and one to two in Cuba. In Spanish Cuba alone, free blacks outnumbered by 30,000 the number of manumitted slaves in all the Southern states in 1800, although the black population of the American South tripled that of Cuba.

Some historians have interpreted this greater opportunity for freedom in the Spanish and the Portuguese colonies as evidence of the relatively flexible and humane nature of the system there and as proof of the Iberian commitment to preparing the enslaved African for citizenship. But others, who argue that demographic and economic factors were supremely important, are more persuasive. They point out that the White *need* for free blacks, not humanitarian concern for black freedom, motivated most Spanish and Portuguese slave owners to emancipate their human property. Because the English, Scots-Irish, and Germans had immigrated to the American colonies in far larger numbers than the Spanish or Portuguese, they were numerous enough to fill most of the positions of artisan, overseer, mariner, cattle tender, and militiaman—the "interstitial work of the economy."[18] But the relatively light Spanish and Portuguese immigration to their colonies left them desperately short of people who could function above the level of manual labor. Therefore, it became necessary to create a class of free blacks, working for whites as wage laborers; otherwise, the economy would not have functioned smoothly for the benefit of White landowners, merchants, and investors. Where Africans were functional as freedmen or freedwomen in the White man's society, they were freed; where they were not, they usually remained slaves, though the Spanish practice of *coartáción* gave slaves the right to work one day a week on their own account in order to accumulate money used to purchase their own freedom. If free blacks had not been needed in Latin American society, or if it had been more profitable to close the door to freedom than to keep it ajar, it is unlikely that slaves would have been manumitted in such large numbers or that the *coartáción* system would have survived.

A second way in which free blacks were vital to the interests of White colonizers in Latin America and the Caribbean was as a part of the system of military defense and internal security. North American and Brazilian slave systems, for example, diverged strikingly in their attitudes toward arming slaves and in creating a community of free blacks. Brazilian colonists could not have repelled French attacks in the late sixteenth century, the Dutch invasion in the second quarter of the seventeenth century, and the French assaults in the early eighteenth century without arming their slaves. "Because the mother country . . . was too weak or unconcerned to offer much assistance," writes Carl Degler, "all the resources of the sparsely settled colony had to be mobilized for defense, which included every scrap of manpower, including black slaves."[19] In the American colonies, by contrast,

the need to arm slaves was comparatively slight. Naval raiders of other European powers intermittently endangered colonial shipping, but the colonies were rarely subjected to external attack. Where they were, principally in South Carolina, slave owners resorted to the Portuguese pattern. Threatened by the Spanish in Florida, the Carolinians passed a law in 1707 requiring every militia captain "to enlist, train up and bring into the field for each White, one able slave armed with a gun or lance."[20] In the Yamasee War of 1715, South Carolinians gladly used slaves to stave off the attacks of their Indian enemies. But this was the exception rather than the rule.

For the internal security of plantation society, armed slaves would have been a contradiction, but free blacks were not. They could be used to suppress rebellion, to repel marauding escaped slaves beyond the plantations, or to invade and defeat maroon communities. But rebellion and marronage occurred primarily in plantation societies where Africans massively outnumbered whites and where the geography favored the creation of communities of escaped slaves. Such was the situation in the English West Indies, where the mountainous island interiors provided ideal refuges for maroons. By freeing slaves, the Caribbean planters secured the loyalty and military service of a corps of islanders who kept the slave-based sugar economy going. In North America the security problem was less severe. The ratio of White to black was more even, and geography did not favor maroon refuges because the interior was occupied by powerful Indian tribes who were only occasionally receptive to runaway slaves. Far from being regarded as loyal adjuncts of White society, the small numbers of free Negroes in the American colonies were usually seen as a threat to the security of the slave system and were therefore often compelled to leave the colony where they had been manumitted.

[18]Carl N. Degler, *Neither Black Nor White: Slavery and Race Relations in Brazil and the United States* (New York, 1971), p. 44.
[19]Ibid., p. 79.
[20]Verner W. Crane, *The Southern Frontier, 1670–1732* (Ann Arbor, MI, 1956), p. 187n.

A third, crucially important, way in which the African was more valuable as a freed person than as a slave in the Caribbean and Latin American colonies was as a sexual partner. "No part of the world," writes one historian, "has ever witnessed such a gigantic mixing of races as the one that has been taking place in Latin America and the Caribbean since 1492."[21] Partly, this racial mixing is explained by the centuries of war and economic relations between Iberian peoples and those from Mediterranean, Middle Eastern, and North African societies. The legacy of these extensive interactions was a plasticity in race relations. The English, by comparison, had remained relatively isolated in their island fortress prior to the late sixteenth century, intermingling hardly at all with people of other cultures.

But the inherited Iberian attitudes, transported to the New World, would probably have faded had it not been for compelling circumstances that encouraged racial mingling in such places as Mexico, Peru, and Brazil. Spanish and Portuguese males emigrated without women to a greater extent than did Englishmen, who came predominantly with their families. In the Spanish and the Portuguese cases, the colonizers carried with them a racial ideology that, although it favored white skin and European blood, was still malleable enough to justify mixing with Indian and African women. In the Latin American colonies, interracial sexual relations were common, as the colonizers took Indian and African women as mistresses, concubines, and wives. Such partnerships caused little embarrassment or social strain, for it was regarded as natural to have sexual relations with or even to marry a woman of dark skin.

Such was not the case with the English. English women had come with English men to the Northern colonies, establishing rough parity between the sexes from the beginning. This balance obviated the need for Indian and African women. In the Southern colonies, where White women were in short supply for four or five generations, African women were also absent because the importation of slaves remained insignificant until the last decade of the seventeenth century. By the time black women were available in large numbers, the numerical disparity between White men and White women had been redressed. It was not so much extreme ethnocentrism as it was the presence of White women that made racial crossings officially disreputable and often illegal, though often practiced privately. If White men had continued to lack English women at the time when African women began flooding into the Southern colonies, then the alleged English distaste for dark-skinned partners would doubtlessly have broken down. Womanless men are not easily restrained by ethnocentrism in finding release for their sexual urges, as was demonstrated by English males in the sugar islands of Barbados, Jamaica, and the Leeward Islands. English women were not as plentiful there as in the mainland colonies. Surrounded by a sea of black women, Englishmen eagerly followed the practice of the Spanish and the Portuguese, consorting with and occasionally marrying their slaves. "Not one in twenty can be persuaded that there is either sin or shame in cohabiting with his slave," wrote a Jamaica planter.[22] To outlaw sexual relations with African women, as was being done in the English mainland colonies in the eighteenth century, Winthrop Jordan has suggested, would have been more difficult than abolishing the sugar cane.[23] Where White women were absent, black women were needed; where they were needed, they were accepted, and laws prohibiting interracial sex and marriage never entered the statute books.

Slavery in the Americas took many forms: in the treatment of slaves, the degree of openness in the system, and the willingness of the

[21]Magnus Mörner, *Race Mixture in the History of Latin America* (Boston, MA, 1967), p. 1.
[22]Long, The *History of Jamaica*, p. 328.
[23]Jordan, *White Over Black . . .* , p. 140.

dominant society to mix intimately with the Africans in their midst. The cultural heritage brought to the New World by the various European settler groups played some role in the formation of attitudes, policies, and laws. But the exigencies of life in the New World, including economic, sexual, and military needs, did far more to shape racial attitudes and the system of slavery.

Summary

The tragic 366-year Atlantic slave trade, one of the most important historical phenomena, was carried out by every maritime European power. On its foundation of injustice and cruelty, it was critical in building both the European colonial empires and the wealth that later led to the Industrial Revolution. In all, some 12 million Africans from Western and Central Africa were brought to the Western Hemisphere, usually with the complicity of warring African societies. Of all the enslaved enduring the Middle Passage to the Americas, only about 4 percent clambered ashore in coastal North America.

For Africans, the horrors of capture, forced march to the coast in coffles, humiliating "inspections," branding, and being loaded into canoes that would take them to the waiting ships were preliminary to what lay beyond. Once aboard the ships that would carry them to the Americas, they faced undernourishment, dehydration, disease, and no provision for basic hygiene. Added to that were punishments rained down upon them by the ship crews, especially if an insurrection was mounted. Not more than one in two captured Africans lived to see the Americas or lasted there more than a few years. Once at their destinations, they faced unending bondage in a life of enslavement, though in differing degrees, depending on where they arrived. Life in North America was more harsh and restrictive in the Southern colonies, where most of the enslaved labored in intense crop regimes. In Latin America the conditions of enslavement were sometimes mediated by the intervening hand of the Catholic Church, and the opportunity for eventual freedom was less out of reach than in the English colonies of North America.

Critical Thinking Questions

1. In the fifteenth century, contact was made between Europeans and African kingdoms. Is the traditional belief in a precontact "culture gap" between Europe and Africa valid, and why or why not?
2. The African slave trade, a tragic chapter in history, might have remained a short-lived event if certain circumstances had not arisen. What were those circumstances, and what were their effects?
3. What was the notorious "Middle Passage" in slave transport, and how might the conditions, events, and reactions associated with it be described?
4. The status of enslaved Africans differed in various regions of the Americas. Did these people fare better in Latin or British America—in what ways and why?

Further Reading

Ira Berlin, *Many Thousand Gone: The First Two Centuries of Slavery in North America* (Cambridge: Harvard University Press, 1998).

Emma Christopher, *Slave Ship Sailors and Their Captive Cargoes, 1730–1807* (Cambridge: Cambridge University Press, 2006).

Carl Degler, *Neither Black Nor White: Slavery and Race Relations in Brazil and the United States* (New York: Macmillan, 1971).

David Eltis, *The Rise of African Slavery in the Americas* (Cambridge: Cambridge University Press, 2000).

David Eltis and David Richardson, *Atlas of the Transatlantic Slave Trade* (New Haven: Yale University Press, 2010).

Gwenolyn Midlo Hall, *Slavery and African Ethnicities in the Americas* (Chapel Hill: University of North Carolina Press, 2005).

Linda M. Heywood and John K. Thornton, *Central Africans, Atlantic Creoles, and the Foundation of the Americas, 1585–1660* (Cambridge: Cambridge University Press, 2007).

Sidney W. Mintz, *Sweetness and Power: The Place of Sugar in Modern History* (New York: Viking, 1985).

Magnus Mörner, *Race Mixture in the History of Latin America* (Boston: Little, Brown, 1967).

Marcus Rediker, *The Slave Ship: A Human History* (New York: Viking, 2007).

Barbara Solow, ed., *Slavery and the Rise of the Atlantic System* (Cambridge: Cambridge University Press, 1991).

Frank Tannenbaum, *Slave and Citizen: The Negro in the Americas* (New York: Knopf, 1946).

Hugh Thomas, *The Slave Trade: The Story of the Atlantic Slavery Trade, 1440–1870* (New York: Simon and Schuster, 1997).

John K. Thornton, *Africa and the Africans in the Making of the Atlantic World, 1400–1600*, 2nd ed. (Cambridge: Cambridge University Press, 1998).

CHAPTER 7

The African Ordeal Under Slavery

LEARNING OBJECTIVES

■ Explain the ways in which Africans coped with their enslavement in North America, from the standpoint of adapting their cultural heritages and interacting with those who held them in bondage.

■ Draw comparisons between the lives of enslaved Africans in the French and Spanish borderlands, the Chesapeake region, the Carolina and Georgia low country, and the North.

■ Discuss how Africans resisted and rebelled against their captivity and give an account of the largest slave revolt in colonial North America.

■ Describe how captive Africans created a culture woven from language, religion, work, and family life, including the respective roles of men and women.

It is easy to assume that Africans, once sold into slavery and brought to the Americas, were simply fitted into a closed system of forced labor where they lived out their lives, abject and de-Africanized, as best they could. With much attention paid to the slave system fashioned by slave owners—the black codes they legislated, their treatment of slaves, the economic development they directed—the slaves themselves are often neglected as active participants in a cultural process. How did they respond to the loss of their freedom and the separation from all that was familiar in their native culture? How did they live day by day in a vastly different environment? To what extent were they acculturated into White European society? To what degree did they mold a new African American culture, distinct from the European culture surrounding them? By studying the interior lives of slaves, we can see African Americans in all their humanness.

Coping with Enslavement

The central problem for Africans who found themselves defined as the property of a European master 5,000 miles from their homeland was to create social spaces and lifeways that would allow them to survive under an oppressive slave regime. This problem was not one of merging a West African culture

137

with a European culture, because the human cargoes disgorged from slave ships did not come from a single African society, nor did they encounter masters from a unified European society. Slaves arriving in North America were culturally diverse, coming from many different tribes with distinct characteristics. In the matter of language, for example, Africans had no common medium of communication, for they spoke a diversity of tongues. Similarly, they had been taken from regions in Africa where kinship systems, social organization, and political structures differed. Hence, arriving slaves did not form "communities" of people at the outset but became communities only by forging a new existence out of the elements of many old cultures and shards of the diversified European cultures that now bounded their existence. "What the slaves undeniably shared at the outset," it has been written, "was their enslavement; all—or nearly all—else had to be created by them."[1]

In the encounter between enslaved Africans coming from diverse cultural backgrounds and the European slavocracy that was somewhat more culturally homogeneous, the preponderance of power exercised by the colonizers must always be kept in mind. Slaves, to be sure, drew on what they remembered from Africa to make life bearable in the Americas. White slave owners were aware of these attempts of their slaves to maintain inherited cultural practices, and they usually allowed this insofar as it did not interfere with the "seasoning" of new slaves. When it impeded adaptation to the new system of life and work, slave masters tried to obliterate such Africanisms. But this engagement involved a continuous struggle between slave and master. The master's ideal was to convert the slave into a mindless drudge who obeyed every command and worked efficiently for the master's profit. But never in the long history of slavery could the

memory, habit, and belief of slaves be entirely wiped away. And never could slavery, however brutal and dehumanizing, completely overawe and cow its victims. Black men and women in the English colonies, as elsewhere, "were able to find the means to sustain a far greater degree of self-pride and group cohesion than the system they lived under ever intended for them to be able to do," not because "the system was more benign than it had been pictured, but rather that human beings are more resilient, less malleable, and less able to live without some sense of cultural cohesion, individual autonomy, and self-worth" than many historians have maintained.[2]

The status difference between slave and free, in other words, was immense, and power was very unequally divided. Yet Africans and Euro-Americans interacted continuously under slavery because both groups were intimately tied together. Masters could set the boundaries of the slave's existence, defining physical location, work roles, diet, shelter, and access to education; but the master had little control over how slaves established friendships, fell in love, formed kin groups, raised their children, worshipped their gods, buried their dead, and organized their leisure time. At this "much deeper and more fundamental level of interpersonal relationships and expressive behavior," Africans in America exercised a degree of autonomy and were thus able to draw on their cultural backgrounds in shaping an African American character.[3]

In this process of adaptation, there was a built-in premium on cultural innovation. This was the case both because of the need for enslaved Africans to adjust rapidly to the power of the master class, which bore so heavily on them, and because of the initial cultural diversity of the Africans brought to the colonies. Thrown together with captives from other tribes and thrust into a system of bondage, "all slaves must have

---

[1]Sidney W. Mintz and Richard Price, *An Anthropological Approach to the Afro-American Past: A Caribbean Perspective* (Philadelphia, PA, 1976), p. 10.
[2]Lawrence W. Levine, *Black Culture and Black Consciousness: Afro-American Folk Thought from Slavery to Freedom* (New York, 1977), p. xi.
[3]David Dalby, "The African Element in American English," in T. Kochman, ed., *Rappin' and Stylin' Out: Communication in Urban Black America* (Urbana, IL, 1972), p. 173.

found themselves accepting, albeit out of necessity, countless 'foreign' cultural practices."[4] Nostalgia for the homeland and for old ways no doubt endured, but the overriding instinct was to survive. This need required rapid adaptation, learning new ways of doing things that ensured survival. It was imperative, therefore, that Africans adopt "a general openness to ideas and usages from other cultural traditions, a special tolerance (within the West African context) of cultural differences."[5] Yet in adopting new lifeways, Africans did not discard what was familiar and habitual. Rather, they adapted customary ways of living, working, worshipping, grieving, celebrating, and associating to the requirements of a brutal and foreign new environment.

Masters were frequently insensitive to the cultural creativity of their slaves and to the local African American lifeways being formed from the time Africans first landed. They preferred to think of their slaves as animals or, in legal terms, as property. Property cannot think and create; animals cannot learn new languages, cultivate crops, create music, and dance. This was the central contradiction in the Atlantic system of chattel slavery—that while treating their human property inhumanely and defining their slaves as less than human, the master class implicitly had to recognize the humanity of their slaves, for the slaves' ability to work, think, and express emotion (and to revolt against, resist, and ridicule their oppressors) told them so.

Regional Variations of North American Slavery

"Saltwater" Africans, as colonists called slaves brought directly from Africa, and their creole offspring, slaves born in America, did not all face the same conditions in North America. African American culture was shaped differently in distinct regions because slavery itself varied markedly. The complexity of black culture in North America can be understood only by considering these distinct, regional black societies shaped over more than a century.

Spanish and French Borderlands

Before a single enslaved African touched soil in the English colonies, slaves by the thousands were present in North America. They came first with fifteenth-century Spanish explorers. Juan Ponce de León's Florida expedition of 1513 included Africans, who served as scouts and ship handlers. As many as one hundred Africans accompanied Lucas Vásquez de Ayllón's 1526 reconnaissance of the South Carolina coast. When a leadership crisis beset the expedition of 600 people, some Africans fled to the Guale Indians and began the mixing of African and Indian blood that continued in North America for centuries.

Another expedition, in 1528, produced the most colorful and talented African of sixteenth-century North America. Estévancio, born in Morocco, accompanied his Spanish master of the Narváez expedition through Florida and was one of four survivors of this ill-fated intrusion into Indian lands. During several years of enslavement in a Florida Indian tribe, Estévancio's talent blossomed as a healer, linguist, guide, and diplomat. When the four survivors fled Florida and made their way through hostile Indian land to Mexico, Estévancio was the indispensable man. In 1539, he was the trailblazer for Coronado's Spanish expedition into what would become Arizona and New Mexico.

The importance of Africans on these arduous expeditions through uncharted territory gave slavery a distinct character in the early Spanish settlements. The slaves did much of the difficult work as field laborers, on supply trains, and in fort and church construction; but they were equally important as soldiers, guides, and linguists. Moreover, they crossed their blood so frequently with the Indians, and sometimes with the Spanish, that slavery had little of the castelike condition of English slaves. Two hundred years after Africans had accompanied the early Spanish expeditions

---

[4]Mintz and Price, *An Anthropological Approach to the Afro-American Past . . .*, p. 24.
[5]Ibid., p. 26.

through the southern parts of North America, African Mexicans represented a significant fraction of settlers in Mexico's northern frontier, including what would become the American Southwest.

Similarly, in the Southeast, Africans carved out economic and social spaces for themselves that had little parallel in the later English colonies. For example, de Soto had dozens of Africans with him as he cut a terrifying swath through Florida in 1639 through 1641, and some of the Africans escaped to live among the Indians. Africans also arrived with the Spanish in the 1560s and helped construct St. Augustine, the Spanish fort in Florida erected in 1565. As its northern outpost, St. Augustine became critical to Spain's Caribbean defense. More than a century later, in 1686, St. Augustine's black militia regiments, both free and slave, fought lustily to dislodge the budding English settlements in South Carolina. For many decades after that, African Spaniards on the Florida frontier demonstrated their military prowess as guerrilla fighters against the South Carolinians. For their bravery, dozens of them received freedom from Florida's Spanish governor in 1738, whereupon they promptly settled in North America's first free black town, Pueblo de Gracia Reál de Santa Terese de Mose (known simply as Mose). Two miles north of St. Augustine, Mose was led by African-born Francisco Menéndez. Though English attacks scattered the free blacks of Mose in 1740, the town regathered in 1752 and lasted until Spain ceded Florida to the British in 1763. A tiny outpost of free blacks in a region based on slave labor, Mose had a short and precarious existence, yet one that offered an important example of enslaved Africans wresting freedom on the edges of European settlement.

French slaves were as important to the development of Louisiana and the Illinois country to the north as they were to Spanish Florida. Arriving with skills as rice growers, indigo processors, metalworkers, river navigators, herbalists, and cattle keepers, the West Africans became the backbone of the economy. Like the male slaves in Spanish Florida, they mingled extensively with Indian women, producing mixed-race children known locally as *grifs*. African women sometimes made interracial liaisons with French immigrants, often soldiers in search of partners.

Always precariously perched in Louisiana with limited numbers of French settlers, French governors used enslaved Africans extensively as militiamen and sometimes granted them freedom for military service. To secure freedom, Africans fought in the Chickasaw War of the 1730s and in the next decade against the Choctaws. For the French, it was doubly advantageous to draw on black military skills because pitting them against hostile Indians reduced the chance of what might have been a disastrous Indian-African alliance. All in all, the chance of gaining freedom in fluid French Louisiana exceeded that of any other colony in the southeastern part of the continent, and the absorption of free blacks into White society, particularly if they were of mixed race descent, was shockingly common from the English point of view. As in all places in the Americas where slavery ruled, violence and brutality were commonplace. But in French Louisiana the desperate need for African skills as well as African labor led to a porous line between White and black—a racial openness seldom found in the English colonies.

Representing the greater racial flexibility on the French frontiers in North America was the shrewd and ambitious Jean Baptiste Pointe Du Sable. Forging north from New Orleans in the 1770s, this mixed-blood immigrant from Saint

RUN away from the subscriber in *Albemarle*, a Mulatto slave called *Sandy*, about 35 years of age, his stature is rather low, inclining to corpulence, and his complexion light; he is a shoemaker by trade, in which he uses his left hand principally, can do coarse carpenters work, and is something of a horse jockey; he is greatly addicted to drink, and when drunk is insolent and disorderly, in his conversation he swears much, and in his behaviour is artful and knavish. He took with him a white horse, much scarred with traces, of which it is expected he will endeavour to dispose; he also carried his shoemakers tools, and will probably endeavour to get employment that way. Whoever conveys the said slave to me, in *Albemarle*, shall have 40 s. reward, if taken up within the county, 4 l. if elsewhere within the colony, and 10 l. if in any other colony, from
THOMAS JEFFERSON.

(Courtesy Thomas Jefferson Runaway Slave advert, from 'The Virginia Gazette', 14th September 1769 (litho), American School, (18th century)/ Virginia Historical Society, Richmond, Virginia, USA/The Bridgeman Art Library)

Domingue, born of a French father and an African mother, became a legendary trapper and hunter in the Illinois country controlled by the French. With his Potawatomi wife, he established himself at the mouth of the Chicago River near Lake Michigan, where he flourished as a trader, miller, and land speculator. From the village of Eschikagou arose the metropolis of Chicago.

The Chesapeake

Slavery in Virginia and Maryland evolved through three different periods. For nearly the first half-century after Africans first arrived in Virginia in 1619, they were treated by the tobacco planters much as were White indentured servants. Life was brutal and often short, for the planters were intent on wringing profit from the tobacco frontier. The Africans were predominantly male, and many of those who did not succumb to disease and the work regimen gained their freedom and became landowners themselves. In this period before the 1660s, when slavery was legalized, they adapted rapidly to White society. This was facilitated by their origins in Angola and Kongo, where Christianity and European cultural forms had taken root in a region of West Central Africa where the Portuguese had great influence. Still, in 1675 there were only about 2,500 Africans in Virginia and half that number in Maryland, and in this still-fluid regime, African and White bond laborers "ran away together, slept together, and, upon occasion, stood shoulder to shoulder against the weighty champions of authority."[6]

Beginning in the 1670s, Chesapeake planters began to import slaves in much larger numbers, and now they came mainly from West Africa instead of Central Africa. By the early eighteenth century, the agricultural labor force was overwhelmingly black. About 96,000 slaves, almost all of them coming directly from West Africa, were marched ashore in Virginia between 1698 and 1774. This influx profoundly Africanized black plantation society. In a period of rapid expansion, Virginia planters used many of these new immigrants to develop new upland plantations. There, they worked in small groups to clear the land and plant tobacco, living in an unruly region remote from the older tidewater settlements. Planters used creole American-born slaves far more frequently in the tidewater area, where sex ratios were becoming better balanced and black family life was developing.

The convergence of African and creole slave societies in Virginia and Maryland began in the 1740s. By this time natural reproduction supplied most of the additional enslaved Africans that Chesapeake planters needed. By the eve of the American Revolution, slaves imported from Africa made up only 10 percent of the annual increase in Virginia's slave population. An increasingly creole black population was reproducing itself, and with this reproduction came a rapid balancing of the sex ratio, which in turn created greater possibilities for family life. Facilitating the growth of black kinship networks was the greater density of slave settlement, the growth of larger plantations where dozens of Africans labored together, and the development of a network of roads and market towns that allowed for greater mobility between plantations. In addition, as the Chesapeake economy began to shift in the 1740s from tobacco monoculture to a mixed economy of tobacco, wheat, and iron production, the nature of black labor began to change. More slaves learned artisan skills, required in a more diversified and urbanized economy. This experience expanded their universe, drawing many away from the dull, backbreaking labor of tending tobacco plants and giving them points of contact with the larger society beyond the single plantation. Still, large numbers of slaves worked on small plantations, and none were ever free from the threat that the debts or death of their master would put them on the auction block and shatter their family.

By the late colonial period, Chesapeake African Americans had achieved considerable "social space" in which to maneuver. They continued

[6]Ira Berlin, "Time, Space, and the Evolution of Afro-American Society in British Mainland North America," *American Historical Review,* 85 (1980): 69.

to live in close proximity to whites, for almost all Virginia and Maryland planters resided on their plantations, regulating their slaves themselves or with overseers. But even though slaves might work from sunup to sundown under the overseer's whip and the master's shadow, and during the Sabbath and holidays, they were largely out of sight and sound of their owners. Black culture grew in the unintended interstices of an institution designed to extract labor from its captives. Because a growing proportion of them were American-born, had established a family life, and labored within an increasingly diversified economy, they were becoming part of a blended African American culture. At the same time, this culture was much more connected to Anglo-American culture and far more shaped by it than in the lowland colonies to the south.

The Carolina and Georgia Low Country

Africans first came to the marshy waterways of the Carolina coast with their West Indian masters who settled in the country, so they had already adjusted to life in the English-speaking parts of the Americas. The Carolina frontier was a rugged, dangerous place in the late seventeenth century, as the colonizers engaged in Indian wars, Indian slave trading, and periodic skirmishes with the Spanish and French. This vulnerability to external enemies made slaves vital to colonial defense, making South Carolina the one colony that offered freedom to any slave "who in time of an invasion kills an enemy."[7] This relative flexibility in the slave system was magnified by the familiarity of West Africans with the semitropical environment of the lowlands. White settlers depended on their slaves to adapt African techniques of rice cultivation and cattle herding to a geography and climate foreign to their masters.

"Transplanted Englishmen," it has been written, "learned as much or more from transplanted Africans as did the former Africans from them. . . . White domination made itself felt, but both whites and blacks incorporated much of West African culture into their new way of life."[8] Far more than on the Chesapeake, Africans shaped the culture in which they labored.

In the early eighteenth century, after the agricultural skills of West Africans had made rice the keystone of the lowlands economy, slavery entered a new phase. Only about 4,000 slaves toiled in South Carolina in 1708, but that number tripled in the next twelve years and then tripled again by 1740, when the nearly 40,000 Africans inhabiting the rice coast outnumbered whites by two to one. This demographic upheaval brought the end of the relatively open, flexible system of slavery in the early years. As large rice and indigo plantations emerged, slaves lived in larger units (much larger than the Chesapeake plantations) and worked under brutal conditions in field gangs. Prosperous planters retreated to the coastal cities, especially Charleston, leaving field labor to the supervision of overseers and black drivers. By 1737, a Swiss newcomer ventured that Carolina "looks more like a negro country than like a country settled by white people."[9]

A notable fracture appeared in the ranks of slaves as the coastal lowlands experienced the "rice and indigo revolution." In the capital city of Charleston, a creole population of African Americans, representing more than half the city's population, lived in close proximity to White society. As house servants, boatmen, dockworkers, and artisans, they became relatively mobile, skilled, and privileged. Some women mixed sexually with slave masters, producing a large mulatto population that formed the basis of a small free black population. Hewing close to White culture, these urban African Americans mastered the

---

[7]Thomas Nairne, *A Letter from South Carolina . . .* (London, 1710).
[8]Berlin, "Afro-American Society in British Mainland North America," p. 56.
[9]Quoted in Peter Wood, *Black Majority: Negroes in Colonial South Carolina from 1670 through the Stono Rebellion* (New York, 1974), p. 132.

The work routines of cultivating, harvesting, and processing rice and indigo, pictured here, were carried out in an environment where heat, humidity, disease, brutality, and incessant labor took a terrible toll on slaves. Next to the sugar regimens in the Caribbean, rice and indigo production was the worst to be found in the Americas.

Source: World History Archive/Image Asset Management Ltd./Alamy

English language and the intricate interracial personal relationships required in the cities to obtain privileges from the ruling whites.

But on the large plantations, black culture moved in the opposite direction. Slaves represented a large proportion of the population and lived in relative isolation from White culture. They tilled truck gardens to supply much of their own food needs and labored in the task system, where the daily work routine was defined by quotas—feet of irrigation ditch to be dug, rows of rice to be harvested, or bushels of rice to pound. Both these developments gave them a degree of independence from close White management. Combined with the fact that so many of them had

recently arrived from Africa, this arrangement led to the forging of a culture that more than anywhere else in British North America was West African in its characteristics. This culture was reflected in their distinctive language patterns, burial ceremonies, religion, and child-naming preferences. For example, Gullah became the primary tongue on the rice coast among slaves. A "pidgin," or mixture of several languages, combined elements of English and a variety of West African dialects. Gullah emerged as the slaves' "central mode of communication and expression, linking together people of widely disparate backgrounds" who, because of their numerical superiority and relative isolation from White society, did not have to assimilate so thoroughly into White culture as did enslaved Africans in the Chesapeake colonies.[10] This greater degree of West African cultural persistence can also be seen in naming patterns. African day names (given for the day of the week on which the child was born) such as Quaco, Juba, Quashee, and Cuba are frequently found in the South Carolina plantation records but far less so in Virginia and Maryland records. On the rice and indigo plantations of the Carolina lowlands, African Americans remained more culturally distant from the world of their captors than in other colonies, and thus culturally closer to Africa.

The same was true in Georgia, the last North American colony to be established by the British. For the first fifteen years after founding the colony in 1733, its proprietors tried to prohibit slavery. But settlers became more and more vocal in demanding slaves—"the one thing needful," they claimed, for economic success. Once the threat of the Spanish in Florida declined in the 1740s, the ban on slavery collapsed, and South Carolina planters flocked to Georgia to institute a slave economy closely resembling what they had left behind in Carolina.

The North

Enslaved Africans in the North made up only 2 to 3 percent of the population in most of New England and Pennsylvania, and up to 8 to 12 percent in Rhode Island, New Jersey, New York, and Delaware. Yet the Northern colonies were more involved in slavery than these figures suggest. New England's merchants and ship captains were deeply involved in slave trading as early as the 1640s, and the northern exports of wheat, fish, and wood products to the slave regimes of the West Indies were central to economic growth. As a small minority in the population, enslaved Africans in the Northern regions toiled differently than on Southern plantations. Infrequently employed in field gangs, they typically worked as artisans, farmhands, or personal servants. Whereas a majority of Southern slaves worked on plantations with many other slaves, the typical Northern slave labored alone or with only a few of his or her countrymen or countrywomen. Moreover, the plantation slave quarters, where blacks could maintain a considerable degree of cultural autonomy and privacy away from the watchful eye of the owner, had no equivalent in northern slave life. Most Northern slaves ate, slept, and lived in the house of the master. All these factors—their low proportion of the population, wide dispersion, and constant contact with whites—made retaining a link to the African past very difficult, while ensuring that acculturation proceeded at a relatively rapid pace. A notable exception to this Northern pattern was the Narragansett region of Rhode Island, where large landowners frequently owned 5 to 40 slaves and one merchant landowner in 1766 owned as many as 238.

In the Northern cities, slavery sank deeper roots than in the countryside. In New York City, where the Dutch had begun a tradition of relying on slave labor during the half-century that they controlled the town, almost 20 percent of the population was African American in 1750 and two of every five householders owned at least one slave. In Philadelphia and Boston in the mid-eighteenth century, slaves made up about a tenth of the population and could be found in the homes of nearly every fifth family. In all three cities more than 1000 black slaves labored for their masters in the decade before the Revolution. These urban blacks were always rubbing elbows with lower-class whites—on the docks, at the markets, in the workplace of the master craftsman, in taverns, and at street entertainments such as cockfights. Slavery in the North was onerous; but its harshest features were mitigated by the absence of death-dealing gang labor in the fields, by the closer living relationship between masters and bond persons, and, in the cities, by the large degree of mobility and privileges that Africans gradually wrung from the master class.

---

[10]Ibid., p. 191.

The assimilationist tendency in the North was somewhat reoriented by the large influx of captives directly from Africa beginning in the 1740s. As the Northern colonies grew rapidly in the eighteenth century, the call for bond labor increased. Larger shipments of slaves arrived, reaching a peak during the late 1750s when the Seven Years' War cut off the supply of White indentured servants from Ireland and Germany. Urban white officials noticed the introduction of African ways—burial ceremonies, dances, song, and other entertainments.

The most vivid evidence of the infusion of an African strain in Northern African American culture was the midcentury introduction in many northern towns of "Negro Election Day," an annual festival that drew blacks from the surrounding countryside to the cities for feasting, parading, dancing, and the election of black kings, judges, and other officials. "All the various languages of Africa, mixed with broken and ludicrous English filled the air," reported a White observer in Newport, Rhode Island, "accompanied with the music of the fiddle, tambourine, the banjo [and] drum."[11] In a ritual of role reversal, blacks in the towns dressed in the clothes of their masters, rode their masters' horses, feasted and drank on tributes exacted from their owners, and symbolically ruled the town for a day. Negro Election Day imitated the masters' election-day festivities, but it was more. It gave Northern slaves an opportunity to express the sorrows of thralldom and also provided a mechanism for them to choose and recognize their own leaders, who acted throughout the year in a semiofficial capacity as adjudicators of disputes and counselors to the black community. Through the "'Lection Day" festivals, black Northerners remembered Africa while giving birth to a consciousness of African American peoplehood.

Despite the infusion of African culture that accompanied the importation from Africa of thousands of slaves between 1740 and 1765, the overall tendency in the North, far more than in the plantation South, was for a speedy merging with Anglo-American culture. Slavery was more benign in the North, slaves were more widely dispersed, and extensive cross-cultural contact eroded African ways. Yet slaves in the North knew that bondage kept them distinct from White society, and no amount of assimilation could alter that intolerable fact.

Resistance and Rebellion

While African-born and creole slaves struggled to adapt to bondage in various geographical and economic regions of North America, they also rankled, resisted, and rebelled in ways that kept their captors constantly aware of the costs of building and maintaining the edifice of slavery. The forms of resistance, like the forms of slavery itself, varied, depending on the circumstances of enslavement and the makeup of the slaves. Resisters, runaways, and rebels had multiple goals: to extract better conditions from masters, to rejoin family members, to obtain a new master, to avenge sadistic overseers, or—most radically—to flee slavery in the hope of finding freedom.

The spirit of resistance among "saltwater" Africans fresh from their homelands was often immediate, spontaneous, and not easy to break. A North Carolinian was sure that newly imported slaves in his or her colony, most of them from Guinea, were far less industrious and more active in resisting slavery than "country-born" blacks.[12] "If he must be broke," warned another observer of the African newcomer, "either from obstinacy, or, which I am more apt to suppose, from greatness of soul, [it] will require hard discipline. You would really be surprised at their perseverance; they often die before they can be conquered."[13] A study of fugitive slaves in eighteenth-century Virginia and South Carolina makes clear that newly imported Africans often ran away and did so in

[11]Quoted in Berlin, "Afro-American Society in British Mainland North America," p. 54.
[12]John Brickell, *The Natural History of North Carolina* (Raleigh, NC, 1911), pp. 272–273.
[13]Quoted in Darold D. Wax, "Negro Resistance to the Early American Slave Trade," *Journal of Negro History,* 51 (1966): 11.

ways that reflected the communal folk ethos that they had known on the other side of the ocean.

When they took flight, Africans often did so in groups, particularly in company with Africans from their own country. In 1773, for example, fourteen freshly imported slaves fled as a group from a Virginia slave merchant, plunging into an unknown countryside in search of refuge.[14] Newspaper advertisements in eighteenth-century South Carolina also reveal this kind of cooperative effort that brought slaves from the same region of Africa together in attempts at escape. The newspapers frequently advertised for groups of runaway "Gambia men" or slaves from the "Fullah Country." The Carolina backcountry as well as the Spanish-Indian Florida frontier acted as a magnet to those who were bent on escape, especially after 1733 when a Spanish decree promised escaped English slaves freedom in Florida. By 1738, enough Carolina slaves had escaped to Florida for the Spanish governor there to form a company of black militia.

This kind of overt rebelliousness often changed as Africans began absorbing the culture of the English-speaking plantation. Living on plantations with other slaves, many of them American-born, new arrivals learned the routine of planting, transplanting, weeding, worming, harvesting, and transporting crops. They also learned how to reduce the tediousness of their tasks and minimize the exertion that slave masters attempted to maximize. Dragging out the job, feigning illness, pretending ignorance, breaking tools, and other forms of "gold-bricking" were ways of avoiding physical depletion and also subtle forms of resistance against slavery itself. Planters like Landon Carter of Virginia complained endlessly that "my people seem to be quite dead hearted and either cannot or will not work."[15] An English observer of American slavery noted that the slave "does not appear to perform half as much as a labourer in England"

and added a comment about "the slovenly carelessness with which all business is performed by the slave."[16]

Enslaved Africans practiced many more direct forms of resistance: truancy, which usually took the form of hiding out in the woods; arson, by which the runaway slave struck against the white man's fields, barns, and houses; crop destruction; poisoning and murder; and organized pilfering, in which groups of slaves requisitioned chickens, livestock, crops, liquor, tools, and household items by moonlight and sold them in black market systems that spread over considerable distances. In every case, they kept the slave system on edge.

The most extreme form of individual resistance was suicide. Believing in the transmigration of the soul to the African homeland, some slaves took the ultimate step to get release from perpetual bondage. One way masters combated this was to cruelly take advantage of the African belief "in the sacredness of the corpse and the importance of respecting the dead."[17] By beheading the corpse of a slave who took his own life the master violated the sanctity of the body and compromised, in the African view, the process of transmigration. In another way of interfering with African deathways, many colonial lawmakers banned slave funeral gatherings or limited the number who could gather, believing that these were assemblages where slave rebellions were hatched.

When creole slaves moved from the field to the house and changed their role from gang laborer to household servant, they learned new ways of resisting. From the slaveholder's point of view, the slaves should be pleased with this advance in position, for it brought them closer to "civilized" life, conferred status on them in the plantation hierarchy, and lightened their work. Although not many slaves resisted this chance for "advancement," accompanied by opportunities

---

[14]Gerald W. Mullin, *Flight and Rebellion: Slave Resistance in Eighteenth-Century Virginia* (New York, 1972), pp. 39–47.
[15]Quoted in Mullin, *Flight and Rebellion . . .* , p. 53.
[16]Quoted in ibid., p. 54.
[17]Erik R. Seeman, *Death in the New World: Cross-Cultural Encounters, 1492–1800* (Philadelphia, PA, 2010), p. 194.

for better food, clothes, and shelter, most knew that the role of domestic servant carried a heavy price, for it brought them into a more intimate relationship with their captors and thus sapped their ability to preserve customary ways practiced in the relative privacy of the slave quarters. The household slave lost full membership in the black community and the chance to be mostly out of sight of the White people of the plantation. New demands to behave in less African ways fell on these slaves with every aspect of their behavior now scrutinized by the master and mistress. Involved in a close, daily relationship with those who dominated their lives, many slaves developed speech problems such as stuttering—an outward sign of an inward difficulty in attempting to act in ways that satisfied the master and mistress but conflicted with inner impulses and feelings. Rebelliousness could not take the same forms as in the field; so in the "big house," drunkenness, malingering, and verbal and emotional contests of will with those whose authority hung over them became the slaves' means of resisting.

Because the plantation was a small world in itself, relatively self-sufficient and encompassing a wide variety of tasks, it required artisans skilled in carpentry, blacksmithing, milling, bricklaying, weaving, coopering, plastering, leatherworking, and butchering. As skilled workers, enslaved Africans became more assimilated into White society, moving more freely between house, field, and workshop, between the plantation and the town, and between the warehouse and the wharf. Other skilled work, such as piloting tobacco- and rice-laden rafts and small boats through the maze of Southern inland waterways, took the slave away from the plantation and out into a larger world.

Captive Africans living in this wider world became skilled and imaginative in their resistance. After running away, they often tried to pass for free blacks in other colonies, hiring themselves out as sailors, trading from carts, and

living in towns with other free blacks and poor Whites. Usually running away as individuals, they used their new skills and resourcefulness to maneuver their way into situations that cloaked their former slave status and to make good their bid for freedom.

Even in the North, where slavery was less harsh, few whites had illusions about the contentedness or submissiveness of slaves. Magistrates continually faced cases of black resistance to slavery from Maine to Delaware. The "fondness for freedom" that led slaves to defy their masters, run away, destroy property, and express their discontent in drunkenness and rowdyism repeatedly tried the patience of Bostonians and other urban dwellers. Puritan clergymen and magistrates attempted to convince slaves that "Your servitude is gentle . . . you are treated, with more than mere humanity, and fed and clothed and lodged, as well as you can wish for." They warned that "if you were free, many of you would not live near so well as you do." But still, wrote a Boston judge early in the eighteenth century, slaves engaged in "continual aspiring" after "forbidden liberty."[18]

In Philadelphia, where the efforts of Quakers to abolish slavery may have produced the most humane practice of slavery in North America, slaves also malingered, balked, and struggled for their freedom. Benjamin Franklin, himself a slave owner, wrote in 1770 to a European friend: "Perhaps you may imagine the Negroes to be a mild-tempered, tractable kind of people. Some of them indeed are so. But the majority are of a plotting disposition, dark, sullen, malicious, revengeful and cruel in the highest degree."[19]

Viewing the enslavement of Africans in North America as an encounter between two cultures, we can see that slaves not only adapted to the death-dealing daily toil of the plantation but also schooled themselves in strategies of survival, resistance, and rebellion. Slave masters extracted labor and obedience from their slaves in

[18]Lawrence E. Towner, "'Fondness for Freedom': Servant Protest in Puritan Society," *William and Mary Quarterly,* 3rd Ser., 19 (1962): 202.
[19]"A Conversation between an Englishman, a Scotchman, and an American," in Verner W. Crane, "Benjamin Franklin on Slavery and American Liberties," *Pennsylvania Magazine of History and Biography,* 62 (1938): 8.

an overall sense—if they had not, slavery would have collapsed as an economic and a social institution. However, they did so with difficulty, never with the degree of success they wished for, and often at the price of destroyed property and even lives.

Revolt, of course, was the supreme expression of rebelliousness. Contrasting the relatively small number of American slave rebellions with the frequent revolts of Brazilian and West Indian slaves, historians have concluded that Africans in America were less rebellious than slaves elsewhere in the hemisphere. Truly, no American parallel exists for the massive slave uprisings that occurred in Jamaica in the late seventeenth century or the wave of insurrections that kept the city of Bahia in northern Brazil in a state of disruption in the early nineteenth century. But almost nowhere was there slavery without violent resistance.

The largest uprising in colonial North America took place in South Carolina in 1739, when about twenty Africans along the Stono River southwest of Charleston obtained a cache of arms, killed several whites, and fled toward the Florida frontier where they hoped to take refuge with the Spanish, as handfuls of slaves had done for years. Burning and plundering plantations as they fled southward, the rebels recruited slaves who swelled the small army to about one hundred. The plan was squashed by the White militia, which quickly intercepted the slave band and, with Indian assistance, defeated the rebels in a pitched battle. Thirty slaves were killed in the White counterattack or were executed after surrendering. South Carolina's frightened legislature stopped imports of new Africans for several years and tightened the screws on slaves' use of passes to move about on Sundays or holidays.

A few other revolts were nipped in the bud, such as the plot to capture Annapolis, Maryland, in 1740; but large-scale rebellions of this kind were rare in the history of American slavery. Nor

is there an American parallel to the semistates created by escaped Africans in Dutch Surinam, English Jamaica, French Guiana, Spanish Cuba, and Portuguese Brazil. In these hideaways, thousands of runaway slaves built their own communities and held out for decades against periodic assaults of colonial troops. Only Spanish Florida, to which hundreds, but not thousands, of slaves fled in the eighteenth century, offers an American parallel.

However, examples such as these do not really prove the greater rebelliousness of Latin American slaves. Rather, they indicate that the chances for the enslaved to mount a successful rebellion increased in inverse proportion to the power of the White community. "The greater number of blacks, which a frontier has," warned one observer in 1741, "and the greater the disproportion is between them and her White people, the more danger she is liable to; for those [blacks] are all secret enemies, and ready to join with her open ones on the first occasion."[20] When enslaved Africans outnumbered European colonizers six or eight to one, they could be counted on to rebel more frequently than when they were a minority or only a slight majority in the population.

By the same token, the incidence of flight from slavery correlated with the chances for successful escape. In Brazil, where Africans and Indians had mixed for generations, more opportunities existed to hide out or join an Indian community beyond the boundaries of White settlement than in colonial North America, where the slave plantations were rarely situated more than one hundred miles from the Atlantic coast and where African-Indian mixing was slight by comparison. Fewer open rebellions in the English mainland colonies do not prove the greater servility of the American slave but indicate only the greater problems faced by potential insurrectionists in rising against their oppressors. Under different conditions, rebelliousness became

---

[20]Benjamin Martyn, *An Impartial Inquiry into the State and Utility of the Colony of Georgia* (London, 1741), quoted in Peter Wood, *Black Majority . . .* , p. 166.

channeled into other forms—more subtle, less dangerous, and often more effective.

Almost all the colonies passed special laws against arson and poisoning in the eighteenth century, an indication of the persistent resistance to enslavement and the hostility of slaves against their masters. In fact, "the sharpest evidence of slave resistance," it has been observed, "is not the historical record of armed revolts . . . so much as the codes that legalized branding, flogging, burning, the amputation of limbs, hamstringing and murder to keep the slaves 'non-violent.' "[21]

That Africans did not lapse into passive dependency and abject obedience is evident in the fear of black rebellion that coursed through White communities. A vivid example can be found in the reaction of the Southern colonies to the onset of the Seven Years' War in 1755. William Shirley, commander of the British forces in North America, complained that nothing could be expected of the Southern militia because if they left their local communities, the slaves would flee en masse to the French, who were promising "liberty & lands to settle upon." Lewis Evans, a Pennsylvania strategist, also conceded that the Southern militia could not make a move: "The thing is impossible," he wrote, "they have . . . scarce whites enough to prevent the defection of their slaves; and if any considerable party should happen to be defeated, when abroad, it could be scarce possible to prevent their total revolt."[22] The governor of Virginia hoped to spare a few militia units for the intercolonial war effort but greatly feared "the combinations of the Negro slaves, who have been very audacious on the defeat on the Ohio [of Braddock's army]." He prayed that "we shall be able to defeat the designs of our enemies and keep these slaves in proper subjection."[23]

Even in the North, it proved impossible to shape slaves into mild-tempered, compliant workers. In New York City in 1712, a group of more than twenty slaves, determined to overthrow their oppressors, set fire to a building and then lay in wait for the White men who came to extinguish the flames. Wielding knives, axes, and guns, they killed nine whites and injured many others before making their escape. It was later reported that "had it not been for the garrison [of English soldiers] there, that city would have been reduced to ashes, and the greatest part of the inhabitants murdered."[24] After suppressing the rebels, officials took about seventy slaves into custody. Forty-three were brought to trial, and twenty-five, including several women and Indian slaves, were convicted. The sentences imposed bespoke the White fear of black insurrection: thirteen slaves died on the gallows, one was starved to death in chains, three were burned at the stake, and one was broken on the wheel. Six others killed themselves rather than endure the White community's retribution.

After the 1712 revolt, New York's legislature quickly passed a new slave code, which strictly regulated the slaves' freedom of movement and stripped away most of the rights that until this time distinguished their lot from that of their Southern counterparts. In neighboring colonies, legislators scurried to impose new restrictions on blacks or, as in Pennsylvania, to pass import duties so high as to make further importations of Africans unprofitable.

Even the medieval torture imposed on the black conspirators of 1712 did not achieve the desired results of cowing Northern slaves into submissiveness. A generation later, a wave of slave unrest swept the eastern seaboard, beginning in New Jersey in 1740 with a few incidents of barn burning. Two enslaved males paid with their lives for this act of rebellion. A few months later, a rash of thefts and fires struck New York City, the largest urban center of slavery in the colonies next to Charleston, South Carolina. Among the buildings ignited was Fort George, which housed the English garrison. Indicted in these incidents were a

[21]Sidney Mintz, "Toward an Afro-American History," *Journal of World History,* 13 (1971): 321.
[22]Quoted in Lawrence H. Gipson, *The Great War for Empire: The Years of Defeat, 1754–1757* (New York, 1946), pp. 14–15.
[23]Ibid., p. 15.
[24]Quoted in Kenneth Scott, "The Slave Insurrection in New York in 1712," *New York Historical Society Quarterly,* 45 (1961): 51.

White tavern keeper, his wife, and an indentured servant girl who served as a prostitute in the tavern. Helped along by some low-grade torture and a promise of immunity, the servant girl confessed that her master was involved with several slaves in a conspiracy to burn the town to the ground and kill all its White inhabitants. The authorities brought two slaves to trial for theft and possible conspiracy. When the conspiracy charge against them could not be substantiated, they were hanged for theft, dying "very stubbornly" on the gallows without confessing to anything more.

A month later, the tavern keeper and his wife were hanged for treason, though they too went to their deaths with closed lips concerning a slave plot. When the servant-prostitute went to the gallows for conspiracy, she died renouncing the statements she had made concerning black insurrectionists. But fear of black revolt and a desire to cow the city's blacks had overtaken the town, and the dragnet began pulling in slaves, who were threatened with torture and execution if they did not reveal the identity of the slave conspirators four. In the following months, White authorities extracted sixty-seven confessions from terrified slaves. Before the trial was over, 150 slaves and twenty five whites had been imprisoned, seventeen slaves and four whites had been tortured and hanged, thirteen slaves had been burned at the stake, and seventy two others transported to the West Indies, Newfoundland, and the Madeira Islands.

Many of those arrested, tortured, deported, or killed may have been innocent victims of the fear and anger that overtook New York in 1740 and 1741, but revolt was certainly in the minds of many of the city's slaves. White New Yorkers knew that slaves, at their core, were indeed insurrectionists and would repeat acts of aggression and rebellion against the White community unless the most draconic measures were taken. Had New Yorkers regarded their slaves as docile and childish "Sambos," no such conspiracy would have been believable, and no such brutal punishment would have been meted out. New Yorkers

were not eager to destroy human property in which they had invested. But they lived with a gnawing fear that their slaves were truculent, resistant workers whose desire for freedom seldom flagged. Incidents such as the one in New York show that even in the Northern colonies, slaves awaited opportunities to cast off their chains or inflict on White society some of the pain that had been apportioned to them.

Black Culture in Colonial America

Resistance and rebellion were forms of attacking the system of slavery, of attempting in piecemeal fashion to end the institution. With power massively stacked against the slave in this quest, it is not surprising that the incidence of organized group resistance was low. More important than counting slave rebellions is understanding how slaves, living within the confining limits of a degrading, brutal system, carved out areas of cultural and personal autonomy in order to make life bearable. Viewing the plantation or the city as "a battlefield where slaves fought masters for physical and psychological survival"[25] enables us to understand the private side of black life and culture in colonial North America.

In investigating the nature of slave culture, several dimensions of the acculturation process must be kept in mind. First, captive Africans came from many cultures in West Africa. Beneath this tribal diversity flowed a number of important shared characteristics; but upon arriving in North America, Africans could forge informal communities only by blending their various heritages within the limiting scaffolding imposed by the slave system itself.

This process of amalgamating specific cultural backgrounds within the context of the European slave masters' culture began with language aboard the slave ships, where on the long Middle Passage enslaved Africans from a range

---

[25]John W. Blassingame, *The Slave Community: Plantation Life in the Antebellum South* (New York, 1972), p. 184.

of language groups devised a variety of pidgins to allow communication. Once on the western side of the Atlantic, there was little motive to retain native tongues because they were cast into a multilingual assemblages of the enslaved. When they bore children, they had little incentive to teach sons and daughters a native language because it was not useful in communicating with masters and slaves of other African nations. Usually the old had to yield to the new.

Second, in adapting to slavery in the Americas, enslaved Africans found it easier to perpetuate or adapt religious values, expressive forms, craft skills, and modes of forming male-female bonds than to re-create formal institutions. A Dahomean priesthood could not survive the transition to the slave South, but voodoo and burial rituals could. Yoruban regal ceremonies had no opportunity to transit the Atlantic, but the ceremonial use of the drum did.

With these two strictures in mind, we can examine how slaves created a new cultural dynamic in colonial America, focusing particularly on religion, work, the family, and aesthetics. The unending struggle of enslaved Africans was to preserve their humanity within the boundaries of a soul-wracking system of compelled labor and to skirt or challenge White control.

Religion

Enslaved Africans brought with them to the Americas a complex religious heritage, and no amount of desolation or physical abuse could wipe out these deeply rooted beliefs. In fact, people enduring the daily stress inherent in the master-slave relationship typically turned for relief to their deepest emotive sources. Thus, religion stood near the center of African American slave existence and religious activities became "areas of considerable potential creativity and social strength."[26]

Though they were born in a variety of societies with many religious differences, most Africans clambering off slave ships in the North American colonies shared certain religious principles and ritual patterns. Widespread among the societies from Senegambia to Angola on the west coast of Africa was belief in a Supreme Creator of the cosmos and a pantheon of lesser gods who were associated with forces in nature such as rain, animals, and the fertility of the earth. These gods had the power to intervene in the affairs of humankind and therefore had to be propitiated. Ancestors, in the West African belief system, also had the power to affect the welfare of village life, for they mediated between the living and the lesser gods. It was, therefore, important to ensure the entrance of deceased family members into the spiritual world with elaborate funeral rites that honored them properly for the role they would play after death. Finally, West Africans believed in spirit possession, by which the gods spoke to men and women through priests and other religious "experts."

Although differing from the religious beliefs of their slave owners, in some cases, especially among slaves brought from the Kongo region, conversion to Christianity had already occurred or "they probably had a greater knowledge of Christianity before embarkation as a result of missionary endeavors."[27] Other Africans also stood on some common ground with their masters. Africans and Europeans shared beliefs about a physical world where everyone lived and an "other world" inhabited by the souls of the dead. Both cultures believed the "other world" could not be seen but could be known through revelations that spiritually gifted persons could interpret. These roughly shared foundations of religious feeling made it possible for a hybrid African Christianity to develop. African religious customs, funeral rites, sacred images, and charms for protection against evil spirits were no doubt attenuated on New World plantations or melded with elements of Christianity. How fast this process happened is murky, but clearly it varied from place to place. In New England, the enslaved were few in number, and the attempts to indoctrinate them into Christian belief were relatively

[26]John Thornton, *Africa and Africans in the Making of the Atlantic World, 1400–1680* (Cambridge, MA, 1992), p. 254.
[27]George Rawick, *From Sundown to Sunup: The Making of the Black Community* (Westport, CT, 1972), p. 32.

strenuous. Both private religious instruction and public churchgoing were common among slaves, and by the mid-eighteenth century many black children were attending schools opened by Anglicans and Quakers in New York and Philadelphia. In the Northern towns, Protestant ministers performed slave marriages and baptized their children. Also, because slaves usually lived within White households in small numbers rather than in slave quarters amid a black community, African ways eroded more rapidly than in the South.

On Southern plantations, slave masters were not so eager to see their coerced laborers instructed in Christianity. Though sluggishly, the missionary wing of the Anglican Church sent its agents into many areas in the eighteenth century, and other churches also began to instruct slaves. Moreover, African beliefs and rituals persisted longer than in the North because on the plantation, the enslaved person could maintain a greater sense of a collective experience and was constantly in touch with their homelands through freshly arriving slaves. Recognizing this influence, slave masters were caught in a dilemma. If the perpetuation of African religion fostered a collective identity and fed the spirit of resistance, then it was imperative to replace it with Christian belief. But at the same time, the owner was loath to have his human property subjected to a new religion with liberatory undercurrents that would make an enslaved African a less willing worker. So, when masters permitted their bondspeople to attend church, it was with the hope that they would learn the Christian ideals of meekness, humility, and obedience, as the missionaries promised, and not the ideals of the brotherhood of humans or the story of the Hebrew flight from oppression.

A clergyman did not last long anywhere in the South if he threatened the slavocracy. Thus, Protestant ministers and Catholic priests lectured slaves that acceptance of Christ was not to be confused with obtaining freedom. Reinforcing this, most colonies passed laws to make it clear that baptism did not place the master under the slightest obligation to manumit his slaves. But try as they might to suppress it, the idea spread among the enslaved in the eighteenth-century

South that baptism was a first step toward freedom. Whether this idea reflected slave familiarity with the Western tradition that no Christian could enslave another Christian or sprang from another source is uncertain. But the equation of baptism and eventual freedom spread. In 1730, following a period of unusual missionary activity in Virginia, a number of baptized slaves circulated the word that their acceptance of Christ entitled them to freedom. Several hundred slaves gathered in Norfolk and Princess Anne counties in Virginia to foment a rebellion, but White planters discovered the plan and hanged four black leaders. Thereafter, resistance to catechizing slaves grew.

The Great Awakening in the 1740s ushered in a new era of activity among those eager to Christianize slaves and a new era of receptivity among the enslaved to the precepts of Christianity. In the Anglican parish of Williamsburg, the capital of Virginia, white ministers baptized nearly 1000 Africans in a single generation from 1746 to 1768. Presbyterians were also active in the Southern colonies beginning about 1740. Samuel Davies, a leading Presbyterian, boasted that he had one hundred slaves in his congregation in Hanover County, Virginia, in 1750, and a few years later claimed that some 300 blacks received instruction from him. The Anglican Jonathan Boucher recorded that he baptized 315 slaves on a single day in 1767. By this time, Anglican, Presbyterian, and Methodist ministers had indoctrinated many enslaved Virginians, especially those living in the vicinity of towns such as Williamsburg and Norfolk.

Investing these efforts with special force was the revivalists' style and message. For a people whose ancestral religion was grounded primarily in an understanding of nature as in-dwelling and whose eschatological vision allowed for no sharp differences between the secular and the sacred, religion and daily life being conjoined, Protestantism always had a limited appeal. Highly literate and rational, sanitized of its mystical elements, and guarded over by professional clergymen who stressed passivity among worshippers, the Protestant service seemed unintelligible or comfortless in the strange and repressive world of the enslaved. But the revivalists of the 1740s and 1750s were different. They preached a personal rebirth, using music and body motion, and invited the dynamic participation of each individual in an intense emotional experience. This had a tremendous appeal to Africans. Here was a religious outlook that had meaning for the daily experience of slave life and shared enough with ancestral styles and beliefs such as spirit possession to allow for the creation of a unique black Christianity. Especially in the ecstatic expression associated with evangelical religion, in the dancing, shouting, rhythmic clapping, and singing, West African spirit possession merged with European Christianity. Indeed, to some degree, African culture influenced White awakeners, especially in a more ecstatic spirituality and in the idea of heaven as a place to be reunified with ancestors.

Slave masters hoped that Christian doctrine, whether of the ascetic, rational variety or the emotional, revivalistic type, would be the opiate of their slaves. Even if their chattels shared nothing of what their labor produced, even if they lost all their rights they could at least comfort themselves with the knowledge that Christianity sanctified the weak, the poor, and the humble. But slaves did not passively accept what the Anglican or Presbyterian minister chose to teach. They drew selectively from White Christianity and shaped their own religious experience to gain control of an aspect of life that was semi-independent from the master's power but also provided a psychological mechanism for channeling anger and shielding aggression in ways that would not bring physical retribution from the White community.

Black spirituals reveal a great deal about this two-edged nature of religion. Many of the slave spirituals were adaptations of White spirituals or a unique blend of African rhythm patterns, Anglo-American melodies, and adapted words, which reflected the pain of the slave experience. Some of the spirituals were called "sorrow songs," and the musical expression of this pain was no doubt cathartic for those who sang them communally. Another theme of the spirituals, however, was that of worth and strength. We cannot know whether such songs as "We Are the People of God," or "I Really Do Believe I'm a Child of God," or "I'm Born of God, I Know I Am" were sung by slaves in the eighteenth century, because it is extremely difficult to date their origins. But there is reason to believe that if slaves found them sustaining in the nineteenth century, they would have created songs and spirituals with similar themes in the pre-Revolutionary period. What is impressive about these songs is that they portray feelings of worthiness and even a belief that slaves will ultimately prevail because they are superior to the masters. In a society that worked to convince slaves of their lack of worth and the poverty of their African culture, the songs show a strong black self-esteem, an abiding feeling of communal fellowship, and a sense of purpose to life. Black religious music demonstrates how difficult it was for White society to remake the black consciousness and to coerce the black slave into internalizing White values.[28]

The theme of resistance and rebellion was also woven into many of the slave songs. The spiritual celebrating Samson, who sang, "If I had my way, I'd tear this building down," may have had only biblical meaning for the whites who sang it on Sunday mornings in the parish churches of the South. But for black workers in the field, the building was the edifice of slavery, and tearing it down meant nothing less than the destruction of the slave system. Similarly, the spiritual "Didn't My Lord Deliver Daniel," which referred to the deliverance of the Hebrews from their enemies, had a more modern meaning for the black slaves who adopted the song as one of their own.

Work

Throughout most of the Atlantic world, from southern New England to the southernmost reaches of Latin America, African labor was vital

<hr/>

[28]Lawrence W. Levine, "Slave Songs and Slave Consciousness: An Exploration in Neglected Sources," in Tamara K. Hareven, ed., *Anonymous Americans: Explorations in Nineteenth-Century Social History* (Englewood Cliffs, NJ, 1971), pp. 99–130.

in the development of agricultural economies. One Southern planter put it succinctly: "The planters in general have throve and grown rich by the help and labour of their slaves, for their lands though ever so fertile are of no use or profit without them."[29]

African American slaves in the English colonies turned daily labor—the very core of their existence and the entire reason for the investment of capital in chattel property—into a contested area and adapted African work habits to New World conditions in a way that made life more bearable. Slaves were aware that the labor they did benefited only the master. But in their daily work, they behaved in a number of ways—shamming sickness, breaking hoes, uprooting freshly planted seedlings, and harvesting carelessly—that signaled their defiance of the exhortations and floggings of the masters, overseers, and drivers. From these responses, masters learned that there were limits beyond which they dare not go, for to push too hard was only to prove the law of diminishing returns. To deny the slaves the traditional Sunday holiday or the usual Christmas respite, for example, could result in less rather than more work being done in the future. Similarly, to set work standards too high only encouraged slaves to accomplish less or to retaliate against their masters. The lesson was clearly stated in 1732 by the South Carolina *Gazette,* which reported that a master who had driven his slaves late into the night, cleaning and barreling a rice crop, found his barn "and all that was in it" burned to ashes by morning.[30]

Masters, of course, wanted to wring from their slaves the maximum amount of work. To do this, they employed a gamut of devices, running from the whip at one end of the spectrum to positive incentives at the other. Many of them concluded that nothing could turn the slave into a willing worker. "I find it almost impossible," complained Landon Carter, one of Virginia's largest slave owners, "to make a negro do his work well. No orders can engage it, no encouragement persuade it, nor no punishment oblige it."[31] In the end, Southern planters learned that, though the White work ethic could never be instilled in those who labored only to produce profits for others, they could get the most from their slaves by delegating authority and creating a hierarchy of black workers. The tasking system, used especially along the rice coast of South Carolina and Georgia, was another method of obtaining satisfactory output and, from the slaves' point of view, of ensuring work boundaries that left them relatively free of direct supervision and time to cultivate their own plots or take their ease. On nearly every rice plantation, the slaves' work rhythm had to be negotiated between African workers and European masters. "Should any owner increase the work beyond what is customary," wrote one South Carolina planter, "he subjects himself to the reproach of his neighbors, and to such discontent amongst his slaves as to make them of little use to him."[32]

Africans also reacted in positive ways to work by developing a "black work ethic." Because most slaves had been seized from agrarian societies, they were already partially prepared for agricultural field work. This part of the adjustment to slavery was probably easier than most others, the more so for women because they had been primarily responsible for crop cultivation in their African homelands. In the colonial South, masters kept most slave women at work in the fields. Reflecting work patterns that were traditional, slaves proved that they would work harder and longer at tasks that required collective labor, but offered resistance to working by themselves. In this preference for collective labor, they demonstrated an attitude toward work that contrasted to the European norm of the

[29]Quoted in Philip D. Morgan, *Slave Counterpoint: Black Culture in the Eighteenth-Century Chesapeake and Low Country* (Chapel Hill, NC, 1998), p. 146.

[30]South Carolina *Gazette,* October 14, 1732, quoted in Wood, *Black Majority . . . ,* p. 293.

[31]Jack P. Greene, ed., *The Diary of Colonel Landon Carter of Sabine Hall, 1752–1776,* 2 vols. (Charlottesville, VA, 1965), II, 733.

[32]Quoted in Morgan, *Slave Counterpoint . . . ,* p. 184.

individual's following his or her "calling" and laboring independently. Their African background had inured them to collective agricultural labor, and they strove to maintain this pattern of work in their lifetime of bondage.

The lives of most slaves were measured out by the requirements of the particular crop they worked: rice, indigo, tobacco, or wheat. But gradually, in the eighteenth century, as staple economies matured and plantation size increased, a growing percentage of slaves escaped field labor. Overseeing other slaves, working in crafts, serving multiple roles in plantation houses, and transporting goods, enslaved Africans found new occupational opportunities that at least partially improved their lives. In the South Carolina low country, about one in four males worked outside the fields by the 1780s, and in the Chesapeake region, perhaps one in three. In the North, at least half of all slaves worked outside agricultural regimens. Notably, women had much less chance of escaping grueling field labor because slave men dominated the crafts and transportation services, leaving domestic work in the planter's house as the only opportunity for women to escape crop labor.

If enslaved craftspeople became common in Northern towns by the mid-eighteenth century, they dominated the work of carpentry, blacksmithing, coopering, shoemaking, and tailoring on large Southern plantations. One Northern visitor in the Chesapeake observed that "the principal planters have nearly everything they can want on their own estates. Amongst their slaves are found tailors, shoemakers, carpenters, smiths, turners, wheelwrights, weavers, tanners, etc."[33] He might have added potters, basket makers, iron makers, boatbuilders, bricklayers, and stonemasons. As wagoneers, boatmen, and fishermen, enslaved Africans also came to dominate the waterways of the South.

Household slaves, coming to enfold the lives of perhaps one of every ten slaves in the most established parts of the South, also found at least some respite from punishing field labor. Men served as gardeners, stablemen, coachmen, grooms, butchers, cooks, and waiting men, whereas women performed as housemaids, nurses and midwives, dairy maids, cooks, poultry women, bakers, spinners, and weavers.

Family

In the family—the close intimate connections between man and woman, parent and child, and brother and sister—slaves developed the most important bastion of defense against the hardships and heartaches of slavery. In West Africa, all social relations were centered in kinship; and kinship lines, stretching backward to include the dead, were vital to the individual in locating himself or herself in the local society. Hence, in developing new lifeways under the ordeal of slavery, Africans had to surmount the horror of being torn from their kinship networks and deprived of their prior status in ancestral societies. For this reason, the task of rebuilding kin groups, within which the most intimate aspects of life were carried out—love, sexuality, birth, child rearing, and death—must have been regarded as supremely important.

From the master's point of view, slave family life was theoretically impossible. Authority was to flow in only one direction—from owner to bond servant and never among slaves themselves. In most English colonies, unlike Spanish and Portuguese America, law prohibited contractual marriage, for chattel could not make contracts. But in reality, domestic life was another area in which slaves and masters struck a bargain. For their part, slave owners found that to prohibit family life interfered with profitably managing the plantation or farm. For the slaves, defining their own social and interpersonal relations within the confines of slave quarters became so important that they were willing to risk the master's ultimate power of life and death over them to secure the right to play an active role in shaping familial relationships.

---

[33]Quoted in ibid., pp. 225–226.

To be sure, slave masters placed obstacles in the way of their bondspeople who attempted to reconstruct African kinship ties in North America. Once formed, a marriage-like relationship was rarely secure because it could precipitously end with the sale of either spouse. This kind of wrenching separation happened repeatedly. Likewise, children were often torn from the family through sale or dealt to the master's children when they married. Also, many masters hired out their slaves, adding to the difficulties of maintaining a stable relationship.

Family life was also stunted by the general shortage of women, although the excess of males was never so pronounced in the British mainland colonies as in the Caribbean islands and many parts of Spanish and Portuguese America. Throughout the seventeenth and eighteenth centuries, Africans were imported in a ratio of about two men to each women. This excess of males, especially in the South, meant that permanent or semipermanent relationships were possible for perhaps half to two-thirds of enslaved males. As natural increase swelled the slave population after 1730, this gender disparity gradually disappeared, but it was not until a generation or so after the closing of the slave trade in 1808 that parity was finally reached. In the North, where enslaved Africans were sparsely held, this problem was intensified because, although the gender ratio was more even than in the South, most slave owners held only one or two slaves, meaning that male and female slaves only occasionally lived together under the same roof. They had to seek partners on neighboring farms or even distant ones.

Still another barrier to satisfactory family life was White male sexual aggression against black women. How many black women were assaulted or lured with favors into sexual relations with White masters cannot be known, although judging from the sizable mulatto population by 1800, the number cannot have been small.

Interracial sex was particularly widespread in the South, where White women were less available to White men and black women more so than in the North. The South Carolina *Gazette* in 1732 called miscegenation an "Epidemical Disease,"[34] and thirty-five years later, a visiting New Englander noted that "the enjoyment of a negro or mulatto woman is spoken of as quite a common thing: no reluctance, delicacy, or shame is made about the matter."[35]

For a black husband to know of or witness the assault of a White slave owner upon his wife was probably the most psychologically destructive and socially disruptive weapon in the White person's arsenal. "In its political contours," one historian points out, "the rape of the black woman was not exclusively an attack upon her. Indirectly, its target was also the slave community as a whole. In launching the sexual war on the woman, the master not only asserted his sovereignty over a critically important figure of the slave community, he would also be aiming a blow against the black man."[36] Sexual exploitation of black women often had traumatic effects on slave attempts to build stable relationships because the male head of the family was usually powerless to defend those closest to him from the most intimate and painful form of attack.

Not all interracial liaisons were cruel and coercive. Many amounted to common-law marriages between slave masters and their female slaves. Most affectionate interracial unions, it appears, began with a White master who came to love a black mistress. Such was the case of Thomas Wright, a Virginian who fathered six children with Sylvia, his chattel property. This couple openly lived together in the 1780s and 1790s, and Wright's attachment to Sylvia led to freeing her, providing for her after his death, and openly recognizing his children, one of whom inherited his father's plantation and married a White woman.

---

[34]Quoted in Wood, *Black Majority . . .* , p. 235.
[35]Quoted in Morgan, *Slave Counterpoint . . .* , p. 406.
[36]Angela Davis, "Reflections on the Black Woman's Role in the Community of Slaves," *Black Scholar,* 3 (1971–1972): 13.

Such relationships, which sometimes endured for the lifetimes of the partners, were nonetheless threatening, both to the slave community and to the White plantation ideal. They spanned the theoretically unbridgeable gap between the slave and free sectors of society, and they often produced children who, though legally slaves, lived in a twilight zone. White paternity and affection for mulatto offspring often led to favored treatment and sometimes to manumission, but for the black male the advantages of this crack in the wall of slavery had to be weighed against the pain that attended the sight of a sister, daughter, or former mate entering the slave master's private world.

Even in the face of these formidable obstacles, Africans in bondage fashioned intimate ties between man and woman, parent and child. Men and women frequently formed monogamous relationships, and if these did not last as long as in White society, a large part of the explanation lies in aspects of the system that were beyond the slave's control—the shorter life span of African Americans, the breakup of marriage through the sale of one or both partners, and the call of freedom that impelled many Africans to run away. Many planters encouraged their slaves to live together and to take up the role of parents, for they found that enchained laborers were more dutiful and less likely to flee when they were tied to a spouse and offspring. It was not so much a concern for the morality of their slaves as an interest in maximizing the output of labor and minimizing insubordination that led owners to promote slave marriage and family life.

Within the black family, what were the roles of the man and the woman? This vexed question has assumed new importance because the idea is prevalent today that the welfare family, headed by a woman, is a replication of a slave matriarchate. In this view, the slave mother, as the noted sociologist E. Franklin Frazier has written, "was generally the recognized head of the family group. She was the mistress of the cabin to which the 'husband' or father often made only weekly visits. Under such circumstances, a maternal group took form and the tradition of the Negro woman's responsibility for her family took root."[37] Following this formulation, it is assumed that the enslaved in the United States emerged after emancipation with only a faint tradition of normal family life. Buffeted by the problems of trying to adapt as free people to an increasingly urban and industrial world, ex-slaves were never able to knit together the same nuclear, two-parent family that served as the norm in the White community. Nor did they necessarily aspire to monogamous nuclear families because that was not the norm in most African societies, where a more flexible definition of kinship produced extended household groupings that embraced more than natal kin.

Although the black matriarchal family structure no doubt existed to some extent in the eighteenth-century Southern colonies, it was probably not the characteristic slave family. Enslaved men were undoubtedly emasculated in important ways because they could not occupy the dominant role in family and community relationships as they had in the villages of Africa. But the black male did assert his authority by supplementing the food supply through trapping and fishing; by organizing the garden plot behind the slave cabin; by disciplining his children; and most of all, by being the principal figure in the active resistance to slavery. Men in bondage did marry enslaved women, and together they established a relatively stable family life, considering the deterrents inherent in the situation. In some cases, slaves were able to preserve these relationships by threatening rebellion. For example, the government of South Carolina, reeling under the blows of the Yamasees in 1715, negotiated a promise of 130 militiamen from Virginia in exchange for an equal number of slave women. But threats of

---

[37]*The Negro Family in America,* quoted in John H. Bracey, August Meier, and Elliott Rudwick, eds., *Black Matriarchy: Myth or Reality?* (Belmont, CA, 1971), p. 8.

a full-scale insurrection if the women were sent northward forced the Carolinians to renege on their part of the bargain.[38]

While African men struggled to preserve their familial role, black women came to occupy a position in the family and in the black community that differed markedly from that of White women. By custom and law in the Anglo-American world, women were regarded as inferior to men and subservient to them in almost all matters. Moreover, on Southern plantations, the ideology of domesticity kept White women confined in the home where they were expected to be the guardians of White virtue and culture. Black women, by contrast, remained indispensably important to both the work of the plantation and the stability of the slave community. They worked in the fields, they worked in the "big house," and they worked in the slave cabin. It was ironic, Angela Davis has written, that the enslaved woman "had to be released from the chains of the myth of femininity. In order to function as slave, the black woman had to be annulled as woman—that is, as woman in her historical stance of wardship under the entire male hierarchy. The sheer force of things rendered her equal to her man. Male supremacist structures could not become deeply embedded in the internal workings of the slave system."[39]

Caught in the net of slavery, the black woman thus maintained a position of strength and autonomy within the black community that made her far more equal to the male than was the case of women in White society. The black family was a partnership of equals in the tasks performed and responsibilities shouldered. In this respect, it bore closer resemblance to Algonquian and Siouian family structure than to European family organization, for in Indian cultures, women were also vitally important in agricultural work, child-rearing responsibilities were shared, and the woman in general maintained a degree of power and autonomy not allowed in Euro-American society.

Because slavery was, above all else, a system for extracting the maximum amount of labor from its victims, it chronically involved cruelties that often made family life almost impossible to maintain. But, in general, North American slaves were better clothed, fed, and treated than those in the West Indies, Brazil, or other parts of the Americas, where settled White society took only shallow root and plantation owners found it more profitable literally to work their slaves to death and then purchase fresh replacements from Africa. When conditions were conducive to sustaining life, slaves were effective in defining a culture of their own. As one black scholar has written: "Slaves were able to fashion a life style and a set of values—an ethos—which prevented them from being imprisoned altogether by the definitions which the larger society sought to impose. This ethos was an amalgam of Africanisms and New World elements which helped slaves . . . 'feel their way along the course of American slavery, enabling them to endure. . . . '"[40]

Aesthetics

What a society values for its beauty and the pleasure it gives can loosely be called *aesthetics*. This is the part of African culture that was most resistant to the brutality of slavery. How to form a pot from clay, style one's hair, arrange fabric over the body, play an instrument, play on words, or use one's voice became parts of the culture that enslaved Africans developed in the American colonies.

Music and dance were central to everyday life in the field where slaves toiled, in the quarters where they lived, and in woods and along riverbanks where they gathered in off-hours. "We are almost a nation of dancers, musicians, and poets," Olaudah Equiano wrote in his

---

[38]David D. Wallace, *South Carolina: A Short History, 1520–1948* (Chapel Hill, NC, 1951), p. 91.
[39]Angela Davis, "The Black Woman's Role," p. 7.
[40]Sterling Stuckey, "Through the Prism of Folklore: The Black Ethos in Slavery," *The Massachusetts Review,* 9 (1968): 418.

autobiographical account of eighteenth-century enslavement.[41] Jefferson (who viewed African culture negatively in most respects) admitted that Africans "are more generally gifted than the whites with accurate ears for tune and time."[42] Dancing was rarely absent when slaves gathered, usually to the accompaniment of drums, rattles, sometimes banjoes, and clapping. In all of this, the African musical and dance heritage remained vibrant. Surviving the Middle Passage, they melded with European musical traditions, particularly in the African appropriation of the violin or fiddle. But always, complex rhythms sounded out with rattles, drums, and gongs were distinctively African.

It is in the realm of music that we can see how the culture of an exploited and brutalized people could "swim uphill" to conquer the hearts and minds of those who claimed cultural superiority. The blues and jazz music of today, though they have gone through many phases, has distinct African origins, and it is no exaggeration to say that the virtuosity and aesthetic appeal of African-derived music has become almost universal. As historian John Thornton has maintained, "the conquest of the musical world of the whole Western hemisphere by music of African origin" took place in spite of the widespread disparagement of African culture.[43] Polyrhythmic music and use of blue notes that did not conform to European scale divisions are only some of the characteristics of African music that began to transform the music of those who enslaved them.

Aesthetic adornment also exhibited African cultural retention while showing cultural borrowing. The designing and shaping of hair, using braiding and plaiting with beads, shells, and strips of material, drew upon homeland fashions and patterns. So did adorning the body with brass wire earrings, beaded armbands and necklaces, and cloth bands draped over or wrapped around the body. Headgear, prized in Africa, made its way across the Atlantic; but in this sartorial area, rapid innovation with beaver and raccoon skins, as well as Scotch bonnets, created African European effects. More important than the exact blending of cultures from two continents was the role of personal adornment in refusing to succumb to the dehumanization of slavery.

How much of African culture survived under eighteenth-century slavery can never be determined quantitatively; nor is it especially important to do so. It is enough to understand that Africans in the English plantations adapted elements of African culture to the demands of a new life and a new environment. Slave masters were doubtless intent on obliterating any Africanism that reduced the effectiveness of slaves as laborers, and they had some success in this. It is also true that slavery eliminated many of the cultural differences among slaves, who came from a wide variety of African cultural groups—Fulanis, Ibos, Yorubas, Malagasies, Ashantis, Mandingos, and others. At the same time, throughout the eighteenth century, unlike in the nineteenth, large numbers of new Africans were arriving each year. Slave importations grew rapidly in the eighteenth century so that probably never more than half the adult slaves were American-born. This continuous infusion of African culture kept alive many of the elements that later were transmuted almost beyond recognition. By fashioning their own distinct culture, within the limits established by the rigors of the slave system, blacks were able to forge their own religious forms, their own music and dance, their own family life, and their own beliefs and values. All these proved indispensable to surviving brutal forced labor. Though slaves might have feigned deference or submissiveness and were severely constrained in many respects, they drew upon important elements of traditional culture and learned to carve out important areas of activity that gave meaning and importance to life.

[41]Robert J. Allison, ed., *The Interesting Life of Olaudah Equiano* (Boston, MA, 1995), p. 36.
[42]William Peden, ed., *Notes on the State of Virginia by Thomas Jefferson* (Chapel Hill, NC, 1954), p. 140.
[43]John Thornton, *A Cultural History of the Atlantic World, 1250–1820* (Cambridge, MA, 2012), p. 386.

Summary

Once enslaved and sold to masters in colonial North America, Africans had to adapt to life under disorientation and oppression. In the process, African American culture took shape differently, depending upon the region—the Spanish and French borderlands, the Chesapeake region, the Georgia and Carolina low country, and the North—because slavery itself varied widely.

Unaccepting of their bondage, enslaved Africans found many ways to resist: escape, truancy, arson, crop destruction, poisoning and murder, organized pilfering, and, as the most extreme way to resist, suicide. Sometimes outright rebellion took place; the largest uprising in colonial North America took place in South Carolina in 1739, though outbreaks occurred in the Northern colonies as well. In general, though, the enslaved Africans had to find ways to survive, while hoping for eventual freedom. Searching for ways to make life bearable, Africans adapted ancient homeland religious values, expressive forms, craft skills, and modes of forming male-female bonds to the realities of life in the American colonies. In their struggle to maintain their humanity within confined circumstances, religion, work, family life, and aesthetics figured prominently.

Critical Thinking Questions

1. Under harsh and restrictive living conditions in the colonies, enslaved Africans were able to forge lifeways and adapt African cultural characteristics to the new realities of their unenviable lives. How were they able to do this?
2. Did enslaved Africans experience, in general, a greater degree of acculturation in the Northern or Southern colonies, and why was this so?
3. Resistance on the part of the enslaved Africans took many forms. What were some of those forms, and what did the enslaved hope to accomplish?
4. The family acted as a bulwark against the sorrows and difficulties of the slave life. What attitudes on the part of whites and what societal circumstances posed a threat to the families of enslaved Africans?

Further Reading

Ira Berlin, *Many Thousands Gone: The First Two Centuries of Slavery in North America* (Cambridge: Harvard University Press, 1998).

Leland G. Ferguson, *Uncommon Ground: Archaeology of Early African America, 1650–1800* (Washington, DC: Smithsonian Institution Press, 1992).

Michael Gomez, *Exchanging Our Country Marks: The Transformation of African Identities in the Colonial and Antebellum South* (Chapel Hill: University of North Carolina Press, 1998).

Graham Russell Hodges, *Root & Branch: African Americans in New York & East New Jersey, 1613–1863* (Chapel Hill: University of North Carolina Press, 1999).

Jill Lepore, *New York Burning: Liberty, Slavery, and Conspiracy in Eighteenth-Century Manhattan* (New York: Vintage Books, 2005).

Phillip Morgan, *Slave Counterpoint: Black Culture in the Eighteenth-Century Chesapeake and Low Country* (Chapel Hill: University of North Carolina Press, 1998).

Gerald W. Mullin, *Flight and Rebellion: Slave Resistance in Eighteenth-Century Virginia* (New York: Oxford University Press, 1972).

Anthony Parent, *Foul Means: The Formation of a Slave Society in Virginia, 1660–1740* (Chapel Hill: University of North Carolina Press, 2003).

William D. Piersen, *Black Yankees: The Development of an Afro-American Subculture in Eighteenth-Century New England* (Amherst: University of Massachusetts Press, 1988).

Marie Jenkins Schwartz, *Birthing a Slave: Motherhood and Medicine in the Antebellum South* (Cambridge: Harvard University Press, 2006).

Erik R. Seeman, *Death in the New World: Cross-Cultural Encounters, 1492–1800* (Philadelphia: University of Pennsylvania Press, 2010).

Mechal Sobel, *Trabelin' On: The Slave Journey to an Afro-Baptist Faith* (Princeton: Princeton University Press, 1988).

John Thornton, *A Cultural History of the Atlantic World, 1250–1820* (Cambridge: Cambridge University Press, 2012).

Peter Wood, *Black Majority: Negroes in Colonial South Carolina from 1670 through the Stono Rebellion* (New York: Knopf, 1974).

CHAPTER 8

The Transformation of Euro-American Society

LEARNING OBJECTIVES

- Describe the mix of Europeans who made up the proto-Americans of the seventeenth and eighteenth centuries, and explain how the social origins of those immigrants figured into the social transformation that took place.

- Discuss the indentured servant system: how it came about; its uses and abuses; and the opportunity, or lack thereof, for servants to rise above the system.

- Characterize the two types of agricultural societies that emerged in eighteenth-century North America; explain how the view of land use and

- acquisition changed and how the conceptual unit of thought shifted from the community to the individual.

- Account for the importance of cities such as Boston, New York, and Philadelphia in creating economic, political, and social change in eighteenth-century North America.

- Define the Great Awakening, discuss the role of George Whitefield and other preachers in this movement, and explain how it reflected a profound cultural transformation that had been in the making for generations.

In 1650, the European population of the colonies clinging to the eastern edge of the continent was about the same as the daytime population of a large university campus today—roughly 50,000. Fifty years later, this number had increased fivefold to a quarter million. By 1750, the number had again increased fivefold, including about 240,000 Africans. Such a rate of population growth was unknown in other parts of the world. By the middle of the eighteenth century, the inhabitants of the English colonies in North America were one-third as numerous as the English themselves, and the rate at which the gap between the two populations was closing led early demographers such as Benjamin Franklin to estimate that before another four generations passed, the colonizers would outnumber the population of England.

Eighteenth-Century European Immigrants

These rapidly multiplying proto-Americans were not only English. The seventeenth-century immigrants had come primarily from

162

England, mixing with a small number of Dutch, Swedes, and Finns already settled along the seaboard and with a small number of Germans, Scots-Irish, French, and Africans who arrived late in the seventeenth century. But eighteenth-century immigration belonged to the non-English. Beginning in the second decade of the century, thousands of Germans, Swiss, Ulster Scots-Irish, and Africans poured into the colonies. Some came voluntarily and some involuntarily. But whether arriving as slaves, indentured servants, or free persons, they drastically altered the gene pool of the existing population. By the end of the colonial period, as the Revolution loomed on the horizon, roughly half the inhabitants of the thirteen colonies had no English blood in their veins. This proportion of non-English was greater than at any time in American history, even after the tremendous influx of Europeans in the late nineteenth and early twentieth centuries.

Historians have told us mostly about the lives of only a tiny fraction of this population. We know a great deal about the political and military leaders, the people who amassed fortunes, and those who because of their high positions in society left their names and opinions in the official and private records of the time. But the cultural change occurring in the century prior to the Revolution bore far more relation to the roughly congruent behavior of thousands of "historically voiceless" individuals than to the actions of leaders whose words and deeds form the basis of most of our written history. After the Revolution, John Adams would write that "the poor man's conscience is clear; yet he is ashamed . . . he feels himself out of the sight of others groping in the dark. Mankind takes no notice of him. He rambles and wanders unheeded. In the midst of a crowd, at church, in the market . . . he is in as much obscurity as he would be in a garret or a cellar. He is not disapproved, censured, or reproached; he is only not seen."[1] Similarly, historians have "not seen" the largest part of colonial society whose footprints are only now being discerned in the sands of time.

Yet the work, the wanderings, the attitudes, and the hopes and fears of the masses of inconspicuous individuals led to cultural change so distinct in North America in the eighteenth century that touring Europeans never tired of setting down the characteristics of the people they saw. What they described was a set of economic activities, forms of social and political organization, and a constellation of values and beliefs that were fused together in what we call a culture. During the first three-quarters of the eighteenth century, this culture was transformed so extensively that a John Smith or a John Winthrop, had he still lived, would have been amazed at what he saw.

The social origins of those who flocked to the colonies in the eighteenth century played a part in the social transformation. From the top layers of European society came almost nobody. In the seventeenth century, a small number of Englishmen at the apex of the social pyramid had taken an active role in colonizing the New World—men such as Walter Ralegh and Richard Grenville in Virginia; the Calverts, who founded Maryland; the insiders at the court of Charles II, who became the proprietors of South Carolina and New Jersey; and a handful of others. But for the most part, they contributed money and organizational ability rather than their lives. Only a few tore free of their moorings in England and immigrated permanently to North America. In the eighteenth century, upper-class immigrants were even rarer. Only an occasional Baron de Graffenried or Count von Zinzendorf, usually leaders of groups of Germans, Swiss, or Scots-Irish immigrants, represented the upper stratum of European society.

Below the nobility were the country gentry; grouped with them on the social scale were officeholders, members of the professions, and the wealthier merchants. These people ran the joint-stock companies that had launched the early seventeenth-century settlements, and they continued to provide most of the investment

---

[1]Quoted in James A. Henretta, *The Evolution of American Society, 1700–1815* (Lexington, MA, 1973), pp. 3–4.

capital necessary for developing Atlantic-wide territories. In the seventeenth century, they contributed substantially to the Atlantic migration, either by coming themselves or by sending their younger sons. The Oxford- and Cambridge-trained Puritan ministers, many of the early merchants of Boston and Philadelphia, and some of the large planters of Virginia, Maryland, and the Carolinas were included in this category. But in the eighteenth century, they came in smaller numbers.

A rung below the gentry were the yeoman farmers of the countryside and the artisan-shopkeepers of the cities. In Europe's social hierarchy, these were respected people who bulked large in the membership of the church and were entitled to participate in the political life of the community. Through hard work, good fortune, or a judicious marriage, they often hauled themselves upward a rung on the social ladder or at least lived to see a son enter one of the professions or embark on a career as a merchant. They may have composed as much as one-third of the immigrants to the colonies. Once there, they provided the backbone of the middle class and often moved rapidly upward in a society that had plenty of room at the top. As a group, they were skilled, industrious, and ambitious; their fortunes advanced much faster than if they had remained at home.

Taken together, these recruits from the nobility, gentry, and middle class of European society accounted for roughly one-half of all those Europeans who traveled the water highway to the west side of the Atlantic in the seventeenth century and probably less than a third of the eighteenth-century immigrants. The remaining colonizers consisted mostly of indentured servants—men, women, and children who lacked sufficient resources to pay their way to the New World and therefore contracted out their labor for a number of years in return for passage. Their backgrounds were mixed. Some were obscure shopkeepers, artisans, schoolteachers, and farmers who were down on their luck or sorely pressed by an economic downturn. Many more had never risen above the subsistence level and could not expect to do so. These were the sturdiest of them. The lowliest were paupers and petty criminals—people who sometimes left England, Scotland, Ireland, and Germany voluntarily and sometimes at the demand of the authorities. Local officials gladly rid themselves of the community's undesirables and reduced the poor taxes by banishing the disinherited to what they promised would be a new life—or a quick death—in the New World. The Scottish Privy Council, for example, in attempting to organize a colonizing expedition to New York in 1669, sent out warrants to local authorities to recruit "strong and idle beggars, vagabonds, Egyptians, common and notorious whores, thieves and other dissolute and lousy persons banished or stigmatized for gross crimes."[2] Between 1718 and 1775, British authorities transported about 50,000 convicts—mostly young males convicted of petty crimes, especially theft—to the American colonies.

Indentured Servants

Since indentured servants represented a large proportion of the eighteenth-century immigrants, it is important to understand the mechanics of the profitable business of transporting them to the colonies. Like enslaved Africans and Indians, White indentured servants were invaluable in a society rich in land but poor in labor. Labor in the colonies, Benjamin Franklin wrote in 1759, "is performed chiefly by indentured servants brought from Great Britain, Ireland, and Germany, because the high price it bears cannot be performed in any other way."[3] Franklin was forgetting that enslaved Africans were as numerous as White servants in 1759, even in his hometown of Philadelphia, and that in the Southern colonies they comprised the bulk of the labor force. But his general point is valid: Colonial North America was being developed by unfree laborers. No matter whether the person was a

[2]Quoted in Peter Gouldesbrough, "An Attempted Scottish Voyage to New York in 1669," *Scottish Historical Review*, 40 (1961): 56.
[3]Quoted in Marcus W. Jernegan, *Laboring and Dependent Classes in Colonial America, 1607–1783* (New York, 1965), p. 55.

small tobacco planter in Virginia, a shopkeeper in New York, a farmer in Connecticut, or a shipwright in Boston, nearly every free colonist wanted a bound laborer by his or her side as soon as he or she had accumulated the £20 to £40—equivalent to several years of income—required to purchase one. Additional labor meant the ability to produce more goods or services, which, in turn, meant greater profits. In an age before machines, commanding the labor of others became crucially important.

The terms of indentured servitude were simple. A servant bound himself or herself by contract to a ship captain for a specified length of time, usually four to seven years. In return, the captain agreed to transport the servant across the Atlantic and place him or her on the auction block in one of the colonial seaports. The ship captain signed the work contract over to the highest bidder. By the terms of the indenture, the servant agreed to serve faithfully in return for food, clothes, shelter, and, at the end of the contract, a small sum of money, occasionally some tools, and sometimes a few acres of land.

The traffic in bound labor became a regular part of the commerce linking Europe and North America. A combination of merchants, ship captains, immigrant brokers, and recruiting agents kept thousands of Europeans on their way to the colonies throughout the pre-Revolutionary period. Like any other cargo, servants were loaded onto boats, carried across the ocean, and sold on the other side. The system provided labor for the established colonists, eventual freedom and the chance for a better life for those caught in the net of European poverty, and profits for the middlemen involved. The system was full of abuses. Just as the trade in Indian and African slaves was ridden with callous disregard for human life, so also the trade in contract White labor was often a dirty business. Kidnapping and shanghaiing of drifters and drunks was endemic. Many unfortunate seaport dwellers woke one morning with a head-splitting hangover to find themselves in the hold of a ship headed across the Atlantic. Once on the ship, they found appalling conditions. The description of Gottlieb Mittelberger, who accompanied a boatload of German servants sailing from Rotterdam to Philadelphia in 1750, conveys some feeling for what those seeking a better life in the American colonies endured:

> During the journey the ship is full of pitiful signs of distress—smells, fumes, horrors, vomiting, various kinds of sea sickness, fever, dysentery, headaches, heat, constipation, boils, scurvy, cancer, mouth-rot, and similar afflictions, all of them caused by the age and the highly-salted state of the food, especially the meat, as well as by the very bad and filthy water, which brings about the miserable destruction and death of many. Add to all that shortage of food, hunger, thirst, frost, heat, dampness, fear, misery, vexation, and lamentation, as well as other troubles. Thus, for example, there are so many lice, especially on the sick people, that they have to be scraped off the bodies. All this misery reaches its climax when in addition to everything else one must suffer through two or three days and nights of storm, with everyone convinced that the ship will go to the bottom with all human beings on board. . . . Children between the ages of one and seven seldom survive the sea voyage; and parents must often watch their offspring suffer miserably, die, and be thrown into the ocean, from want, hunger, thirst, and the like. I myself, alas, saw such a pitiful fate overtake thirty-two children on board our vessel, all of whom were finally thrown into the sea.[4]

Mittelberger described how shipmates turned on each other after reaching the limits of endurance. But mostly they recalled the villages from which they had come: "Oh! If only I were back at home, even lying in my pig-sty!" Probably one-quarter of those embarking from European ports never lived to see the forests of the New World or, in their weakened condition, died shortly after arrival—a mortality rate approximating that

[4]Gottlieb Mittelberger, *Journey to Pennsylvania*, Oscar Handlin and John Clive, eds. and trans. (Cambridge, MA, 1960), pp. 12–15.

of the Atlantic slave trade. For those who did survive the ordeal, the dangers of "seasoning" in North America—the acclimatization to a new environment—lay ahead. In addition, they faced a physical and psychological adjustment to a new master. Especially in the Southern colonies, agricultural labor took a deadly toll among those whose masters tried to extract as much labor as possible during the years of the work contract. Adding to the difficulty of the servant's life was the right of the master to forbid marriage. Because it invariably led to pregnancy among female servants, and thus a loss of time, most masters denied their servants a family life.

Given the harshness of the indentured labor system, it is not surprising that colonial newspapers were filled with advertisements for runaway servants, interspersed with notices for runaway slaves. Servants knew the penalties for this: whipping and additional service, usually reckoned at twice the time lost to the master, but sometimes, as in Pennsylvania, calculated at a five-to-one ratio and in Maryland at ten-to-one. Even so, servants fled their masters by the hundreds and occasionally staged minor insurrections. When war came, they flocked to enlist in the British army. Many masters were willing to take the compensation paid by the army and let a balky servant go.

The great goal of every servant was to obtain a place on the ladder of opportunity—or what *seemed* to be such a ladder from a vantage point in the villages of Scotland, Ireland, and Germany. But as one historian has reminded us, "it will not do simply to assume that freed servants, especially those from the tobacco fields, were in any mental or physical condition to start vigorous new lives, or that long and ripe years of productivity lay ahead of them."[5] Although it is extremely difficult to follow the lives of freed servants, an informed study of White servitude indicates that out of every ten indentured servants, only one attained a position as a farmer in comfortable circumstances, and one more achieved the status of artisan. The other eight died before they obtained their freedom or became propertyless day laborers, vagrants, or denizens of the local almshouse after completing their indentures.[6] The life chances of a servant were better than this in the seventeenth century but worsened thereafter, as the early fluidity of society shrank. Though a handful of servants prospered or achieved fame—revolutionary leaders such as Daniel Dulany, Charles Thomson, and John Lamb—the statistical probability for rising even to the middle class was slight. Among the mass of those who sought opportunity in the British American colonies, it is the story of relentless labor and ultimate failure that stands out. The chief beneficiaries of the system of bound White labor were not the laborers themselves but those for whom they labored.

Land, Growth, and Changing Values

Out of the combination of fertile land, a pool of bound laborers, and the ambition of thousands of small farmers and artisans who labored independently, two types of agricultural society emerged in eighteenth-century North America. In the North, small communities made up of farmers and artisans dotted the landscape. New Englanders engaged in mixed farming, which included harvesting the forests for timber used in barrels and ships, and farming the offshore waters for fish that provided one of the staples in the diet of the fast-growing slave population of the West Indies. The Middle Colonies specialized in producing corn, wheat, beef, and pork. By the mid-eighteenth century, they were provisioning not only the West Indies but also parts of Spain, Portugal, and England. A large percentage of free men owned land; and, though differences in ability and circumstances led gradually to greater

[5]Richard Hofstadter, *America at 1750: A Social Portrait* (New York, 1972), p. 61.
[6]Abbot E. Smith, *Colonists in Bondage: White Servitude and Convict Labor in America, 1607–1776* (Chapel Hill, NC, 1946), pp. 297–300.

social and economic stratification, the truly rich and abjectly poor were few in number, and the gap between them was small in comparison with European society. Most men lived to acquire a farm of at least fifty acres. They extracted from the soil a modest income that allowed for security from want while providing a small inheritance for their children.

In the Southern colonies, where tobacco, rice, indigo, and timber products predominated, many yeomen farmers also struggled independently, although they were dispersed across the land rather than clustered in New England–style villages. Historians have noticed these men far less than the plantation owners with slaves and indentured servants. But the usual picture of a Southern plantation society made up of immensely wealthy men exploiting the labor of huge gangs of black slaves is overdrawn. Perhaps as many as 40 percent of the Southern whites worked as tenant farmers or agricultural laborers, and of the remaining men who owned land, about two of every three in the Chesapeake region worked farms of 200 acres or less. In North Carolina, farms were even smaller and men of real wealth rarer. In South Carolina, the opposite was true; slaveholding was more widespread, plantations tended to be larger, and planters of substantial wealth represented a larger proportion of the population. As early as 1726, in St. George's Parish, 87 of 108 families held slaves. A generation later, in St. Bartholomew Parish, about 250 White families owned more than 5,000 slaves.[7] On the eve of the American Revolution, the governor of South Carolina assured a prospective rice planter that "you'll never make yourself whole with less than thirty Negroes."[8]

On the whole, probably not more than 5 percent of the White landowners were wealthy enough by mid-eighteenth century to possess a plantation worth £1,000—not too different from the North.

Similarly, those owning large numbers of Africans were not numerous. The number of those enslaved in the South increased rapidly in the eighteenth century, rising from about 20,000 in 1700 to 240,000 in 1750. But a majority of White adults held no slaves at all at midcentury, and those who operated plantations with more than twenty slaves probably did not exceed 10 percent of the White taxables. South Carolina excepted, the South throughout the pre-Revolutionary period was dominated numerically by small landowners whose holdings, if perhaps twice the size of the average New England farm, were not more than half again as large as the typical farm in Pennsylvania, New Jersey, or New York.

Nonetheless, the ideal in the South was the large plantation where black slaves would make the earth yield up profits sufficient to support the leisured life. Statistically speaking, not many White colonists in the South achieved the dream. But that is what people worked for, and they came to identify the quest for material comfort with the exploitation of African slave labor in an era when the Northern colonists were beginning to phase out White bound labor and turning to an Atlantic-wide market economy in which both goods and labor were freely exchanged.

The Protestant work ethic, which purportedly propelled people upward by inculcating a life of frugality, industriousness, and closely calibrated economic activity, perhaps operated less dynamically among Southern colonists than among their Northern counterparts. But the abundant, fertile land of the South and the wider availability of enslaved Africans after 1690 provided all the incentive necessary to incubate an aggressive, competitive society. Much folklore about Southern cavaliers reposing under magnolia trees has been handed down in the history books, but in the eighteenth century, European colonizers in the South as avidly pursued wealth

[7]Frank J. Klingberg, *An Appraisal of the Negro in Colonial South Carolina: A Study in Americanization* (Washington, DC, 1941), pp. 58–60; William Langhorne, "An Account of the Spiritual State of St. Bartholomew's Parish" (1752), *South Carolina Magazine of History*, 50 (1949): 200.
[8]Quoted in Philip D. Morgan, *Slave Counterpoint: Black Culture in the Eighteenth-Century Chesapeake and Low Country* (Chapel Hill, NC, 1998), p. 35.

and material comfort as European colonizers in the North. If the warm climate of the South bred languor, it was also true that farmers in the South had no long, frozen winters when there was little to do but mend harness and chop wood. The typical New England farm produced just one crop each year, but a South Carolina rice or indigo plantation produced two crops. Moreover, the restraints of a New England community orientation and the Puritan bias against the accumulation of wealth that was not used in socially useful ways never hindered entrepreneurial activity in the South. Also, organized religion was only shallowly rooted in most of the Southern colonies, and the community orientation never took hold because communities themselves were few and far between.

Paradoxically, one of the effects of the growth and success of the colonies in eighteenth-century British America was to shatter the utopian dream of the first generation that communities could be built where men and women worked for the commonweal, not only for themselves. The Puritan work ethic and an atmosphere of seemingly limitless opportunity encouraged men to work hard at their callings. That was to the good. And their labors had generally been rewarded with success. So was that. But living where the ratio of people to land was so favorable compared with the societies from which they came, many colonists developed an aggressive outlook that patterned their behavior. What was to hold back a person in these uncharted expanses of land and unclaimed river valleys, as soon as the Indians were gone? In Europe, the absence of uncultivated lands ripe for exploitation and the grinding poverty that enshrouded the lives of the great mass of people induced in peasants a mentality where little was expected. "The frontier zone between possibility and impossibility barely moved in any significant direction, from the fifteenth to the eighteenth century," writes Fernand Braudel.[9] But it moved in North America. A competitive, entrepreneurial spirit began to take hold where anything seemed possible.

Religion and commitment to community, which acted as brakes on competitive, individualistic behavior, were by no means dead in the eighteenth century. But in general, defining one's life as a preparation for the afterlife declined. Even in the seventeenth century, Roger Williams had deplored the "depraved appetite after the great vanities, dreams, and shadows of this vanishing life, great portions of land, land in this wilderness, as if men were in as great necessity and danger for want of great portions of land, as poor, hungry seamen have, after a sick and stormy, a long and starving passage."[10] In the eighteenth century, land became ever more regarded not simply as a source of livelihood but also as a commodity to be bought and sold speculatively as a means of building a fortune. Benjamin Franklin's little how-to-do-it best seller, *The Way to Wealth,* caught the spirit of the aggressive entrepreneurial eighteenth century. "Every man is for himself," lamented a prominent Philadelphian in 1706, only a generation after Penn had planted the seed of his "Holy Experiment."[11] Two generations later, the lieutenant governor of New York, who had grown up in the colony, put it more explicitly: "The only principle of life propagated among the young people," wrote Cadwallader Colden, "is to get money and men are only esteemed according to what they are worth—that is the money they are possessed of."[12] A contemporary in Rhode Island echoed the thought when he wrote, "A man who has money here, no matter how he came by it, he is everything, and wanting [lacking] that he's a mere nothing, let his conduct be ever so reproachable."[13]

---

[9]Fernand Braudel, *Capitalism and Material Life, 1400–1800,* George Weidenfeld, trans. (New York, 1973), p. ix.
[10]Quoted in Francis Jennings, *The Invasion of America: Indians, Colonialism, and the Cant of Conquest* (Chapel Hill, NC, 1975), p. 181.
[11]Quoted in Gary B. Nash, *Quakers and Politics; Pennsylvania, 1681–1726* (Princeton, NJ, 1968), p. 303.
[12]Quoted in Henretta, The *Evolution of American Society . . . ,* p. 99.
[13]Quoted in Carl Bridenbaugh, *Cities in Revolt; Urban Life in America, 1743–1776* (New York, 1964), p. 140.

"A man who has money" was also an avid consumer. In an early stage of consumerism, colonists by the mid-eighteenth century were buying imported English goods as never before. Imported cloth replaced homespun and Staffordshire china replaced crude earthenware. On one morning, Benjamin Franklin's wife surprised him by serving his porridge not in the usual earthenware bowl and a pewter spoon but in "in a china bowl with a spoon of silver." Often running into debt, colonists quadrupled their imports of English goods between 1740 and 1770—an increase partly due to a ballooning population but also by an increase in wealth at the top and middle strata of society.

As acquisitive values took hold, the individual replaced the community as the conceptual unit of thought. The advice of the forefathers, such as the Puritan minister John Cotton, to "go forth, every man that goeth, with a public spirit, looking not on your own things only," or John Winthrop's maxim that "the care of the public must oversway all private respects," carried less and less weight in eighteenth-century society. A French visitor, who took up residence in New York, described this psychological reorientation:

> An European, when he first arrives, seems limited in his intentions, as well as in his views; but he very suddenly alters his scale. . . . He no sooner breathes our air than he forms schemes, and embarks in designs he never would have thought of in his own country. . . . He begins to feel the effects of a sort of resurrection; hitherto he had not lived, but simply vegetated; he now feels himself a man, because he is treated as such; . . . he begins to forget his former servitude and dependence. . . .[14]

This shift of attitudes, although it promoted phenomenal growth and unleashed economic energies, paradoxically led toward material success that contained within it the seeds of social strain. The demand for land east of the Appalachian Mountain barrier grew rapidly after 1740, as the population rose through immigration and natural increase. Especially, in New England, ungranted land in the coastal region was a thing of the past, and the division and redivision of original land grants among sons and grandsons progressed as far as it could go without splitting farms into unviably small economic units. New land—on the Maine frontier, in western Massachusetts and Connecticut, across the Appalachians in Pennsylvania, Virginia, Maryland, and the Carolinas—was the obvious solution to the problem of overcrowding. Land companies emerged in the mid-eighteenth century to claim the valuable lands to the west. Their investors understood the enormous appreciation in value that would occur as the next generation came of age and sought *lebensraum* to the west. But blocking a westward movement were interior Indian peoples, as well as the French and the Spanish.

The Cities

Even though only about 5 percent of the eighteenth-century colonists lived in cities (none of which exceeded 16,000 in 1750), the commercial capitals of coastal North America were the cutting edge of economic, social, and political change. Almost all the alterations associated with the advent of capitalist society occurred first in the seaport towns and then radiated outward to the villages and farms of the hinterland. In the colonial maritime centers, part of the web of global economic life, the transition first occurred from a barter to a commercial economy; where a competitive social order replaced one based on ascribed status; where a hierarchical and deferential polity gave way to participatory and contentious civic life; and where factory production began to replace small-scale artisan-style production.

In the Atlantic-facing towns of Boston, Newport, New York, Philadelphia, and Charleston, the competitive and acquisitive ethos took hold more rapidly than in rural areas. This tendency did not mean that artisans and laborers always

[14]J. Hector St. John Crèvecoeur, *Letters from an American Farmer* (New York, 1957), pp. 54–56.

worked feverishly to move up the ladder of success. Craftsmen who commanded four or five shillings a day knew that weather, sickness, and the inconstancy of supplies made it difficult to work more than 250 days a year, which earned an income of £35 to £60—equivalent to $7 to $12 thousand today. Hence, laboring people did not regard themselves as failures if they did not acquire substantial property. Their desire was not to reach the top but to get off the bottom. Yet they came to expect a "decent competency," as it was called, and did not anticipate the hand-to-mouth existence of the laboring poor everywhere in Europe. Many of those who started as blacksmiths, carpenters, coopers, and shipwrights rose to the level of shopkeeper or even merchant. A handful did even better, such as William Phips, a sheep farmer and ship's carpenter from Maine who rose to the governorship of Massachusetts, or Benjamin Franklin, a poor printer who came to stand for the opportunities for upward mobility that many thought differentiated the American colonies from Europe.

In the half-century between 1690 and 1740, Boston, New York, and Philadelphia blossomed into commercial centers that rivaled Britain's Hull, Bristol, and Glasgow. This urban growth reflected the development of the hinterlands to which they were commercially linked. More and more, these seaports were drawn into the international marketplace of the Atlantic basin. Increasingly, economic decisions were dictated by an emerging commercial ethic that rubbed abrasively against traditional restraints on entrepreneurial activity. The older economic ethic, medieval in origins, rested on the assumption of a world made up of many semiclosed economies, each operating in a nearly self-sufficient way. A city, according to this model, was connected to the immediately surrounding area, but the area itself remained self-contained.

By the early eighteenth century, the North American seaports had become a part of a wide Atlantic basin network that linked them not only to their hinterlands but also to Newfoundland, the West Indies, Portugal and Spain, England and Ireland, and West Africa. Economic decisions were made under the new order of things, not with reference to local and public needs but according to laws of supply and demand that operated internationally. In this wider market, indifferent to individuals and local communities, the flow and price of commodities, as well as labor and land, were dictated by the invisible laws of the international marketplace. If grain fetched eight shillings a bushel in the West Indies, for example, and only five in Boston, then a New England merchant felt entitled to send all the wheat he could purchase from local farmers to the more distant buyer.

Not until war in Europe created a genuine crisis did the full extent of the tension between the new entrepreneurial freedom and the older concern for the public weal become manifest. Such a moment occurred in Boston during Queen Anne's War (1702–1713) when Andrew Belcher, one of the town's largest grain merchants, decided to ship large quantities of wheat to the West Indies, where prices were higher than in Massachusetts. Threatened with a bread shortage and appalled that a leading townsman would put profits ahead of the welfare of the community, ordinary Bostonians descended on one of Belcher's ships, which was about to sail with 6,000 bushels of grain. Sawing through the rudder, they tried to run the disabled ship aground in order to seize the grain from its holds. Such food shortages rarely occurred in the American colonies, usually only during wartime, when unusual amounts of grain were needed for military provisioning. But when they did, urban people demanded to be fed at prices they could afford, regardless of the merchants' strictures that the laws of supply and demand must rule.

The urban social strain that grew with the spread of the individualistic and entrepreneurial ethic became more evident in the European wars of 1739 to 1747 into which the colonies were drawn. New England was drained of manpower and resources in King George's War (1744–1748), as its inhabitants engaged in costly attempts to overcome the French enemy to the north. But the war also offered opportunities for merchants and others to run up profits through

BOSTON IN 1772.

From a map of The Town of Boston, in New England, by Capt. John Bonner.

THE FAINTER LINES SHOW STREETS OF 1880.

Map of Boston, 1772, by Captain Bonner.

(Courtesy of the University of Texas Libraries, The University of Texas at Austin)

war contracts and privateering. "A covetous self-ish spirit" ran through the people, lamented one Massachusetts spokesman, and "every man looks at his own things, and not at the things of others." Gone was a "public spirit" and in its place stood a "greedy desire of gain."[15] Another commentator noted that food prices had escalated sharply during the war and that all around Boston, men were turning from their professions to become buyers and butchers of livestock. By intercepting Boston's meat supplies and withholding them from the market, they could drive up prices and take over the function of the town's butchers and hucksters. Known as "forestalling,"

[15]Nathaniel Appleton, *The Cry of Oppression* (Boston, MA, 1748), pp. 36–37.

this amounted to a sort of economic warfare between rural and urban society. The war against the French had not unified Massachusetts but instead had set one element against another in the pursuit of private gain.

The fissuring of an interdependent economic community appeared again in the action of merchants in other colonies during King George's War. Foodstuffs exporters in New York and Philadelphia piled up profits by trading illegally with the French and the Spanish enemy in the West Indies. Diverting food supplies from New England to the Caribbean, where the enemy paid high prices in order to feed their slaves, they smuggled their way to fortune. "How surprising it is that for the sake of private gain, his Majesty's declared enemies should be thus openly assisted to destroy his subjects," cried the *Boston Evening Post*.[16] This betrayal of the public good by private economic interest padded the food bill of every Bostonian. War had fueled the free market, with everyone from the lowliest tar aboard a privateer to the largest war contractor and merchant smuggler seeking to capitalize on new opportunities for gain.

The throwing off of governmental and ideological restraints, and the enthronement of the concept of self-interest, provided the perfect rationale for rapidly developing a vast area of land blessed with abundant natural resources and peopled by ambitious, tough-minded, innovating Europeans. The new system of values legitimated private profit-seeking, promoted the abandonment of economic regulation, and projected a future in which men's energies were cut loose from age-old mercantilist controls instituted to promote the good of all. This, it was argued, would produce a far better common good. Thus, two conceptions of economic life and social relations jostled for ascendancy.

Such thinking paralleled emerging values in England and Europe. There too a new model of economic and social life had emerged, predicated on the notion that the market mentality was preferable to the older corporate ideal of persons attuned to the public good because that idealistic model refused to take people as they really were. Self-denial, moral rectitude, and the subordination of private to public interests lay as dead weights on the economic order. National prosperity required something different—acceptance of the notion that "the self-seeking drive appeared more powerful than institutional efforts to mold people's actions."[17] If each individual sought his or her own improvement, all these separate efforts would produce, through a mysterious process later described by Adam Smith as the "invisible hand," a natural harmony and a prosperous, free society. People could not be compelled to work for the good of the whole. But left to sort out their wants and to pursue their own material desires in open competition, they would collectively form an impersonal market that would regulate human affairs to everyone's advantage.

Changing Social Structure

Population growth and economic development, carried on for a century and a half by opportunistic individuals, changed both the structure of colonial society and the attitudes of the people toward social structure—but changed them in opposite directions. Most seventeenth-century Europeans on both sides of the Atlantic accepted the naturalness of hierarchy in human affairs, the inevitability of poverty, and the right of those in the upper stratum of society to rule those below them. The belief was general that social gradations and internal subordination were not only sanctioned by God but also were essential to the maintenance of social cohesion. Therefore, care was taken to differentiate individuals by dress and titles, in social etiquette, and even in penalties imposed in criminal proceedings. Puritans, for example, did not simply file into church on Sunday mornings and occupy the pews randomly. Instead, a church committee "doomed" each seat according to the social rank of the person in the

---

[16]*Boston Evening Post*, February 1, 1748.
[17]Joyce Appleby, "The Social Origins of American Revolutionary Ideology," *Journal of American History*, 64 (1978): 944.

community. Thus, Puritans never entered their church without being reminded where they stood in the ranks of the community.

The philosophical commitment to hierarchy was strongest among the elite, but most of immigrant society was lower-middle class in its composition. With land widely available, the spectrum of wealth remained relatively narrow throughout most of the seventeenth century. Even in the cities, where the redistribution of wealth proceeded the fastest, the dawn of the eighteenth century witnessed a colonial society that was mostly middle class in character. In the Hudson River valley and in the Southern colonies, a handful of large plantation owners had made their mark, but the largest slave owners in Virginia at the beginning of the eighteenth century still owned fewer than 100 slaves, and not more than a handful of people had as much as £2,000 to leave to their heirs. As late as 1722, one of Philadelphia's richest merchants died with personal possessions worth just over £1,000—a sizable estate but unimpressive by European standards.

In the eighteenth century, and especially in the half-century before the Revolution, the customary commitment to hierarchy and deference waned at the same time that social stratification increased. Social attitudes and social structure were moving in opposite directions. Below the elite, free whites developed an egalitarian ideal. The middling sort of people, wrote a Philadelphian in 1756, "enjoy and are fond of freedom, and the meanest among them thinks he has a right to civility from the greatest."[18] Such comments were common. The Frenchman J. Hector St. John de Crèvecoeur was surprised to see hired workers who "must be at your table and feed . . . on the best you have," and the schoolteacher Philip Fithian wrote of "labourers at the tables and in the parlours of their betters enjoying the advantage, and honour of their society and conversation."[19]

For most American colonists, then, the ideal was a society where a wealthy aristocracy did not dominate and grind a mass of poor whites into the dust. When Benjamin Franklin toured the English countryside in 1772, he was appalled at what he saw and raised thanks that America was different. He described "landlords, great noblemen, and gentlemen, extremely opulent, living in the highest affluence and magnificence" alongside "the bulk of the people, tenants, extremely poor, living in the most sordid wretchedness, in dirty hovels of mud and straw, and clothed only in rags." Ignoring Indians and Africans, he wrote, "I thought often of the happiness of New England, where every man is a freeholder, has a vote in public affairs, lives in a tidy, warm house, has plenty of good food and fuel, with whole clothes from head to foot, the manufacture perhaps of his own family."[20] The German Gottlieb Mittelberger summed up the twin ideals of economic equality and democratic scorn for authorities and authoritarian institutions. Pennsylvania, he said, was "heaven for farmers, paradise for artisans, and hell for officials and preachers."[21]

If Franklin and Mittelberger reflected the growing celebration of America's egalitarianism, they also knew that eighteenth-century society, even for White colonists, was moving away from this New World ideal. As the old deferential attitudes gave way to brash, assertive, individualistic modes of thought and behavior—what would become known as "the democratic personality"—society became more stratified, and wealth became less evenly distributed. Population growth and economic development in the eighteenth century enriched many of those with capital to speculate in land, buy slaves and servants, or participate in trade. In Boston, Newport, New York, Philadelphia, and Charleston, stately townhouses testified to the fortunes being acquired in trade, shipbuilding, and land speculation. Probably, the last of these was the most

[18]Quoted in Hofstadter, *America at 1750 . . .* , p. 131.
[19]Ibid., p. 141.
[20]*The Writings of Benjamin Franklin*, 10 vols., Albert H. Smyth, ed. (New York, 1907), V: 362–363.
[21]Mittelberger, *Journey to Pennsylvania*, p. 48.

profitable of all. "It is almost a proverb," wrote a Philadelphian in 1767, "that every great fortune made here within these fifty years has been by land."[22] By the late colonial period, it was not unusual to find merchant land speculators with estates valued at £10,000 to £20,000. Even in the rural areas of the North, wealthy farmers amassed estates worth £4,000 to £5,000. In the South, plantation magnates built even larger fortunes, for the rapid importation of African slaves after 1720 accelerated the rate at which profits could be extracted from the cultivation of tobacco or rice. By the eve of the Revolution, the great planters of the Chesapeake region, men such as Charles Carroll, Robert "King" Carter, and William Byrd, had achieved spectacular affluence. Their estates, valued at £100,000 or more, were equivalent in purchasing power to a fortune of about 20 million dollars today. It was not unusual to see 300 to 400 slaves toiling on such plantations, whereas in the late seventeenth century, the largest slaveholder on the continent had no more than 50 bound laborers.

Although the rapid increase in population and large-scale capital investment in land and slaves enabled a small number of people to accumulate fortunes that would have been noteworthy even in English society, the development of the colonies also created conditions in which a growing number of persons were finding it difficult to keep bread on the table and wood in the fireplace. This was especially the case in the cities, where social stratification proceeded most rapidly. All the major cities built almshouses and workhouses in the second quarter of the century to provide for those who could not care for themselves—the aged, indigent, sick, insane, and orphaned. Between 1725 and 1760, the poor in the cities increased more rapidly than the urban population as a whole, and after about 1750, poverty was no longer confined to the old or physically depleted.

Boston, the first utopian settlement in British North America, was the first to feel the pinch of economic hardship. The city had grown to about 12,000 in 1720 and increased to 16,000 in the next two decades. But from 1740 until after the Revolution, the city's population stagnated while New England's economy languished. Expenditures for poor relief edged upward in the 1730s and grew faster than the population in the 1740s. In 1753, the Overseers of the Poor reported to the Massachusetts legislature that poor relief expenditures in Boston were double that of any town of comparable size "upon the face of the whole earth" by the reckoning of those acquainted with such matters. Though this may not have been true, it was certain that a large number of people in the town were in real distress. In 1757, the Overseers reported that "the poor supported either wholly or in part by the town in the alms-house and out of it will amount to the number of about 1000," and those receiving private charity from churches and philanthropic organizations swelled the total.[23]

The differing abilities of people to manipulate their economic environment, capitalize on the freedom to exploit White and black labor, and obtain title to Indian land were eventually recorded on the tax lists of the community, where each person's wealth was set alongside that of his or her neighbors. Processing these tax lists, historians have found that population growth and economic development led toward a less even distribution of wealth and an increase in the proportion of those without property in virtually every community. The change occurred slowly in rural areas but proceeded more rapidly in the seaboard centers of commercial activity.

If poverty touched the lives of a growing part of the urban laboring class, it was the usual condition on the edges of colonial settlement. Here, the gap between rich and poor hardly existed because the rich were nowhere to be found. The social order of the mid-eighteenth-century frontier was even cruder than rural society on the edge of the continent a century before. Whether in the towns of western Massachusetts

---

[22]*Pennsylvania Magazine of History and Biography*, 1 (1877): 277.
[23]*Records Relating to the Early History of Boston*, 39 vols. (Boston, MA, 1881–1909), 14: 240, 302.

and Connecticut, founded in the second and third quarters of the eighteenth century by the sons of Yankee farmers; or the lands along the Mohawk River in New York and the Susquehanna River in Pennsylvania, which represented the hopes of the German and Scots-Irish immigrants; or the backcountry of Maryland, Virginia, and the Carolinas, which sponged up some 250,000 souls in the late colonial period, frontier society was composed of small farmers and rural artisans who all stood roughly on the same plane. They purchased land cheaply, often for as little as four shillings an acre, and struggled to carve farms from land previously occupied (and often cultivated) by Native people. Many hoped to produce surplus crops for market within a few years. But with only the help of one's sons and a few farm animals, this goal often took most of a farmer's life. Others struggled only to make enough improvements on a piece of land so that other settlers pushing westward on the next wave of settlement would find it attractive enough to pay a price that rewarded their labor.

On the New England frontier, where people pushed westward and northward in groups, they founded new towns and churches as they went, quickly reproducing the institutions of eastern society. While poor, these simple villagers and farmers lived a life in which institutional ligaments had not been altogether severed. But southward from New York on the east side of the Appalachian slopes, frontier society existed in what many observers took to be a semibarbarous state. William Byrd described one of the largest plantations on the Virginia frontier in 1733 as "a poor dirty hovel, with hardly anything in it but children that wallowed about like so many pigs."[24] Charles Woodmason, an Anglican minister who spent three years tramping from settlement to settlement in the Carolina backcountry

in the 1760s, was appalled at what he found. "For through want of ministers to marry and through the licentiousness of the people, many hundreds live in concubinage—swapping their wives as cattle, and living in a state of nature, more irregularly and unchastely than the Indians."[25] Woodmason had all the English prejudices usually harbored against the Presbyterian Scots-Irish, the main inhabitants of the region. But the crudeness of life he described actually existed. After preaching at Flat Creek to "a mixed multitude of all classes and complexions," he paled at their after-service "revelling, drinking, singing, dancing, and whoring" and threw up his hands that "most of the company were drunk before I quitted the spot—they were as rude in their manners as the common savages, and hardly a degree removed from them." Some of what he saw made him close his eyes in horror, but he kept them open long enough to observe the young women who "have a most uncommon practice. . . . They draw their shift as tight as possible to the body, and pin it close, to show the roundness of their breasts, and . . . their petticoat close to their hips to show the fineness of their limbs—so that they might as well be in Puri Naturalibus—Indeed nakedness is not censurable or indecent here, and they expose themselves often quite naked, without ceremony—rubbing themselves and their hair with bear's oil and tying it up behind in a bunch like the Indians—being hardly one degree removed from them."[26]

The Great Awakening

Nowhere did the line between social and economic change, on the one hand, and religion on the other, crumble more swiftly than in the emotional and ideological upheaval called the Great Awakening. More than a solely religious movement, this period of sustained religious

[24]Quoted in Richard R. Beeman, "Social Change and Cultural Conflict in Virginia: Lunenburg County, 1746 to 1774," *William and Mary Quarterly*, 35 (1978): 445.
[25]Charles Woodmason, *The Carolina Backcountry on the Eve of the Revolution*, Richard J. Hooker, ed. (Chapel Hill, NC, 1953), pp. 15, 33.
[26]Ibid., pp. 56, 61.

enthusiasm reflected a profound cultural transformation that had been building for several generations.

At its core, the Great Awakening was "a search for new sources of authority, new principles of action, new foundations of hope" among people who had come to believe that the colonial churches "no longer met the spiritual needs of the people."[27] The Awakeners preached that the old sources of authority were too effete to solve the problems of the day, too encrusted with tradition, hypocrisy, and intellectualism to bring hope and faith to a generation that was witnessing the remaking of the world of their fathers. A new wellspring of authority was needed, and that source, the evangelists preached, was the individual himself. Like the Quaker "inner light," which dwelled in every man and woman, the "new light" within the awakened would enable them to achieve grace through the conversion experience. When enough people were "born again," as the evangelists of the Great Awakening phrased it, they would forge a new sense of community, achieve a new brotherhood of man, and restore the city on the hill. The Awakening, in its way, was a "revitalization movement," similar to those that occurred periodically in Indian societies when new leaders rejected corrosive changes and urged their followers to return to the traditions of the past.

The Awakening's first stirrings in the colonies occurred in the 1720s in New Jersey and Pennsylvania and then in the 1730s in Jonathan Edward's church in Northampton, Massachusetts. But not until 1739, with the arrival of George Whitefield from England, did it strike with full force. Whitefield was a master of open-air preaching and had trekked across the English countryside for several years preaching the word of God. A diminutive man with a magnificent voice, he began a barnstorming trip along the east coast of North America that evoked a mass response of a sort never witnessed before in the colonies. Thousands turned out to see him; with each success his fame grew. Especially in the cities, which were the crucibles of social change, his effect was extraordinary. People fought for places in the churches to hear him or congregated by the thousands in open fields to receive the "divine fire" he kindled.

Some of Whitefield's appeal can be attributed to his genius for dramatic performances, his perfection of the art of advanced publicity, and his ability to simplify theological doctrine and focus the attention of masses of people on one facet of religious life—the conversion experience. Stunned by his electrifying performances, where he cast away written sermons, where his spastic body movements and thundering voice replaced dry, logical, rigidly structured sermons, thousands experienced the desire to "fly to Christ." But it was the message as well as the medium that explains why people flocked to hear Whitefield. He assaulted traditional sources of authority, called upon people to become the instruments of their own salvation, and implicitly attacked the upper-class notion that the simple folks had no minds of their own.

When Whitefield began his American tour in 1739, upper-class leaders did not perceive the social dynamite buried deep in his message. After all, his preaching produced thousands of conversions and filled the churches that had been languishing for more than a generation. Whitefield refocused those who heard him on the importance of religion, so it is no wonder that he was welcomed as "an angel of God, or as Elias, or John the Baptist risen from the dead."[28] But Whitefield's popularity soon waned among the gentry because he was followed by itinerant Awakeners whose social radicalism was far less muted, and because of the effects the evangelists' message had on the lower orders. Roaming preachers like Gilbert Tennant infused evangelical preaching with a radical egalitarianism that left many former supporters of Whitefield

[27]William G. McLoughlin, *New England Dissent, 1630–1833: The Baptists and the Separation of Church and State* (Cambridge, MA, 1971), p. 335.
[28]Perry Miller, *Jonathan Edwards* (New York, 1949), pp. 166–167.

Image of "George Whitefield Preaching to a Great Crowd."
(Courtesy of Library of Congress Prints and Photographs Division [LC-USZ62-137507])

sputtering. Tennant attacked the established clergy as unregenerate and encouraged people to forsake their ministers. "The sapless Discourses of such dead Drones" were worthless, he proclaimed.[29] James Davenport, another itinerant preacher, told huge crowds that they should drink rat poison rather than listen to the corrupt clergy. Even more dangerous, Davenport indicted the rich and powerful, criticized the growing gap between rich and poor, and exhorted ordinary people to resist those who exploited and deceived them. Only then, he cried, would the Lamb Jesus return to earth.

Crowds followed Davenport through the towns, singing and clapping so that "they look'd more like a Company of *Bacchanalians* [italics in original] after a mad Frolick, than sober Christians who had been worshipping God," as one distressed Boston newspaper complained.[30] Respectable people became convinced that revivalism had gotten out of hand. Revivalism had started out as a return to religion among

[29]Ibid., p. 166.
[30]*Boston Evening Post*, August 2, 1742.

backsliding Christians but now was turning into a social experience that profoundly threatened the established leaders, who stressed order, discipline, and submissiveness from laboring people. The fear of the Awakeners' attacks on genteel literate culture, on wealth and ostentatious living, was epitomized in New London, Connecticut, in 1743, when Davenport scandalized the gentry by inducing a huge crowd

> to burn "sundry good and useful treatises, books of practical godliness, the works of able divines," as well as "hoop petticoats, silk gowns, short cloaks, cambrick caps, red heeled shoes, fans, necklaces, gloves, and other such apparell." While psalms and hymns were sung over the pile, the preacher added his own pants, "a pair of old, wore out, plush breaches." This, commented one critic, would have obliged him "to strutt about bare-arsed" had not the fire been extinguished.[31]

By 1742, New England and the middle colonies were being crisscrossed by itinerant gospelers and haranguers, all of them labeled social incendiaries by the established clergy. Of all the signs of social leveling that conservatives saw springing from Evangelicalism, the one they feared the most was the practice of public lay exhorting. Within the established churches, there was no place for laypersons to compete with the qualified ministry in preaching the word of God. Nor was there room for "self-initiated associations of the people meeting outside of regularly constituted religious or political meetings." To do so was to relocate authority collectively in the mass of common people.[32]

Almost as dangerous, lay preachers corrupted the idea of sacred space by going outside the church to unconsecrated profane space—streets, fields, and barns, where they kindled spiritual renewal. This attack on "the notion of sacred space

was also an attack on the entire social and political order, a bold attempt to introduce what contemporaries saw as 'Anarchy and Confusion' into the peaceable kingdoms of New England."[33] Lay exhorters shattered the monopoly of the educated clergy on religious discourse. They put all people on a plane in matters of religion, gave new importance to the oral culture of common people, and established among them the notion that their destinies and their souls were in their own hands instead of the hands of the elite clergy. They turned the world upside down by allowing those who had traditionally been consigned to the bottom of society to assume roles customarily reserved for educated, adult men. Lay exhorters, preaching the Lord's truth extemporaneously, crossed class lines and defied assigned sexual and racial roles. Especially infuriating to established clergymen was the evangelicals' willingness that lay women might speak publicly if spiritually moved. "The encouraging [of] WOMEN, yea GIRLS to speak in the assemblies for worship," declaimed the shocked Charles Chauncy, "is a plain breach of that *commandment of the LORD,* where it is said, *Let your WOMEN keep silence in the churches.*"[34]

The Great Awakening thus represented far more than a religious revival. Through it, ordinary people haltingly enunciated a distinctive popular ideology that challenged inherited cultural norms. As many historians have noted, the Awakening represented a groundswell of individualism, a kind of protodemocratic spirit that anticipated the Revolution. Especially, among the middling people of colonial society, who partook of spontaneous meetings, assumed new power in ecclesiastical affairs, and were encouraged by the evangelists to adopt a skeptical attitude toward dogma and authority, the revival years involved an expansion of political consciousness and a new feeling of self-importance. But

---

[31]J. M. Bumstead and John E. Van de Wetering, *What Must I Do to Be Saved? The Great Awakening in Colonial America* (Hinsdale, IL, 1976), p. 90.
[32]Harry S. Stout, "Religion, Communications, and the Ideological Origins of the American Revolution," *William and Mary Quarterly*, 34 (1977): 527.
[33]Susan Juster, *Disorderly Women: Sexual Politics and Evangelicalism in Revolutionary New England* (Ithaca, NY, 1994), p. 22.
[34]Quoted in ibid., p. 31.

among the lowliest members of society, including impoverished city dwellers, servants, slaves, and those who struggled to gain a foothold on the treacherous slopes of economic security, the Awakening experience did not propel them forward toward democratic bourgeois revolution but backward to an earlier age when it was conceived that individuals acted not for themselves, always striving to get ahead at the expense of their neighbors, but instead pulled together as a community. Hence, the dispossessed harked to the anti-entrepreneurial, communalistic tone permeating the exhortations of the radical evangelists such as Tennant, who preached that in any truly Christian community "mutual *Love* is the *Band* and *Cement*. . . . For men, by the Neglect of its Exercise, and much more by its Contrary, will be tempted, against the *Law of Nature*, to seek a *single* and independent State, in order to secure their Ease and Safety."[35]

Radical Awakeners were not preaching class revolt or the end to wealth-producing commerce. What they urged was "a thorough reconsideration of the Christian ethic as it had come to be understood in the America of the 1730s."[36] Nor were those who harked to the Awakeners inspired to foment social revolution, for in fact the seeds of overt political radicalism were still in the germinative stage. But the multitudes that were moved by the spiritual intensity and emotional warmth of the revivalists, in the North in the 1740s and in the South during the next decade, began to believe that it was justifiable in some circumstances to take matters into their own hands. This is why Jonathan Edwards, a highly intellectual, latter-day Puritan minister, was seen by the commercial elite and their clerical allies as "the grand leveler of Christian history," even though sedition and leveling were not what he had in mind.

Producing the greatest flow of religious energy since the Puritan movement a century before, the Great Awakening also supplied "the most pertinent and usable model for radical activists in the years that lay ahead."[37] Originating as an outpouring of the heart, the Awakening built on the tensions and contentions in colonial society that had grown from generations of social and economic change. Church by church, Awakeners learned that to advance their minority rebellious ideology they must persuade the majority or, if necessary, withdraw to establish new churches. In the process, they assaulted "the institutional structures that sheltered orthodoxy and fortified its authority."[38] Finding their allies among the common people, the Awakeners challenged traditional customs of social deference and developed new arguments justifying the rights of minorities. Thus, the Great Awakening became a "practice model" that would have an immense importance in the political crisis leading toward the American Revolution.

Summary

By the middle of the eighteenth century, people living in the English colonies in North America were already one-third as numerous as the English themselves. Those of European descent included the English, Dutch, Swedish, Finnish, Swiss, German, and Scots-Irish. Not only the nationality but also the social origins of these people influenced the social transformation that took place. In the seventeenth century, the gentry and middling farmers and artisans of European society made up about one-half of all those Europeans coming to the western side of the Atlantic; in the eighteenth century, they probably accounted for less than a third. The remaining colonizers were, in the main, indentured servants,

[35]Gilbert Tennant, *Brotherly Love Recommended* (Philadelphia, PA, 1748).
[36]Alan Heimert, *Religion and the American Mind from the Great Awakening to the Revolution* (Cambridge, MA, 1966), p. 32.
[37]Patricia V. Bonomi, *Under the Cope of Heaven: Religion, Society, and Politics in Colonial America* (New York, 1986), p. 152.
[38]Ibid.

part of a system of labor that was rife with abuses but still provided the hope for ascending the ladder of success.

As the desire for land grew, so did the hunger for money and goods. Thus, acquisitive values took root. In the seaboard towns of Boston, Newport, New York, Philadelphia, and Charleston, these values were embraced more rapidly than in rural areas. Respect for the traditional social hierarchy dwindled, and individualistic modes of thought and behavior (characterizing "the democratic personality") gained ground. Paradoxically, throwing open the doors of opportunity led to a more stratified society marked by the increasingly uneven distribution of wealth. The ideological underpinnings of the Great Awakening, a widespread explosion of religious enthusiasm from the 1730s to the 1750s, strengthened impulses toward challenging established authority and served as a "practice model" in events leading toward the American Revolution.

Critical Thinking Questions

1. The indentured servant system, like the slave trade involving Africans and Indians, was characterized by abuse and suffering. How was the life of an indentured servant similar to, yet different from, that of a slave?
2. A desire for material success arose in eighteenth-century British America. What contributed to this, and what lifestyle, social, and philosophical effects did it create?
3. The Great Awakening has been called "the most pertinent and usable model for radical activists in the years that lay ahead." What characteristics of this movement would justify such a statement?

Further Reading

Bernard Bailyn, *Voyagers to the West: A Passage in the Peopling of American on the Eve of the American Revolution* (New York: Knopf, 1986).

T. H. Breen, *Marketplace of Revolution: How Consumer Politics Shaped American Independence* (New York: Oxford University Press, 2004).

Richard Bushman, *The Refinement of America: Persons, Houses, Cities* (New York: Knopf, 1992).

Jon Butler, *Becoming America: The Revolution before 1776* (Cambridge, MA: Harvard University Press, 2000).

David Hackett Fischer, *Albion's Seed: Four British Folkways in America* (New York: Oxford University Press, 1989).

Aaron S. Fogleman, *Hopeful Journeys: German Immigration, Settlement, and Political Culture in Colonial America, 1717–1775* (Philadelphia: University of Pennsylvania Press, 1996).

Alison Games, *Migration and the Origins of the English Atlantic World* (Cambridge: Harvard University Press, 1999).

James Henretta and Gregory Nobles, *Evolution and Revolution: American Society, 1600–1820* (Lexington: D. C. Heath, 1987).

Rhys Isaac, *The Transformation of Virginia: 1740–1790* (Chapel Hill: University of North Carolina Press, 1982).

Frank Lambert, *Inventing the "Great Awakening"* (Princeton: Princeton University Press, 1999).

Ned C. Landsman, *From Colonials to Provincials: American Thought and Culture, 1680–1760* (New York: Twayne Publishers, 1997).

Gary B. Nash, *The Urban Crucible: Social Change, Political Consciousness, and the Origins of the American Revolution* (Cambridge: Harvard University Press, 1979).

Sharon V. Salinger, *"To Serve Well and Faithfully": Labor and Indentured Servants in Pennsylvania, 1682–1800* (Cambridge and New York: Cambridge University Press, 1987).

Billy G. Smith, *The "Lower Sort": Philadelphia's Laboring People, 1750–1800* (Ithaca: Cornell University Press, 1990).

CHAPTER 9

Wars for Empire and Indian Strategies for Survival

LEARNING OBJECTIVES

- Trace the trading relations between the Iroquois and the Dutch, French, and English; note how the Iroquois used diplomacy to their advantage.

- Describe how the Creek confederation of the Southeast, especially under Chief Brims, used a policy of aggressive neutrality in dealing with the English, French, and Spanish.

- Discuss the importance of Cherokee support to the Carolinians and indicate the strains placed on Cherokee loyalty by the Carolinians, including the matter of the German mystic Gottlieb Priber.

- Explain how interaction with European societies over many generations transformed Indian culture in ultimately detrimental ways; use fur trading, warfare, political organization (particularly that of the Creeks and the Cherokees), and the use of alcohol as reference points.

- Discuss cultural persistence among the interior tribes and why this was the case.

Between 1675 and 1763, three European powers—France, Spain, and England—employed diplomacy and war in a struggle for trade and territory in the vast area between the Mississippi River and the Atlantic Ocean, and in the waters of the Caribbean. Both the trade and the territory they coveted in North America required them to be in continual touch with the powerful tribes of interior North America. Our history books have largely forgotten what was obvious to people living in this period—that European authorities, whether in New Spain, New France, New England, or elsewhere in North America, were continually negotiating, trading, and fighting with and against various Indian societies, and filing reports, requests, and complaints to the home governments concerning the state of Indian affairs. Those in charge of colonial affairs in Madrid, Paris, and London were almost as well informed about the Indian inhabitants of the territories that they claimed as about their own colonists.

In this three-cornered fight for a continent, Native peoples are often imagined as merely the objects of European power, manipulated like pawns on a continental chessboard before finally being swept from the board altogether. This view is part of the myth of the overwhelming cultural superiority and military force of the European colonizers and the Indians' acquiescence when confronted with it. But the power of the Europeans has been greatly exaggerated and that of Native societies greatly underestimated, though certainly the power equation was tilting toward the English and the French by the 1720s. More accurately, Indian societies of the interior were not only reciprocally involved in the complicated maneuvers among contending European powers but also played a dynamic role in the unfolding of events. They could not turn back the clock or drive the Europeans back into the sea. But the interior tribes were far stronger than the less populous coastal tribes that had succumbed to the invaders in the seventeenth century. They were, therefore, able to interact with the Europeans in a much different way.

Throughout the eighteenth century, Indians helped to shape their own history. Pitted against each other and sometimes divided among themselves, the European powers had too few resources to overpower the inland tribes. They had to rely on Indian allies to maintain themselves even in the limited areas they occupied. Understanding the Europeans' weaknesses gave Indian nations an opportunity to exercise initiative and to gain much in exchange for their support. That they were eventually the losers does not obscure the fact that the interaction was truly a two-way process. Europeans used Indians to enhance their own power, and Indians used Europeans in precisely the same way.

Iroquois Diplomacy

Only by looking at European imperial rivalry from the Indian point of view can we understand the real nature of cross-cultural contact in North America. For example, while European governors and colonial bureaucrats put millions of words on paper, moved armies and navies across an ocean, and engaged thousands of people in the manufacture and shipment of Indian trade goods—all as a part of empire-building—the Iroquois, never numbering more than 2,000 warriors and 10,000 people after devastating epidemics from 1647 into the mid-1670s had more than halved their population, were adroitly pursuing their own self-interest and shaping events in North America. The French historian La Potherie wrote in 1722: "It is a strange thing that three or four thousand souls can make tremble a whole new world. New England is very fortunate in being able to stay in their good graces. New France is often desolated by their wars, and they are feared through a space of more than 1500 leagues of the country of our allies."[1] A generation later, an Indian "expert" in New York warned the governor that "on whose ever side the [Iroquois] Indians fall, they will cast the balance."[2]

For the first two-thirds of the seventeenth century, the Iroquois involvement in trade with Europeans pivoted on their connection to the Dutch. Superior Dutch woolens, guns, and other metal goods made the connection valuable to the Iroquois, though their militant quest for beaver, with which to conduct trade, cost them heavily.

By the mid-1660s, however, sharp challenges to the Dutch by English and French rivals obliged the Iroquois to find new trading partners. Almost simultaneously, the French and the English eagerly became their suitors. In New France in 1661, royal government supplanted the joint-stock company that had colonized north of the Iroquois since early in the century. With royal government came 1,000 soldiers to pursue an aggressive policy of French territorial expansion. By the early 1680s, France had consolidated its hold in the St. Lawrence River valley and established a string of trading posts and forts along an arc that swung north and west of the English settlements

---

[1]Quoted in Anthony F. C. Wallace, "The Origins of Iroquois Neutrality: The Grand Settlement of 1701," *Pennsylvania History*, 24 (1957): 235.
[2]Archibald Kennedy to George Clinton, 1746, Clinton Papers, vol. 3, Clements Library, University of Michigan.

like a long, encircling arm. Into Iroquoia, along with the French fur traders and farmers, came black-gowned Jesuits.

While reckoning with this new French intrusiveness, the Iroquois also had to adjust to the English conquest of New Netherland in 1664. For the remainder of the century, the Iroquois split between pro-English and pro-French groups, sometimes with tragic results. Making the Iroquois situation all the more fragile was the fact that the French and English, busily trying to remove each other from the map of North America in two wars that were local versions of major Anglo-French conflicts in Europe, leaned hard on their Iroquois allies to help defeat their enemies.

In replacing the ruptured Dutch chain of trade, the Iroquois at first gravitated toward the French. In this context, Jesuit priests found a welcome in many Iroquois villages, though the desire of the "Black Robes" for a thoroughgoing change of behavior as well as of belief caused tension. Slowly, as the English traders presented superior woolen cloth and offered high prices for beaver skins, the French connection began to wear thin. By the 1680s, with the balance tipping toward the English, the Iroquois expelled Jesuit priests from their villages.

If the English reminded the Iroquois of the Dutch in their disinterest in converting Indians to Christianity, they also seemed alike in their avidity for the skins of fur-bearing animals. At first, the Iroquois welcomed this tendency. As in the earlier beaver wars against the Huron, the Iroquois turned aggressively toward their western neighbors. Needing captives to replace their disease-ridden ranks as well as pelts to fuel the trade for English goods, the Iroquois battled Miamis, Illinois, Ojibwas, Foxes, Shawnees, and Ottawas in the 1670s and 1680s. From the north, in the closing decades of the seventeenth century, came stinging raids from the French. Whether aligning with the French or the English, the Iroquois found themselves seeking cross-cultural alliances

to achieve the dominance in the West that was indispensable in maintaining the fur trade.

King William's War, from 1689 to 1697—for Europeans a battle for economic and territorial ascendancy in North America—was so traumatic for the Iroquois that they came to understand that their survival depended on extricating themselves from the imperial wars of their European trading partners. "You are pleased to recommend us to pursue our enemies the French vigorously, which we will endeavor to the utmost for they are your enemies also," a Mohawk chief promised the English in 1689. "Yea, if all our people should be ruined and cut in pieces, we will never make peace with them."[3] And so it was that the Mohawks and other Iroquois tribes spilled their blood in a series of bungled assaults on Quebec in 1690 and 1691. In these poorly supplied joint expeditions of Native and English warriors, the Iroquois often destroyed pro-French Iroquois who still remained in villages near Montreal or along Lake Ontario. But they paid dearly for these fratricidal attacks and were humbled by a French-Indian attack on the Mohawks in 1693, a heavy blow that evoked a caustic Mohawk comment: "You tell us we are one heart one flesh and one blood. Pray let us know the reason why you do not come to our assistance according to your former promise that we may live and die together."[4] The Iroquois sustained further poundings from western and northern enemies and a formidable invasion of Iroquoia, in 1696, by 2,000 French soldiers marching with their Native allies.

By the end of the seventeenth century, after years of exhausting warfare, it became apparent to all parties involved that though the English vastly outnumbered the French, the English could not defeat the Canadians because of disunity among the English colonies and the unwillingness of the government at home to supply military forces. Nor could the French destroy an Anglo-Iroquois alliance or forge a Franco-Iroquois alliance because they lacked sufficient

[3]Quoted in Daniel K. Richter, *The Ordeal of the Longhouse: The People of the Iroquois League in the Era of European Colonization* (Chapel Hill, NC, 1992), p. 162.
[4]Quoted in ibid., p. 175.

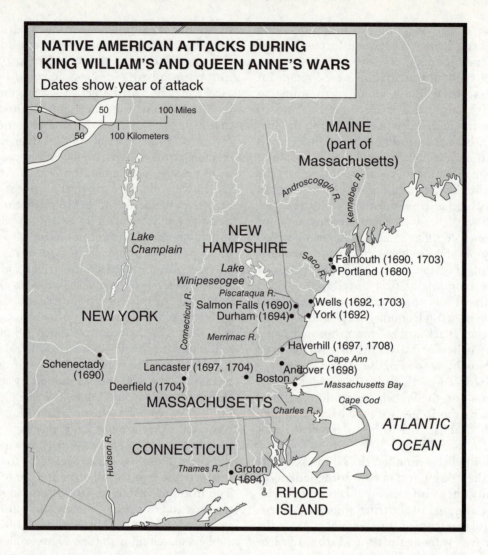

NATIVE AMERICAN ATTACKS DURING
KING WILLIAM'S AND QUEEN ANNE'S WARS
Dates show year of attack

military strength for the former and suffered a competitive disadvantage in the fur trade that prohibited the latter. The Iroquois retained the strategic geographical position in the northern part of the continent. But in spite of expanding their influence over tribes to the south and west of them, they paid dearly in maintaining a pivotal role in the fur trade. By the end of the seventeenth century, hard hit by French attacks, war weary, and suffering disastrous population losses, they sought a formula for maintaining their security while withdrawing from the attritional warfare.

The solution to their problem was sudden and bold. In the summer of 1700, the Iroquois, along with several dozen other tribes, entered negotiations with both the English and the French, signing treaties almost simultaneously at Montreal and at Albany a year later. To the French, they promised neutrality in any future war between England and France—a great gain for the French, who had often been stung by Iroquois military forays. To the English, who now lost a military ally, the Iroquois ceded their western hunting lands, conquered a half-century before from the Hurons. By this clever piece of diplomacy, the Iroquois implied that their primary allegiance was still to the English. But it was only a symbolic land cession, for the English had no ability to occupy or control this territory; in fact the lands in question had recently been reconquered by the French and their allies, the Wyandots. To complete their compromise negotiations, the Iroquois made peace with the tribes to the west of them, while urging the English and the French "to put a stop" to their destructive animosities so "that we may have the benefit of the peace concluded between the two Kings in Europe."[5]

For almost half a century after 1701, the Iroquois policy of balancing one European power with another worked well. The Five Nations (which became the Six Nations after the addition of the Tuscaroras in 1722) disengaged from the costly beaver wars, pursued their role as fur suppliers, and increased their population by absorbing remnants of coastal tribes decimated by Europeans and elements of western tribes they had themselves conquered. The test of the "Grand Settlement of 1701" came immediately. Less than a year after the Iroquois concluded their treaties at Albany and Montreal, another Anglo-French war broke out. But while the French and their local Indian allies put the torch to towns along the New England frontier, the Iroquois remained on the sidelines, exhorting "you both to make peace together," as one Iroquois spokesman told the French governor of Canada.[6] Though they were tempted to strike at the French, whose Indian allies still harassed them, the Iroquois were confirmed in their opinion that the English were unreliable military allies when New York refused to come to New England's aid. Afraid of jeopardizing their profitable fur trade and the black market traffic they were conducting with the French Canadian enemy, the New Yorkers kept their minds to commerce and, according to some Massachusetts authorities, even marketed in Albany plunder from devastated New England frontier towns. The Iroquois's one

act of assistance was to send three Mohawks and one Mahican to London with two prominent New Yorkers to argue for English assistance in the war against Canada. Arriving in London in 1710, they paid their respects to Queen Anne, stopped the show when they attended the theater, ran down a stag in the royal park, and were followed by throngs everywhere they went. But this was only a diversion. For more than a generation, the Iroquois rebuilt their torn society through diplomacy rather than war.

This Mohawk chief, Sa Ga Yeath Qua Taw No Tow in his language and called Brant by the English, arrived in London in 1710 to parley with Queen Anne. His grandson, Joseph Brant, made the same trip sixty-five years later and joined the British to thwart American independence. The Dutch painter Verelst captured Brant with his spectacular tattooing, which the London press said won "not . . . so much terror as regard."

(Courtesy Historical/Corbis)

---

[5]Quoted in ibid., p. 206.
[6]Quoted in ibid., p. 219.

At the conclusion of Queen Anne's War in 1713, the English made substantial gains in North America. France ceded the territory they claimed in Nova Scotia, Newfoundland, and Hudson's Bay to England; recognized the sovereignty of the British over the Iroquois (the Iroquois made no such concession); and permitted English traders to open commerce with the western tribes that had previously been linked to the French. But these paper concessions meant little, for the English could not implement them by occupying the areas they had gained or by establishing trading posts deep in the interior. Not for another generation would the English find the strength to concern themselves with these distant regions. For now, they fixed their attention on the buildup of population between the coast and the Appalachian Mountains. Only in constructing a fort and trading post at Oswego on Lake Ontario did England take advantage of the French concessions. The final act of the imperial drama, and the fate of the Iroquois and more western tribes, was postponed for forty years.

Creek Diplomacy

Just as a time of trouble impelled the Iroquois to disengage from attritional warfare by substituting council fire diplomacy for the battlefield, the Creek confederation of the Southeast mastered the principles of *realpolitik* following the Yamasee War of 1715 to 1717. Like the Iroquois, the Creeks had been a defensive and loosely integrated confederacy before European settlers arrived. They too capitalized on European trade to become the most formidable society in a vast region coveted by England, France, and Spain. And like the Iroquois, they initially enhanced their strength but then suffered from the intensification of warfare fueled by the European trade connection. Less than two decades after the Iroquois cemented their "playoff system" between the English and the French, the Creeks had made themselves "the custodians of the wilderness

balance of power in the South."[7] Through a quarter-century of adroit maneuvering, they extended and withdrew promises to the English, French, and Spanish in order to extract trade and military concessions. At the same time, they maintained their autonomy. Just as the English attempted to play Creeks and Cherokees against each other—"how to hold both as our friends, for some time, and assist them in cutting one another's throats without offending either," as one Carolinian put it—the Creeks worked to keep French, English, and Spanish pitted against each other, with no one of the European powers gaining dominance over the other two. So skillful was the Creek leader Chief Brims in this strategy that one Englishman opined that he was "as great a politician as any Governor in America."[8]

The new policy of aggressive neutrality was a logical course for the Creeks to follow after flagrant abuses by the Carolina traders infected the trading alliance with the English earlier in the century. Greatly aroused, the Creeks had declared war against their exploiters, but their inability to persuade the Cherokees to join them in an all-out offensive against the English thwarted their efforts in the Yamasee War. Thereafter, they pursued a policy of limited cooperation. Despite their defeat in war and heavy population losses from smallpox, this was far from a passive strategy. Instead, Indian leaders regathered their people's strength while interacting advantageously with the foreigners in their country.

Creek politics had to be devised within the context both of intra-Indian rivalries and of Anglo-French-Spanish rivalry. Ever since the English had arrived in South Carolina and harassed the northern frontier of Spanish Florida, Spain had dreamed of mounting an expedition by land and sea that would wipe out English pretensions in the region. The Spanish made such an attempt in 1702, but it failed abysmally, producing only an English counterattack two years later that laid waste to the Spanish missionary frontier in Florida. The English attacked French trading

[7]Verner W. Crane, *The Southern Frontier, 1670–1732* (Ann Arbor, MI, 1956), p. 260.
[8]Ibid., pp. 260–261, 263.

posts on the lower Mississippi and along the Gulf of Mexico in 1708. But more successful in striking at nascent French power was the military expedition in 1711, primarily composed of Native allies, aimed at the Choctaws, the principal Indian allies of the French. Yet none of these assaults on the frontier outposts of rival European nations succeeded in establishing English control in the lower South. It was this design of English hegemony that the Creeks hoped to prevent while still maintaining trade connections with them.

In the aftermath of the Yamasee War, the Creeks tried to restore the balance of power by making overtures to the Spanish, against whom they had fought at English instigation for many years. First, Chief Brims sent his son to St. Augustine in 1716 with instructions to allow the Spanish to build a fort at Coweta, the principal town of the Lower Creeks. Then he sent other Creek emissaries to faraway Mexico City to seal an alliance. A year later, Creek leaders conferred with the Senecas, more than 1000 miles to the north, and with the English in Charleston. By 1717, they had fashioned a complicated arrangement by which some of their villages would remain within the Spanish orbit and some within the English. They signed a treaty with South Carolina that left them free to trade with whomever they pleased but set fixed rates in their trade with the English, guaranteed ammunition and arms for use against tribes not friendly to the English, and established a policy of mutual accountability for Creeks and Carolinians who committed crimes or injuries against each other.

Brims sealed his strategy of dynamic equilibrium by commissioning one son as his principal emissary to the English and another son as main emissary to the Spanish. English Carolinians and Spanish Floridians, both struggling unsuccessfully for the upper hand with the Creeks, attempted to persuade Brims to name "their" son his successor. Until he died in 1733, Brims maintained the policy of playing Spanish and English against each other. The Creeks continued to aid

the Yamasees, with whom the English were intermittently at war, and they continued to attack the Cherokees, with whom the English were closely allied. The English attempted various strategies to coerce the Creeks into an unqualified English connection—interference in Creek political affairs, trade embargoes, and the threat of a joint Cherokee-English war against them. These tactics brought the Creeks closer to the English and convinced them to break off their traditional support of the Yamasees, but the Creeks still preserved their autonomous position and remained the pivotal force in the region. The Creeks, wrote the Assembly of South Carolina in 1737, "have been treated with as allies but not as subjects of the Crown. . . . They have maintained their own possessions, and preserved their independency."[9] Numerically strong and diplomatically skilled, the Creeks preserved their central position for many years after the Yamasee War. Their emissaries ranged for thousands of miles, parleying with the Spanish in St. Augustine, Vera Cruz, and Mexico City; with the English in Charleston and London; with the French at Fort Toulouse on the Alabama River; and with headmen of other Indian nations from the Florida border to the Great Lakes. At times, they carried out simultaneous negotiations with two warring European powers, just as the Iroquois had conducted dual negotiations at Montreal and Albany in 1701.

After Brims's death, the Creeks preserved their policy of neutrality at critical junctures. In 1739, when England declared war on Spain, the Carolina government pressured the Creeks to join General James Oglethorpe (who had founded the colony of Georgia between South Carolina and Florida only seven years before) in an assault on St. Augustine. Although warriors from a few villages joined the English expedition, which ended in disaster, most of the Creeks remained out of the fray, convinced that the key to Creek survival was trading with whoever offered the best prices but allying militarily with no single European power. The Creeks might well have congratulated

---

[9]*The Colonial Records of South Carolina, Journal of the Commons House of Assembly, Nov. 10, 1736–June 7, 1739*, J. H. Easterby, ed. (Columbia, SC, 1951), p. 75.

Tomochichi, who was born before the first English set foot in the Carolinas, sat for his portrait with his nephew in 1734. Ear piercing and body painting (or tattooing) were common among Native Americans. Tomochichi's nephew holds an eagle, signifying his clan membership.

(Courtesy North Wind Picture Archives/Alamy)

themselves for adhering to their policy, for the Cherokees who joined the English brought back smallpox that spread disastrously in the Cherokee towns in 1740 to 1741. In the next year, a Creek headman gave new expression to the old strategy: "The [Creek] land belonged to the English as well as the French and indeed to neither of them. But both had liberty to come there to trade."[10]

In the 1740s, when France joined Spain in war against England, the Creek policy of neutrality was again put to the test. Summoning headmen from the Upper Creek towns to Charleston in 1746, the governor of South Carolina promised bountiful rewards if the Creeks would join an English military assault on Fort Toulouse, the main French bastion on the Alabama River. Back in their own country, however, Creek leaders vetoed the project, again thwarting the English in obtaining the Indian support for driving the French from the lower South. South Carolina attempted again to mobilize the Creeks and Cherokees for attacks on the French in 1747. Failure was again the result when Malatchi, the youngest son of Brims and a pro-French chief, gained recognition as emperor of the Lower Creeks. Malatchi had been at the Charleston conference in 1746 and had refused to let the Carolina governor browbeat him with threats of withdrawing the English trade. He returned to the Lower Creek villages, spoke against the English plan, and then ceremoniously visited St. Augustine and Fort Toulouse to inform the Spanish and the French of the English proposals. Creek leaders summarily told the English that they were welcome to trade in Creek country but could not build forts and should expect no Creek support for military expeditions against the Spanish or the French.

Cherokee Diplomacy

The Cherokees, numbering about 8,500 in 1750, were numerically stronger than the Iroquois and Creeks, and the English regarded their allegiance, or at least their neutrality, as indispensable to security in the region from Virginia to Georgia. Settled in the Appalachian Mountains to the west of the Carolina and Georgia settlers, and known for the valor of their warriors, they had been allied to the English in trade and war since the late seventeenth century. Faced with other Indian enemies, the Carolinians came to regard Cherokee support as a cornerstone of their Indian policy. The Cherokees were aware of this view. They understood that they had played the decisive role in the Yamasee War of 1715 to 1717, maneuvering, as the Carolinians admitted, in the best tradition of European power politics. "The last time they were here [in Charleston] they insulted us to the last degree," complained Carolina leaders in 1717, "and indeed by their demands (with which we were forced to comply) made us their tributaries."[11]

The support of the Cherokees wavered after the Yamasee War, especially in the 1730s. The abuses of English traders during that decade aroused their ire, and when an immigrant German mystic, Gottlieb Priber, reached them in 1736, he found them ripe for his visionary message. Priber's genuine respect for Indian culture and his disaffection from European society, which he regarded as hopelessly corrupt, made him welcome in the Cherokee towns. Priber preached about the need to establish communal states in the English colonies, based on Plato's *Republic*. Wherever he went, he was regarded as a dangerous radical, for very few colonizers wanted to abandon the concept of private property and return to an Arcadian past. But the Cherokees' values were much closer to Priber's, and they esteemed him for teaching them the use of weights and measures so they could protect themselves against dishonest traders. Priber also cautioned them to maintain their freedom by trusting no Europeans and encouraged them to cultivate trade connections with the French at New Orleans as a way of diminishing the English influence. His plan for Indian survival in the South depended on a confederacy of all the region's

---

[10]Quoted in M. Eugene Sirmans, *Colonial South Carolina: A Political History* (Chapel Hill, NC, 1966), p. 198.
[11]Quoted in David D. Wallace, *South Carolina: A Short History, 1520–1948* (Chapel Hill, NC, 1951), p. 90.

major tribes and an iron resolve among the Indians to surrender no territory, make no concessions to any European power, and continue the balance-of-power strategy in relations with the French, English, and Spanish. He also planned a city of refuge within Cherokee territory for criminals, debtors, and escaped slaves, who would live interracially and communally without regard to marriage. That the Cherokees regarded him as "a great beloved man" indicates how his radical ideas about race and gender politics resonated in the Cherokee mind, even while they maintained close relations with the Carolinians.

A sign that Cherokee strength endured long after the Iroquois grasp on the northern region faded appeared when South Carolina authorities ordered Priber's arrest in 1739. The Cherokees refused to surrender him. But in 1743, while making his way to the French in New Orleans, the Creeks captured him and turned him over to the English. He died in prison in Frederica, Georgia, much to the regret of his Cherokee friends.

In 1748, the South Carolina government further antagonized the Cherokees by refusing to honor a treaty of mutual support when the Upper Creeks attacked the Cherokees. In response, the Cherokees fell upon abusive White Carolina traders, demonstrating that they did not regard themselves as English dependents. Making periodic overtures to the French, the Cherokees kept the English off balance.

That the dependency of the English on the Cherokee was at least as great as Cherokee dependence on the English was plainly admitted in 1750, when the governor of South Carolina reminded the assembly that "it is absolutely necessary for us to be in friendship with the Cherokees, for all they are reckoned to be about 3000 gunmen, the greatest nation we know of in America except the Choctaws. . . ."[12] Because the Choctaws had long been tied to the French in the lower Mississippi area, the Cherokees provided a critical buffer between the English and their French enemies. Recognizing this, the Crown committed £6,000 for presents to the Creeks and Cherokees in 1749 and 1750, sterling testimony to the English regard for maintaining the alliance. Further proof of the English dependence on their Indian allies came with the doubling of South Carolina expenditures for Indian presents between 1750 and 1758, reaching £14,837 in the latter year.[13]

Transformations in Indian Society

During the first half of the eighteenth century, the interior Indian nations of North America demonstrated their capacity for adapting to the presence of Europeans and for turning their economic and political interaction with them to their own advantage. For a century and a half, the Indians had observed European societies and their culture. Native peoples drew selectively from what they saw, adopting through the medium of the fur, skin, and slave trade European articles of clothing, weapons, metal implements, and a variety of ornamental objects. Incorporating material objects, such as the iron hatchet and copper kettle, weakened some Native skills, though agriculture, fishing, and hunting remained the mainstays of Indian subsistence and were practiced more efficiently by the use of European sharp-edged implements such as the hoe, knife, and fishhook. Likewise, scissors, needles, and thimbles made it easier for Indian women to stitch and decorate clothing. However, pottery making declined, and the hunter became more dependent on the gun. Skill in fashioning beautiful clay pots or arrowheads ebbed. Metal awls and knives "bequesthed anything carved from bone, antler, or wood a degree of detail unimaginable with stone tools," while Native artisans used imported glass and copper to ornament hair combs, ear pendants,

[12]David H. Corkran, *The Cherokee Frontier: Conflict and Survival, 1740–1762* (Norman, OK, 1962), p. 15.
[13]Sirmans, *Colonial South Carolina . . .* , p. 275; Wilbur R. Jacobs, ed., *Indians of the Southern Colonial Frontier: The Edmond Atkin Report and Plan of 1755* (Columbia, SC, 1954), pp. 27n, 31n.

peace pipes, war clubs, ceremonial masks and many other artifacts.[14]

Interaction with European societies over many generations transformed Indian culture in ways that boded ill for the future. By looking at several aspects of life among the interior tribes—trade, warfare, political organization, and the use of distilled spirits—we can sort out the overall effects of Indian contact with Europeans, while at the same time exploding some of the myths that have clouded Native American history for years.

The Fur Trade

The fur trade is the proper place to begin a consideration of the transformation of Indian societies because from almost the first moment of contact, it joined Native Americans and Euro-Americans as partners in the emergent Atlantic market economy. For a long time, historians of the fur trade focused on the rugged trappers and colorful fur company entrepreneurs, making folk heroes of them while all but ignoring the Indians' role or the effects of the fur trade on Native societies. Studies in recent years, however, have restored Native Americans to the central role they played in the fur trade.

Native peoples had traded extensively over long distances for centuries before Europeans arrived; indeed, the exchange of goods was fundamental to most aboriginal economies. Some tribes, such as the Jumanos in the Southwest and the Great Lake Ottawas, were long-distance traders, moving the goods of one tribe to another across vast distances. The simple commodity exchange of the precontact period also served to maintain social and territorial relations among neighboring tribes. Profit was not involved, so the trade tended to reinforce peaceful relations rather than inciting competition and conflict. Exchanging material goods went hand in hand with political relations.

The arrival of Europeans eager to trade ushered in a new epoch for Native peoples. Each side had something to gain. However, the success of these new trade encounters depended on meshing native ideas about reciprocity with European goals of making profits and establishing footholds in new territories. From the Indian point of view, trade was carried on within the context of a political and social alliance and, accordingly, was surrounded by ceremonial gift giving. Haggling over prices appalled them at first, for, according to their values, trade was an aspect of friendship.

Native people did not seek trade goods because they wished to become part of an acquisitive, bourgeois culture but because they recognized the advantages, within the matrix of their own culture, of goods fashioned by societies with a more complex technology. The utility of European trade goods, not the opportunities for profit provided by the fur trade, drew Native Americans into it. "The beaver does everything perfectly well," one Indian fur trapper asserted; "it makes kettles, hatchets, swords, knifes, bread . . . in short, it makes everything."[15] From the Indian point of view, beaver skins were easy to obtain and the trade goods bartered on reasonable terms. "The English have no sense," said one Indian. "They give us twenty knives . . . for one beaver skin."[16]

Whatever the tensions created by the encounter of tribal and European bourgeois values in the fur trade, supplying pelts to the Europeans on a large scale required a reallocation of human resources and a reorganization of the tribes' internal economies. Subsistence hunting to acquire the food requirements of a tribe turned into commercial hunting, limited only by the quantity of trade goods desired. Native males spent far more time away from the villages trapping and hunting, and the importance of their activity to the life of the tribe, which soon became dependent on trade goods, undermined the relatively

[14]Daniel K. Richter, *Before the Revolution: America's Ancient Pasts* (Cambridge, MA, 2011), p. 141.
[15]Quoted in James Axtell, *After Columbus: Essays in the Ethnohistory of Colonial North America* (New York, 1988), p. 167.
[16]Quoted in Colin G. Calloway, *New Worlds for All: Indians, Europeans, and the Remaking of Early America* (Baltimore, MD, 1997), p. 45.

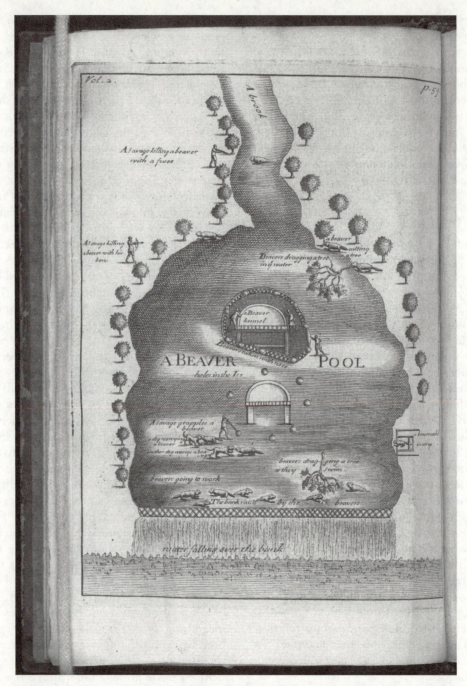

"A Beaver Pool," in Louis Armaud de Comte d'Arce, Baron de Lahoutan, *New Voyages to North America* (London, 1703). Sent to New France at age 17 as a French military officer, Baron de Lahontan spent a decade exploring the Great Lakes region, where he took extensive notes on Algonkian native life. In this depiction of a beaver dam, industrious beavers at the upper and lower right are dragging trees to build the dam, while native dogs on the left are worrying beavers. The beaver pelt, greatly prized in Europe for hats, was an important trade commodity.

(Courtesy The Beinecke Rare Book & Manuscript Library)

egalitarian matrilineal base of society. Women were also drawn into the new economic organization of villages, for the beaver, marten, or fox, once killed, had to be skinned and the skins scraped, dressed, trimmed, and sewn into robes. Among some tribes the trapping, preparation, and transporting of skins became so time consuming that food resources had to be procured in trade from other tribes. Ironically, the reorientation of tribal economies toward the fur trade dispersed villages and weakened the localized basis of clans and lineages. Breaking up in order to be nearer the widely spread trapping grounds, Indian villagers moved closer to the nomadic woodland existence that Europeans had charged them with at the beginning of contact.

Involvement in the fur trade also altered the relationship of Native Americans to their ecosystem. In their traditional cosmology, many Indian cultures regarded the destinies of human and animal as linked, for both inhabited a spiritual world governed by a Great Creator. This spiritual symbiosis between human and animal life imposed obligations on hunters and animals alike. As one historian observes, "Man and Nature both had to adhere to a prescribed behavior toward one another."[17] The Indian hunter knew that he must never take more animals than he needed and must treat their bodies with respect; the animals in return must not resist capture but must "consciously surrender themselves to the needy hunter." In this sense, killing was ordained, and the hunter was engaged in a "holy occupation."[18]

The tremendous destruction of animal life triggered by the advent of trade with Europeans altered the spiritual framework within which hunting had traditionally been carried out. Trappers declared an all-out war on the beaver and other fur-bearing animals, which was in effect a repudiation of the human's traditional role within the cosmos. The spiritual relationship between human and animal had not been broken, but it was severely tested.

A final effect of the trade was to broaden the scale of intertribal tensions, which often led to war. Precontact trade had been based on intertribal cooperation. But Europeans of different nationalities competed for client tribes in the fur trade, and the tribes were therefore sucked into the rivalry of their patrons. In addition, as furs became depleted in the hunting grounds of one tribe, they could maintain their trade connection with the Europeans only by conquering more remote tribes whose hunting grounds had not yet been exhausted, or by using armed force to intercept the furs of other tribes as they were being brought to trading posts near the coast. The Mohawks of the Hudson River valley drove the Mahicans away from Dutch traders, from 1624 to 1628, in order to ensure their preeminent position in the fur trade. Likewise, the Iroquois decimated and dispersed the Hurons of the eastern Great Lakes region in the mid-seventeenth century as a part of their drive for "beaver hegemony." By the end of the century, the Iroquois themselves were exhausted and their population depleted by the incessant warfare they had engaged in while attempting to maintain the role of fur-trade broker for the entire Northeast.

Warfare

"Myth contrasts civilized war and savage war," writes Francis Jennings, "by accepting the former as a rational, honorable, and often progressive activity while attributing to the latter the qualities of irrationality, ferocity, and unredeemed retrogression."[19] The point is important because a particularly emotional component of the stereotype of the American Indian has always been the blood lust that supposedly inspired "warfare that was insane, unending, continuously attritional from our point of view [and] . . . so integrated

---

[17]Calvin Martin, *Keepers of the Game: Indian-Animal Relationships and the Fur Trade* (Berkeley and Los Angeles, CA, 1978) p. 73.
[18]Ibid., p. 115.
[19]Francis Jennings, *The Invasion of America: Indians, Colonialism, and the Cant of Conquest* (Chapel Hill, NC, 1975), p. 146.

into the whole fabric of Eastern [Indian] culture, so dominantly emphasized within it, that escape from it was well-nigh impossible."[20] In point of fact, Native societies in North America were relatively free of warfare, especially if compared with European societies of this era.

Before the arrival of Europeans, intermittent violence between tribes did occur. Indian warriors fought to gain status, to arrange the killing of a tribe member, to use a captive to fill one's thinning ranks, or to expand a tribe's territorial claims. Europeans were adept at playing on these intertribal hostilities as they sought Indian allies after planting their first settlements.

But the nature of precontact Indian war was far different from the wars known in Europe, both in duration and in scale of operations. In the Thirty Years' War (1618–1648), rival armies employed terror tactics that wasted entire towns and indiscriminately killed women and children as well as men. Unlike Europeans, Native Americans could not conceive of total war that was fought for months or even years, that did not spare noncombatants, and that involved the systematic destruction of towns and food supplies. Indians conducted wars more in the manner of brief forays, with small numbers of warriors engaging the enemy and one or the other side withdrawing after a few casualties had been inflicted. Roger Williams wrote that in New England, the Indian wars "are far less bloody and devouring than the cruel wars of Europe" and related that "when they fight in a plain, they fight with leaping and dancing, that seldom an arrow hits, and when a man is wounded, unless he that shot follows upon the wounded, they soon retire and save the wounded."[21] John Underhill, hero of the Pequot War, thought that the intertribal hostilities were "more for pastime than to conquer and subdue enemies." Even in hand-to-hand combat, the Natives "fell on pell mell after their feeble manner; indeed it hardly deserves the name of fighting."[22] Warfare was a ritualistic encounter, waged not to shed as much of the enemy's blood as possible nor to devastate the enemy's villages and crops, but to make a convincing show of force.

Willingly drawn into the fur trade and eventually dependent on it, Indian societies embarked on intensified intertribal conflict. Added to the level of killing was the effect of European weaponry, which Natives mastered quickly. Adding flintlock muskets to their traditional tomahawk and bow and arrow, the tribes inflicted far greater casualties in their conflicts than in the precontact period. Yet war never became what it was for Europeans. An Iroquois war party that "seemed on the brink of triumph could be expected to retreat sorrowfully homeward if it suffered a few fatalities . . . [because] casualties would subvert the purpose of warfare as a means of restocking the population." In fact, replacement of population was itself a motive in the Iroquois wars against the Hurons and other tribes in the seventeenth century. The "mourning war"— an attempt to replace people lost to disease with captives, and thus to ensure social continuity— was closely connected with the war to control fur sources. "Vacant positions in Iroquois families and villages were both literally and symbolically filled [by war captives]," writes one historian, "while [Iroquois] survivors were assured that the social role and spiritual strength embodied in the departed's name had not been lost."[23]

Political Organization

Contact with European societies profoundly changed the political organization of Native American societies. This varied from society to society, but the examples of the Creeks and the Cherokees are instructive. Though they belonged

---

[20]Ibid., p. 149, quoting Alfred L. Kroeber, *Cultural and Natural Areas of Native North America* (Berkeley and Los Angeles, CA, 1939), p. 148.
[21]Quoted in Jennings, *The Invasion of America . . .* , p. 150.
[22]John Underhill, *News from America*; or, *A New and Experimentall Discoverie of New England* (London, 1638).
[23]Daniel K. Richter, "War and Culture: The Iroquois Experience," *William and Mary Quarterly*, 40 (1983): 535–536.

to different linguistic groups and frequently warred against each other, their political structures before European intrusions were similar, and they encountered the same historical forces in the seventeenth and eighteenth centuries—disease, trade, war, and land encroachment. Since the collapse in the early sixteenth century of the Mississippian chiefdoms, a significant feature of the traditional political structures was the local autonomy of towns and clans. It was to the town, not to the "confederacy," that the Creeks and Cherokees gave their primary loyalty. Town and clan leaders sometimes tried to coordinate the policy of various towns, but no party in disagreement with a majority decision was compelled to act against its wishes. Thus, in the early years of engagement with Europeans, towns or groups of towns often parleyed separately with the newcomers, made particular agreements with traders, and acted semi-independently in military affairs.

Disease transmitted by arriving Europeans disrupted and often shattered town-centered Creek and Cherokee life, thereby leading to new clusterings of the survivors. It was amid population decline that Creeks and Cherokees, from the mid-seventeenth century forward, began to adapt their political structures to the trade, war, and diplomacy involved in extensive interaction with Europeans. Towns began to align depending on their proximity to French or English traders. A split between the Upper Creek and Lower Creek towns, for example, developed because the former lived within the French trading orbit, whereas the latter had easier access to the English. Similarly, the towns of the Overhill Cherokees gravitated toward the French, and the Middle and Lower Cherokees traded with the English. The need to deal with English, French, and Spanish traders and governments also obliged the towns to move toward firmer confederacies in which coordinated action would give them greater strength in their dealings with outsiders.

Another political change involved a gradual move toward centralized tribal leadership and the establishment of patrilineal dynasties among the headmen or "micos." This change altered the traditional structure and criterion of leadership.

Before contact with Europeans, leadership was local and descended in the dominant matrilineal clan of the village. But in the eighteenth century, the tendency was to create supratown chiefs and to allow their power to pass on to their sons rather than to their sisters' sons. One cause of these shifts was that English, Spanish, and French authorities wanted to deal with one chief rather than many and tended to promote and support the candidacy of the chief's son, consistent with the European view of male-dominated social and political organization. This European attempt to influence the internal politics of Native societies was meant to further the colonizers' control in their dealings with Indian military allies and trading partners. Also favoring the development of patrilineal institutions was the intensified hunting, trading, and warring of the eighteenth century, which generally elevated the importance of male roles in Native society.

Europeans also influenced the political dynamics of Creek and Cherokee societies by supporting the candidacy of a particular headman's son or even to commission certain individuals in order to facilitate communication and cooperation. The English tried to establish Ouletta, the son of the Creek Chief Brims, as their client. When he died, they transferred their recognition to the Spanish candidate, his brother Seepeycoffee. Annual gifts, essential for good relations, were distributed through commissioned headmen, thus enhancing their prestige within their own society. The English practice of picking particular headmen with whom to negotiate conferred power on those who often had not earned their authority in the traditional way, according to matrilineage and honor, but simply through the intervention of an external authority. In time, a commission from colonial officials became important in the degree of influence wielded by a particular chief.

Intermarriage with an Indian woman was another way of gaining influence in a tribe, particularly if the woman was from an influential clan. Named Coosaponakeesa at birth, the woman who became famous as Mary Musgrove Bosomworth, a niece of Brims, married three

Englishmen in succession. The first was the son of Indian trader John Musgrove. Though she was fiercely anti-English on occasion, her husbands attained positions of great importance within the Creek confederation and she became a key figure herself as an inter-cultural mediator. Thus, through commissioning client headmen and marrying Indian women, the Carolinians worked to strengthen the pro-English faction in the Creek confederacy and to wield influence in their political decisions.

Although recruiting headmen in a way that benefited the English upset traditional lines of political authority, it was also a purposeful adjustment of traditional political practices by Indian peoples who faced new and powerful invaders bearing highly desirable trade goods. By modifying the customary criteria of kinship, the Creeks selected leaders better equipped to act in their interest. Greater access to the English or Spanish came by marrying one's sister to a European, by accepting a commission, or by having a European father. In none of these cases were the Creeks simply passive objects responding to White initiative. In a period of shifting power among the European groups present in the region, the Creeks were "coping creatively in a variety of ways with the different situations in which they found themselves."[24]

Like the Creeks, the Cherokees changed their political practices in the eighteenth century in response to new needs related to war and trade with Europeans. Before about 1730, the nearly autonomous village was the locus of Cherokee political authority. Little need existed for the political unification of towns. But tension with their Creek neighbors, encouraged by the English, and intermittent hostilities with the English themselves created a need for political centralization. By midcentury the Cherokees had formed a supravillage political organization. Civil chiefs or "priests," under the leadership of Old Hop, gathered together the fragmented authority of the

earlier period and formed a tribal "priest state" in which the Cherokee towns coordinated decision making.

When this step proved inadequate in the difficult, strife-filled years after midcentury, warriors began to assume the dominant role in tribal councils. The warrior commanded great respect before this time but was outranked by the civil chiefs. By the 1760s, adapting to a new era of strife, the Cherokees made "warring and warriors an unambiguous part of the good life" and gave the war chiefs new and coercive political authority over the nation.[25] By this process, the Cherokees made political changes that enabled dozens of villages to unify and pool their strength.

Alcohol

A final aspect of culture change, which was both cause and effect, was the use of distilled spirits. Rum became an important item in the Indian trade because traders pushed it hard and because Indians acquired a taste for it. Indian traders and coastal merchants reaped economic benefits from the Natives' desire for rum and therefore worked to increase the volume of the trade. From the Indian point of view, alcohol became important in internal and intertribal relations. The quality of English over French rum became a major consideration in diverting the Northern fur trade from Montreal to Albany. The decision of the Georgia government to allow no traffic in alcohol—a part of their attempt to reform the Indian trade in the 1730s—brought only protests from the Creek leaders, who understood the debilitating effects of rum on Creek society but were unwilling to give up the power they enjoyed as distributors of it.

How were Indian societies affected by the use of distilled spirits? Some scholars have seen alcohol as a painkilling device used by people caught between two cultures. Unable to maintain their traditional ways of life after becoming dependent

[24]Robert F. Berkhofer, Jr., "The Political Context of a New Indian History," *Pacific Historical Review*, 40 (1971): 364.
[25]Fred Gearing, "Priests and Warriors; Social Structures for Cherokee Politics in the 18th Century," American Anthropological Association *Memoir*, 93 (1962): 102.

on European material goods, but equally unable to gain acceptance into White society, Indians, it is argued, turned in despair to rum. In this view, drunkenness was a way of escaping internalized feelings of unworthiness that came from prolonged contact with a White society that called Natives "savages" and "barbarians." Drunkenness provided at least temporary flight back to a romanticized past and gave momentary salve in resolving a painful crisis of identity.

The difficulty with this explanation is that whatever its value in revealing the causes of alcoholism in modern society, it does not satisfactorily explain drunkenness among either Indians or Europeans in the eighteenth century. Europeans were not known for identity crises in pre-Revolutionary society; yet their alcoholic consumption was staggering even by modern American standards and was far greater than among Natives in this period. If nothing else, mere availability assured this tendency. The spigots in thousands of colonial taverns rarely ran dry, but distilled spirits were available only intermittently to Natives spread over thousands of square miles of the interior.

By understanding that consuming alcohol has different meanings in different cultures and that drunken behavior takes many forms according to varying cultural norms, we can better appreciate the role of alcohol in Indian societies. Anthropologists and historians have recently argued that for Indians in the early period of European contact, drinking was primarily "an institutionalized 'time-out' period from ordinary canons of etiquette." Only later did it become a form of social protest and a means of release from despair. In the seventeenth and early eighteenth centuries, Indians imbibed rum for cultural reasons that made sense within the context of their own culture—"expansive conviviality, the letting down of customary decorum, and

in some cases, serious dignified drinking into a comatose state."[26] Indians incorporated the consumption of alcohol into a value system that earlier had adopted the smoking of tobacco not only as a way to nurse sociability and generosity— "passing the pipe"—but also as a custom invested with religious functions and meanings. When one trader observed that Carolina Indians went about drinking solemnly "as if it were part of their religion," he was unconsciously noting "a virtual means of achieving an altered state and communing with spiritual powers."[27]

Alcohol became important in Euro-Indian relations in another way. Colonial leaders and traders commonly distributed it as a prelude to negotiations for land or trade goods. If many eighteenth-century commentators are to be believed, this custom was all to the advantage of the colonizers because Indians became befuddled and then easily swindled. This outcome, however, was probably the exception rather than the rule. Indians did not relish being cheated any more than Europeans, and according to the testimony of many traders, they were as skillful at driving a bargain as their White trading partners. The distribution of alcohol at the beginning of negotiations was, in their terms, a ritual for ensuring a mutually beneficial contract. So long as Indians had more than one place to trade, it was hardly good business practice for traders to drive them into the arms of competitors by getting them drunk and stealing their furs.

This is not to deny that sharp practices occurred. On occasion unauthorized traders brought casks of rum to an Indian village, watched it eagerly consumed, and left with a winter's harvest of furs and skins. But Europeans complained about being "held up" by Indians as often as Indians complained about European trickery. And when the trading was conducted at frontier posts or in Indian villages, it was not

---

[26]Nancy Oestreich Lurie, "The World's Oldest On-Going Protest Demonstration: North American Indian Drinking Patterns," *Pacific Historical Review*, 40 (1971): 321; Craig MacAndrew and Robert B. Edgerton, *Drunken Comportment, A Social Explanation* (Chicago, IL, 1969).

[27]James Merrell, *The Indians' New World: Catawbas and their Neighbors from European Contact through the Era of Removal* (Chapel Hill, NC, 1989), p. 39.

to the trader's advantage to cheat Natives who had been robbed of their senses by the demon rum. Indians took their furs where they could obtain the best prices and the amplest supply of trade goods. Their extraordinary mobility over land and inland waterways, combined with the availability of more than one European supplier, made it imperative for colonial traders to maintain a relationship that satisfied the Indians. When the traders did not, as in the case of the Carolina traders, the Indians took their trade to the French, to the Spanish, or to rival traders in Georgia and Virginia.

When Indian societies lost their land, their autonomy, and their confidence in their traditional belief system, drinking could change from a form of social relaxation to a solvent for internalized aggressive impulses against whites. This seems to have been the case among some of the remnants of coastal tribes, which by the eighteenth century had lost their land and their power. They existed only as clients of White society, and the chronic and debauched drinking that many observers described may indicate their precarious inner state. Almost powerless and unable to express their hostility toward whites, their frustrations accumulated and were turned inward. Only drinking, and in extreme cases suicide, provided release from this situation.

The costs of alcohol abuse mounted rapidly by the 1720s, when the flow of rum and brandy into Native villages, even those of strong, interior Indian societies, grew from a trickle to a torrent. As one historian of the Iroquois has put it, "No less than modern drug lords, the traders at Oswego [the English trading post on Lake Ontario] dispensed death, and Iroquois leaders were powerless to stop them." One Iroquois leader protested bitterly to Albany officials in 1730, "You may find graves upon graves along the lake, all which misfortunes are occasioned by

selling rum to our Brethren."[28] Four decades later, Mohawk sachems lamented that "our grown people have become so addicted to liquor that unless some stop be put thereto we shall soon be a ruined people."[29] In South Carolina, where the rum trade began early but did not dominate the Indian desire for European items, alcohol represented four-fifths of the trade goods purchased by the Natives in 1770, according to the British agent to the Choctaws. Two years later, traveling through Choctaw towns, the agent "saw nothing but rum drinking and women crying over the dead bodies of their relations who have died by rum."[30]

All over North America, whether in the region colonized by the French, Spanish, or English, by the mid-eighteenth century, Indians were paying a terrible price to quench their thirst for liquor. Native women may have suffered the most. Drinking binges produced unspeakable domestic violence, created animosity in Indian villages, weakened the constitution of bodies already under assault from European diseases, endangered yet unborn children of pregnant Indian women, impoverished the tribes that drank away the profits from trading animal pelts, sharpened the White image of the violent "savage" Indians, and ate away at the individual self-respect and communal pride that precontact Indian values inculcated. The Indian trader John Lawson described the tragic abuses of Native women. He saw Indian men who "when they have a design to lie with a woman . . . strive to make her drunk" and then "take the advantage to do with them what they please, and sometimes in their drunkenness, cut off their hair and sell it to the English, which is the greatest affront can be offered them."[31] Englishmen seized the same advantage. Virginia's William Byrd enjoyed "Jenny, an Indian girl, [who] had got drunk and made us

[28]Richter, *The Ordeal of the Longhouse . . .* , p. 266.
[29]Quoted in David L. Preston, *The Texture of Contact: European and Indian Settler Communities on the Frontiers of Iroquoia, 1667–1783* (Lincoln, NE, 2009), p. 198.
[30]Quoted in Peter C. Mancall, *Deadly Medicine: Indians and Alcohol in Early America* (Ithaca, NY, 1995), p. 94.
[31]John Lawson, *A New Voyage to Carolina*, . . . Hugh T. Lefler, ed. (Chapel Hill, NC, 1967), pp. 211–212.

good sport."[32] "In alcohol's empire," writes one historian, "Indians suffered."[33]

Cultural Persistence

Although the interior tribes blended a wide variety of European trade goods into their material culture and adapted their internal economies and political structures to meet new situations, they held fast to traditional culture in other ways. Iroquois, Creeks, Cherokees, and other tribes were unimpressed with most of the institutions of European life and saw no reason to replace what they valued in their own culture with what they disdained in the culture of others. This perspective applied to the newcomers' political institutions and practices, their systems of law and justice, religion, education, family organization, and child-rearing practices. In all these areas, Native Americans carefully observed European customs but saw little worthy of emulation. Indeed, so far as they could ascertain, these institutions often failed to work successfully in the Europeans' own societies.

Anglican missionaries of the Society for the Propagation of the Gospel were plagued by this paradox in their efforts to convert Indians to Christianity. Why, asked Native men and women, should they convert to a system that, despite its claims of superiority, was ridden with crime, social disorder, and political factionalism? "[The Indians] are for the most part great lovers of justice & equity in their dealings," wrote Robert Maule, an Anglican missionary in South Carolina in 1709, "and I have asked some of them whether they would learn to be or had any desire to become of the White men's religion. They have plainly told me no; what's the matter said I, why so? Because, replies they,

Backarara [the White man] no good; Backarara cheat; Backarara lie, Backarara drink brandy, me no love that."[34] Clergymen in the Carolinas repeated the same message in reporting to London. Most of the settlers, wrote a plaintive Charles Woodmason at the end of the colonial period, lived "after a loose and lascivious manner. . . . The manners of the North Carolinians in general, are vile and corrupt—the whole country is a stage of debauchery, dissoluteness, and corruption. . . . Polygamy is very common, . . . bastardy no disrepute—concubinage general."[35] Was it any wonder, then, that he was unable to convince the Indians of the superiority of the White way of life?

John Lawson, an official in the Carolinas in the early eighteenth century, captured the essence of why Natives shunned cultural borrowing aside from prizing material objects. "They are really better to us," he wrote in 1708, "than we are to them; they always give us victuals at their quarters, and take care we are armed against hunger and thirst. We do not do so by them (generally speaking) but let them walk by our doors hungry, and do not often relieve them. We look upon them with scorn and disdain, and think them little better than beasts in human shape, though if well examined, we shall find that, for all our religion and education, we possess more moral deformities and evils than these savages do, or are acquainted withal."[36] Indians were not secretive in their disdain of White culture. When it was suggested to the Iroquois in 1744 that they send some of their young men to Virginia for a European-style education, they counterproposed that "if the English Gentlemen would send a dozen or two of their children to Onondaga, the great Council would take care of their education, bring

---

[32]William Byrd, *The Secret Diary of William Byrd of Westover, 1709–1712*, Louis B. Wright and Marion Tinling, eds. (Richmond, VA, 1941), p. 245.

[33]Mancall, *Deadly Medicine . . .* , p. 85.

[34]Robert Maule to Society for the Propagation of the Gospel [June 3, 1710], SPG Mss, A5, No. 133 (microfilm of Library of Congress transcripts), UCLA Research Library.

[35]Charles Woodmason, *Carolina Backcountry on the Eve of the Revolution: The Journal and Other Writings of Charles Woodmason, Anglican Itinerant*, Richard J. Hooker, ed. (Chapel Hill, NC, 1969), pp. 80–81.

[36]Lawson, *A New Voyage to Carolina*, p. 243.

them up in really what was the best manner and make men of them."[37]

In marriage and social relations, it was much the same. Although Europeans often disparaged Native customs of companionate marriage or serial monogamy and accused them of "licentiousness," "debauchery," and "faithlessness" in their sexual practices, domestic relations among the Indians, as a few European observers admitted, were entirely satisfactory to them and seemed much better than those of their European critics. Shortly after his arrival in the colonies, Thomas Paine reported the opinion of an "American savage" concerning Christian marriages: "Either the Christian's God was not so good and wise as he was represented," the Indian avowed,

> or he never meddled with the marriages of his people; since not one in a hundred of them had anything to do either with happiness or common sense. Hence as soon as ever you meet, you long to part; and not having this relief in your power, by way of revenge, double each other's misery. Whereas in ours [Indian marriages], which have no other ceremony than mutual affection, and last no longer than they bestow mutual pleasures, we make it our business to oblige the heart we are afraid to lose; and being at liberty to separate, seldom or never feel the inclination. But if any should be found so wretched among us, as to hate where the only commerce ought to be love,

we instantly dissolve the band. God made us all in pairs; each has his mate somewhere or other; and it is our duty to find each other out, since no creature was ever intended to be miserable.[38]

In sum, though Native societies embraced an array of material goods and modified their political structures, many aspects of Indian life endured in the long period of interaction with Europeans. Indian societies were as selective as European societies in borrowing from the cultures they encountered. They incorporated what served them well and rejected what made no sense within the framework of their own values and modes of existence.

Despite many areas of cultural persistence, the involvement of Native societies in the European trade network brought many changes that worked to the Native Americans' disadvantage. Trade hastened the spread of epidemic diseases, raised the level of warfare, depleted ecozones of animal life, and drew Indians into a far-flung market economy in which "they eventually destroyed the basis for the very economy they were trying to practice."[39] Over a long period of time, the fur trade constricted the economic freedom of Native societies, for they reorganized productive relations within their own communities to serve a trading partner who, through the side effects of the trade, became a trading master.

Summary

Between 1675 and 1763, France, Spain, and England engaged in a struggle for trade and territory in the region between the Mississippi River and the Atlantic Ocean and in the waters of the Caribbean. In so doing, they used diplomacy and war in their continual interactions with the powerful Native tribes of interior North America, who did much the same, with varying degrees of success. For almost half a century after 1701, the Iroquois policy of balancing one European power with another worked well. The Creeks followed a similar course of "aggressive neutrality" in their relations with the Europeans. The numerically superior Cherokees also kept the English off balance by their overtures to the French while encouraging English dependence, just as they depended on the English.

---

[37]Quoted in A. Irving Hallowell, "The Backwash of the Frontier: The Impact of the Indian in American Culture," in Paul Bohannan and Fred Plog, eds., *Beyond the Frontier: Social Process and Cultural Change* (Garden City, NY, 1967), p. 325.
[38]Philip S. Foner, ed., *The Complete Writings of Thomas Paine*, 2 vols. (New York, 1945) 2:119–120.
[39]Jennings, *The Invasion of America . . .* , p. 87.

Interaction with European societies over time transformed Indian culture in ways that ultimately spelled decline for the Native people. Through trade, warfare, and the use of alcohol, the overall effects of contact with Europeans worked to the disadvantage of the tribes. Even so, many aspects of Indian life survived the long period of interaction with Europeans, reflecting the selectivity of Indians in borrowing from the European societies they encountered and their ability to adapt their political organization as North America was swept by militant European rivalry.

Critical Thinking Questions

1. How do the Iroquois-French and Iroquois-English treaties of 1700 illustrate the Iroquois approach to "managing" these two groups of Europeans?
2. What strategy did Chief Brims of the Creeks use against the French, English, and Spanish, and how successful was it?
3. Why did Cherokee support of the Carolinians weaken after 1730, and why was it necessary for the English to rebuild that support?
4. Which aspects of European culture and lifestyle did the interior tribes accept, and which not (and why not)?

Further Reading

Kathryn E. Holland Braund, *Deerskins and Duffels: The Creek Indian Trade with Anglo-America, 1685–1815* (Lincoln: University of Nebraska Press, 1993).

Colin Calloway, *New Worlds for All: Indians, Europeans, and the Remaking of Early America* (Baltimore: Johns Hopkins University Press, 1997).

James Taylor Carson, *Searching for the Bright Path: The Mississippi Choctaws from Prehistory to Removal* (Lincoln: University of Nebraska Press, 1999).

John Demos, *The Unredeemed Captive: A Family Story from Early America* (New York: Knopf, 1994).

Gregory Dowd, *War under Heaven: Pontiac, the Indian Nations, and the British Empire* (Baltimore: Johns Hopkins University Press, 2002).

W. N. Fenton, *The Great Law and the Longhouse: A Political History of the Iroquois Confederacy* (Norman: University of Oklahoma Press, 1998).

Andrew Frank, *Creeks and Southerners: Biculturalism on the Early American Frontier* (Lincoln: University of Nebraska Press, 2005).

Eric Hinderaker, *The Two Hendricks: Unraveling a Mohawk Mystery* (Cambridge: Harvard University Press, 2010).

Jon Parmenter, *The Edge of the Woods: Iroquoia, 1534–1701* (East Lansing: Michigan State University Press, 2010).

Theda Perdue, *Cherokee Women: Gender and Culture Change, 1700–1835* (Lincoln: University of Nebraska Press, 1998).

David L. Preston, *The Texture of Contact: European and Indian Settler Communities on the Frontiers of Iroquoia, 1667–1783* (Lincoln: University of Nebraska Press, 2009).

Daniel R. Richter, *Facing East from Indian Country: A Native History of Early America* (Cambridge: Harvard University Press, 2001).

Claudio Saunt, *A New Order of Things: Property, Power, and the Transformation of the Creek Indians, 1733–1816* (Cambridge: Cambridge University Press, 1999).

Michael Witgen, *An Infinity of Nations: How the Native New World Shaped Early North America* (Philadelphia: University of Pennsylvania Press, 2012).

CHAPTER 10

The Seven Years' War and Its Aftermath

LEARNING OBJECTIVES

- Cite the causes and primary effect of the population explosion, especially in the English colonies, in the first half of the eighteenth century.

- Explain the factors and events precipitating the Seven Years' War; include details on the purpose and outcome of the Albany Congress of 1754.

- Analyze the strategies employed by the Iroquois, Cherokees, and Creeks in the Seven Years' War, pointing out strengths and weaknesses; explain why the Peace of Paris, signed in 1763, came as a blow to these Native peoples.

- Characterize the relations between Indians and whites after 1763; incorporate discussion of Pontiac's Revolt and the Proclamation of 1763, with its creation of a racial boundary from Maine to Georgia.

- Assess the effects of the Seven Years' War on White communities from the perspectives of economic change; alienation from the mother country; social transformation and the widening gulf between the rich and poor, particularly in the cities; the lure of the frontier; and factional politics.

For the first third of the eighteenth century, interior tribes such as the Creeks, Cherokees, and Iroquois maintained a state of equipoise with European colonial societies by artfully playing one colonizing power against another and serving periodic reminders to the Europeans that Indian trade and military assistance were as valuable to the Europeans as the latters' trade goods were to Native Americans. "To preserve the balance between us and the French," wrote New York's Indian secretary, "is the great ruling principle of modern Indian politics."[1] Indians were useful to Europeans, Europeans were useful to Indians, and power, though tipping toward the Europeans, was roughly divided between them. But in the second third of the eighteenth century, historical forces, both in international politics and in the more limited sphere of the colonizers' communities, ended the equilibrium between Indian and European peoples while deeply dividing colonial society itself.

---

[1]Peter Wraxall, *An Abridgment of the Indian Affairs*, Charles H. McIlwain, ed. (Cambridge, MA, 1915), p. 219.

Population Increase

In North America, an explosive population buildup, especially in the English colonies, created such a shortage of land on the coastal plain that by the 1750s, thousands of land-hungry settlers were breaching the mountain gaps in the Appalachians in search of new territory. From a population of a quarter million in 1700, the English colonies grew to 1.2 million in 1750 and increased another 400,000 in the next decade. Three-quarters of this increase came in the colonies south of New York. The advance agents of this enormous westward rush were eastern land speculators. They had only to watch the German and Scots-Irish immigrants disembarking daily at Baltimore, Philadelphia, and New York to understand that fortunes could be made by those who laid claim to land west of the existing settlements.

With capital provided by London investors, the Virginia tobacco planters and the northern merchants formed land companies in the 1740s and 1750s to capitalize on this demographic explosion. The Ohio Land Company, organized in 1747, laid claim to half a million acres in the Ohio valley. The Susquehannah Land Company, organized five years later, declared rights to hundreds of thousands of acres in Pennsylvania. In the next decade, the Delaware Company, Miami Company, Indiana Company, and other private syndicates all raced to establish claims. Some, like the Susquehannah Company, advertised that their purpose was to "open the most effectual door for carrying the light of the glorious Gospel of Christ among the numerous tribes of Indians that inhabit those inland parts." But nobody doubted that the principal object was land.[2] To this end, colonial agents tirelessly pressured Indian leaders to cede and sell their lands in order to pave the way for new White settlements. The farther west the colonizers moved, the closer they came to the Western trading empire of the French and the Indian nations allied to them.

The Seven Years' War

On the other side of the Atlantic, the revival of international rivalries hastened this showdown west of the Appalachian Mountains. In 1748, France and England had seemingly resolved the differences that had led them to war in 1744, but even as the ink was drying on the articles of conciliation, they prepared for a renewal of hostilities. The powerful merchant element in England, supported by American clients, called for a destruction of French overseas trade. Even before events in Europe brought formal declarations of war, fighting began in the North American interior. By the time it was over, in 1763, France had surrendered its vast North Atlantic claims. This outcome rearranged the balance of power in Europe and North America, while shattering the Indians' precious system of balancing European powers, the key to maintaining their leverage in a precarious, fast-changing world.

In the 1740s, English fur traders from Virginia and Pennsylvania pushed deep into the Ohio valley, establishing outposts on the Ohio River and its tributaries. By 1749, the French commander at Fort Miami, south of Detroit, reported that about 300 English traders were operating in the Ohio country, luring Indians into their trade orbit. For decades, people with a sense of geopolitics had realized that the struggle for the continent hinged on control of the trans-Allegheny West. For more than a century, the English had been content to populate the narrow coastal plain, leaving the continental heartland to their rivals and obtaining their share of the Indian trade through connections centered at Albany and Charleston. Now they challenged the French where the French interest was vital. The British were now poised to sever Canada from Louisiana.

France's choices were to resist or to surrender the continent to the English and Spanish. The French chose the former. Determined to block further English expansion, they established forts

---

[2]Petition of Subscribers to the Susquehannah Company, 1755, in Julian P. Boyd, ed., *The Susquehannah Company Papers* (Wilkes-Barre, PA, 1930), 1: 255.

throughout the Ohio valley and tried to pry various Indian tribes loose from their English connections. The Iroquois, Shawnees, and Delawares of the Ohio region listened to French overtures that only an alliance with the French would guarantee their survival. "The English," warned one French emissary in the early 1750s, "are much less anxious to take away your peltries than to become masters of your lands . . . and your blindness is so great, that you do not perceive that the very hand that caresses you, will scourge you, like Negroes and slaves, so soon as it will have got possession of those lands."[3]

Though the tribes were aware of the westward surging White population, they were unwilling to break the connections with English traders that brought them commodities that the French could not match in price and quality. Moreover, English strength in their region was a reality, but French talk of trade south of the Great Lakes was only a promise. In 1752, France began a campaign to alter this situation, attacking English trading posts and building forts of their own. By 1754, they had driven the English traders out of the Ohio valley, established themselves as far east as the forks of the Ohio River, near present-day Pittsburgh, Pennsylvania, and smartly rebuffed the ambitious young Colonel George Washington, who attempted to expel them from Fort Duquesne.

Internal division crippled English attempts to respond to this bold French campaign. This failure was starkly revealed at the Albany Congress of 1754, where the thirteen colonies attempted to unify for military purposes and through united action to woo the all-important Iroquois out of their neutrality. One of the main purposes of the Congress was to demonstrate to the Iroquois that fighting resolved and cohesion prevailed in the English colonies. But while the colonies' delegates attempted to work out a plan of confederation, land agents from Connecticut and Pennsylvania plotted to purchase Iroquois lands west of the Susquehanna River—an intrigue in which lesser Indian chiefs signed away land while knowing that the councils of the Iroquois nations would not sanction such transactions. With Virginians not even sending a delegate to the Congress, the attempt at intercolonial cooperation fell to pieces, and the Iroquois left the conference convinced that the English were "like women: bare and open and without fortifications."[4]

Statesmen in the capitals of Europe decided to force a showdown. What ensued is known as the Seven Years' War, or the French and Indian War—a sprawling global conflict that its most recent historian calls "the most important event in eighteenth-century North America."[5] London dispatched two Irish regiments under the command of General James Braddock. Orders from Paris sent 3,000 regulars to the French strongholds at Louisbourg on Cape Breton Island, guarding the St. Lawrence River, and at Quebec. The year it took Braddock to make his way across the Atlantic and then lead his army, reinforced by American enlistees, across Virginia and into the western wilderness was the last of his life. Less than twenty miles from Fort Duquesne, the French and their Indian allies ambushed the British Americans in 1755 and routed Braddock's reputedly invincible army of 2,200 with an attacking force one-third as large. Two-thirds of the English force were killed and wounded; the survivors fled, leaving artillery, horses, cattle, and supplies behind.

For the rest of 1755, Indian raiders terrorized Virginia and Pennsylvania frontier settlements. For years they had nursed grudges against White land encroachers and ungenerous traders. Now was their opportunity to align themselves with the French and to even scores that went back decades. Among the first to strike at the English, Scots-Irish, and German communities were the

[3]Quoted in William J. Eccles, *The Canadian Frontier, 1534–1760* (New York, 1969), p. 158.
[4]E. B. O'Callaghan, ed., *Documents Relative to the Colonial History of the State of New York* (Albany, NY, 1855), 6: 870.
[5]Fred Anderson, *Crucible of War: The Seven Years' War and the Fate of Empire in British North America, 1754–1766* (New York, 2000), p. xvii.

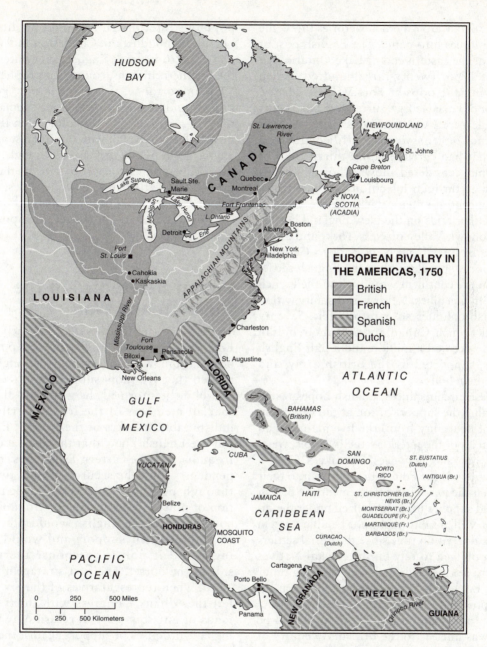

EUROPEAN RIVALRY IN THE AMERICAS, 1750

- British
- French
- Spanish
- Dutch

Delawares, who, a generation before, had been cheated out of their tribal lands in eastern Pennsylvania. Just as they had streamed westward as refugees from colonial oppression, now they sent thousands of European refugees fleeing eastward as they burned, killed, and pillaged along the Pennsylvania frontier. "Almost all the women and children over Susquehanna have left their habitations, and the roads are full of starved, naked, indigent multitudes," cried one colonist.[6]

---

[6]Quoted in Douglas E. Leach, *The Northern Colonial Frontier, 1607–1763* (New York, 1966), p. 200.

In 1756 and 1757, French victories threw the English colonies into panic. The English post at Oswego, at the eastern end of Lake Ontario, fell in August 1756. Twenty-three hundred British and provincial troops at Fort William Henry, at the foot of Lake George, surrendered in August 1757. So desperate was the English situation that the governor of Pennsylvania, terrified at Indian attacks that had carried within thirty miles of Philadelphia, considered allowing hostile Indians free passage through his colony if they promised to concentrate their attacks on the Virginia frontier. Other raids on the New England border, in the Mohawk Valley of New York, and along the entire frontier from New York to Georgia, led to gloomy speculations in the English settlements that the continent would fall to the French and their Indian allies. Never was disunity within the English colonies so painfully felt. Seventy thousand French Canadians and their Indian allies had taken on a million and a half English colonists, supported by the British army, and whipped them hollow.

In these circumstances, English hopes rested on obtaining the support of (or, at the very least, pledges of neutrality from) the five main Indian confederacies of the interior—the Iroquois, western Delawares and Shawnees, Cherokees, Creeks, and Choctaws. If the French drew them into their camp, even the massive reinforcements of British troops and supplies being mobilized under the direction of William Pitt might not be able to stem the Gallic tide. At no time since the initial settlers had been obliged to rely on the coastal Natives for food to see them through the "starving time" were the English colonists so dependent on Indian support.

How Indian support or neutrality could be secured was unclear to the British. A century of intermittent hostility and the frantic hungering after the Indians' western lands during the previous decade suggested that the allegiance of the populous interior tribes would be difficult to obtain. Edmond Atkin, Charleston Indian trader and soon to become English Superintendent of the Southern Indians, sounded a prophetic note: "The importance of Indians is now generally known and understood. A doubt remains not, that the prosperity of our colonies on the continent, will stand or fall with our interest and favor among them. While they are our friends, they are the cheapest and strongest barrier for the protection of our settlements; when enemies, they are capable by ravaging in their method of war, in spite of all we can do, to render those possessions almost useless."[7]

Indian Strategies in the Seven Years' War

The case of the Iroquois is illustrative of the English vulnerability to which Atkin pointed. In negotiations with the French, the English pretended that Iroquois support was a certainty and bluntly informed the governor of Canada that all members of the Iroquois tribes were indisputably subjects of the King of England.[8] But the English knew that the allegiance of the Iroquois and the eastern Delawares, their dependents, could be secured in only two ways: through purchase or through a demonstration of power so great that the Iroquois would conclude that the English would prevail with or without their support and would accordingly find it politic to choose the winning side at the outset. The first stratagem failed in 1754, when representatives of the Six Nations left the Albany Congress with thirty wagonloads of gifts but gave in return only tantalizing half-promises of support against the French, who continued to score major victories in the next three years. Only when paid as mercenaries, such as in 1757 when about 500 Mohawks

---

[7]Wilbur R. Jacobs, ed., *Indians of the Southern Colonial Frontier: The Edmond Atkin Report and Plan of 1755* (Columbia, SC, 1954), pp. 3–4.
[8]Governor Clinton to Governor of Canada, October 10, 1748, in O'Callaghan, ed., *Documents Relating to History of New York*, 6: 492.

collected £33,602 for services rendered to the English forces in New York, would the Iroquois support the Anglo-Americans.[9]

Colonial leaders made further attempts during the next two years to get the Iroquois to subdue the attacking Delawares, who had driven the Pennsylvania settlers away from their frontier settlements. Pennsylvania itself was deeply divided between pacifistic Quakers, who believed that Scots-Irish frontiersmen were only reaping what they had sown through years of abusing and defrauding Indians, and militant Anglicans and Presbyterians, who wanted taxes passed for a stern counteroffensive against the attackers. "The Indians learned our weakness, by being informed of our divisions," wrote the colony's official interpreter in 1757, after a conference convened for the purpose of buying off the Delawares' wrath.[10]

Not until October 1758 did the English get a promise from the Iroquois to halt the Delaware attacks on the Pennsylvania settlements. Agreement was reached at Easton, Pennsylvania, where the Indians left the conference with a wagon train of gifts. It is easy to suppose that these Indian concessions were simply a response to White stimuli. From the Indian point of view, however, the Easton Treaty had a different meaning. The Iroquois made no military commitment to the English. And in exchange for pledging their neutrality and promising to quiet the hostile Delawares, they resecured a vast tract of land west of the Susquehanna River that they had ceded to Pennsylvania four years before at the Albany Congress. This outcome restored their territorial security west of the Alleghenies.

Except for the half-hearted support of the Mohawks, the easternmost of the Six Nations, the Iroquois either maintained their neutrality or, as in the case of the Senecas, fought with the French in the campaigns of 1757 and 1758. The Mohawks' allegiance to the English is explained by their proximity to the English trading center at Albany, by the huge amounts they were paid for their services, and by the fact that William Johnson, appointed British Superintendent of the Northern Indians, had married a Mohawk woman and lived among them for years. Colonial leaders who had attempted to woo the Iroquois in the dark years from 1754 to 1758 found that the Six Nations steadfastly pursued their traditional policy of disengagement from European wars.

In 1759, however, the Iroquois reversed their position. Feelers by Johnson in February led him to report that if the English mounted an expedition against the French stronghold at Fort Niagara "or elsewhere, through the country of the Six Nations," he could convince most of the Iroquois "to join His Majesty's arms."[11] Assessing the Anglo-French military situation, the Iroquois reformulated their policy. After four years of French victories, the tide had turned in the British favor in July 1758, when Louisbourg and Fort Frontenac, the strategic centers of French power at opposite ends of the St. Lawrence, fell before Anglo-American assaults. In November 1758, the French abandoned Fort Duquesne at the forks of the Ohio River. By the end of the year, the upper Ohio valley was in English hands for the first time in four years. William Pitt had mobilized the fighting power of the English nation, putting more men in the field than existed in all of New France, and the colonists had put aside their intramural squabbling long enough to stem the French tide.

While English victories helped to move the Iroquois away from their long-held position of neutrality, the English capture of French ships bringing trade goods to Montreal vastly improved the English position in wooing the Six Nations. In April 1759, the Iroquois chiefs came to the Mohawk town of Canajoharie and

[9]Wilbur R. Jacobs, *Diplomacy and Indian Gifts: Anglo-French Rivalry Along the Ohio and Northwest Frontiers, 1748–1763* (Stanford, CA, 1950), p. 178.
[10]Lawrence H. Gipson, *The British Empire before the American Revolution*, 14 vols. (New York, 1936–1969), 7: 58.
[11]Ibid., p. 342.

The Indians giving a Talk to Colonel Bouquet in a Conference at a Council Fire, near his Camp on the Banks of Muskingum in North America, in Oct. 1764.

In his left hand, an Indian orator, either a Shawnee or Delaware chief, holds a wampum belt over the obligatory council fire to initiate a diplomatic negotiation with Colonel Henry Bouquet, who had led an expedition against the Ohio River valley Indian tribes at the end of the French and Indian War in 1763. In the following year, Bouquet pressed the defeated Indians, pictured here, to hand over all English captives taken by the tribes during the long war. This lithograph appeared in a contemporary book by William Smith, *An Historical Account of the Expedition against the Ohio Indians in the year 1764* (Philadelphia, 1766).

(Courtesy Library of Congress Prints and Photographs Division [LC-USZ62-104])

promised 800 warriors for an attack on Fort Niagara, the strategic French fur-trading depot on Lake Ontario. The Iroquois had calculated correctly: the French were going down to defeat in North America and were an unreliable trading partner. If the Iroquois policy of *realpolitik* failed at all, it was in not perceiving that the maintenance of French power in North America was essential to their long-range interests.

The Cherokees also played power politics during the Seven Years' War but less successfully than the Iroquois. From 1753 to 1754, the governor of Virginia worked hard to gain Cherokee support for Washington's attempt to dislodge the French at the forks of the Ohio, believing that only with Indian support could the English overcome the larger French forces. The Cherokee chiefs responded by promising the Virginians 1000 warriors; but at the same time, they pressed South Carolina for better trading prices and consulted with the French at Fort Toulouse on the Alabama River. They expressed interest in reviving the old Virginia-Cherokee trade, which in the past had been employed by the Cherokees to remind the Carolinians that their trade was desirable but not irreplaceable. In the end, their promise to send warriors to join Washington on his foray into the wilderness disappeared like smoke.

In 1755, when the Virginians came again to seek support for Braddock's campaign, the Cherokees promised hundreds of warriors to gain a trade with Virginia on more favorable terms than the Carolinians offered. Well aware that South Carolina and Virginia were close to blows in their struggle for control of the Cherokee trade, the Cherokees withheld the warriors when trade negotiations failed. When Braddock suffered his disastrous defeat a few months later, he had only eight Natives with his army.

In May 1755, South Carolina agents met the Cherokee leaders deep in the backcountry for treaty making. When the Cherokees agreed to recognize the English king as their sovereign and to cede some of their lands to the Crown, the Carolinians believed that they had accomplished a major breakthrough in luring the Indians out of their neutrality. In exchange, they pledged to supply more trade goods at lower prices and to build a fort in Cherokee country that would offer protection against French and Creek enemies.

How badly the English misunderstood Indian uses of diplomacy soon became clear. Although the governor of South Carolina boasted that the treaty of 1755 added "near 10,000 people to his Majesty's subjects and above 40,000,000 acres to his territories," the Cherokees regarded themselves as subject to British authority only so long as it served mutually satisfactory goals.[12] About 300 Cherokees fought with the Virginia militia on the colonists' western frontier in 1757, but they agreed to serve not as allies but as mercenaries. When they were not paid according to agreement, they promptly plundered Virginia frontier settlements in order to collect by force what the White government had failed to give them. The process was repeated in the next year, but this time Virginia frontiersmen began ambushing hundreds of Cherokees returning from battle and living off the land as they made their way home. Thirty Cherokees lost their lives at the hands of their allies in 1758. Spurring the Indian-hating Virginians was the colony's £50 scalp bounty, meant to apply to enemy Indians such as the Shawnees. To avaricious Virginians, scalps were scalps, whether Cherokee or Shawnee. Each earned its bearer the equivalent of a year's income as a frontier farmer.

A few such incidents were enough to fan into a roaring blaze the anti-English embers that pro-French factions had kept alive in the Cherokee towns. Messengers went out to the Creeks and Chickasaws, and by the winter of 1758 to 1759, talk of Indian retaliation had spread across the southern frontier. English agents countered with the warning that an English blockade of French shipping in North America would make

[12]Quoted in David H. Corkran, *The Cherokee Frontier: Conflict and Survival, 1740–1762* (Norman, OK, 1962), p. 61.

it impossible for the Natives to obtain guns, ammunition, and even normal trade goods from the French.

Nonetheless skirmishing from Virginia to South Carolina continued on the western edge of colonial settlement, soon turning the southern sector of the Seven Years' War into a war with the Cherokees. With 1,300 militia, Governor William Henry Lyttelton of South Carolina invaded Cherokee territory in 1759, the onset of a three-year war that razed dozens of Cherokee villages. The peace treaty he extracted from the Cherokees blamed the Indians for all that had happened. The Cherokee chiefs signed it under duress, but it inflamed them more.

The war erupted again in 1760. This time the Cherokees were far more united in opposing the English. The new governor of South Carolina, William Bull, soon recognized that the united Cherokees outmatched the largest force of militia he could put in the field. Bowing to circumstances, he agreed to a treaty that made concessions to the Cherokees on "terms that perhaps may not be thought suitable, according to the rules of honor, observed among Europeans," as he delicately put it.[13] The arrival of 1,300 crack Scottish troops under Sir Jeffrey Amherst and the subsequent expedition against the Cherokees again proved the difficulties of fighting Indians in their own territory. Bogged down in the hilly terrain, ambushed at every turn, the expedition "accomplished little, except possibly to boost Cherokee morale."[14] Badly stung, the British force returned to Charleston. Shortly thereafter, Fort Loudoun, the main English garrison in Cherokee country, surrendered to a Cherokee siege. But 1,800 British regulars, joined by 700 provincial militia, tried again in the summer of 1761. This time, by burning Cherokee villages and crops, they succeeded. With supplies from the French virtually cut off, the Cherokees submitted to a peace treaty that acknowledged English sovereignty and established the eastern boundary of the Cherokee territory.

Throughout the Rebellion of 1759 through 1761, the Cherokees made attempts to enlist the support of the Creeks. Two generations before, the refusal of the Cherokees to join the Creeks in the Yamasee War against the Carolinians had deprived the Creeks of their victory. Now the Creek decision to remain neutral cost the Cherokees decisively. Left to fight the English themselves, the Cherokees struggled against food shortages, lack of gunpowder, and a smallpox epidemic. The only trade goods reaching them from the French, ironically, were provided by New England ship captains, who brought contraband supplies to the French forts on the Gulf of Mexico. The desperate shortage of trade goods forced the Cherokees back to ancient customs—fashioning clothes from deer and bear skins, and tipping their arrows with bone points instead of trader's brass. Cut off from an alternate supply of trade goods and unable to organize a pan-Indian offensive, they joined the French as losers in the Seven Years' War.

Whereas the Iroquois made common cause with the English once French weaknesses were evident and whereas the Cherokees alternately allied with and fought against the English, the Creeks held fast to the policy of neutrality that had been the hallmark of their diplomacy since the Yamasee War. Their major concerns were trade and the maintenance of political sovereignty. Through the 1750s and early 1760s, the Creeks ranged from the Cherokee country to the French trading posts at Fort Toulouse and Mobile, accepting presents from both English and French and driving hard bargains for more favorable terms in the deerskin trade. Pro-French, pro-English, and neutralist factions argued bitterly in the Creek towns. But by 1757, British naval superiority had strangled French shipping. This outcome undermined the arguments of the Creek leaders who were advocating a pan-Indian, anti-English rebellion of Shawnees, Cherokees, Creeks, Chickasaws, and Catawbas. The English solidified their position with the Creeks in 1758

[13]Quoted in M. Eugene Sirmans, *Colonial South Carolina; A Political History* (Chapel Hill, NC, 1966), p. 335.
[14]Ibid., p. 336.

and 1759 by showering them with presents. Sensitive to the possibility that the Cherokee insurgency might spread, Governor Henry Ellis of Georgia spent the spring of 1760 trying to "set every person of influence upon endeavoring to create a rupture between those two nations—the Creeks and Cherokees."[15]

While refusing to join the Cherokees, the Creeks used their neighbor's rebellion for their own benefit. When English trade goods became scarce or when prices rose, they dropped the word to English traders that the arguments of the Cherokees and French had taken on a new persuasiveness. Actually, the outbreak of the Cherokee rebellion had divided the Creeks. The pro-French faction continued to urge the Cherokees on to greater efforts against the English and even murdered eleven English settlers in an attempt to precipitate an English attack that would galvanize the Creek nation behind the Cherokees. The Carolina and Georgia governments failed to rise to the bait, however. The decision not to respond to the murder of the traders or even to demand that the Creeks put the murderers to death showed the precarious position of the Southern colonists and their need to keep the Creeks neutral.

In spite of Cherokee victories in 1760 and in spite of their desire to check English expansionism, the Creek strategic options were crucially limited by the inability of the French to supply an alternate flow of vital weapons and trade goods. At a grand meeting of the French, the Cherokees, and the Creeks at Fort Toulouse in March 1761, the French had no munitions, presents, or trade goods to back up their talk of expelling the English from North America. English victories in the North had nearly sealed the fate of the French on the continent. For a half-century, the Creeks had maintained their neutrality and kept open a profitable trade with both the French and the English. In the process, however, they had become dependent on the European trade connection, which was shortly to be monopolized by the English.

Anglo-American victories in the North began in 1759 with the capture of Fort Niagara, continued with General James Wolfe's dramatic victory at Quebec, and culminated in the following year with the fall of Montreal. These events marked the end of hostilities in North America. Almost two centuries of French presence on the continent was coming to an end.

For the Indian nations that had demonstrated such independence of action and impressive power during the Seven Years' War, the Peace of Paris came as a hammer blow. Unlike the coastal tribes, whose numbers and autonomy had ebbed through contact with European colonizers, the interior tribes had grown more politically cohesive, militarily formidable, and technologically developed as a result of their connections with the English, French, and Spanish. Although becoming dependent on the European trade, they turned this dependency to their own advantage so long as more than one source of trade goods existed. They had mastered the European style of diplomatic intrigue, used it to serve their own self-interests, and proved their ability to evade or defeat numerically superior European forces.

But while playing a powerful role on land, the Indian nations possessed not a shred of power to control the ocean separating Europe and North America or the trade goods that flowed across it. In the end, this was the factor that undermined their strength. Control of the Atlantic by the British navy dealt a near-fatal blow to the playoff system, for the French in North America without trade goods were hardly better than no French at all. The inability to obtain French trade goods diminished Native Americans' room for maneuver and rendered futile the nascent pan-Indian movements against the English. Had the interior tribes been unified under French arms and supplies, the designs of the French imperialists to rule the continent might have materialized.

By the terms of the Peace of Paris, signed by England, France, and Spain in 1763, Canada and all of North America east of the Mississippi

---

[15]Quoted in W. W. Abbot, *The Royal Governors of Georgia, 1754–1775* (Chapel Hill, NC, 1959), p. 80.

River became English territory. France ceded the lands west of the Mississippi to Spain. Spain ceded Florida to England. From that year onward, English sway in the eastern half of North America was unchallenged in the courts of Europe. No longer could the Creeks, Cherokees, or Iroquois employ the playoff system to gain advantages in trade, since only one source of trade goods remained. Also, hostilities between the colonies, which Indian groups had often exploited, subsided as the thirteen English provinces unified to an unprecedented degree. Two centuries of European rivalry for possession and control of eastern North America had ended with dramatic swiftness. Iroquois, Cherokees, Creeks, and other interior tribes were now forced to adjust to this reality.

Indian-White Relations after 1763

At the conclusion of a long global war, the English government planned a continental Indian policy in North America, a dramatic departure from a century and a half of allowing each colony to conduct its own Indian affairs. Stung by how most of the North American tribes had given their allegiance to the French in the Seven Years' War, the English government now intended to separate Native Americans and colonizers, in order to guarantee the integrity of Indian territory. "It is just and reasonable, and essential to our interest, and the security of our colonies," stated the King's proclamation in 1763, "that the several nations or tribes of Indians with whom we are connected, and who live under our protection, should not be molested or disturbed in the possession of such parts of our dominions and territories as, not having been ceded to or purchased by us, are reserved to them, or any of them, as their hunting grounds."[16]

By the terms of the Proclamation of 1763, full of goodwill promises to Native peoples,

British policy-makers created a racial boundary from Maine to Georgia, roughly following the crestline of the Appalachian Mountains. Colonial governors were ordered to forbid "for the present and until our further pleasure be known" any surveys or land grants beyond the Appalachian watershed. "All the lands and territories lying to the westward of the sources of the rivers which fall into the sea from the west and northwest" were specifically reserved for Indian nations. All White settlers already beyond the Appalachian divide were charged to withdraw east of the line.

The Proclamation of 1763 is one of the most poignant documents in American history and one of the noblest promises issued by an imperial power to indigenous, colonized people. Historians who subscribe to the "frontier thesis" of Frederick Jackson Turner have argued that this attempt to dam up the energy of restless westward-looking Americans alienated the colonists and provided a major impetus for throwing off the restraining yoke of the mother country. Other historians, while agreeing that the proclamation was an irritant contributing to revolutionary sentiment, point out that those most alienated by it were the large land speculators of the eastern seaboard, who boiled at seeing such a fabulous source of profit put beyond their grasp. What has rarely been noted is that for several years before the bureaucrats in London drew the 1763 boundary, the Indian tribes of the interior—from the Senecas, Ottawas, Illinois, Miamis, and Sioux of the North to the Cherokees, Creeks, and Choctaws of the South—had themselves been attempting to fix a territorial line that would limit White expansion. Their attempts were inspired by their certainty that, contrary to the language of the Proclamation of 1763, they did *not* live under English "protection" but in fact could protect their own interests and ensure their survival only by throwing off English "protection" and fighting to preserve their land.

Though the interior Native peoples had no way of counting the population increase in the

---

[16]Quoted in Francis Paul Prucha, *American Indian Policy in the Formative Years: The Indian Trade and Intercourse Acts, 1790–1834* (Lincoln, NE, 1970 rpr.), p. 5.

thirteen colonies, they were keenly aware that waves of settlers were moving into their tribal hunting grounds almost on the heels of the Anglo-American armies that had pushed the French out of the Ohio valley beginning in 1759. More than half of the population increase occurred in New York, Pennsylvania, and Virginia. Land-hungry speculators and immigrants began pouring into the western parts of the colonies as soon as the French were expelled. Both before and after England issued the Proclamation Line of 1763, land poachers were staking out claims to lands to which the English, by the terms of their own treaties with Indian tribes, had no claim. Creek lands, for example, were guaranteed by a treaty signed in 1733, and the limits of White settlement in Cherokee territory had been set at the end of the Cherokee War in 1761 in a treaty with the government of Virginia. Yet neither of these treaties stopped White land speculators and settlers from swarming into Indian territory, knowing that their provincial governments had neither the desire nor the power to do much about it.

Though now deprived of French aid, the Indian response was to meet force with force. Bloody clashes pockmarked the Southern frontier in the early 1760s, as Indians and settlers fought over Native lands that the provincial governments had guaranteed to the tribes. Some Indian leaders attempted to form another pan-Indian defensive league, even at the risk that the English would cut off their supply of trade goods. Meanwhile, the colonists did their best at a series of conferences to wheedle land cessions from the Creeks and the Cherokees, while privately they fanned enmity between the major tribes.

The determination of the Southern tribes to resist English encroachments, even with the French removed from the continent, was vividly displayed in 1763 by the refusal of the Creeks to surrender their tribesmen who had murdered fourteen White land poachers. The Creeks, on the other hand, were unable to forge a Southern Indian alliance when such a unified Indian movement might have joined a major Indian uprising in the Northwest to give the Native peoples their best advantage of the eighteenth century.

If the Indian reaction to the Anglo-American victory over France was not one of cowed submission in the South, it was even more aggressive in the North. In June 1761, the Senecas, always the most pro-French of the Six Nations, carried a red wampum belt (signifying an intention to go to war) to Detroit, where the British army was garrisoned among the various tribes that had formally fought with the French—the Delawares, Shawnees, Ottawas, Hurons, Chippewas, Wyandots, and Potawatomies. The Senecas took the lead in resisting the new English Indian policy, which curtailed trade, increased British garrisons, required the Indians to bring their furs to the British forts, ended the system of annual "presents" that Indian leaders regarded as a kind of rent for land occupied by British forts, prohibited trade in rum, and in general instituted trading terms far less satisfactory to the Indians than those existing before the war. The Senecas had an additional incentive for taking to the warpath. General Amherst, the commander in chief of the Anglo-American forces during the Seven Years' War, had rewarded some of his officers with Seneca lands near Niagara in violation of a treaty between the Iroquois and the New York government. Such generosity at their expense was not lightly regarded in the Seneca towns.

The Senecas proposed a coordinated attack by the Northern tribes on all the English outposts that ranged along the Great Lakes and as far south as Pittsburgh. Acting together, the tribes would drive the English out of the Ohio valley, out of Iroquois country, and back across the mountains to the Piedmont. Whether this "nativistic" plan included a resolve to give up the English trade altogether is uncertain, although it is possible that after many years of trade difficulties, they considered no trade at all preferable to a restricted trade at pinched prices. Although the Western tribes rejected the Seneca plan after long discussion, they were far from pleased by what they heard from Sir William Johnson, the Northern Indian superintendent, at a Detroit conference. Johnson claimed he came to brighten "the chain of friendship" and spoke glowingly of the king's concern for the welfare "of all his subjects." But he promised nothing in regard to the high price of trade goods, the unavailability of rum, the stoppage of annual presents, and the inadequate supplies of ammunition now allotted to the tribes. These, he said, were matters of official policy beyond his control.

Although Johnson reported optimistically to General Amherst at the conclusion of the conference, boasting that he left Detroit with matters "settled on so stable a foundation there that unless greatly irritated thereto, they will never break the peace," the fact was that the Indians, for all their show of amity, were deeply embittered.[17] The most experienced English trader in the Ohio valley, George Croghan, accurately perceived the situation. The Indians "had great expectations of being very generally supplied by us, and from their poverty and mercenary disposition they can't bear such a disappointment."

Adding to the inflammatory state of affairs were the preachings of Neolin, a charismatic Delaware prophet. Just when the English were cutting off guns and gunpowder to which the Indians had become accustomed and were threatening the Indians' land base, Neolin began a journey through the Delaware territories, preaching that Native Americans must return to "their original state that they were in before the White people found out their country." The alternative, he argued, was slow extinction at the hands of the settlers swarming across the mountains. Several traders described the renaissance of traditional Native culture preached by the Delaware prophet. Neolin's vision, conveyed to him in dreams by the Master of Life, was that the Indians' salvation lay not in adopting Christianity and European culture but in returning to ancient customs. They must forswear and abandon the material objects of European culture. Population increase must be curbed through

abstinence so that the difficult return to the old ways could be accomplished. Indians could escape the desperate trap they were in only by regaining sacred power.

Neolin's message resonated not only in Delaware country but also among other Western Indian nations. It called not only for cultural renaissance but also for revolutionary resistance. "Wherefore do you suffer the whites to dwell upon your lands?" he asked. "Drive them away; wage war against them. I love them not. They know me not. They are my enemies, they are your brothers' enemies. Send them back to the lands I have made for them. Let them remain there."[18] Throughout 1762, Neolin's admonitions were passed by word of mouth and on inscribed deerskin parchment from one Native village to another.

Neolin's plan for propitiating the Master of Life's anger with the Indians' dependence on European guns and alcohol did not prescribe a complete return to traditional Delaware culture. Instead, it proposed a blend of Native and European elements. Some of the old customs, such as war rituals and polygamy, were not to be revived, and some Christian concepts, such as written prayers and a written "Bible" or "Great Book," were to be retained. But Neolin's appeal for the de-Europeanization of Delaware culture amounted to an independent, creative, and sacred response to the bleak situation that confronted interior tribes after the defeat of the French. After his disciples carried his message throughout the Western territories, large numbers of Indians, acting on his advice to boycott European trade goods, hunted only to supply their own needs. Most spectacularly, an Ottawa leader named Pontiac became a convert to Neolin's doctrine and made it the spiritual underpinning of the uprising he led against the English beginning in May 1763.[19] According to a French account, Pontiac inspired his warriors with a speech that reflected Neolin's nativism.

---

[17]Quoted in Howard H. Peckham, *Pontiac and the Indian Uprising* (Chicago, IL, 1961), p. 86.
[18]Anthony F. C. Wallace, *The Death and Rebirth of the Seneca* (New York, 1970), p. 118.
[19]Ibid., pp. 120–121.

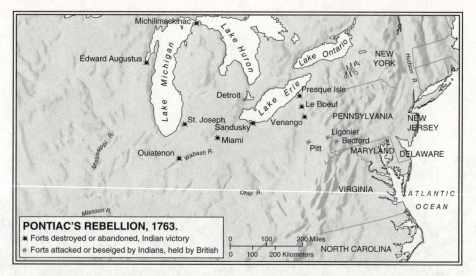

PONTIAC'S REBELLION, 1763.
★ Forts destroyed or abandoned, Indian victory
⚔ Forts attacked or beseiged by Indians, held by British

0   100   200 Miles
0   100   200 Kilometers

Source: Map 10 in *Atlas of Great Lakes Indian History,* edited by Helen Hornbeck Tanner. Copyright©1987 by the University of Oklahoma Press. Reprinted by permission of the Publisher and the Newberry Library.

"It is important for us, my brothers," he exhorted, "that we exterminate from our lands this nation which seeks only to destroy us."[20] Under this banner Pontiac led an assault on Fort Detroit, the strongest British Great Lakes garrison. While the Ottawas laid siege to the fort, other tribes rubbed out the British outposts in the western Great Lakes region. But the Indians were unable to overwhelm the three major British forts at Detroit, Niagara, and Pittsburgh. The war dragged on through the summer with several thousand traders and settlers falling to Indian ambushes and assaults. When news of the war reached London, the government hurriedly issued the Proclamation Act. Military reinforcements arrived from the East, creating a standoff by summer's end. Pontiac fought sporadically for another two years, and the English colonies hummed with rumors that he was conspiring with Creek and Choctaw chiefs to organize a grand alliance of eighteen Indian nations. But lacking vital supplies of powder, shot, and guns, the tribes were forced to sue for peace. Without the presence in North America of another European power, they could not overcome their supply problems.

In one tragic incident stemming from Pontiac's uprising, frontiersmen showed that neither Crown nor colonial government meant much to them in their hatred of Indians. Stung by Pontiac's marauders, who had set upon Pennsylvania's western settlements, Scots-Irish farmers avenged themselves on a small band of peaceful, Christianized Conestoga Indians—a "small native island in a vast colonial sea"—who farmed a few acres and peddled their wares among the whites with whom they lived as neighbors and friends. After butchering six defenseless Conestogas, the "Paxton Boys," as they called themselves, invaded the workhouse in Lancaster, where magistrates sheltered fourteen other Conestogas to protect them from the enraged frontiersmen. The Paxton Boys slaughtered them as the Indians sat in a circle with hands joined and prayers on their lips. One Conestoga held a copy of the friendship treaty signed by William Penn in 1701, where Indians and Quakers pledged "that they shall forever hereafter be as

---

[20]Quoted in Peckham, *Pontiac and the Indian Uprising,* p. 119.

EVENTS OF INDIAN HISTORY.
Massacre of the Indians at Lancaster by the Paxton boys in 1763.

Engraving of "Paxton Boys Expedition" (1763) or "The Massacre of Indians at Lancaster" (1841 etching).
(Courtesy Corbis)

one head and one heart and live in true friendship and amity as one people."[21]

A month later, the Paxton Boys organized a march on Philadelphia to convince the legislature that it was far too timid in raising troops to defend the frontier. With clubs and pitchforks, they threatened to make as much blood run in Philadelphia as it had in Lancaster. Benjamin Franklin, now famous for his experiments with electricity, sprang into action. After helping to organize the militia in Philadelphia to repulse the marching frontiersmen, Franklin took up his pen

to write *A Narrative of the Late Massacres . . . of a Number of Indians,* a scorching condemnation of the "Christian White savages" who massacred the friendly, acculturated Indians. Although the perpetrators of lynch law were never tried or punished, Franklin's impassioned indictment of them aroused the conscience of many Pennsylvanians. "The only crime of these poor wretches," he wrote, "seems to have been, that they had a reddish brown skin, and black hair; and some people of that sort, it seems, had murdered some of our relations. If it be right to kill men for such

---

[21]*Minutes of the Provincial Council of Pennsylvania,* 10 vols. (Harrisburg, 1851–1852), II: 15–17; James H. Merrell, *Into the American Woods: Negotiatiors on the Pennsylvania Frontier* (New York, 1999), pp. 284–285.

a reason, then should any man with a freckled face and red hair kill a wife or child of mine, it would be right for me to revenge it by killing all the freckled red-haired men, women, and children, I could afterwards anywhere meet with."[22]

Though Pontiac's resistance movement collapsed, the major interior tribes preserved their political autonomy in the decade prior to the outbreak of the American Revolution. "The Six Nations, Western Indians, etc.," wrote William Johnson to London in 1764, "having never been conquered, either by the English or French, nor subject to their laws, consider themselves as a free people."[23] Yet preserving political independence could not stem the tide of frontier land speculators and farmers. By itself, this demographic pressure was enough to overcome all the efforts of the English government to fashion an Indian policy based on fair trade relations and respect for land boundaries.

The main points of English Indian policy—prevention of encroachment on Indian lands and equity in the Indian trade—fell into a shambles in the decade before the Revolution. Staggering under an immense debt accumulated in fighting the Seven Years' War, the English government abandoned their interior garrisons after Pontiac's Revolt and scrapped their plan to coordinate and control the Indian trade and Indian affairs of the various colonies. Reliance was placed on drawing lines on maps—lines that theoretically separated Indians and colonizers. After 1764, when a whole cluster of issues concerned with imperial authority in the colonies threw the colonists into a quasi-revolutionary state, the Proclamation Line of 1763 existed only on paper, and neither colonists nor Indians took it seriously. Colonial governors, often closely connected with land speculators, bombarded colonial administrators in London with reasons why exceptions should be made to the Proclamation Act. These included scores of false assertions that interior tribes had abandoned their claims to various parcels of land west of the Appalachians. When London denied such requests, the governors turned their heads and permitted land grants, surveys, and private purchases of land from Indian tribes such as the Creeks and the Cherokees, who did not recognize the right of the English government to demarcate boundaries. When White farmers and trappers moved onto land still claimed by the Natives, they were usually left to fight it out among themselves. Nobody in England could discover a means of compelling the Americans in the West to obey Crown commands at a time when even along the Atlantic seaboard the king's authority was under challenge.

For the interior tribes, the alternatives were limited after Pontiac's abortive revolt. They could seek other Indian allies to forge another pan-Indian uprising, as did one faction of the Creeks led by The Mortar, who had been staunchly anti-English for decades. Or they could seek private revenge for White depredations and land grabbing, as did Logan, a displaced Cayuga living on the Virginia frontier, whose family had been wiped out by outlaw frontiersmen and who led a party of warriors in retaliatory raids that set off the brief but bloody Lord Dunmore's War in 1774. Or they could continue to seek French support in New Orleans while hoping for a renewed French presence on the continent, as did the Choctaws. Or they could bow to the White tidal wave and sell off their land, piece by piece at the best price possible, to private individuals and land companies that knew that they could safely ignore both the Proclamation of 1763 and colonial statutes forbidding such purchases.

The Colonizers' Society after 1763

Although the Seven Years' War is primarily remembered as the climactic military struggle in which Anglo-American arms finally overcame the hated French in North America, it was also a war that deeply affected White communities.

---

[22]Franklin, *A Narrative of the Late Massacres,* in Leonard Labaree et al., eds., *The Papers of Benjamin Franklin* (New Haven, CT, 1959), XI: 142–169, quoted sentences on p. 55.
[23]Quoted in Prucha, *American Indian Policy . . .,* p. 19.

It was a war that convinced the American colonies of their growing strength and maturity yet ironically left them debt-ridden and weakened in manpower. It brought the greatest infusion of English capital in their history, yet rendered them unusually sensitive to the disadvantages of the British mercantile connection. It propelled the commercialization of life, especially in the seaport towns, yet exposed the social costs of the transition to the market economy.

War contracts and the general quickening of the economy brought some degree of prosperity to many White colonial Americans during the war years. But after the triumphant victories over the French in 1759 and 1760, the war theater moved to the Caribbean, and now a commercial downturn struck hard. Especially along the seaboard, unemployment, high prices, and a great increase in war-widowed families caused a crumbling of economic security. The greatest hardships fell upon the laboring classes, which included many artisans who occupied positions on the middle rungs of the social ladder. It was they who had the smallest savings and the thinnest margin between profit and loss and who devoted the largest proportion of their budgets to food, rent, clothing, and fuel—expenses that could be little trimmed when times worsened. The war had created a class of wealthy merchants, but it also left many communities strewn with crippled, widowed, and destitute persons. Pauperism spread in all the colonial cities, and authorities struggled for ways of providing for the poor.

If all colonists had suffered equally in the aftermath of the Seven Years' War, the depression of the early 1760s might have unified colonial society. It might have served to warn Americans that while growing more muscular in numbers, they were becoming less powerful in their ability to control violent fluctuations in the Atlantic economy. This perception of the problem as externally caused dominated thinking among merchants, large landowners, lawyers, and government officials, and the drastic overhaul of imperial policy instituted by the English Parliament at the end of the war gave credence to this point of view. It was apparent that an invigorated customs service, cracking down on colonial smugglers, dried up profits on the illegal importing of French tea and sugar. Equally clear, establishing English vice-admiralty courts in the colonies placed violators of the Navigation Acts beyond the forgiving attitudes of local juries. It was also plain that the Currency Act of 1764, restricting issuance of paper money in New York and Pennsylvania, further dampened an already depressed trade. And the Stamp Act of 1765 obviously laid additional levies on communities still trying to pay off a heavy war debt. For many Americans, the post-1763 parliamentary legislation and the contractionary actions of their British creditors signaled that a maturing American people might now have their necks pinned to the ground by the paw of an insensitive British lion.

Many in the lower levels of the White communities shared this feeling of alienation from the mother country. Interwoven with this perception was another strand of thought. War, it was understood, had required financial sacrifice from everyone in the form of higher taxes. Furthermore, war had spilled much blood, primarily the blood of the lower classes. That was the usual way of things. But many were disturbed that eight years of conflict had left many communities swarming with the poor while a few people stood high above their neighbors. This social transformation, occurring most dramatically in the cities, was apparent to all who witnessed the urban mansions of the merchants rise in the 1760s at the same time that large almshouses were under construction to house the multiplying destitute. "Some individuals," charged a New Yorker in 1765, "by the smiles of providence, or some other means, are enabled to roll in their four-wheeled carriages, and can support the expense of good houses, rich furniture, and luxurious living. But is it equitable that 99, rather 999, should suffer for the extravagance or grandeur of one? Especially when it is considered that men frequently owe their wealth to the impoverishment of their neighbors?"[24]

---

[24]*New-York Gazette*, July 11, 1765.

This was the language of emerging class tension, bred out of ancient feelings of self-worth by those who labored with their hands, nurtured by periodic adversity, and extended and clarified by the depressing aftermath of the Seven Years' War.

For many colonists who struggled for security in the wake of the Seven Years' War, moving to new land in the interior seemed a solution to their problems. By itself, the population buildup was a powerful incentive for such a move, and the attraction of the frontier was increased by depressed conditions in many coastal communities. For those who exercised this Western option, the overall result was an increase in tension with the Native Americans into whose lands they pushed. For those who remained behind, economic problems had to be worked out in their own community or within communities to which they migrated in search of opportunity. Thus, it was that the depression that enveloped coastal communities beginning in 1760 was accompanied by political turmoil.

It was not political power itself that those at the lower levels of these communities groped for after the Seven Years' War but an equitable system in which they could pursue their modest goals. When their economic security was threatened, they responded by attempting to influence, not dominate, politics and to redress grievances rather than dismantle the system of upper-class domination of politics inherited from their fathers. Yet they began to move toward radical politics in order either to conserve the corporate community ideal of the past or to pry open the doors of opportunity in the new entrepreneurial age. Such forays into political activism, first nurtured during the Great Awakening, had a cumulative effect. A sense of their own power grew as their trust in those above them shrank and as their own experience expanded in making decisions, exercising leadership roles, and challenging those who were supposed to be wiser because they were wealthier. Hence factional politics intensified in the late colonial period. As never before, members of the lower ranks began to act for and of themselves, pushing forward their own leaders, making their muscle felt, and wreaking bitter violence—as in the Stamp Act riots of 1765—against those they construed as their enemies. In this sense, the Seven Years' War that gave the Anglo-Americans supremacy in North America, the Seven Years' War that placed the interior Indian tribes in an increasingly untenable position, was also the Seven Years' War that initiated the rupture between colonists and mother country and that led to political divisiveness within the colonizers' communities.

Summary

During the second third of the eighteenth century, historical forces ended the equilibrium between Indian and European peoples, as well as dividing colonial society itself. A major factor playing into this was the population explosion, especially in the English colonies, that by the 1750s had impelled thousands westward beyond the Appalachians in search of land. Add to this, the growing tensions between the French and English, both European powers, the result was what some regarded as "the most important event in eighteenth-century North America": The Seven Years' War, also known as the French and Indian War.

To survive this major conflict, the Iroquois, Cherokees, and Creeks all engaged in "power politics" with both the English and the French—the Iroquois with notable success, and the Cherokees and Creeks with less success. In the end, the English prevailed; and in the 1763 Peace of Paris, signed by England, France, and Spain, Canada and all of North America east of the Mississippi River became English territory, France ceded the lands west of the Mississippi to Spain, and Spain ceded Florida to England. The reaction of the Indians to the English victory was aggressive in the South and even more so in the North, exemplified by Pontiac's uprising and resistance movement in 1763. This movement collapsed, as did, in the decade before the Revolutionary War, the English Indian policy, leaving the Native tribes to find their own ways to survive. Among the ruins of war, the White colonists, too, especially those in the lower ranks, had to find their own path, which included the pursuit of an equitable economic and social system during a period of postwar recession. While their growing numbers and strength built the self-confidence of American colonists in general, political factionalism increased as small farmers and urban artisans made demands for a more participatory political system.

Critical Thinking Questions

1. Who was most successful in terms of policy toward the French and English during the Seven Years' War—the Iroquois, Cherokees, or Creeks—and why?
2. Who was Neolin, what was his vision, and what influence did he have?
3. As fallout from the expense of carrying on the Seven Years' War, the English Indian policy fell into disarray. What consequences followed?
4. An economic depression settled on coastal communities beginning in 1760. What changes did this make in the political thinking and actions of White colonists in the lower levels of these communities?

Further Reading

Fred Anderson, *Crucible of War: The Seven Years' War and the Fate of Empire in British North America, 1754–1763* (New York: Vintage, 2000).

Colin G. Calloway, *The Scratch of a Pen: 1763 and the Transformation of North America* (New York: Oxford University Press, 2006).

Gregory Evans Dowd, *War under Heaven: Pontiac, the Indian Nations, and the British Empire* (Baltimore: Johns Hopkins University Press, 2002).

John Mack Faragher, *A Great and Noble Scheme: The Tragic Story of the Expulsion of the French Acadians from Their American Homeland* (New York: W. W. Norton, 2005).

Eric Hinderaker, *Elusive Empires: Constructing Colonialism in the Ohio Valley, 1673–1800* (New York: 1997).

Francis Jennings, *Empires of Fortune: Crowns, Colonies, and Tribes in the Seven Years' War in America* (New York: W. W. Norton, 1988).

Michael N. McConnell, *A Country Between: The Upper Ohio Valley and Its Peoples, 1724–1774* (Lincoln: University of Nebraska Press, 1992).

James H. Merrell, *Into the American Woods: Negotiators on the Pennsylvania Frontier* (New York: W. W. Norton, 2000).

Jane T. Merritt, *At the Crossroads: Indians and Empires on a Mid-Atlantic Frontier, 1700–1763* (Chapel Hill: University of North Carolina Press, 2003).

Gary B. Nash, *The Urban Crucible: The Northern Seaports and the Origins of the American Revolution* (Cambridge: Harvard University Press, 1986).

Greg O'Brien, *Choctaws in a Revolutionary Age, 1756–1830* (Lincoln: University of Nebraska Press, 2002).

Timothy J. Shannon, *Indians and Colonists at the Crossroads of Empire: The Albany Congress of 1754* (Ithaca: Cornell University Press, 2000).

Matthew C. Ward, *Breaking the Backcountry: The Seven Years' War in Virginia and Pennsyhlvania, 1754–1765* (Pittsburgh: University of Pittsburgh Press, 2003).

Richard White, *The Middle Ground: Indians, Empires, and Republics in the Great Lakes Region, 1650–1815* (Cambridge: Cambridge University Press, 1991).

CHAPTER 11

The Tricolored American Revolution

LEARNING OBJECTIVES

■ Describe the beginnings of abolitionism in the Northern colonies, highlighting the efforts of the Quaker humanitarian John Woolman.

■ Discuss how the Revolutionary War created opportunities for enslaved people; include an account of Dunmore's Proclamation and its effects; the pro-British freedom fighter "Colonel Tye"; blacks who fought for the American cause, such as James Armistead, Rhode Island's First Regiment, and James Forten; and the freedom-seeking Elizabeth Freeman.

■ Give an account of the exodus at the end of the Revolutionary War in 1783 of Africans who gained their freedom by fleeing to the British, and discuss the role of Thomas Peters in the exodus, first to Nova Scotia and then to Sierra Leone.

■ Characterize the following free black leaders in terms of their vision and accomplishments: Jupiter Hammon of Long Island, Prince Hall of Boston, and Richard Allen of Philadelphia.

■ Explain how the Revolutionary War affected Native Americans; analyze their motivations in choosing sides, the part played by the Mohawk leader Thayendanegea, the effects created by George Rogers Clark's invading mini-army, and the fate of the Cherokees.

Every textbook properly lavishes attention on the American Revolution because it gave America independence from Great Britain and created the United States of America. But until recent years, textbooks have largely ignored the Indian and African American peoples of North America who fought in the Revolution and were deeply affected by its outcomes. This chapter makes no attempt to recount the complicated events that led to the Revolution, nor to detail the military struggle that ended with the British capitulation at Yorktown in 1781, nor to analyze the breathtaking attempts of state and local governments to fashion constitutions and new rulebooks by which White Americans might live as a free and an independent people. Rather, this chapter focuses on the connections among red, White, and black peoples of the Revolutionary era and the way that the Revolution altered these relationships.

The Abolitionist Impulse

For African Americans, the period following the Seven Years' War was one of both hope and despair. In the Northern colonies, a handful of reformers raised the banner of abolitionism sufficiently high to make the question of slavery a public issue for the first time since Africans had been marched ashore in Jamestown in 1619. Quaker humanitarians such as Benjamin Lay, John Woolman, and Anthony Benezet led the way and were joined by New England ministers, black spokespeople, and emerging revolutionary radicals. All of them argued that slavery was immoral and contradicted the principles of liberty and opportunity that demarcated the American experience from that of postfeudal Europe.

In developing a rationale for revolution in the decade after the Seven Years' War and in mounting propaganda attacks on England, colonial leaders found themselves asking questions not only about the nature of English authority and its legitimate limits in the colonies, but also about the character of the colonial society they had built. The revolutionary arguments about "the natural rights of man," the "consent of the governed," the meaning of "freedom" and "tyranny," and the naturalness of equality contained intellectual dynamite. These stirring words and phrases led toward social and political territory where even the most radical patriot leaders had not intended to go. They were primarily concerned with the threatening actions of Parliament and the king's ministers. But when they spoke of unalienable rights or the dignity of all men or abuses of power, they unconsciously pointed a finger at themselves. The more they used catchwords such as "slavery" and "tyranny" to describe British imperial reforms, the more difficult it became to ignore domestic slavery, which,

by the 1760s, enchained about one-fifth of the population in the colonies.

People on both sides of the Atlantic and on both sides of the Anglo-American argument pointed out the contradiction. How could Americans treat Africans "as a better kind of cattle . . . while they are bawling about the rights of human nature?" asked one English official.[1] An American patriot chided his countrymen: "Blush ye pretended votaries for freedom! ye trifling patriots! who are making a vain parade of being advocated for the liberties of mankind, who are thus making a mockery of your profession by trampling on the sacred natural rights and privileges of Africans; for while you are fasting, praying, nonimporting, nonexporting, remonstrating, resolving, and pleading for a restoration of your charter rights, you at the same time are continuing this lawless, cruel, inhuman, and abominable practice of enslaving your fellow creatures."[2]

The principles invoked in defense of colonial freedom were thus used to indict the system of labor that undergirded the colonial economy of the South and supported economic enterprise in the North. Slavery insulted the principles for which revolutionaries were preparing to fight. "Oh the shocking, the intolerable inconsistence! . . . This gross, barefaced, practiced inconsistence!" cried Samuel Hopkins, a Congregationalist minister of Rhode Island on the eve of war.[3]

Not only the dehumanization of Africans under slavery but also the accompanying degradation of whites concerned many who declared their opposition to slavery in the pre-Revolutionary decade. John Woolman, whose abolitionist efforts of the 1750s were widely ignored, was convinced that slaveholding, even by the kindliest of masters, "depraved the mind in like manner and with as great certainty as prevailing cold congeals water." The absolute authority exercised by the master over the slave established "ideas of

[1]Quoted in Winthrop Jordan, *White Over Black: American Attitudes toward the Negro, 1550–1812* (Chapel Hill, NC, 1968), p. 291.
[2][John Allen], *The Watchmen's Alarm to Lord N—h* (1774), in Bernard Bailyn, *The Ideological Origins of the American Revolution* (Cambridge, MA, 1967), p. 240.
[3]Quoted in ibid., p. 244.

things and modes of conduct" that molded the attitudes of children, neighbors, and friends of slaveholders.[4] As Woolman traveled through the colonies, he became convinced that slavery was indelibly fixing the notion of White superiority in the White mind. Such an idea was incompatible with both the Christian concept of the brotherhood of all humans and rationalist thought of the eighteenth century that stressed natural equality. Because most slaves were employed in servile labor and lived in abject conditions, whites grew to look upon them "as a contemptible, ignorant part of mankind."[5] The outward condition of the slave, the result of White desire for material gain, was taken to correspond with the inward condition of the displaced African. But for Woolman, the slave's outer degradation was a function of the White person's "inner corruption." White people, in the process of enslaving the African, had enslaved themselves. The imprisonment of Africans and their progeny was external and physical, whereas for the whites it was internal and spiritual. In either case, the implications for the health of American society were fearful to contemplate.

Complementing Woolman's work was that of Anthony Benezet. Since 1750 the deeply ascetic Quaker had been instructing black Philadelphians in his humble home and in 1770 convinced the Quaker leaders to open an "Africans' School." Convinced that black children had the same intellectual potential of White youths, he spread his message of racial equality aimed at knocking the props beneath the argument that innate African inferiority justified their enslavement. By the 1770s, Benezet's efforts had led many conscience-stricken Quakers to free their slaves. But the big breakthrough came when Benezet, by now the premier antislavery pamphleteer on both sides of the Atlantic, led the Philadelphia Quakers in 1774 to ban the ownership of enslaved people. It would take persistence to break through the noncompliance of many Quakers, but the die had been cast: for the first

time in the western world, a religious body had forsworn inhuman bondage.

From the increasing awareness of White racial prejudice and the immorality of slavery sprang the Pennsylvania Abolition Society, founded just a few days before gunfire erupted at Concord and Lexington in April 1775. The incompatibility of enslaving Africans with the principles that White colonial society claimed as the foundation of its uniqueness began to gain wide recognition. In response, a number of Northern colonies abolished the slave trade or taxed it out of existence as the storm clouds gathered. Slavery, however, was not abolished, so even though a small number of merchants were forced to reroute their ships, this cost other colonial whites little or nothing. Not until 1780 would Pennsylvania pass the first gradual abolition act, the first of its kind in the western world.

In the South, the ideological war against slavery got nowhere. The 1760s, in fact, saw the largest slave importations of any decade in the colonial period. In South Carolina, enslaved Africans imported between 1760 and 1770 exceeded those brought in during the previous quarter-century, and in the early 1770s, the influx increased again. The massive capital investment in black labor made the question of abolishing slavery almost academic in the parts of the country where it counted most. In Virginia, which had a White population equivalent to that of Sacramento, California, or Jersey City (New Jersey, today), the capital investment in slaves was about £5.5 million, or, in today's money, about 1 billion dollars. Who would compensate slaveholders for this property? Thus, while African Americans heard of pamphlets advocating abolition and even pondered reports that the legislatures of Virginia and other colonies were debating the issue, slaveholders with large sums invested in the situation organized to turn back the campaign that sought to eliminate what had become their primary source of wealth, power, and prestige. The abolitionist critique of American society resounded loudly

---

[4]Quoted in Gary B. Nash, "Slaves and Slaveholders in Colonial Philadelphia," *William and Mary Quarterly*, 3rd Ser., 29 (1973): 243.
[5]Quoted in Jordan, *White Over Black*, p. 273.

where only one of every ten American slaves lived; it was seldom listened to where the other nine toiled.

Struggling for Liberty

We can only imagine how the spirits of enslaved Africans must have been lifted by eavesdropping on their master's dinner-table conversations, working in taverns and coffeehouses where Revolutionary politics were hatched, and reading or hearing about pamphlets pronouncing the necessity of ending slavery. What is certain is that many coerced laborers acted on their hatred of their clanking chains to petition for their freedom in ways calculated to prick the conscience of the master class. Couched cautiously at first, their petitions became bolder as the war approached. "We expect your house [the legislature] will . . . take our deplorable case into serious consideration, and give us that simple relief which, as men, we have a natural right to," remonstrated four slaves in rural Massachusetts in 1773. Six years later in Connecticut, blacks echoed these claims to freedom: "We do not ask for nothing but what we are fully persuaded is ours to claim," for "we are the creatures of that God, who made of one blood, and kindred, all the nations of the Earth." Therefore, "there is nothing that leads us to a belief, or suspicion, that we are any more obliged to serve them [our masters] than they us, and . . . can never be convinced that we are made to be slaves."[6]

By its very nature, the Revolutionary War created unprecedented situations and opportunities for the enslaved. A wave of black insurrectionary activity coursed through South Carolina in the 1760s. In 1765, more than one hundred slaves made a concerted attempt to establish a refugee colony in the interior. White Charlestonians became alarmed the next year when black men took literally the White rhetoric concerning liberty and equality by parading through the streets chanting "Liberty, Liberty!"

White authorities put the city under arms for a week as rumors of insurrection spread through the colony. A nervous legislature quickly passed a three-year prohibitive tariff on imported Africans, which choked off the flood of nearly 7,000 captives who had tumbled ashore in 1765.

With the huge movement of both civilian and military populations in and out of nearly every major seaport from Savannah to Boston between 1775 and 1781, urban slaves had unprecedented chances for making their personal declarations of independence and for destabilizing the institution of slavery. Similarly, in the countryside, as Tory and Whig militia units crisscrossed the terrain, plundering the farms and plantations of their enemies, enslaved men and women found ways of tearing holes in the fabric of slavery.

A turning point in the calculation of enslaved Africans came in November 1775 when the royal governor of Virginia, Lord Dunmore, issued a dramatic proclamation that offered freedom to slaves and indentured servants who could escape their masters, reach the king's forces, and swear support for the suppression of the American rebels. Against this concrete offer of unconditional freedom, slaves had only the chance that the American patriots would respond to calls for abolition and follow the urgings of the first abolition society established in Pennsylvania just a few months before. Waiting for freedom as a White gift at some indeterminate point turned out to be a poor substitute for immediate freedom. When word of Dunmore's Proclamation spread quickly through the South, slaves fled their masters to British troops, where officers formed them into the Black Regiment of Guides and Pioneers. Some marched in uniforms with the chilling inscription on their breasts, "Liberty to Slaves."

Dunmore's Proclamation galvanized the South against England, for it conjured up the vision of a large body of free blacks, armed by the British, abroad in the land. The Proclamation, wrote one prominent Southerner, tended "more effectually to work an eternal separation between

[6]Quoted in Benjamin Quarles, "The Revolutionary War as a Black Declaration of Independence," in Ira Berlin and Ronald Hoffman, eds., *Slavery and Freedom in the Age of the American Revolution* (Charlottesville, VA, 1983), p. 290.

1775

By His Excellency the Right Honorable JOHN Earl of DUNMORE, His
MAJESTY's Lieutenant and Governor General of the Colony and Dominion of
VIRGINIA, and Vice Admiral of the same.

A PROCLAMATION.

AS I have ever entertained Hopes, that an Accommodation might have
taken Place between GREAT-BRITAIN and this Colony, without being
compelled by my Duty to this most disagreeable but now absolutely necessary
Step, rendered so by a Body of armed Men unlawfully assembled, firing on His
MAJESTY's Tenders, and the formation of an Army, and that Army now on
their March to attack His Majesty's Troops and destroy the well disposed Subjects of this Colony. To defeat such treasonable Purposes, and that all such
Traitors, and their Abettors, may be brought to Justice, and that the Peace, and
good Order of this Colony may be again restored, which the ordinary Course
of the Civil Law is unable to effect; I have thought fit to issue this my Proclamation, hereby declaring, that until the aforesaid good Purposes can be obtained, I do in Virtue of the Power and Authority to ME given, by His Majesty, determine to execute Martial Law, and cause the same to be executed
throughout this Colony; and to the end that Peace and good Order may the
sooner be restored, I do require every Person capable of bearing Arms, to resort
to His MAJESTY's STANDARD, or be looked upon as Traitors to His
MAJESTY's Crown and Government, and thereby become liable to the Penalty
the Law inflicts upon such Offences; such as forfeiture of Life, confiscation of
Lands, &c. &c. And I do hereby further declare all indented Servants, Negroes,
or others, (appertaining to Rebels,) free that are able and willing to bear Arms,
they joining His MAJESTY's Troops as soon as may be, for the more speedily
reducing this Colony to a proper Sense of their Duty, to His MAJESTY's
Crown and Dignity. I do further order, and require, all His MAJESTY's Leige
Subjects, to retain their Quitrents, or any other Taxes due or that may become
due, in their own Custody, till such Time as Peace may be again restored to this
at present most unhappy Country, or demanded of them for their former salu-
tary Purposes, by Officers properly authorised to receive the same.

GIVEN under my Hand on board the Ship WILLIAM, off NORFOLK,
the 7th Day of NOVEMBER, in the SIXTEENTH Year of His Majesty's Reign.

DUNMORE.

(GOD save the KING.)

Dunmore's Proclamation (November 1775), broadside.

(Courtesy Library of Congress Prints and Photographs [rbpe.1780180b])

Great Britain and the Colonies—than any other expedient, which could possibly have been thought of." Another put it more graphically: "Hell itself could not have vomited anything more black than this design of emancipating our slaves."[7]

Eight hundred to 1000 black Virginians broke for the British army in late 1775. Making personal declarations of independence, they achieved liberty by joining those whom White American patriots called enemies of freedom. Among one wave of eighty-seven were twenty women, sixteen men, twenty-two girls, and twenty-seven boys under sixteen. This tells us that many fled as families, and in this group half a dozen were babes in arms.[8] Reaching Dunmore, who had retreated from Williamsburg to Norfolk, where the British navy lay at anchor, the black refugees were folded into the Ethiopian Regiment, commanded by the loyalist son of the prominent Virginia planter, William Byrd III. In general, the appraisal of Joseph Galloway, a Philadelphia loyalist, characterized the African American population as the Revolution began. "The Negroes," wrote Galloway, "may all be deemed so many intestine [internal] enemies, being all slaves and desirous of freedom, and would, was an opportunity offered them, take up arms against their masters."[9] This black war for independence in North America occurred in every part of the country and was especially intense whenever slaves were within running distance of the British army or navy.

When Lord Dunmore retreated to British naval ships in Chesapeake Bay, it became difficult for enslaved people bent on freedom to reach his forces. Stalking these bold attempts at self-liberation was a killer even more dangerous than the White slave patrols. Sweeping eastern North America, smallpox spread through the jammed British ships and, in Dunmore's words, "carried off an incredible number of our people, especially blacks."[10] When the British withdrew to New York City in mid-1776, enslaved Virginians had to await another day.

When this day arrived in late 1779, after the war moved south, the greatest black rebellion in North America erupted. British forces invading Virginia struck far into the interior, all the way to the doorstep of Jefferson's Monticello. Washington, Jefferson, Thomas Nelson (governor of Virginia), Patrick Henry, and many other worthies that we celebrate as Founding Fathers gasped as their enslaved workers fled in droves. "This is the general case of all those who were near the enemy," wrote Richard Henry Lee to his brother in mid-1781.[11] A Hessian officer serving the British army believed that by now more than 4,000 blacks of all ages here encamped with the British forces.

The pursuit of freedom through flight to the British, although it can never be exactly calculated, was so large that the British army was often hard pressed to provision the escapees. Probably two-thirds of Virginia's slaves were young children, women with infants, physically depleted men and women over forty-five, and men whose flight would have left their families at the mercy of revengeful masters. After accounting for those in situations that made flight nearly impossible, it can be estimated that a third of the slaves who may have been considered eligible escapees, two-thirds of them male, sought their freedom behind British lines. In South Carolina and Georgia, a similar proportion of adult men and women fled to the British during the Southern campaigns between 1779 and 1783.

In the North, where hardly more than one-tenth of the half-million enslaved Africans lived, the hungering for freedom was no less intense,

[7]Quoted in Benjamin Quarles, *The Negro in the American Revolution* (Chapel Hill, NC, 1961), p. 20n.

[8]Gary B. Nash, *The Forgotten Fifth: African Americans in the Age of Revolution* (Cambridge, MA, 2006), pp 27–28.

[9]Benjamin F. Stevens, ed., *Facsimiles of Manuscripts in European Archives Relating to America, 1773–1783* (London, 1889–1895), 24, No. 2097.

[10]Quoted in Nash, *The Forgotten Fifth . . .* , p. 29.

[11]Quoted in Gary B. Nash, *The Unknown American Revolution: The Unruly Birth of Democracy and the Struggle to Create America* (New York, 2005), p. 336.

even though slavery was milder than in the plantation South. Even in the budding capital of American abolitionism, where many believed that the city's slaves were docile and contented, White Philadelphians were shocked when a "gentlewoman," walking near Christ Church, was insulted by a black man only a few weeks after Dunmore's Proclamation. When the White woman reprimanded him, he shot back, "Stay you d[amne]d White bitch 'till Lord Dunmore and his black regiment come, and then we will see who is to take the wall."[12] When the British occupied Philadelphia for nine months beginning in September 1777, hundreds of bondspeople fled to the British, confirming one Lutheran leader's belief that it "is almost universal among the Negroes in America" that they secretly hoped for the British to whip the Americans "for then all Negro slaves will gain their freedom."[13]

In New York City and its surrounding hinterland, slave flight was even greater. The chattel property of Quaker John Corlies is illustrative. Named Titus by his master, this 21 year old fled his owner in 1775 and headed south to join the black regiment being formed by Lord Dunmore. Renaming himself Colonel Tye, he was soon back in northern New Jersey organizing other slaves and free blacks to fight against the Americans. For five years, he led a local guerrilla band that terrorized the patriot farmers of northern New Jersey. Known as "one of Lord Dunmore's crew," Tye died from battle wounds and lockjaw.[14] Known all over New Jersey, he stood as a symbol of black rebellion and a beacon of hope. Tye and thousands of other enslaved blacks show that the high-toned rhetoric of natural rights and moral rectitude that accompanied the onset of the Revolution had only a limited power to soften the hearts of American slave masters. To be sure, several thousand masters freed their slaves; but as a proportion of all slave owners, these manumitters were insignificant compared

with those who refused to give up their investment in human property. The American Revolution brought to the fore a sharp collision between human rights and property rights; that the latter prevailed among the majority of slave owners confirmed Adam Smith's hard-nosed proposition that morality could rarely, if ever, transcend economic interest.

Though blacks like Colonel Tye were numerically dominant among the half-million black Americans in choosing the British side, many free blacks and a small number of slaves fought for the American cause. These were the minority celebrated by William C. Nell, the first black American historian, who in the 1850s held high the abolitionist banner by pointing to the blood shed for the "glorious cause" by black Americans in the time of the nation's birth. Among those whom Nell celebrated in his *Colored Patriots of the American Revolution* (1855) was Prince Whipple, the slave of a New Hampshire officer, who pulled the stroke oar carrying George Washington across the Delaware River in a piercing snow and sleet storm on Christmas night, 1776. Another was James Armistead, a Virginia slave whose master gave him permission to enlist under Lafayette, the French general who came to fight with the Americans. Armistead played a dramatic role as a double-spy, infiltrating the British lines at Yorktown while posing as a runaway Virginia slave and bringing back to the American forces crucial information that gave the Americans the upper hand in the climatic battle of the war. In 1786, the General Assembly of Virginia emancipated Armistead (who would call himself James Lafayette thereafter).

Most famous of all were the men of Rhode Island's mostly black First Regiment (later dubbed the Black Regiment). Desperate to flesh out his manpower-starved army, Washington agreed in 1778 to a proposal to raise a regiment of Rhode Island enslaved men, who would be

---

[12]*Pennsylvania Evening Post*, December 14, 1775.
[13]*The Journals of Henry Melchior Muhlenberg,* 3 vols. (Philadelphia, 1942–1958), III: 78.
[14]Graham R. Hodges, *African-Americans in Monmouth County during the Age of the American Revolution* (Madison, WI, 1997), pp. 13–23.

given their freedom if the legislature compensated their masters for the loss of their laborers. Like other states, Rhode Island had dipped into the bottom of the social barrel to recruit poor White men for the First Regiment, decimated by disease, absenteeism, and outright desertion, and now had hit rock bottom. About 200 strong, and fighting side by side with Wampanoag men, the First Regiment's liberated slaves fought in a series of rolling battles all the way to Yorktown, where in October 1781 Washington picked the regiment to storm the British Redoubts 9 and 10, the strongholds that held the key to victory.

Among the free black men who fought with the Americans was a man who became the new nation's wealthiest free black, a considerable essayist, an eloquent abolitionist, and the progenitor of a talented family of children and grandchildren. James Forten's great-grandfather had been brought in chains from Africa to the Delaware River and had been one of the first slaves in Pennsylvania to buy his freedom. Forten's father, born free, was a sailmaker, and he sent his son James to Anthony Benezet's school, where he learned to read and write, and imbibed many of the kindly Quaker's principles about the universality of humankind. In 1781, at age 15, Forten signed onto Stephen Decatur's twenty-two-gun privateer as a powder boy and began a career of heroic acts that would gain him fame in Philadelphia. "Scarce wafted from his native shore, and perilled upon the dark blue sea," wrote Nell, "than he found himself amid the roar of cannon, the smoke of blood, the dying and the dead."[15] This purplish passage referred to the bloody engagement of Decatur's *Royal Louis* with the British ship *Lawrence*, in which Forten was the only survivor at his gun station. But Forten's colors showed even truer on the next voyage, when the British captured his ship after a battle at sea. The British captain's son befriended Forten, who was offered free passage to England and the patronage of the captain's family. "NO, NO!" replied Forten, "I am here a prisoner for the liberties of my country; I never, NEVER, shall prove a traitor to her interests."[16] His offer spurned, the British captain consigned Forten to the *Old Jersey*, the rotting deathtrap prison ship anchored in New York, where thousands of Americans died. Released seven months later as the war was drawing to a close, the 16-year-old Forten made his way shoeless from New York to Philadelphia. At the time, however, his exploits were atypical, for few black Americans had reason to be infected by patriotic fever.

One who was certainly infected was Mumbet, who renamed herself Elizabeth Freeman after she took her freedom suit to court and won in 1781 at the hands of an all-White male jury. Upon hearing of the newly ratified Massachusetts constitution, whose preamble stated that "all men are born free and equal," Mumbet asked the court if this noble principle did not apply to her. Two years later, the state's highest court upheld the jury's decision. A household slave had become the agent of change in New England's most populous state.

Exodus of Pro-British Slaves

For thousands of American slaves who fought for "life, liberty, and the pursuit of happiness" on the British side, the end of the war in 1783 ushered in a perilous era. There could be no staying in the land of the victorious American revolutionaries, for the new United States was still slave country from North to South, and the blacks who had fought with the British were particularly hated and subject to reenslavement. But where would England send the American black loyalists? The West Indian sugar islands were built on slave labor and had no place for a large number of free blacks. England itself wished no influx of ex-slaves because London and other major cities already felt themselves burdened by growing numbers of impoverished blacks requiring public support. The answer to the problem was Nova Scotia, the easternmost part of the former New

---

[15]William C. Nell, *Colored Patriots of the American Revolution* (repub. New York, 1968), p. 167.
[16]Ibid., p. 170.

France that England had acquired at the end of the Seven Years' War. Here, amid the sparsely scattered old French settlers, the British relocated the black Americans who had fought alongside them.

Thomas Peters came to embody the exodus of the pro-British American blacks in 1783. Kidnapped from the Yoruba tribe in what is now Nigeria and brought to North America by a French slave trader, Peters had been purchased in Louisiana about 1760. He resisted enslavement so fiercely that his master sold him into the English colonies. By 1770, Peters became the property of an immigrant Scots planter on North Carolina's Cape Fear River. Here he toiled while the storm brewed between England and the colonies.

Peters's plans for his own declaration of independence may have ripened as a result of the rhetoric of liberty he heard around his master's house, for William Campbell had become a leading member of the Sons of Liberty in Wilmington, North Carolina. When twenty British ships entered the Cape Fear River in March 1776 and landed royal troops, Peters seized the moment and escaped. After fighting for seven years with the British-officered Black Pioneers, he was evacuated in 1783, along with his family, from New York City by the British, with several thousand others, to start life anew in Nova Scotia. The whims of international war and politics had destined him to pursue the struggle for survival and the quest for freedom in this unlikely corner of the earth.

The reception by the White Nova Scotians, including several thousand disbanded British soldier-settlers looking for a new lease on life, was decidedly frigid. White Nova Scotians were no more willing than the Americans had been to accept free blacks as fellow citizens and equals. Attacks on free black citizens convinced Peters and other black leaders after six years of travail in Nova Scotia that they must pursue their dream of freedom and equality elsewhere. Carrying a petition from several hundred black families, Peters made his way to London in 1790. There he was able to work out a plan to transport the black Nova Scotians to the west coast of Africa, where English abolitionists were already planning a refuge for England's poor free blacks.

This extraordinary mission to England—undertaken by an uneducated ex-slave who dared to proceed to the seat of British government without any knowledge whether he would find friends or supporters there—proved a turning point in black history. Peters returned to Nova Scotia in the fall of 1791 with a promise that a fleet of ships would arrive the next spring to carry the ransomed sons and daughters of Africa back to their homelands. Peters traveled on foot from village to village, spreading the word that English merchants and abolitionists had chartered the Sierra Leone Company to launch a new society of those wishing to return to Africa from scattered parts of the British Empire. On January 15, 1792, under sunny skies and fair wind, a fleet of British ships stood out from Halifax harbor, laden with several thousand Africans who fervently desired to "kiss their dear Malagueta," the Malagueta pepper or "grains of paradise" that grew prolifically in the region for which they were heading. After a difficult voyage, Thomas Peters, according to legend, led his shipmates ashore in Sierra Leone, singing "The day of jubilee is come, return ye ransomed sinners home."[17] In less than four months he died of fever and was buried in Freetown, the aptly named capital of the new African nation. Although the British compatriots led by Peters were only a fragment of the black Americans of the Revolutionary era, they were the advance guard of the back-to-Africa emigrationists who sporadically in the first half of the century would abandon hope for freedom and equality in the United States and return to Africa in one small wave after another.

The War Comes to an End

At the end of the Revolutionary War, thousands of black Americans had gained their freedom from conscience-stricken masters or by escaping

---

[17]Quoted in Gary B. Nash, "Thomas Peters: Millwright and Deliverer," in David G. Sweet and Gary B. Nash, eds., *Struggle and Survival in Colonial America* (Berkeley and Los Angeles, CA, 1981), p. 83.

from bondage. Some aged slaves had masters who chose to free them rather than support them in their unproductive, declining years. Most who had been manumitted were in the North or in the upper South. In the North, they could look to certain states for hope that the end of slavery might soon come. Pennsylvania passed a gradual abolition law in 1780; in Massachusetts, slavery was abolished by judicial decision in 1783; in Vermont, the constitution of 1777 declared slavery illegal. Connecticut and Rhode Island followed suit. All states except South Carolina and Georgia halted the importation of slaves. Yet in New York and New Jersey, where thousands of people were still trapped in slavery, gradual abolition laws would not be passed for another generation.

Small but significant gains had been made in making the new nation truly free. Yet by the end of the war in 1783, much of the early Revolutionary rhetoric about natural rights had ebbed, though reformers continued to remind Americans that to build a free republic on the foundations of slavery was a dangerous and ideologically compromised proposition. Reform-minded White Americans confronted two main problems. The first was economic: How would slave owners be compensated? The second was social: How would freed people fit into the social fabric of the new nation? Solutions to these two thorny problems hinged, in turn, on a willingness to make economic sacrifices and on an ability to envision a biracial republican society. A number of gradual abolition plans came before the public, several from the hands of Virginians, but none succeeded. Northerners as well as Southerners lost the abolitionist fire and would never rekindle it in their own generation. By the time they were in their graves, the best opportunity for abolishing slavery had been lost.

For some half-million black Americans who saw the flame of freedom flickering out at the end of the war, the road ahead was confused and discouraging. Slavery was ebbing in the North, but it was surging in the South—the result of a rising black birthrate that made further importation of African slaves almost unnecessary.

Moreover, those who remained enslaved had to struggle ahead after suffering the exodus of many of the most physically vigorous and politically able. Emerging from the war, the African American population included a disproportionate number of older slaves, women with small children, and those physically broken or emotionally paralyzed by the slave experience. Gradually the slave population regained gender balance. By 1790, nearly 660,000 slaves faced a bleak future with only a Southern free black population of 32,000 offering some hope.

Free Black Leaders

Despite the heavy losses of black males in the prime of life, vigorous and visionary free black communities began to form in the North. The largest were in the maritime towns because that was where work, companionship, and black churches were most available. But hardly any sizable town between Maine and Maryland failed to develop a subcommunity of free blacks, and in each place men and women emerged as leaders. By looking at several of them, we can trace the pathways that led from the barrenness of life under slavery to creative, though often obstructed, lives under freedom.

Jupiter Hammon of Long Island exemplifies the cautious, tentative yearning for freedom among the enslaved who could not make a clean break from their masters—and from the detested institution of slavery. Born in 1711 as the chattel property of the prominent Lloyd family of merchants and manorial landlords, Hammon served as a valued house servant. Early converted to Christianity, he wrote poetry filled with ecstatic yearnings for salvation in the afterlife. When the Lloyds fled Long Island after the British occupied New York City in 1776, Hammon, already 65 years old, willingly stayed at their side. He continued to preach the gospel of the redeeming salvation that would come to those, black and White alike, who accepted Christ.

Even in this cautious house servant, sparks of the freedom fighter smoldered. His *A Winter Piece* in 1782 urged the moral reformation of

African Americans and exhorted them to retain their African identity while trapped in slavery. After the war, Hammon adopted a gradualist approach to the abolition of slavery. In his last written piece, *An Address to the Negroes in the State of New York,* published as the Constitutional Convention was gathering in Philadelphia in 1787, Hammon "hoped that God would open their eyes [i.e., those of White Americans], when they were so much engaged for liberty, to think of the state of the poor blacks, and pity them."[18] Hammon imbibed much of the conservative message in Christianity that urged the dispossessed to look for release in the afterlife, but even this black minister had edged his way toward using his literary gifts for the cause of black freedom.

In the new nation, the human material out of which postwar black society would have to be constructed included thousands who were less cautious than Hammon. Yet some of them had played their hands carefully during the war because they had already secured a small stake in American society. Such a man was Prince Hall of Boston. Enslaved to a Boston merchant and a worshipper at School Street Church shepherded by the New Light revivalist Andrew Crosswell, Hall was about 40 when the war broke out. He received his freedom in 1770 and very quickly played a role in the five petitions that Boston's blacks placed before the legislature just before the war. Several of these remonstrances against slavery came from a group of fourteen black Masons, Hall among them, who had joined a Masonic lodge formed by one of the British regiments that was occupying the Massachusetts capital. "We expect great things from men who have made such a noble stand against the designs of their *fellow-men* to enslave them," read one petition. Another petition declared that "we have in common with all other men a natural right to

our freedom . . . as we are a freeborn people and have never forfeited this blessing by any compact or agreement whatever."[19]

Hall might have joined the British forces before they retreated from Boston in March 1776. But instead, he cast his lot with the land of his birth. After the war, Hall became a leader of Boston's small black community. Although a judicial decree abolished slavery in 1783, most black freedmen and freedwomen found only ill-paid work and deep prejudice against them. In 1786, when Shays's Rebellion swept Massachusetts, Hall tried to offset White hostility by offering what he called the Commonwealth's "meanest members in this time of trouble and confusion" to fight against the agrarian insurgents.[20]

Spurned by the governor and discouraged at their plight, Hall led Boston's free black community in an entirely different direction. Hardly six weeks after offering to march against the Shaysites, Hall petitioned the legislature on behalf of the city's African Americans to support a plan for returning to Africa. Believing that they would never escape the racism that hobbled them, they wished "earnestly . . . to return to Africa, our native country . . . where we shall live among our equals and be more comfortable and happy, than we can be in our present situation."[21] This was probably the first colonization impulse—an early form of black nationalism—to emerge in the new American republic. When Hall's repatriation plan failed, he continued to organize, protesting the exclusion of black children from tax-supported free schools, protesting against the kidnapping of free blacks into slavery, and calling for the end of the slave trade. Death silenced his voice in June 1807, just six months before the Atlantic slave trade legally ended.

We can see a different postwar strategy at work in the grappling for identity and the future of black Americans of Richard Allen.

---

[18]Quoted in Gary B. Nash, *Race and Revolution* (Madison, WI, 1990), p. 63.
[19]Quoted in Sidney Kaplan and Emma Nogrady Kaplan, *The Black Presence in the Era of the American Revolution, 1770–1800* (Amherst, MA, 1989), pp. 11, 13.
[20]Ibid., p. 205.
[21]Ibid., pp. 207–208.

Twenty-four years younger than Prince Hall, Allen had grown up enslaved to Benjamin Chew, a wealthy, conservative lawyer and officeholder in Pennsylvania. Chew sold Allen's family to a Delaware farmer in the early 1770s, and it was here in about 1777 that Allen experienced a religious conversion at the hands of itinerant Methodists. Allen's new master also fell to the power of the Methodist message, and, nudged along by economic necessity, became enough convinced of the sin of slaveholding to allow Allen and his brother to purchase their freedom. In 1780, with the war still raging, Allen began a six-year religious sojourn, interspersing work as a sawyer, wagon driver, and shoemaker. Stints of itinerant preaching to black and White audiences carried him by foot over hundreds of miles to villages, crossroads, and farms. In the mid-1780s, Allen received the call to preach in Philadelphia to free blacks who were worshipping at St. George's Methodist Church, a rude, dirt-floored building in the German part of the city.

Allen soon increased the black Methodist flock with his oratory skills and steady demeanor. He joined another recently released slave, Absalom Jones, in launching the Free African Society of Philadelphia, the first black mutual aid association in the new nation. This led to a desire for an independent black church. However, Allen's fervent Methodism brought him into conflict with other emerging black leaders, who wished for a nondenominational or "union" church. Thus, within a few years, two black churches took form—one Methodist, the other Episcopalian. In both cases the guiding idea was that black Americans emerging from slavery should form independent black churches because, as the Philadelphia black leaders phrased it, "men are more influenced by their moral equals than by their superiors" and "are more easily governed by persons chosen by themselves for that purpose than by persons who are placed over

Richard Allen, engraving.

(Courtesy Kean Collection/Getty Images)

them by accidental circumstances."[22] In this quietly radical message, they planted the seed of black self-reliance in the capital city of American abolitionism.

Both as places of refuge and citadels of strength, the emerging independent black churches gave free blacks and those still in bondage a sense of peoplehood within a White republic that was increasingly hostile to the free black presence. The "coming out" from White churches, as it was expressed, involved a painful and sometimes dangerous process of rebirthing. The desire "to worship God under our own vine and fig tree," as Allen put it, was in essence a desire to stand apart from White society, avoiding both the paternalistic benevolence of its racially liberal members and the animosity of its racially intolerant members.[23] The distancing from whites

---

[22]"Address of the Representatives of the African Church [of Philadelphia]," quoted in Gary B. Nash, *Forging Freedom: The Formation of Philadelphia's Free Black Community, 1720–1840* (Cambridge, MA, 1988), p. 113.

[23]*The Life Experience and Gospel Labors of the Rt. Rev. Richard Allen, to Which is Annexed the Rise and Progress of the African Methodist Episcopal Church in the United States of America* (Nashville, TN, 1983), p. 26.

allowed former slaves to strike out on independent courses in other areas of concern. From Allen's church, Mother Bethel, flowed petitions and sermons against slavery and the slave trade, plans for black schools and mutual aid societies, protests against race discrimination in the city of brotherly love, and, on occasion, emigrationist schemes.

Hammon, Hall, and Allen represent the different forms taken by the quest for self-definition and security as African Americans emerged from the revolution. Between the 1780s and the 1820s, during the life span of the Revolutionary generation, black Americans by the thousands wrestled to find an identity, trying to reconcile their consciousness of being African with that of being American. For the most part, they had to solve this problem by maintaining a dialectical relationship between the two parts of their identity. This is what W. E. B. Du Bois called "two unreconciled strivings; two warring ideals in one dark body, whose dogged strength alone keeps it from being torn asunder."[24]

The Indians' Revolution

For some 150,000 Native Americans composing eighty-five nations east of the Mississippi River, the American Revolution was also a time to "try men's souls." Their guiding principles, cherished for generations of interaction with European colonizers, were political independence and territorial preservation. African Americans, who had neither liberty nor land, fought for the former in order someday to gain the latter. Native Americans, who had both, struggled to preserve what they had. Like most black Americans, most Indian tribes concluded that their revolutionary goals could best be achieved through fighting *against* the side that proclaimed the equality of all men and with the side that the Americans accused of trampling on their natural, irreducible rights. Nearly two centuries of abrasive contact with colonizing Europeans compelled the choice,

for it was the settler-subjects of the English king who most threatened Indian autonomy, just as royal power before the Revolution had attempted to protect Indian land from White encroachment by means of the Proclamation Line of 1763 and the regulation of trade. American Indians fought an anticolonial war against those attempting to slip their colonial yoke.

Choosing Sides

But deciding to fight with the British came only after a period of determined neutrality. Both the British and the Continental Congress also hoped for Indian neutrality because each blanched at the thought of having powerful Indian nations on the other side of the affray. But before the war got beyond its early months, Native leaders had to make a choice. Washington was able to get pledges of support from the small Penobscot and Abenaki tribes in Maine, from the Stockbridge Natives in Massachusetts, and from the Catawbas of North Carolina. But these were severely weakened and already dependent Native peoples. Where the great reservoirs of Native fighting manpower resided were in Iroquoia, the Ohio River valley, the Kentucky hunting grounds of the Cherokee, and the interior Creek lands of the Lower South. In wooing these nations, the British had the upper hand because they were better able to supply the goods that Natives prized and because they could pledge the sanctity of tribal lands—a promise that the rebelling Americans were not prepared to make.

The Iroquois were at the center of this struggle for Native support. Neutrality seemed the best policy; but if the Iroquois stayed out of the war, would the war stay out of Iroquoia? The Mohawk leader, Thayendanegea, or Joseph Brant, thought this unlikely and worked to bring the Iroquois to the side of the British. At age 13, Thayendanegea had served in the Seven Years' War, fighting alongside British Superintendent of Northern Indians William Johnson against

---

[24]W. E. Burghart Du Bois, *The Souls of Black Folk* (New York, 1970), p. 3.

the French. Eight years later, he aided the colonists again by battling against Pontiac's Indian insurgents, who tried to expel the British soldiers and the encroaching Americans from the Ohio country. But by the 1770s, Thayendanegea understood that despite the trading alliance the Iroquois had maintained with the Northern colonies for generations and despite the close ties that the Mohawks (the easternmost of the six Iroquois nations) cherished with William Johnson, his people were now seriously threatened by the rapidly growing White population. Barely 20,000 White colonists inhabited New York in 1700, but by 1770, their number had increased to 160,000. Many times, rapacious New York land speculators and frontiersmen had swindled the Mohawks out of land. So as war clouds gathered in 1775, Thayendanegea, 33 years old, took ship to London to see what the English king would offer the Iroquois for their support in a war that, while still not formally declared, had been in the shooting stage since early in the year. Like his grandfather, Chief Hendrick, who had been among the Iroquois chiefs who traveled to London to consult with Queen Anne sixty-five years before, Thayendanegea was greeted as royalty in England. His mission was to determine how life, liberty, and the protection of property might best be preserved by his people. His decision, made before leaving London, anticipated a majority of Indian tribes in the next few years—that only by fighting against the independence-seeking Americans could Indian tribes themselves remain independent. He returned to New York a few weeks after the Declaration of Independence; served with the British General, William Howe, at Long Island in the first major defeat of Washington's army; and then in November 1776 began a long trek through the lands of the Iroquois and their confederates in the Ohio country to spread the message, as he wrote, that "their own country and liberty" were "in danger from the rebels."[25] Thayendanegea's diplomatic mission brought

most of the Iroquois into the war on the British side in the summer of 1777. Long after the war, he recalled that "Every man of us thought that by fighting for the King we should ensure to ourselves and children a good inheritance."[26] He was inflating the case, however, because most of the Oneidas and the Tuscaroras enlisted in the American cause.

The Embattled Iroquois

During the war Thayendanegea seemed to be everywhere—at Oriskany in August 1777 when the British and their Indian allies defeated the Americans who were trying to reach the besieged Fort Stanwix, which controlled access to the western Mohawk Valley and the Great Lakes; at Cherry Valley in the summer of 1778 when the Iroquois drove thousands of American farmers from their fields in southern New York and northern Pennsylvania; and at skirmishes in the campaign of 1779 when the American general, John Sullivan, invaded Iroquois country, burning towns and pursuing his blunt motto: "civilization or death to all American savages." For the entire war, Thayendanegea played a leading role in virtually eliminating the New York and Pennsylvania backcountry (a major grain and cattle-growing area on which the Continental army had depended for supplies) from contributing much to the war effort. "A thousand Iroquois and five hundred Tory rangers," writes one historian, "were able to lay in waste nearly 50,000 square miles of colonial territory."[27]

The summer of 1779 tested the pro-British Iroquois sorely. Washington made the destruction of the Iroquois his priority. Committing one-third of his army, he carried out a scorched earthy policy to "lay waste all the settlements around [Iroquoia] . . . that the country may not be merely overrun but destroyed." Led by General John Sullivan, the American forces greatly outnumbered the Iroquois warriors and Brant's

[25]Barbara Graymont, *The Iroquois in the American Revolution* (Syracuse, NY, 1972), p. 109.
[26]Quoted in Nash, *The Unknown American Revolution* . . . , p. 250.
[27]Anthony F. C. Wallace, *The Death and Rebirth of the Seneca* (New York, 1972), p. 146.

Volunteers (farmers and craftsmen from interior New York and Pennsylvania who stood with the English king). As the Iroquois withdrew to the west, Sullivan's army razed Native villages, burned 160,000 bushels of corn, and girdled thousands of fruit trees, leaving them to die. "There is not a single town left in the country of the Five Nations,"[28] Sullivan reported to Washington. The winter of 1779 to 1780, bringing bitter cold and the deepest snow in recent years, was a nightmare of dying, dysentery, and displacement for some 3,000 Iroquois people, most of whom took refuge in the British fort at Niagara on the shore of Lake Ontario.

Thayendanegea vowed revenge. Sullivan had destroyed Iroquois villages, granaries, and orchards, but not warriors. "The nests are destroyed," recounted one American officer, "but the birds are still on the wing." He was right. After Washington withdrew his invading army, he sent them south to counter the southern campaign of the British general, Lord Charles Cornwallis. Steaming back eastward in the spring of 1780 came Iroquois war parties that devastated American farmlands and villages in the Schoharie Valley of New York as thoroughly as their own villages had been wiped out.

Though never militarily defeated during the war, the Iroquois lost about one-third of their people, and most of their settled towns and orchards, but even worse, they were abandoned by their British allies at the peace talks in Paris, left to cope with aggressive, combat-seasoned, and land-hungry Americans. Thunderstruck that British diplomats sold them out to their American enemies, the Iroquois signed dictated treaties that dispossessed them of most of their land and consigned them to reservations that within a generation became "slums in the wilderness." Thayendanegea spent the last twenty years of his life trying to lead the Iroquois in adjusting to the harsh new realities by which a proud and an independent people found that the pursuit of happiness by White Americans required red Americans to surrender life, liberty, and property.

A War of Conquest

While wars in Iroquoia and western New York and Pennsylvania devastated both Native and American farming and village life, another longstanding contest reached a climax between the Ohio River and the Great Lakes. The shaky grip of British claims in this vast territory provided a stage onto which the young George Rogers Clark could stride to seize his place as one of the heroes of American storybooks. When the war erupted, the 23-year-old Clark was living restlessly near Jefferson's Monticello. What he loved was the vast forested region to the west, and what he hated were the Indians who lived there—Shawnee, Ottawa, Huron, Potawatomi, Kickapoo, Winnebago, Chippewa, Sauk, and Fox. Now he schemed to conquer what history books called the Old Northwest, while neutralizing British-backed Native assaults through Virginia's backdoor.

Of the many tribes that would meet Clark's invading mini-army, the Shawnee were the most militant. They had allied with the Cherokee to attack encroaching Virginians even before the Continental Congress declared independence. "From being a great nation," the Shawnee sorrowfully told the Cherokee in May 1776, "[we are now] reduced to a handful." Once they had "possessed lands almost to the seashore," but "red people who were once masters of the whole country [now] hardly possessed ground enough to stand on." Knowing that the White settlers intended to destroy them, the Shawnee argued that it was "better to die like men than to dwindle away by inches."[29] Several years of skirmishing with intruders such as Daniel Boone prepared them for Clark's invasion.

Raising seven companies of militiamen in early 1778, Clark targeted the small British forts at Kaskaskia and Vincennes, in today's Illinois and Indiana. In what many in his small

---

[28]Quoted in Nash, *The Unknown American Revolution . . .* , pp. 346–347.
[29]Quoted in Gregory Evans Dowd, *A Spirited Resistance: The North American Indian Struggle for Unity, 1745–1815* (Baltimore, MD, 1992), p. 47.

From an Original Drawing in the Possession of James Boswell Esq.

JOSEPH THAYENDANEKEN

The Mohawk Chief

Thayendanegea, known to the English as Joseph Brant, sat for his portrait on both sides of the Atlantic. This portrait was painted by George Romney, one of London's best-known portrait painters. It may have been painted when Brant was in London in 1775, parleying with King George III and his ministers about Iroquois allegiance to England in the war brewing in the colonies. William Leete Stone, *Life of Joseph Brant-Thayendanegea*. Published by A. V. Blacke, New York, 1838.

Source: Courtesy of the Library of Congress.

contingent regarded as a suicide mission, Clark marched through icy rivers and across 180 miles of frozen terrain to attack the English outpost at Vincennes. Though outnumbered four to one by 500 British regulars and their Native allies, Clark fooled the fort's defenders into believing that his force was much larger. Convinced that he faced disaster, the British commander surrendered without a shot. This event marked the beginning of a momentous collapse of pan-Indian efforts to drive the White frontier fighters out of their Kentucky, Ohio, and Indiana homelands.

For the Shawnee people, who had captured Daniel Boone in the winter of 1777 to 1778 and laid siege to the frontier town of Boonesborough that threatened Shawnee territory between Kentucky and Virginia, the war in the West brought terrible destruction. Some Shawnee villages tried to remain neutral, and a few pledged allegiance to the Americans; but most villages gravitated toward the British. Clark's invasion of Shawnee country in the summer of 1780 began annual search and destroyed missions to burn Shawnee crops and villages, deeply disrupting the Indian cycles of subsistence farming and hunting. Supplied by the British from their Detroit fort, the Shawnee, like the Iroquois, were shocked when the British sued for peace in 1783 and abandoned their Shawnee allies to the victorious Americans. At an exchange of prisoners in July 1783, a gloating American officer taunted the Shawnee: "Your fathers the English have made peace with us for themselves, but forgot you their children, who fought with them, and neglected you like bastards."[30] Still ahead lay invading American armies equipped with the knowledge that Clark and his contingent had gained in their forays into the vast trans-Appalachian region.

The Divided Cherokee

For the powerful Cherokee, the American war for independence, the matter of choosing sides was agonizing. In their villages, on both sides of the Appalachians, they had choked at seeing a huge swath of their hunting lands ceded away by Iroquois delegates at the Treaty of Stanwix in 1768. Other cessions followed, four times between 1770 and 1775. This led to growing tension between young war chiefs, counseling the red path of war, and the older civil chiefs desperately trying to maintain the White path of peace.

This tension reached a climax in March 1775, at the Treaty of Muscle Shoals, where a group of North Carolinian land speculators of the Transylvania Land Company persuaded headmen such as Attakullakulla (Little Carpenter to the English) and Oconostota to cede 27,000 square miles of prime Cherokee hunting land between the Kentucky and Cumberland rivers in exchange for 10,000 pounds of trade goods. This was clearly in defiance of the English Proclamation Act of 1763. It was also the final straw for militant young Cherokee warriors, led by Dragging Canoe, the son (or possibly the nephew) of Attakullakulla. Dragging Canoe left the treaty in a rage, swearing to make the ceded lands "dark and bloody." He put it squarely to the British "that he had no hand in making these bargains but blamed some of their Old Men who he said were too old to hunt and who by their poverty had been induced to sell their land but that for his part he had a great many young fellows that would support him and that they were determined to have their land."[31]

Even before the Declaration of Independence, Dragging Canoe's young warriors kept his vow. Falling upon what they regarded as White trespassers who were pouring into Cherokee lands from Virginia, the Carolinas, and Georgia, the young Cherokee warriors bloodied the ground with a vengeance. However, failing to obtain support from the powerful Creek nation to their south and far from British trade sources, the militant Cherokee found themselves short of ammunition and other supplies. This situation left them vulnerable to Southern militia eager

[30]Quoted in ibid., p. 174.
[31]Quoted in Colin G. Calloway, *The American Revolution in Indian Country: Crisis and Diversity in Native American Communities* (New York, 1995), p. 195.

to "carry fire and sword into the very bowels of their country," to extirpate the Cherokee and drive them, as Jefferson recommended, beyond the Mississippi River.[32] In the summer and fall of 1776, nearly 6,000 Southern militiamen, not yet engaged in the fight against the British, punished Cherokee towns severely, burning food and supplies, destroying orchards, razing villages, killing many women and children, and capturing runaway slaves.

While the war for independence raged in the South, splitting the White population into Patriot and Loyalist camps, the Cherokee struggle continued. The British capture of Augusta and Savannah, Georgia in 1778 to 1779 opened a new supply line along the Savannah River for the British to furnish Dragging Canoe's warriors the guns, ammunition, and food that kept them on the warpath. This led to another Virginia expedition of militiamen against the irreconcilable Cherokees in April 1779, and another was mounted in June 1780. In the later punitive expedition, Virginia governor Thomas Jefferson explicitly charged the militia officers to take "great care that no injury be done to the friendly part of the [Cherokee] nation" which "have our faith pledged for their protection." What followed was not the destruction of Dragging Canoe's militant Cherokee but rather the "friendly" Cherokee. The 700 militiamen, led by the Indian-hating John Sevier, stopped short of their targeted Cherokee enemies and instead, maintaining that the neutralist Cherokee were foxes in sheep's clothing, stormed seventeen accommodationist Cherokee towns, where they burned 1000 houses and lodges and destroyed 50,000 bushels of corn. Then marching to Chota, the Cherokee's "beloved town," Sevier's men killed thirteen men who offered no resistance, thrusting aside Cherokee ceremonial chief Nancy Ward, who begged the Virginians to honor their pledge of protection. Sevier returned in March 1781 to destroy another fifteen towns of the conciliatory Cherokee who had fled in panic.

The militant Cherokee and Shawnee raided sporadically in the interior throughout the war but were able to mount a sustained assault on the Americans. The war deeply divided the Cherokees with Dragging Canoe leading the young Cherokees southward and westward to establish new towns along the Chickamauga and Tennessee rivers, where they remained militantly anti-American. But the Spanish entry into the war on the American side spelled their defeat. When British-controlled Mobile in today's Alabama fell to the Spanish navy in February 1780 and Pensacola in today's Florida in April 1781, the lifeline to British supplies that had sustained Dragging Canoe's warriors and their villages was severed. By the time the White revolutionaries were ratifying their new constitution in 1788, the Cherokees had lost three-quarters of their land and seen half their towns destroyed. The Chickamaugan Cherokee secessionists, weary of the war, sued for peace while hoping that the Spanish would supply them with the trade goods upon which they relied.

After the War

Some Indian tribes, mostly small ones surrounded by White colonists and greatly reduced in population by disease and earlier wars, fought with the Americans. The Passamaquoddy and Penobscot in Maine, who had sustained bitter losses in the Seven Years' War in fighting against New Hampshire rangers, now fought alongside these rangers against the British. The Stockbridge in Massachusetts, an amalgam of remnant Indians from the Hudson River valley in western Massachusetts who had fought alongside Robert Rogers' Rangers in the Seven Years' War, served with Washington's troops at Boston in 1775 and later in New York, New Jersey, and Canada. The Oneida in New York, and the Tuscarora and Catawba in North Carolina all signed allegiance to the Americans and contributed scouts and warriors to the revolutionary cause. But the Indians who pledged support, usually because they were dependent on American trade and surrounded by a sea of White

---

[32]Quoted in ibid., p. 197.

settlers, reaped little benefit from their efforts. Although grateful state governments compensated a number of Native warriors after the war, this act did little to protect the tribes from the land-hungry Americans in the postwar rush for more land.

In the end, the Indians were disastrous losers in the Revolutionary War. This was partly because they were less successful than the White colonists in overcoming intratribal and intertribal factionalism; partly because the supplies of European trade goods on which they depended—especially guns, powder, and shot—were seriously disrupted during the war; and partly because they were abandoned to the Americans by their British allies at war's end. Facing a White society in 1783 that was heavily armed and determined to occupy the vast trans-Appalachian region, nations such as the Iroquois and the Cherokee were forced to cede most of their land. The American victory over the British was "the greatest blow that could have been dealt us," heard the Spanish governor of St. Louis from the Indian chiefs in 1784.[33] The prewar White population buildup that had exhausted the land supply along the coastal plain found a safety valve as thousands of settlers spilled across the mountains after 1783, frequently in violation of treaties contracted by their own elected governments. Aiding these frontiersmen, many of them war veterans, were state and national governments that understood that the Western lands, once the Native inhabitants had been driven away, were the new nation's most valuable resource. The sale of Western lands would provide the revenue both to liquidate the huge war debt and to underwrite the expenses of a nation of tax-shy people.

In pursuing such a policy White Americans sacrificed the sanctity of their own laws and treaty obligations, and abandoned the revolutionary ideal of just and equitable relations among men. Some White leaders, such as George Morgan, were troubled by this outcome. Morgan, a former Indian trader and agent for the Continental Congress, wrote in 1793:

At what time do a people violate the Law of Nations, as the United States have done, with regard to the North Western Indians? Only when they think they can do it with impunity. Justice between nations is founded on reciprocal fear. Rome whilst weak was equitable; become more strong than her neighbors, she ceased to be just. The ambitious and powerful are always unjust. To them the Laws of Nations are mere chimeras.[34]

But most Americans were unwilling to apply the principles that animated their struggle for independence in their relations with the Native inhabitants of the trans-Appalachian region. Indian land, like black slave labor, was one of the new republic's preeminently important resources. The White Americans' revolution was fought in the East for release from the British Empire but was also fought in the West to create an empire of their own.

The pro-British stance of the Native Americans cannot be counted as a failure of judgment on their part. Had they sided with the Americans, they would have fared no better, as the dismal postwar experience of several pro-American tribes, such as the Tuscaroras and Oneidas, demonstrates. Allying with the British was realistically the only chance of halting the flood of American settlers, perhaps as many as 50,000, who by clandestine purchase and defiance of royal authority had swept across the Appalachians before the war. If they were "too numerous, too lawless and licentious to be restrained," as General George Gage explained, how could the Shawnee, Cherokee, Miami, or Iroquois further their struggle to retain their lands and independence by siding with the American revolutionaries?[35]

[33]Quoted in ibid., p. xv.
[34]Quoted in Randolph C. Downes, *Council Fires on the Upper Ohio: A Narrative of Indian Affairs in the Upper Ohio Valley Until 1795* (Pittsburgh, PA, 1969), p. 249.
[35]Quoted in Richard White, *The Middle Ground: Indians, Empires, and Republics in the Great Lakes Region* (Cambridge and New York, 1991), p. 340.

The wartime pro-British attempts at intertribal confederation, though they could not prevent an American victory, played a large role in mounting the next great Indian resistance movement, from about 1783 to 1815, when White Americans, having won a war of national liberation, now embarked on a war of national expansion. Thayendanegea's wartime exertions and his efforts to foster international cooperation, after another trip to London in 1785, led to fierce Indian resistance in the Old Northwest. Similarly, in the Old Southwest, Hoboi-Hili Miko (known by whites as Alexander McGillivray), a Creek headman whose Scots-Irish father had married a Creek woman, galvanized Creek resistance to land-hungry South Carolinians and Georgians. "Our lands are our life and breath," he wrote, "if we part with them, we part with our blood. We must fight them."[36] Fearing assassination at the hands of Georgian officials, McGillivray told a friend:

> If I fall by the hand of such [assasins], I shall fall a victim in the noblest of causes—that of failing in maintaining the just rights of my country. If every peaceable mode of obtaining a redress of grievances having proved fruitless, then having recourse to arms to obtain it, be marks of the savage, and not of the soldier, what savages must the Americans be. . . .[37]

Thayendanegea and McGillivray were the exemplars of pan-Indian resistance. From the work of a host of such war-tempered Native leaders arose a new generation of resistance leaders—Black Hawk, Tecumseh, and others. The tribes of the Ohio River valley fought desperately in the postwar era to protect their homelands, only to lose against overwhelming odds when state militias and federal armies, whom they had defeated in the late 1780s and

early 1790s, returned with larger and larger forces to invade their land. By this time the humanitarian language of the Northwest Ordinance of 1787 had been all but forgotten. "The utmost good faith," promised the Continental Congress in its last significant act, "shall always be observed towards the Indians; their lands and property shall never be taken from them without their consent; and in their property, rights and liberty, they never shall be invaded or disturbed, unless in just and lawful wars authorized by Congress; but laws founded in justice and humanity shall from time to time be made, for preventing wrongs being done to them, and for preserving peace and friendship with them."[38] As the strengthening of state militias and the creation of a national army progressed in the 1790s, Indian societies learned how hollow were the phrases of the Northwest Ordinance. Armed conflict replaced "utmost good faith." The republic's greatest wartime hero, now its first president, captured the national mood when he wrote, "The gradual extension of our settlements will as certainly cause the savage as the wolf to retire; both being beasts of prey though they differ in shape."[39]

In reaching conclusions about the character and outcome of the American Revolution, fair mindedness requires us to recognize that the conflict fought by White Americans for life, liberty, and the pursuit of happiness compelled most nonwhite Americans to take the British side in quest of the same goals. African and Native Americans were animated by the doctrine of natural rights as surely as were the signers of the Declaration of Independence, and they were moved by self-interest just as were White revolutionaries. Most of them took the other side to gain or preserve these rights and to pursue their own interests, which had been hammered

---

[36]McGillivray to James White [superintendent of Indian Affairs for the United States], April 8, 1791, *American State Papers, Indian Affairs* (Washington, DC, 1832), VII: 18.
[37]McGillivray to James White, *American State Papers*, VII: 18.
[38]Quoted in Horsman, "American Indian Policy in the Old Northwest, 1732–1812." *William and Mary Quarterly*, 3rd Ser., 18 (1961): 40.
[39]Washington to James Duane, September 7, 1783, quoted in ibid., p. 38.

out during generations of interaction in North America.

In their struggle against the White revolutionaries, most African and Native Americans lost at least in the proximate sense. *Their* colonial experience would not be over when White Americans overthrew their colonial master. What they won, however, was a piece of history, for they kept lit the lamp of liberty and passed on their own revolutionary heritage to their children and their children's children. The founding principles of the American Revolution lived on in the nineteenth-century struggles of Denmark Vesey, Nat Turner, Frederick Douglass, Black Hawk, Tecumseh, Sequoyah, and a host of other black and red leaders.

Summary

The connections that had existed among the red, White, and black peoples of North America for many generations were profoundly altered by the American Revolution. In the Northern colonies—but little in the South—White reformers raised an outcry against slavery, making it a public issue for the first time. The enslaved Africans themselves encountered new situations and opportunities arising from the Revolution. During the war, some grasped the offer of freedom under Dunmore's Proclamation of 1775, and some contributed to the American victory as free blacks or emancipated slaves. After the war, those who had supported the English cause relocated to Nova Scotia and, later, Sierra Leone. Thousands of black Americans were manumitted in the North or upper South, though most of those enslaved in the South watched their dreams of freedom die. In a burst of creativity, free blacks formed churches, schools, and community societies as they strove to claim their inalienable rights.

Like most black Americans, most Indian tribes chose to align themselves with the English. As at so many other flashpoints in relations with Europeans, the Iroquois claimed the dominant Indian role in the North. However, the end result was that both Native and American farming and village life in Iroquoia and western New York and Pennsylvania were devastated. Farther west, George Rogers Clark marched his mini-army into the area between the Ohio Valley and the Great Lakes, and proceeded to rain destruction upon various Native tribes, most notably the Shawnee. In the South, the Cherokee effort against the American revolutionaries was thwarted by the Spanish entrance into the war on the American side. At the end of the war, the Cherokees had lost three-quarters of their land and witnessed the destruction of half their towns. In sum, the Indians were tragic losers in the Revolutionary War for three major reasons: they could not surmount their intratribal and intertribal factionalism, their access to the European goods upon which they relied was disrupted by war, and their British allies abandoned them to the Americans at the end of the Revolution. Even those who fought on the American side faced the seizure of their ancient homelands by land-hungry settlers.

Critical Thinking Questions

1. Why did many enslaved Africans flee to the British during the American Revolution, and what path did these Africans choose once the Americans had prevailed?
2. What happened to abolitionist fervor by the end of the Revolutionary War, and what might account for this?
3. What was George Rogers Clark's motivation for invading the area between the Ohio River and the Great Lakes, and what was the outcome for the Shawnee people?
4. Did Native peoples, in the main, support the American or British during the Revolutionary War, and would the results for them have been much different if they had supported the opposite side?

Further Reading

Alexander X. Boyd, *Captives and Voyagers: Black Migrants across the Eighteenth-Century British Atlantic World* (Baton Rouge: Louisiana State University Press, 2008).

Colin G. Calloway, *The American Revolution in Indian Country: Crisis and Diversity in Native American Communities* (Cambridge: Cambridge University Press, 1995).

David Brion Davis, *Inhuman Bondage: The Rise and Fall of Slavery in the New World* (New York: Oxford University Press, 2006).

Gregory Dowd, *A Spirited Resistance: The North American Indian Struggle for Unity, 1745–1815* (Baltimore: Johns Hopkins University Press, 1992).

Douglas R. Egerton, *Death or Liberty: African Americans and Revolutionary America* (New York: Oxford University Press, 2009).

Sylvia Frey, *Water from the Rock: Black Resistance in a Revolutionary Age* (Princeton: Princeton University Press, 1991).

Alan Gilbert, *Black Patriots and Loyalists: Fighting for Emancipation in the War for Independence* (Chicago: Chicago University Press, 2012).

Joseph T. Glatthaar and James Kirby Martin, *Forgotten Allies: The Oneida Indians and the American Revolution* (New York: Hill & Wang, 2006).

Barbara Graymont, *The Iroquois in the American Revolution* (Syracuse: Syracuse University Press, 1972).

Tom Hatley, *The Dividing Paths: Cherokees and South Carolinians through the Revolution Era* (New York: Oxford University Press, 1993).

Rhys Isaac, *Landon Carter's Uneasy Kingdom: Revolution and Rebellion on a Virginia Plantation* (New York: Oxford University Press, 2004).

Maurice Jackson, *Let This Voice Be Heard: Anthony Benezet, Father of Atlantic Abolitionism* (Philadelphia: University of Pennsylvania Press, 2009).

Sidney Kaplan and Emma Nogrady Kaplan, *The Black Presence in the Era of the American Revolution*, rev. ed. (Amherst: University of Massachusetts Press, 1989).

Gail D. MacLeitch, *Imperial Entanglements: Iroquois Change and Persistence on the Frontiers of Empire* (Philadelphia University of Pennsylvania Press, 2011).

Gary B. Nash, *The Forgotten Fifth: African Americans in the Age of Revolution* (The Nathan I. Huggins Lectures) (Boston: Harvard University Press, 2006).

_____, *The Unknown American Revolution: The Unruly Birth of Democracy and the Struggle to Create America* (New York: Viking, 2005).

Cassandra Pybus, *Epic Journeys of Freedom: Runaway Slaves of the American Revolution and Their Global Quest for Liberty* (Boston: Beacon Press, 2006).

Benjamin Quarles, *The Negro in the American Revolution* (Chapel Hill: University of North Carolina Press, 1961, 1996).

Alan Taylor, *The Divided Ground: Indians, Settlers, and the Northern Borderland of the American Revolution* (New York: Knopf, 2006).

Alfred Y. Young, Gary B. Nash, and Ray Raphael, eds., *Revolutionary Founders: Rebels, Radicals, and Reformers in the Making of the Nation* (New York: Knopf, 2011).

Ellen Wilson, *The Loyal Blacks* (New York: G. P. Putnam's Sons, 1976).

CHAPTER 12

The Mixing of Peoples

LEARNING OBJECTIVES

- Offer reasons why racial intermingling was far more prevalent in colonial Latin American societies than in the North American colonies.

- Characterize sexual mixing between Natives and Europeans, noting how this differed in the various regions of colonial North America.

- Describe the intermixture of whites and blacks in the North American colonies; explain the eighteenth-century change in views on interracial sex.

- Discuss the racial mixing of African and Indian peoples and in which regions this was common and uncommon.

- Summarize how the red, White, and black populations mixed at the end of the eighteenth century in North America; include discussion of the reasons for White resistance to assimilation, the differing demographic histories of Africans and Native Americans, and the role played by the unequal distribution of power among the three peoples.

While Native Americans, Africans, and Europeans worked out their economic, political, and social destinies in the context of Atlantic imperial rivalry, they also interacted with each other at the most intimate and personal levels. This sexual mixing of individuals of different genetic stocks is usually called *miscegenation*, a word invented 140 years ago by Negrophobic journalists to discredit Abraham Lincoln's position on the plight of African Americans. For many decades, racial crossing was mostly the concern of those attempting to prove inherent qualitative differences of various "racial" groups in a society. This pseudoscientific exercise then became the basis for warning against racial mixing.

For historians, anthropologists, and sociologists, however, racial mingling is the process of acculturation and assimilation—the very human mixing of cultural elements and the absorption of one culture into another.

New scientific breakthroughs in molecular biology oblige us to remember that racial categories are only social constructions and that the vast majority of us combine elements of "African," "Indian," and "European" genetic inheritances. DNA analysis, tracing mitochondrial and Y chromosome structures inherited through the female and male lines respectively, shows definitively that the Americas were a stew of mingled gene pools. Even a White supremacist today, establishing a purely "White" enclave in remote North Dakota, has been dumbstruck to find that DNA analysis shows he is descended from 88 percent European stock and 14 percent sub-Saharan African.[1]

This breakthrough in the genetic code, unknown to our ancestors, does nothing to negate the way seventeenth- and eighteenth-century inhabitants of North America thought and acted. They thought of themselves as members of one "race" or another, though they could argue passionately about just how many races existed. If people of different "races" intermingled, their children were simply "theirs." But the cultural arbiters above them insisted on inventing new categories to label the offspring of such racial crossings. Thus, the discussion that follows traces how cultural power brokers understood themselves racially and how historians have studied and interpreted the interaction of people from different cultural and geographical origins.

Most thinking on the subject of racial intermingling in North America starts with the arresting notion that Europeans on this continent did not intermix with Africans and Indians nearly as much as in colonial Latin American societies. Nor did Africans and Indians mix to the same degree. Latin America was the area of the world where the most extensive blending of gene pools in human history has taken place. North America, where Europeans, Indians, and Africans also converged during roughly the same period of time, is notable for the general absence of such intermixture. The census figures of modern North and South America confirm this belief. They show, for example, that only 20 percent of Venezuelans are classified as White, that only 11 percent of Panamanians are White, that mulattoes in Brazil make up a much larger portion of the population than in the United States, and so forth. Although the criteria for defining membership in a particular racial group vary greatly from place to place, the principal point is not in dispute—that widely practiced interracial sexual liaisons produced a dramatically larger proportion of mestizos (European

Indian), mulattoes (European African), and mustees (African Indian) in the southern half of the Americas than in the northern half.

Two ideological factors have been advanced to explain this trend. First, before the European colonization of the Western Hemisphere, the Spanish and the Portuguese had a history of interacting with people of different cultures, particularly with dark-skinned people, whereas the English did not. Through centuries of war and trade with the Berbers, Moors, and other peoples of the Middle East and North Africa, Iberian society had already absorbed new cultural and genetic elements and developed flexible attitudes about the sexual mixing of peoples. The English, by contrast, had remained within their island fortress, sheltered from other cultures and therefore predisposed toward viewing interracial contacts with suspicion and even alarm.

A corollary to this argument is that the permissive attitude of the Catholic Church toward non-Christian people, the Roman system of law (which protected the slave), and the paternalistic attitudes of the Iberian governments combined to make racial intermixture acceptable and therefore common in the Americas, where Spain and Portugal confronted Indians and Africans in large numbers. By contrast, English Protestantism was unusually rigid in admitting "savage" people to the church. English law had nothing to say on the subject of enslavement, leaving colonists free to create rigid institutions to contain their bound laborers. Moreover, the English government exercised less authority in its colonies, especially in the matter of treating subordinate non-English groups. Given these differences in prior experience, in institutions and attitudes, and in governmental policy, it was not surprising that the history of interracial mixing should be so different in the colonies of Spain and Portugal and in the colonies of England.

Interwoven with these ideological factors are social and demographic conditions that deeply influenced cultural interaction in various parts of the Americas. The availability of White women;

[1]*Los Angeles Times*, November 17, 2013, p. A22.

the ratio of Europeans, Africans, and Native Americans in a given area; the extent to which Indians could be pressed into forced labor systems; and the need to employ non-Europeans in positions of importance—all helped shape the dynamics of intercultural mixing. It made sense that in areas where European women were in short supply, White men overcame the racial prejudices they had brought to the Americas to consort with women of another race. Similarly, where Indians or Africans were relatively numerous, intermixture was far more common than where they were relatively scarce. In New England, where Indians had been devastated by epidemics in the early years of European settlement, little red-White mixing occurred. In Mexico, where Spanish men were engulfed by the densely settled Indians, a great deal of mingling transpired.

Indian-European Engagement

Interaction between Natives and Europeans preceded all other contacts and influenced what later occurred. In New England, and later in the mid-Atlantic colonies of New York, New Jersey, Pennsylvania, and Delaware, sexual mixing between Europeans and Indians was very limited. Englishmen had immigrated to these regions with their families, or, if they were single men, found enough single women to satisfy their needs for marriage partners. Parity between the sexes was established quickly and continued throughout the colonial period. Reinforcing this gender balance was a powerful cultural factor. Immigration by family ensured the rerouting of an entire cultural superstructure to which racial mingling was highly threatening, especially given the view, almost universal among whites, that their culture was superior to those of Native Americans and Africans. Cotton Mather, the influential early eighteenth-century Puritan minister, shrank in horror at the "half Frenchified Indians" and "half

Indianized French" who raided pure-blooded New England villages.[2]

In the Northern colonies, red-White mixing was also limited by the relatively small number of Indians. Epidemic diseases and war rapidly reduced the coastal Native societies during the initial period of contact, and the remaining survivors generally lived at a distance from the colonists, though in some areas such as Cape Cod and Martha's Vineyard remnant tribes lived amongst colonists. Another area where European immigrants lived in close contact, often on opposite sides of a river, was in the Schoharie Valley. Here, German settlers lived with only occasional violence with Oneida and Mohawk Natives for several generations, forging "longstanding economic, linguistic, religious, and personalities that had transformed the identities of both peoples."[3] Still, even here intercultural marriage was uncommon. The zone of intimate sexual relations continued to exist mostly on the edges of White settlement, where fur traders often took Indian wives, or had frequent sexual contact with Native women.

One notable case of intermarriage in Iroquois-New Yorker borderlands involved William Johnson, the Northern Superintendent of Indian Affairs, who took several Mohawk wives. Later knighted for his military exploits, Johnson gained great influence with the Mohawk, who renamed him Warraghiyagey, meaning "man who undertakes great things." This tribute was conferred in large part because Johnson had deviated so radically from the White norm by dressing in Mohawk garb, accepting Mohawk customs, and learning their language, as few White people cared to do. "Something in his natural temper," wrote a contemporary, "responds to Indian ways."[4] However, few followed the example of even a high imperial official when it came to matrimony, so long as European women were available. It was said that Johnson's precedent-shattering

[2]Quoted in Colin Calloway, *New Worlds for All: Indians, Europeans and the Remaking of America* (Baltimore, MD, 1997), p. 179.
[3]David L. Preston, *The Texture of Contact: European and Indian Settler Communities on the Frontiers of Iroquoia, 1667–1783* (Lincoln, NE, 2009), p. 187.
[4]Quoted in ibid., p. 154.

At least a dozen Mexican painters in the eighteenth century openly acknowledged the mixing of Europeans, Africans, and Native Americans as those shown here. Each panel represents how intermixing produced children with various degrees of Spanish, African, and Indian blood. A new vocabulary, displayed in the captions for each panel, evolved to describe the degrees of mixing.

(Courtesy Album/Oronoz/Newscom)

common-law marriage, noteworthy enough to attract the attention of the London newspapers, led to eighteen other red-White unions, but even so the number is insignificant.

In the Chesapeake colonies, a different demographic pattern prevailed in the first few decades. With few exceptions, White women were unavailable in Virginia until about 1620. Yet White men had little recourse to Native women. Several early eighteenth-century Virginia commentators believed that this was the case because the early colonizers found Indian women distasteful. William Byrd, no stranger to the pleasures of the flesh with women of different skin colors, claimed that the English were imbued with a "false delicacy" in the early years and thus could not bring themselves to sleep with Indian women. Byrd believed that the Chesapeake tribes had been offended by this rejection and could never "persuade themselves that the English were heartily their friends, so long as they disdained to intermarry with them." Robert Beverley, author of *The History and Present State of Virginia,* took a similar view, regretting that intermarriage had never occurred and convinced that the Indians had been eager for it.[5]

The limited evidence bearing on this question does not support such views, however. A large part of the predominantly male Virginia colony came from the English lower class, including many who had military experience in Ireland, the Spanish Netherlands, and other parts of the world. They were not known for squeamishness, and their later willingness to consort with African women suggests the infrequent sexual contact with Native women is related to Indian rather than European desires. The English did not establish themselves as conquerors in the early years, as had the Spanish and the Portuguese. Therefore, the Chesapeake tribes were under no compulsion to yield up their women. A month after the Rolfe-Pocahontas marriage, Thomas Dale

was spurned by Powhatan, who refused to allow another daughter to marry the Virginia governor. As for Native women, they had little reason to admire White men, who could hardly keep themselves alive in the early years and who launched attacks on Indian villages once they had gathered strength.

The one case of intermarriage within the White community involved John Rolfe and Pocahontas. Although their love for each other was apparently genuine, this was a political marriage. It is sometimes claimed that the King's Council, by deliberating whether Rolfe had committed high treason in marrying an Indian princess, discouraged any further intermarriage. But the charge under consideration was high treason for marrying the daughter of a quasi-enemy, and Pocahontas and Rolfe were fêted in London wherever they went, including the royal court. By the early eighteenth century, the Board of Trade was pushing an official policy of intermarriage in the American colonies, indication enough that moral scruples were not offended in England by thoughts of the commingling of red and White blood.

By the end of the second Indian war in 1644, the Native population in the tidewater area had shriveled to only a small fraction of the White population. By the conclusion of Bacon's Rebellion in 1676, when White women were much more available, only a few Natives remained within the areas of White settlement. This fact puts in perspective Governor Alexander Spotswood's claim in 1717 that the "inclinations of our people are not the same with those of [the French] nation" regarding intermarriage.[6] Racial prejudice no doubt would have limited such partnerships. But neither the need nor the opportunity for Indian-White marriages remained. French "inclinations" in New France were different, not so much because of variations in national character as because of different needs. Even along the

---

[5]William Byrd, *Histories of the Dividing Line Betwixt Virginia and North Carolina,* William K. Boyd, ed. (Raleigh, NC, 1929), p. 3; Robert Beverley, *The History and Present State of Virginia,* Louis B. Wright, ed. (Chapel Hill, NC, 1960), pp. 38–39.
[6]R. A. Brock, ed., *The Official Letters of Alexander Spotswood . . . ,* Virginia Historical Society Collections (Richmond, VA, 1885), 2: 227.

St. Lawrence, where Frenchmen commonly took Indian wives or mistresses, European women were much preferred. But Indian women remained preferable to no women at all. The same was true in Spanish Florida where "Spanish-Indian marriage began immediately and continued persistently through two centuries of Spanish occupation."[7]

The only English region in which the demographic profile even roughly approximated that in the Spanish and French North American colonies was the Southeast—the Carolinas and Georgia. In the early years, White women were relatively unavailable, but Native women could easily be found. The result was considerable contact between English and Scottish men and Indian women, much as in French Canada and the Spanish Southwest. Unembarrassed sexual relations between the two peoples seem to have been the rule. This conduct was especially true of the fur traders who operated in the interior regions and would not give up the satisfactions of Indian "she-bed-fellows," as one eighteenth-century commentator called them. Women were specifically designated by the tribes as "Trading Girls" and were given special haircuts to denote that their role was to satisfy the traders while getting money "by their natural parts." Only these women were available to White men, however, for Indian males "are desirous (if possible) to keep their wives to themselves, as well as those in other parts of the world."[8]

While traders consorted with Native women in the interior, White Carolinians confronted Indian women sold into slavery in the coastal settlements. During the first half-century of the colony's history, the large number of children of Indian mothers and White fathers in Charleston testified to the extensive European-Indian sexual encounters there. White men outnumbered White women in South Carolina by more than thirteen to nine as late as 1708, and womanless men were not reluctant to avail themselves of Native

women. In Georgia, no less a figure than Thomas Bosomworth, chaplain of Oglethorpe's utopian colony, found it respectable to marry a Creek woman in the early years of settlement. Many others followed his example, including John McDonald and Alexander Cameron, deputy Indian commissioners to the Cherokees in the late colonial period.

Aside from the lower South, the limited degree of red-White sexual intermingling forecast the overall failure of the two cultures to merge, though the porous boundaries between the two peoples had led to incessant interaction. The amalgamation of Indians and whites never proceeded very far in eighteenth-century North America because Native people were seldom eager to trade their culture for one they found inferior and because the colonists found the Indians useful only as trappers of furs, slave catchers, consumers of European trade goods, and military allies. All these functions were best performed outside the White communities. Consider the striking contrast to the Spanish colonies in the Americas, where the lack of White women and the subjugation of Native laborers brought the two peoples into intimate contact, thus producing a large mestizo population. The most conservative estimates show that mestizos reached 25 percent of the population in early nineteenth-century Spanish America. Many of these individuals rose to positions of artisan, foreman on the *encomiendas*, militiaman, and even collector of tithes and taxes. But in colonial North America, the half-Indian, half-White person, usually the product of a liaison between a White fur trader and a Native woman, remained mostly within Indian society. A considerable number of the male offspring became fur traders themselves or intermediaries between English and Indian society. Others, such as Thayendanegea (Joseph Brant) of the Mohawks and Alexander McGillivray of the Creeks, became noted leaders of Indian resistance in the second half

---

[7]Kathleen Deagan, "Accommodation and Resistance: The Process and Impact of Spanish Colonization in the Southeast," in David H. Thomas, ed., *Columbian Consequences*, vol. 2 (1990), p. 305.
[8]John Lawson, *A New Voyage to Carolina*, Hugh Lefler, ed. (Chapel Hill, NC, 1967), pp. 189–190.

of the eighteenth century. Although historians have not yet systematically studied the American mestizos, whom whites sneeringly called "half-breeds," it appears that these persons were the Native Americans most alienated from White society. One Virginian in 1757 wrote that traders who consorted with Indian "squaws" left their offspring "like bulls or bears to be provided for at random by their mothers. . . . As might be expected," he pointed out, "some of these bastards have been the leading men or war captains that have done us so much mischief."[9]

The one case in which transculturation between Indians and Europeans did occur involved Indianized whites rather than the Europeanized Indians. Throughout the colonial period, much to the horror of White leaders, small numbers of colonists ran away to Indian settlements, or, when they were captured in war and had lived with a tribe for a few years, often refused to return to White society. This "reversion to savagery," as those who insisted on the superiority of White culture regarded it, has attracted the attention of American novelists since the late eighteenth century. For White colonists the prospect of their own people preferring the Native way of life was a disturbing anomaly. "None can imagine what it is to be captivated, and enslaved to such atheistical, proud, wild, cruel, barbarous, brutish (in one word) diabolical creatures as these, the worst of the heathen," wrote a seventeenth-century Puritan.[10]

In spite of such fantasy characterizations, the colonizers had to live with the fact that some of their own kind found life in Native villages preferable to life in Anglo-American society. To make matters worse, virtually no Indians took the reverse route, choosing to remain in White society after exposure to it. "By what power does it come to pass," asked J. Hector St. John Crèvecoeur, the famous Frenchman who lived in America for more than a decade in the late colonial period, in his celebrated *Letters from an American Farmer*,

that children who have been adopted when young among these people, can never be prevailed on to readopt European manners? Many an anxious parent I have seen after the last war [Seven Years' War], who at the return of peace, went to the Indian villages where they knew their children had been carried in captivity; when to their inexpressible sorrow, they found them so perfectly Indianised, that many knew them no longer, and those whose more advanced ages permitted them to recollect their fathers and mothers, absolutely refused to follow them, and ran to their adopted parents for protection against the effusions of love their unhappy real parents lavished on them! . . . There must be in their social bond something singularly captivating, and far superior to anything to be boasted of among us; for thousands of Europeans are Indians, and we have no examples of even one of those Aborigines having from choice become Europeans.[11]

The phenomenon of the "White Indians" is partially explained by the Indian custom of adopting into their communities as full-fledged members any persons captured in war. This practice became more important as disease and intensified warfare depleted the tribal populations in the century after the Europeans washed ashore. In many instances a bereaved Native family adopted a European captive to replace a lost child or other relative. This integration of newcomers into the kinship system and into the community at large, without judgmental comparisons of the superiority of the captor's culture, made it easy for the captured "outsider" to make a rapid personal adjustment. A White child taken into Indian society was treated on equal terms and prepared for any role open to others of his or her age. That a number of whites and blacks who had fled to

[9]Quoted in James Hugo Johnston, *Race Relations in Virginia and Miscegenation in the South, 1776–1860* (Amherst, MA, 1970), p. 169.
[10]Quoted in Roy Harvey Pearce, "The 'Ruines of Mankind': The Indian and the Puritan Mind," *Journal of the History of Ideas*, 13 (1952): 205.
[11]J. Hector St. John Crèvecoeur, *Letters from an American Farmer* (New York, 1957), pp. 208–209.

THE
NARRATIVE
OF THE
CAPTIVITY AND RESTORATION
OF
Mrs. *Mary Rowlandson,*

Who was taken Prifoner by the INDIANS with feveral others, and treated in the moft barbarous and cruel Manner by thofe vile Savages : With many other remarkable Events during her TRAVELS.

Written by her own Hand, for her private Ufe, and now made public at the earneft Defire of fome Friends, and for the Benefit of the afflicted.

Title page of *A Narrative of the Captivity, Sufferings, and Removes of Mrs. Mary Rowlandson.*
(Courtesy Fotosearch/Getty Images)

Indian communities or had been captured by them became chiefs is dramatic evidence of the receptiveness of Indian cultures to "outsiders."

The most talked-about and troubling cultural conversion in New England was that of Eunice Williams. In 1704, when she was 8, Eunice and her minister father's family was captured when a Mohawk party allied to the French descended on Deerfield, Massachusetts, and overpowered the entire village. Dozens of the Deerfield captives perished on the punishing march of more than 300 miles through snow to the Mohawk village of Kahnawake, north of Montreal. Here Eunice spent the rest of her life. Growing up Mohawk, she became Catholic. At age 16 she married a young Mohawk. Repeatedly, she refused to return to her family, who were sent back to Massachusetts as part of a prisoner exchange. She forgot English, forgot Protestantism, and forgot her biological family. In many churches of New England, Puritans prayed for her "redemption" from "captivity." But Eunice had found a faithful and loving husband and had raised two daughters (who would later marry Mohawk men). Marguerite Arosen, Eunice Williams's Mohawk name, thought of a return to her Deerfield home as captivity rather than redemption.[12]

European colonists differed sharply in incorporating the "other" from a different culture. Though a number of White families adopted Indian children, the general pattern was to isolate the newcomer socially. "It was not that the Indian could not be raised 'up' to the level of civilization," writes one student of the subject, "but rather the lack of an equivalent desire on the part of whites to welcome and assimilate the Indian, and the absence of any established cultural means that would mediate the transition from one culture to the other in a manner that was psychologically sound."[13] Even Christianized Indians trained in White schools, such as the Mohegan Samson Occum (1723–1792), were expected to return to Native society rather than occupy a place of dignity among whites. White colonists always regarded Native Americans as aliens and rarely allowed them to live within White society except as servants or dependents. Operating from mostly small communities and regarding Natives not only as inferior but also as barbaric, the colonizers "erected a defensive wall of heightened consciousness of superiority" in order to keep out those who seemed so threatening.[14] This unwillingness to incorporate Indians into their communities created a wall blocking a merging of two cultures. By contrast, Florida's Spanish governor described how the Indians were "settled amongst our plantations . . . and are as it were a people interwoven with us."[15]

Across the Color Line

White-black intermixture in colonial America is a more complicated phenomenon because Europeans and Africans were always in close proximity, both where White women were plentiful and where they were scarce. This physical and psychological closeness led to widespread sexual contact, but it rarely involved intermarriage. At first glance, one might imagine that the rarity of racial intermarriage stemmed from a deep-seated White aversion to blackness itself, but if this was the case, how can we explain what countless observers of eighteenth-century society claimed to see—that "the country swarms with mulatto bastards," as one Virginian crudely put it.[16] Such comments do not define interracial mingling with statistical precision, but eighteenth-century censuses help to clarify the point. In Maryland in 1755, a special census showed that 8 percent of the Negroes in the colony were mulatto. In

---

[12]See John Demos, *The Unredeemed Captive: A Family Story from Early America* (New York, 1994) for the full story of Eunice Williams.

[13]A. Irving Hallowell, "American Indians, White and Black: The Phenomenon of Transculturation," *Current Anthropology*, 4 (1963): 527.

[14]Ibid., p. 528.

[15]Quoted in Calloway, *New Worlds for All . . .* , p. 185.

[16]Quoted in Johnston, *Race Relations in Virginia . . .* , p. 170.

Rhode Island, the census of 1783 revealed that 16.5 percent of the Negroes were of mixed blood. A register of slaves for Chester County, Pennsylvania, in 1780 listed 20 percent of the Negroes as mulattoes.[17] In all three areas, White females were almost as numerous as White men, indicating that even when White women were available, White men frequently had sexual relations with black women.

These contacts would probably have been even more extensive if black women had been available in the period when White women were in short supply. However, enslaved Africans did not arrive in the English colonies in significant numbers until the end of the seventeenth century, and by that time the number of White women in all but the infant colony of South Carolina nearly equaled the number of White men. In the Southern plantations in 1720, the slave population was about 50,000; not more than about 10,000 of these could have been adult black females. At the same time, some 70,000 adult White colonists inhabited the Southern colonies, of whom almost half were women. This state of affairs contrasts starkly with the situation in Portuguese Brazil, Spanish Peru, Spanish and French North American colonies, and even the English islands in the West Indies. In all these zones of contact, European women were relatively unavailable for much longer periods of time.

The example of the English Caribbean colonies provides further evidence that prior attitudes did not determine the nature and degree of racial intermingling. English women were not present in roughly equal numbers with White men until deep into the second century of settlement, so African women were unhesitatingly exploited to fill the gap. Even married White plantation owners "keep a mulatto or black girl in the house or at lodgings for certain purposes," reported one traveler, and a famous eighteenth-century historian of the English sugar islands colorfully pronounced

that "he who should presume to show any displeasure against such a thing as simple fornication, would for his pains be accounted a simple blockhead."[18]

In the mainland colonies, however, interracial sex brought private pleasure but public condemnation. The latter was mainly a late seventeenth-century development. Not until 1662, when Virginia passed a law imposing a fine for fornication between White and black partners that was twice the usual amount, did an unambiguous law appear on the books that expressed public distaste for racial intermingling. White legislators banned interracial marriage in Virginia in 1691, in Massachusetts in 1705, in Maryland in 1715, and thereafter in Delaware, Pennsylvania, North Carolina, and Georgia.

The key change in the eighteenth century was not a marked increase in miscegenation, reflecting heightened private urges, but a shifting of public attitudes among White leaders toward racial mixing. The grand jury in Charleston, South Carolina, for example, inveighed against "the too common practice of criminal conversation with Negro and other slave wenches in this province" in 1743.[19] Similar comments can be found in other colonies. But with the black population growing rapidly and slavery becoming deeply rooted in colonial society, lawmakers discovered that, although they could not manage biology, they could at least police the bloodlines of the dominant group through laws prohibiting interracial marriage. Under these laws, mulattoes could never be legitimate and would always be classified as black.

With slavery touching the lives of most inhabitants, White colonists worked to contain the black population in a tight web of authority and to assert their dominance. One way of accomplishing this goal was to emphasize the heathen or "savage" condition of the African that justified slavery on the one hand and made sexual

---

[17]Edward B. Reuter, *The Mulatto in the United States* (rpr. New York, 1969), pp. 112–114; Evarts B. Greene and Virginia D. Harrington, *American Population before the Federal Census of 1790* (New York, 1932), pp. 69–70.
[18]Quoted in Winthrop Jordan, *White Over Black: American Attitudes toward the Negro, 1550–1812* (Chapel Hill, NC, 1968), p. 140.
[19]Quoted in ibid., p. 140.

contact legally impermissible on the other. A variety of laws and public statements described the offspring of White-black copulation as "spurious" or "mongrel." Moreover, mulattoes received no higher standing than pure-blood blacks and in law were regarded as fully black. This treatment contrasted sharply with the situation of the mulatto in almost every other part of the Americas, where three-tiered racial systems had evolved. But sexual relations with black women continued. Desire could not be legislated out of the White emotional apparatus, and if the laws and public pronouncements did not correspond with private urges, little harm was done so long as laws preserved the domination of whites by disowning children of mixed racial inheritance.

By the early eighteenth century, racial attitudes toward Indians and African Americans began to diverge. This split was closely tied to striking differences in the nature and degree of sexual contact that characterized red-White and black-White relationships. White attitudes toward the black man cannot be dissociated from the fact that sexual relations, especially between White men and black women, were frequent and usually coercive. White men banned interracial marriage as a way of stating with legal finality that the African American, even when free, was not the equal of the White man. Likewise, sexually exploiting black women outside of marriage enhanced White male power. Racial intermingling, so long as it involved free White men and enslaved black women, intimately and brutally proclaimed the superior rights and strength of White society.

Sexual contact of this character had no parallel in the case of Indian women. When accessible to fur traders, the Indian woman was not in the hapless position of a slave woman, nearly defenseless to resist the advances of a master with power of life and death over her. If a Native woman chose to submit to a White man, it was usually on mutually agreeable terms. Furthermore, Indian men rarely molested female prisoners, believing that intercourse with a potential clan member was incestuous. In these differences

lay the source and meaning of a fear that has long preoccupied White Americans—the fear of black men lusting after White women. This vision of the "black rapist" pictures black men rising not in quest of their freedom but in pursuit of White women. Many scholars have explained this fear as White male guilt, originating in the sexual exploitation of black women and triggering an image of the black avenger filled with anger and poised to retaliate against those who first enslaved him and then plundered his woman.

This element of sexual fear rarely enters the literature concerning the Indian. Because guilt was rarely aroused by the noncoercive contacts with Native women, White men, when they encountered hostile Indian males, rarely pictured them as sexual avengers. In the eighteenth century, the Indian was almost never caricatured as the frenzied rapist, lurking in the bush or stalking White women. Indeed, the Indian male was sometimes viewed as a peculiarly asexual creature. This perception, in turn, created a confused image in the White mind of a hostile, and yet sexually passive, "savage." His hostility was not doubted; but the hostile Indian was commonly regarded as a man with knife in hand, bent on obtaining the scalp of the White encroacher. It was imagined that hostile black men had focused on a different part of the anatomy in their quest for revenge.

The contrast to the sexual dynamics of Spanish-Indian contact is striking. The Spanish brought enslaved Africans to their colonies much earlier than did the English and brought them in larger numbers proportionate to their European masters. What is more, with not enough colonists to serve all the middle-range occupational niches in their societies, the Spanish used Africans as craftsmen, supervisors of enslaved Indians, and even as militiamen. This practice gave many African males a status far above that of field laborer. No doubt, status-seeking Spaniards avoided marriage with Africans, and some colonial officials tried to obtain a royal ban on African-Spanish intermarriage. But all such attempts were doomed. Nobody, as one historian puts it, "was successful in keeping Spaniards, Indians, and Africans out of each other's gene pools."[20] This racial fusion did not stymie racial prejudice, but it modulated it. The offspring of Spanish mixed-race marriages faced discrimination and thwarted ambition, and those with African ancestry had more limited chances than those of Indian ancestry. Not for many generations would Mexicans, for example, celebrate the creation of "the cosmic race" produced by the mingling of African, Indian, and Spanish blood. But if prejudice remained, the fusion continued.

In the North American colonies, the English emphatically rejected racial fusion, objecting strongly not to sexual relations with dark-skinned women but to conferring status on Africans by accepting such intermingling as legitimate or by admitting its biological product to White society. Determined to prohibit a rise in the social status of those who labored at the bottom of society, White colonizers blocked the mulatto from occupying a position midway between White and black. The smallest portion of African blood classified a person as black; and to be black was almost always to be a slave. The "mulatto escape hatch" in Latin American society that Carl Degler has described hardly existed in British North America, for there was little need to call upon Africans or mulattoes for important, status-conferring services, and the well-rooted institution of the White family, an outgrowth of a family pattern of settlement, gave special reasons for excluding the living evidence of a sexual congress that threatened the purity of White culture. The single exception was South Carolina, which maintained the social-sexual system of the West Indies, where so many of its planters had originated and where White women were in short supply. By prohibiting racial intermarriage, winking at interracial sex, and defining all mixed offspring as black, White society found the answer to its labor needs; its submerged sexual desires; its compulsion to maintain its culture purebred; and the problem of maintaining, at least in theory, absolute social control.

This calculus of sexual politics was the peculiar legacy of British North America, linked not so much to the national prejudices of the English as to the historical circumstances of English, Irish, and Scottish settlement there. This outcome is demonstrated by the status of the mulatto in English Jamaica. By the mid-eighteenth century, more than 90 percent of the Jamaican population was black, and White men greatly outnumbered White women. Such a distorted demographic history demanded a system in which black women were available to White men without scruple and where mulatto offspring could rise to places of importance. This is precisely what happened. Miscegenation occurred on a massive scale, and by 1733, the White legislature conferred privileges and property on mulattoes. The same was true in South Carolina, which never banned interracial marriage and conferred higher status on mulattoes.

Between African and Indian

The convergence of African and Indian peoples is the least studied subject in the history of race relations in early North America. Moreover, the terminology and institutions created by White Americans have disguised the degree of red-black intermixing by defining the children of mixed red-black ancestry as black and often using the term *mulatto* to define half-African, half-Indian persons. DNA analysis is revealing that red-black intermixing was far more common than previously believed, and this is being confirmed by scores of family stories now being publicly aired.

In New England, where the coastal tribes had been terribly reduced before more than a trickle of Africans had arrived, little cross-fertilization was possible. It is notable, however, that in the few places, such as Cape Cod and Martha's Vineyard, where Natives did survive, their mixture with a small number of free Negroes was extensive by the late eighteenth century. This mixture also occurred in a number

---

[20]Jorge Klor de Alva, "*Mestizaje* from Spain to Aztlan," in *New World Orders: Casta Painting and Colonial Latin America* (New York, 1996), p. 60.

of New England towns along the coast, where many enslaved Indians from South Carolina had been imported in the early eighteenth century. A census in South Kingston, Rhode Island, in 1730 showed 333 enslaved blacks and 223 enslaved Indians; the resulting intermixture of blood is not to be wondered at. A report in Massachusetts in 1795 stated that the blacks of Massachusetts "have generally . . . left the country and resorted to the maritime towns. Some are incorporated, and their breed is mixed with the Indians of Cape Cod and Martha's Vineyard."[21] Years later, Herman Melville wrote of the African-Indian whalers who went to sea from Nantucket Island.

In New York, which contained the largest slave population north of the Chesapeake, intermixture of slaves and Indians, though unquantifiable, was far from unusual. Negro and Indian slaves had formed a blood bond in 1712, when they joined hands in an insurrection in New York City. Thereafter, provincial officials knew that the best place to look for escaped Africans was among the small local tribes that remained on Long Island and in the Hudson River valley. It was in the cities of the North, however, that the enslaved were concentrated, and these were the places where Indians in the second half of the eighteenth century only occasionally resided.

In the Chesapeake colonies, the possibility of African-Indian fusion was also reduced by the sheer force of circumstances. When Indians were relatively numerous in the tidewater region of Maryland and Virginia, slaves were present only in small numbers. In 1670, fewer than 2,000 enslaved Africans inhabited the Chesapeake region, and by the end of Bacon's Rebellion in 1676, the Indian population in the regions settled by whites was insignificant. Nonetheless, many small coastal tribes gave refuge to runaway slaves. The descendants of these Africans, who mixed with White colonizers as well, formed isolated tri-ethnic communities in Delaware, Maryland, Virginia, and North Carolina. The Wesorts of Maryland are one example. The name *Wesort*

came to differentiate "we-sort-of-people" from "you-sort-of-people." Baptismal and marriage records tell the story of seven families that made up the core of this mixed race of people. One family traces back to the 1670s, when an enslaved African married an Irish maidservant. Since then, black, red, and white bloodlines blended into one group, creating distinctive physical features. The majority of Wesorts have straight brown or black hair. Some have Indian facial features, but blue eyes are not uncommon. Today, other triracial societies such as the Lumbees, Red Bones, and Brass Ankles maintain their distinctive identities from Alabama to New York.

Only in North Carolina, South Carolina, and Georgia did Natives and Africans in substantial numbers confront Europeans simultaneously. Here was the one area in British America where the situation mirrored that prevailing in most regions of Spanish and French colonization.

The colonizers' position of numerical inferiority led to gnawing fears that Indians and slaves would combine forces and overpower them. Keeping Africans and Indians apart, therefore, became a priority. Such fears were well grounded, for during the pre-Revolutionary period the Natives of the Southeast remained numerous in White areas of settlement and, combined with the enslaved Africans, greatly exceeded the White population. White South Carolinians, for example, were outnumbered by their black and their Indian slaves after decades of colonization. Even by the mid-eighteenth century, only about 25,000 whites inhabited the colony along with some 40,000 black slaves and 60,000 Indians gathered in the towns of the Creek, Cherokee, Choctaw, Chickasaw, and subsidiary tribes. Twenty years later, on the eve of the Revolution, the White population had increased to about 50,000, but the slave population had increased even faster to about 80,000. South Carolinians lived surrounded by those who, if they could find a means for concerted action, might overwhelm them at any moment. Only through the greatest

---

[21]Quoted in Kenneth W. Porter, "Relations between Negroes and Indians within the Present Limits of the United States," *Journal of Negro History*, 17 (1932): 311.

vigilance and through policies designed to keep their enemies divided could White South Carolinians remain in control of the unstable triracial ground on which they all stood.

That White Carolinians were able to maintain their grip testifies to their ability to play one Native tribe against another and to their partial success in keeping enslaved Indians and Africans divided. The policy, as one Carolinian put it, was "to make Indians and Negroes a check upon each other lest by their vastly superior numbers we should be crushed by one or the other."[22] One way to accomplish this goal was to prohibit African Americans, whether slave or free, from traveling in Indian country as traders or traders' helpers. Also, White authorities repeatedly asked Indian tribes to return fugitive slaves and pressed the Creeks, Cherokees, and other tribes to sign treaties with clauses stipulating that escaped slaves must be turned over to the Carolina government. In addition, White Southern legislatures offered bounties to Indians for capturing and returning escaped slaves. The legislatures also dispatched patrols to prevent slaves from reaching Indian country. Fostering suspicion of Africans among the Indians was another way to keep mutual aid between the two groups to a minimum. "It has been always the policy of this government," wrote Governor Lyttelton in 1738, "to create an aversion in them [Indians] to Negroes."[23]

Incorporating enslaved blacks into the South Carolina militia during Indian wars served a double purpose. Without them, the Carolinians would have been hard pressed to defeat their Tuscarora, Yamasee, or Cherokee enemies; also, the use of black soldiers helped to remind the Indians that Africans were not their friends. Half the Carolinian force that Governor Charles Craven led against the Yamasee in 1715 was black, and another black company marched with Captain Pight in the same campaign. When these forces proved incapable of defeating the Yamasees, the Assembly called for a "standing army" of 1,200 men, including "400 negroes or other slaves."[24] The 1740 expedition against Spanish St. Augustine included seventy-three slaves. Thereafter, a growing fear of black insurgency dampened White desire to use black troops. Caught up in the Cherokee War, the South Carolina assembly defeated a motion to equip 500 slaves "to serve against the savages."

Just as White colonists used slaves to quash Indian uprisings, they employed Indians to put down black rebellions. In the most spectacular black insurrection in the South, the Stono Rebellion of 1739, the South Carolina government recruited "settlement" Indians to pursue the Africans, who had eluded White militia and were fleeing to Spanish Florida. The assembly equipped the Indians with clothes, guns, and ammunition, and promised £50 for each slave brought back alive or £25 for each slave returned dead. Other attempts were made at warding off black rebellions by relocating Indian tribes into areas where large numbers of slaves were developing the rice and indigo plantations. This policy, originated in the early eighteenth century, was pursued with special vigor in the 1730s, when the buildup of the slave population kept Carolina pulsating with fears of black rebellion. In 1737, White leaders requested Cherokee warriors "to come down to the settlements to be an awe to the Negroes."[25]

In spite of these efforts to promote hatred between Indians and Africans, Native communities harbored many slaves throughout the colonial period. Measuring this phenomenon precisely is impossible, but the persistent inclusion in Indian treaties of a clause providing for the return of escaped slaves indicates that the bounties offered Indians for slave catching often produced little response. The Tuscarora tribe, for example, gave

---

[22]Quoted in William S. Willis, Jr., "Divide and Rule: Red, White, and Black in the Southeast," *Journal of Negro History*, 48 (1963): 165.
[23]Ibid.
[24]David D. Wallace, *South Carolina: A Short History, 1520–1948* (Chapel Hill, NC, 1951), p. 88.
[25]Willis, "Divide and Rule . . . ," p. 175.

refuge to a large number of captive Africans in the period before the outbreak of war in 1711. When war came, these Africans fought alongside the Tuscaroras, and one of them, named Harry, was said to have designed the Tuscarora fortress on a tributary of the Neuse River. Four years later, during the Yamasee uprising, fugitive slaves were also active in the raids on White settlements. Even after the Yamasees had given up their struggle, they refused to return their black friends, which, according to one Carolina official, "has encouraged a great many more [slaves] lately to run away to that place."[26]

Because the Yamasees were located along the coast between the English settlements and the Spanish outposts in Florida, slaves had additional reason to flee in this direction. As early as 1699, the Spanish issued a royal decree promising protection to all fugitive English slaves and repeated this offer periodically during the first half of the eighteenth century. Even after the Yamasee War, the Indians not only encouraged Carolina slaves to join them but also engaged in slave-stealing raids on outlying plantations. In 1738, twenty-three slaves escaped from Port Royal and made their way to St. Augustine. They joined an enclave of free Negroes where thirty-eight escaped slave men, many with families, were already settled. When Governor Oglethorpe of Georgia launched his attack on St. Augustine in 1740, he faced the combined resistance of Spanish, Indians, and former Carolina slaves, who repulsed the expedition in which the Carolinians invested more than £7,000. Two years later, the Spaniards retaliated with an attack on Georgia; among the invasion forces was a regiment whose Negro commanders "were clothed in lace, bore the same rank as the White officers, and with equal freedom and familiarity walked and conversed with their comrades and chief."[27]

The Creeks also harbored runaway slaves and adopted them into their lineages. In 1725, a Spanish delegation arrived at Coweta, the principal town of the Lower Creeks, with an escaped Carolina slave who served as interpreter between the Creeks and the Spanish. Still another refugee African was an interpreter between the French and the Creeks during this period. The threat of losing slaves to the Creeks was great enough in 1722 for South Carolina's governor to issue a proclamation prohibiting Creeks from entering the White settlements, since their visits, purportedly for the purpose of trade, were encouraging large numbers of captive Africans to follow them back into the interior. As late as the 1760s, the Carolinians were pressing the Creeks for the return of runaway slaves. Although blacks were occasionally handed over, hundreds remained in the Indian territory, blending their cultures with those of the Creeks, Cherokees, and others.

By fashioning the harshest slave code of any of the colonies, by paying dearly for Indian support at critical moments, and by militarizing their society, White Carolinians restricted the flow of black slaves into the backcountry. The Cherokee hill country never became the equivalent of the mountain hideaways of runaway Africans in Jamaica or the Brazilian *quilombos* as a refuge for runaway slaves. But neither was the policy of fostering hatred between the two groups entirely successful. Throughout the eighteenth century, slaves ran away and joined Indian settlements. On occasion, when the price was high enough or the need to propitiate the Carolinians great enough, Indians returned black runaways to their White masters. But in most cases, the fugitive slaves disappeared into Indian society, where they took Indian wives, produced children of mixed race, and contributed to African-Indian acculturation in the same fashion as those slaves who lived with settlement Indians in the coastal region. So common was African-Indian contact in the Southern colonies that the term *mustee* entered the Southern vocabulary in order to categorize the offspring of African and Indian parents.

In spite of the considerable contact between Indians and Africans, their relations never ripened into an affinity of oppressed peoples to

---

[26]Quoted in Chapman J. Milling, *Red Carolinians* (Chapel Hill, NC, 1940), p. 153.
[27]Kenneth W. Porter, "Negroes on the Southern Frontier, 1670–1763," *Journal of Negro History*, 33 (1948): 68.

unite against their oppressors. Never in the colonial period did Creeks, Cherokees, and other Southern tribes work in a concerted way to unite with enslaved Africans. The problems of communication, language, and cultural differences made this difficult. More important, Indian groups, especially after the Yamasee War of 1715, were more intent on using White society for their own ends than eliminating the colonists altogether. In their steadfast adherence to self-interest, they acted variously toward Africans. Sometimes they held them as slaves; sometimes they gave them refuge and adopted them into village life; sometimes they returned enough of them to satisfy White demands; and sometimes they hunted them down for pay. Only when an Indian tribe had a firm trading connection outside the English orbit, such as the Apalachees of Spanish Florida, were the enslaved Africans of English colonists welcomed without qualification.

In the final analysis, the mixing of peoples in eighteenth-century America depended on both demographic and historical circumstances. By 1770, some 2.3 million persons lived east of the Allegheny Mountains; but of these, about 1.75 million were White, some 450,000 were black, and only about 100,000 were Indian. Such a preponderance of whites stood in stark contrast to almost every other part of the Americas. All other factors aside, this would have guaranteed a fairly low level of racial mixing, although recent DNA analysis, still very partial, shows that the merging of gene pools was much larger than previously reckoned.

Where people of different racial ancestry did live in close proximity, considerable interracial contact occurred. White colonists in North America did not sanction interracial liaisons, as in many European colonies, but this attitude reflected not only a difference in settlement patterns but also the special concern for the preservation of family-centered "civilized society." Whatever prior attitudes may have been brought by the Spanish to New Mexico, the French to Canada, or the English to the West Indies, these colonists represented small minorities of the population in their New World environments. Short

of defeating their own purposes, they could not have implemented the strict ethnocentric social attitudes and laws that the White colonists legislated in North America. What is surprising is that the color line remained so porous in a society where the dominant group was making such strenuous claims for keeping its bloodstream pure. The gap between public pronouncements, as expressed in laws prohibiting miscegenation, and actual social practice, as visible in the large mixed-blood population, can be explained only by the desire of White men to maintain social control while straying across the color line for casual sexual relations.

Blending and Bleeding: The Mixing of Red, White, and Black

By the end of the eighteenth century, American society, some 4 million strong, was far from knitting together a blended culture. More than 200 years of European colonization and the continuous interaction of three large and internally diverse cultural groups had left a conglomeration of cultural entities. Each cultural bloc was rich with experiences—from soul-wracking to uplifting—varying traditions, folkways, and a multitude of hopes for the future.

The complex interaction of the three cultural groups was filled with paradoxes. English newcomers to the Americas claimed that they wished to assimilate Indians and Africans, but they found that the most effective way to exploit the land of one and the labor of the other was to follow a nonassimilationist policy. Bringing Christianity to non-Christians was an expensive and time-consuming enterprise, best left to men of the cloth. But Protestant England had only a pale version of the black- and brown-robed Jesuits and Franciscans who brought the "true message" to Native Americans. Puritan, Anglican, Presbyterian, Baptist, Dutch and German Reformed, and Quaker churchpeople made only minimal efforts to instruct Indian tribes in Christian doctrine, and most of the efforts were inspired by the expectation that conversion would go hand in hand with pacification and political control. To be sure, in the Great Awakening a small wave of missionizing attempts made evangelical inroads among Native people and enslaved Africans, but the Awakeners themselves were regarded by polite society as disruptive and dangerous for attempting to dissolve social, sexual, and racial boundaries. In the late colonial period and even more so after the American Revolution, Christian doctrine spread among the enslaved in the upper South. But throughout South Carolina and Georgia, planters carefully shielded Africans from the potentially radical message of Christianity. Thus, a large majority of them died strangers to Christian religion. In education it was the same: the enslaved were educated in those things that enabled them to work more effectively; but slave owners discouraged or stifled education as a path of inquiry, knowing its potential to cultivate aspirations regarded as inappropriate to those whose servitude was lifelong. However, in the North, free African Americans, after the Revolution, flocked to Protestant churches of their own and formed schools attached to these churches.

A handful of reformers and churchpeople kept alive the humanitarian impulse, believing that by uplifting Africans and Indians from what they regarded as heathenism, these peoples could be assimilated into Anglo-American society. But most eighteenth-century whites regarded the two cultural minorities in their midst as unassimilable. This is evident when the emancipation of slaves in the Revolutionary era brought cries for their repatriation to Africa. So far as the assimilation of Indians was concerned, nothing could have been less desirable to European colonists, who coveted Indian land but not land with Indians on it.

Also working against assimilation was the inner need of White colonists to justify the exploitation of Africans and Indians by insisting on the wide gap that separated "savagery" from "civilization." By definition, assimilation would narrow this gap, making Africans and Indians more like Europeans. But when mighty master and lowly slave, or "rational European" and "unreasoning savage" were admitted to be fellow humans, either in outward manners or inner capacity, then the rationale of domination and exploitation would crumble. This need to deny a likeness and to oppose measures that would increase the similarity of peoples in colonial society was an important reason for resisting the Christianization of enslaved Africans. It also worked to convince White colonists that Indians were unassimilable. One of the mistaken notions about colonial Americans that endured in England was that the settlers would happily receive the missionaries of the Anglican Society for the Propagation of the Gospel, which hoped to convert both slaves and Indians to the word of Christ. The Bishop of London summed up this misconception of the colonial desire for assimilation when he "referred to Negroes as 'truly a part of our own nation'—which was just what the colonists were sure Negroes were not."[28] The same was true for Indians.

A second paradox was that White Americans developed the most negative attitudes toward the cultural minority in its midst that was most valuable to it—African Americans—and held the more positive attitudes toward the cultural minority that stood only as an obstacle to White society once their military assistance was no longer needed—Native Americans. Colonial society grew in size and strength in direct relationship to an increase in slaves and a decrease in "land-cluttering" Indians. Yet it was the black African upon whom the colonists fastened the most indelibly negative images. The key to this irony was that the colonist almost always encountered Africans as slaves and thus came to think of them as abject and less than human creatures. But the English settlers met Indians as adversaries or half-trusted allies. The Native maintained the freedom to come and go, to attack and kill, to give and withhold support, and to retain political sovereignty. Though hated

---

[28]Jordan, *White Over Black . . .* , p. 208.

for many of these things, Native people earned a grudging respect. The Anglo-Indian relationship in the eighteenth century was rarely that of master and slave with all rights and power concentrated on one side. Instead, when Indian and European colonizer met, they entered power relationships in which each side, with something to offer the other, maneuvered for the superior position. The Indian was the ultimate loser in most of these interchanges, but that outcome does not obscure the fact that Anglo-Americans confronted Indians as formidable adversaries rather than as chattels. Though they were exploited, excluded, and often decimated in their contacts with Europeans, Indians often maneuvered from a position of strength.

Africans in North America, by contrast, were rarely a part of any political or business equation. Mostly they had their labor to offer, and even that was not subject to contractual agreement. Captive Africans were not powerless in their dealings with White society, but they were deeply disadvantaged as compared with Indians. This uneven distribution of power in black-White relations could not help but affect attitudes. Unlike the Natives, the Africans were rarely able to win the respect of the European settlers because their situation was rarely one where respect was required or even possible. Trapped in a relationship where most of the power was on the other side, Africans, as they became more and more important to the colonizers' economy, sank lower and lower in the White settlers' estimation. Meanwhile the male Indian, though hated, was respected for his fighting ability, his dignity, his ability as interpreter, and even his oratorical skill, whereas the female Indian was important as consort and cultural intermediary. American colonists sometimes scoffed at the efforts of the Enlightenment philosophers to depict the American Native as a "noble savage," the archetype of natural beauty and virtue and uncorrupted by materialistic Western civilization; yet their image of the Indian came to have a positive side. The sociology of red-White and black-White relations had differed greatly over many generations. From these variations evolved

distinct White attitudes, in both cases adverse but in different ways.

A third paradox in the collision of cultures was that the group that was enslaved, degraded, and despised survived and flourished in North America, whereas the group that maintained more freedom, power, and European respect suffered a ghastly depopulation and cultural malaise. It does not minimize the pain, humiliation, and brutality of slavery to point out that Africans in North America were remarkably successful demographically, particularly in contrast to most other areas of the Americas. Although black mortality was substantially higher than White mortality, black fertility was close to the White norm, while slave mortality in eighteenth-century North America was far lower than anywhere else in the Americas. This does not necessarily reflect more humane treatment on North American plantations. More important was the more favorable disease and climatic environment of North America. The Caribbean islands were known as graveyards for White and black alike, and in the Latin American countries, tropical diseases swept away enslaved Africans like leaves in a windstorm.

A comparison of slave life in Virginia and in Jamaica illustrates the point. The slave populations of the two colonies were almost equal in 1775, with Virginians owning about 200,000 slaves and the Jamaicans about 193,000. But between 1700 and 1775, Virginia had imported not more than 80,000 slaves, whereas in Jamaica importations were more than four times as great. Life for enslaved Africans on eighteenth-century Southern plantations, however brutal, was healthier than in other parts of the Americas; and, because of a more favorable sex ratio than in other plantation areas, the chances of family life were greater.

By contrast, the Indian tribes east of the Appalachian Mountains, and in the Spanish Southwest and Florida as well, suffered disastrous population losses in the first two centuries of contact with Europeans. Although they were not struck down in the same catastrophic proportions as the indigenous people of Mexico and most parts of Latin America, their mortality rate and natural decline stood in stark contrast to the natural increase of enslaved Africans. In areas of White settlement along the coastal plain, only remnants of the Native population remained on the eve of the Revolution. Connecticut, for example, counted only 930 Indians in a census in 1762; Massachusetts found 1,681 in 1764; Virginia listed only 130 in 1774; and Rhode Island tabulated 1,482 in the same year.

Several factors explain the different demographic histories of Africans and Native Americans. First, Africans were far more resistant than Indians to European epidemic diseases and by the mid-eighteenth century were being immunized, like whites, against smallpox, the biggest killer of all. Hardly an Indian tribe in the eastern part of the continent escaped the dread disease. The European's invisible ally had decimated the eastern Massachusetts tribes even before the Puritans arrived and struck hard again in the early years of White settlement. The Iroquois were scourged many times in the seventeenth and eighteenth centuries. A raging smallpox epidemic in 1738 cost the Cherokees nearly half their population, and the Catawba population of North Carolina was similarly reduced by half during a single epidemic in 1759. Smallpox swept through the Creek towns in the last years of the seventeenth century and continued to diminish the number of Creeks in the following decades. Far less important as a killer were the wars that Natives fought with European settlers and with each other at the instigation of their trading partners. But these too took a toll on life that was not duplicated among enslaved Africans. Still another cause of Indian depopulation was alcohol. Though it killed slowly in contrast to smallpox and other epidemic diseases, it also counted victims by the thousands.

All the lethal factors that decimated Indian villages throughout eastern North America touched enslaved Africans only lightly. This difference was not coincidental. White colonists did not possess direct control over bacteriological and demographic factors, but they eagerly sought to increase the slave population while reducing the Indian population. To this end they instituted

policies that influenced, if they did not control, population curves. Blacks, for example, were inoculated against smallpox and given medical treatment in case of sickness. For a plantation owner to do this was only to preserve one's property, just as the owner would attempt to maintain the health of horses and other farm animals. If Indians, however, contracted an epidemic disease, the colonist could only give thanks that God had seen fit to diminish their numbers in order to make more room for "civilized" persons. European colonists consciously waged bacteriological warfare only occasionally by spreading smallpox through infected trade goods, but they were uninterested in arresting epidemic disease among the Indians in contrast to their slaves. With alcohol it was the same. The rum that masters rationed out to slaves at holiday time and sometimes at week's end as a reward for work accomplished was distributed by traders among Indian tribes in order to create not only dependency but also addiction. Rum was a liquid form of control used by White colonists in their dealings with both Africans and Indians. But it was intended to sustain life among black Americans while destroying life among Indians.

War, which was the third killer, was also controlled to some extent by White colonizers. Black rebellion, of course, was quelled as quickly as possible, for it directly threatened the labor system and social dominance by whites. But White colonists often artfully encouraged war with and among Indians. As soon as they knew they could outmatch local tribes, colonists in the seventeenth century found reasons for warring on coastal tribes. For example, Emanuel Downing, John Winthrop's brother-in-law, thought that a war with the Narragansett Indians would be of "very considerable" advantage to the colony because it would be a sin in God's eyes for the Puritans "having power in our hands, to suffer them to maintain the worship of the devil which their paw wawes often do." He then predicted the history of the next century by pointing out that "if upon a just war the Lord should deliver them [the Narragansetts] into our hands, we might easily have men, women, and children enough to exchange for Moors [Africans], which will be more gainful pillage for us than we conceive."[29]

Downing's willingness to please God while serving the colonists' material needs was a typical seventeenth-century justification of war against local tribes. In the eighteenth century, White leaders couched such arguments in secular language and then applied them to strong interior tribes rather than to small coastal societies. In this changed context, the policy shifted to creating animosities between Indian groups. "If we cannot destroy one nation of Indians by another," wrote South Carolina's governor in 1717, "our country must be lost."[30] This was not only the most effective deterrent to pan-Indian uprisings against the Europeans but also contributed to the general population decline of Indians.

Thus, although escaping slavery in most cases, Native Americans found themselves confronting a mushrooming European population that sought the land they occupied and found Indians useful mostly as auxiliaries in the destruction of other Indians. This situation had not been true for most of the colonial period, for so long as the European population was small, so long as it was divided among Spanish, French, and English contenders for continental supremacy, and so long as the fur and skin trade was a major factor in the colonial economy, Natives had been indispensable to the colonizers. By the mid-eighteenth century, however, the Indian trade had become a minor part of the colonial economy. Fishing and ship-building in New England, grain and livestock production in the Middle Colonies, and tobacco, rice, and indigo production on Southern plantations had become the mainstays of the economy. By 1763, the elimination of France as an imperial rival removed the need for Indian military support. Meanwhile, the tremendous growth of population in the two generations before the Revolution put relentless pressure on Native

American domains. Finally, with American victory in the war for independence, Indians east of the Mississippi River were nearly out of options in a chess game tilted ominously against them.

A final paradox was that Indian societies treasured many of the values that English settlers and other Europeans had braved the Atlantic to reestablish in the New World. Idealistic Europeans saw the "wilderness" of North America as a place where tired, corrupt, materialistic, self-seeking Europeans might begin a new life centered on the frayed but vital values of reciprocity, spirituality, and community. From John Winthrop to William Penn to John Woolman to Oglethorpe, the European notion of building a virtuous society in the Americas coursed through the dream-life of the newcomers. Yet as time passed and Europeans became more numerous, some philosophically inclined whites began to believe that the people in North America who best upheld these values were the people being driven from the land.

Even some hard-bitten, unsentimental colonists recognized that Native society, though by no means without its problems and its own disreputable characters, put White society to shame. The English commissioners investigating Bacon's Rebellion in 1676 wrote a scorching letter to the government of Virginia asking them to stop the land grabbing of settlers who already had title to all the land they could use but "still covet and seek to deprive them [the Indians] of more, out of mere itch of luxury rather than any real lack of it, which shames us and makes us become a reproach and a byword to those more moral heathens."[31] Three-quarters of a century later, Thomas Pownall, governor of Massachusetts, lambasted the colonists for violating their own principles, writing that "the frauds, abuses, and deceits that these poor people have been treated with and suffered under have had no bounds."[32] Edmond Atkin, an Indian trader of South

---

[29]Quoted in Almon E. Lauber, *Indian Slavery in Colonial Times within the Present Limits of the United States* (New York, 1913), p. 311.
[30]Quoted in Wallace, *South Carolina: A Short History, 1520–1948*, pp. 91–92.
[31]*Virginia Magazine of History and Biography*, 14 (1906–1907): 274.
[32]Quoted in Georgiana C. Nammack, *Fraud, Politics and the Dispossession of the Indians: The Iroquois Land Frontier in the Colonial Period* (Norman, OK, 1969), p. 31.

Carolina who knew Indians from years of intimate contact, wrote in 1755:

> No people in the world understand and pursue
> their true national interest, better than the
> Indians. . . . Yet in their public treaties no people
> on earth are more open, explicit, and direct.
> Nor are they excelled by any in the observance
> of them. . . . With respect to . . . all ruptures of
> consequence between the Indians and the white
> people, and the massacres that ensued . . .
> the latter were first the aggressors; the Indians
> being driven thereto under oppressions and
> abuses, and to vindicate their natural rights.[33]

Many European observers admired the Native traits of morality, generosity, bravery, and the spirit of mutual caring. Indians seemed to embody these Christian virtues almost without effort, whereas colonizing Europeans, attempting to build a society with similar characteristics, were pulled in the opposite direction by the natural abundance around them—toward individualism, disputatiousness, materialism, and the exploitation of fellow humans. Some colonial moralists also made the point that Indians hewed closer to the precepts of Christianity than most of the settlers. "As a nation," John Brickell wrote of the Delawares, "they may be considered fit examples for many of us Christians to follow. They certainly follow what they are taught to believe more closely, and I might say more honestly, in general, than we Christians do the divine precepts of our Redeemer."[34]

By embodying virtues around which Europeans had hoped to reorganize their society, the Indian was a disturbing reminder of the retrogression of White colonists in their New World setting. English, Germans, Scots-Irish, Swedes, Spanish, Dutch, French Huguenots, and others were proud of "taming the wilderness"; building thriving seaports, towns, churches, schools, and governments along a thousand miles of coastal plain from Maine to Florida. They had chosen productivity and acquisitiveness but pursued these at the cost of principles earlier regarded as central to the dreams for regenerated lives in the Americas.

In the complex interaction of Native Americans, Europeans, and Africans, the distribution of power between dominant and subordinate groups must always be kept in mind. It largely dictated the formal outcome of the cultural confrontation. Laws, institutions, boundary lines, trade agreements, settlement patterns, and much else emerged as they did because White colonizers were ultimately stronger than native occupiers of the land or Africans brought to the Americas in chains. All social, economic, and political relations had to be mediated, however, because European power was not absolute. Still, the colonizers' power grew in raw numbers and political cohesiveness in the eighteenth century.

Yet the pathways of power did not always dictate the history of cultural interchange. The culture of Africans and Indians—their agricultural techniques, modes of behavior, styles of speech and dress, food preferences, music, dance, and other aspects of daily existence—became commingled with European culture in ways not automatically determined by the status differences of the three groups. For example, "the status of the master's child vis-à-vis his slave governess," write Mintz and Price, "would surely affect his learning of a style of command in dealing with slaves. But his speech, his food preferences, his imagery, his earliest ideas about men and women, and a good deal more of what would become in time his characteristic quality as an individual would be learned from someone far below him in status, but otherwise very much in control of him."[35] Most of this Africanization of European culture occurred within the intimate personal encounters of slaves and masters and their families—relationships that

---

[33]Wilbur Jacobs, ed., *Indians of the Southern Colonial Frontier: The Edmund Atkin Report and Plan of 1755* (Columbia, SC, 1954), p. 38.
[34]"John Brickell's Captivity," *American Pioneer*, 1 (1842): 47–48, quoted in James Axtell, "The White Indians of Colonial America," *William and Mary Quarterly*, 32 (1975): 86.
[35]Sidney W. Mintz and Richard Price, *An Anthropological Approach to the Afro-American Past: A Caribbean Perspective* (Philadelphia: Institute for the Study of Human Issues, 1976), p. 16.

took place daily within the context of work, domestic service, and interracial sex.

The Indianization of European culture occurred within a different context. Expanding rapidly and pushing west across the Appalachian Mountains after their successful revolution against England, White Americans saw themselves as a new people—an amalgam of European settlers toughened in the North American "wilderness." But foreign travelers, while also picturing the colonists as a "new" people, discerned a people who bore the stamp of generations of contact with Native Americans. Even before the American Revolution, the Swedish visitor Peter Kalm believed that "the French, English, Germans, Dutch, and other Europeans who have lived for several years . . . near and among the Indians, grow so like them in their behavior and thought that they can only be distinguished by the difference of their color." Traveling through the United States at the end of the eighteenth century, the Frenchman Moreau de Saint-Mery believed "the American is the perfect mean between the European and Indian."[36]

"New World it is," we are reminded, "for those who became its peoples remade it, and in the process they remade themselves," whether red, White, or black.[37]

Summary

Native Americans, Africans, and Europeans interacted with one another not only in the larger context of Atlantic imperial rivalry but also at the most intimate person-to-person levels. For various reasons, Latin America was where the most extensive blending of gene pools in human history occurred. In North America, where Europeans, Indians, and Africans also lived together during about the same period, such intermixture was much more limited.

The complex mixing of red, White, and black people was not, in theory, acceptable to colonial America's leaders, who wanted to preserve the purity of White blood lines. Yet crossing racial boundaries could never be entirely stopped. Intermingling between red and White peoples varied by region: In New England and the mid-Atlantic colonies, it was limited; in the Chesapeake colonies, despite the famed marriage between Pocahontas and John Rolfe, intimate interaction was also spare; only in the Southeast—the Carolinas and Georgia— did the demographic picture even come close to that in the Spanish and French North American colonies, where White men, generally lacking White female consorts, eagerly sought native partners. In contrast, White-black intermingling in colonial America was more complicated because Europeans and Africans were always in close proximity, despite whether White women were plentiful or scarce. This proximity resulted in widespread sexual contact between White males and enslaved females, usually coerced, but rarely involved intermarriage. Finally, red-black mixing, though the least studied of race relations in early North America, has been found, through DNA analysis, to have been more common than originally believed. Even though White Europeans generally held sway over red and black populations in early North America, their culture nonetheless bore the indelible mark of the Africans and Native peoples with whom they lived.

Critical Thinking Questions

1. Latin America experienced an extensive blending of Europeans, Indians, and Africans during the colonial period, whereas North America is notable for the general absence of such intermixture during the same period. Why might this be the case?
2. In what English region was Indian-European sexual mingling most common, and why?

---

[36]Quoted in Calloway, *New Worlds for All . . .*, pp. 2, 6.
[37]Mintz and Price, *An Anthropological Approach to the Afro-American Past . . .*, p. 44.

3. What might explain the phenomenon of "White Indians," such as Eunice Williams?

4. In the eighteenth century, what were the striking differences in the nature and degree of sexual contact that characterized red-White versus black-White relationships?

5. Only in North Carolina, South Carolina, and Georgia were both Natives and Africans of sufficient number to worry Europeans about a joining of the two peoples in rebellion. Did such a joining ever take place? Why or why not?

Further Reading

Cynthia Cumfer, *Separate Peoples, One Land: The Minds of Cherokees, Blacks, and Whites on the Tennessee Frontier* (Chapel Hill: University of North Carolina Press, 2007).

Elizabeth A. Fenn, *Pox Americana: The Great Smallpox Epidemic of 1775–82* (New York: Hill and Wang, 2001).

Jack Forbes, *Black Africans and Native Americans: Color, Race, and Class in the Evolution of Red-Black People* (Oxford: Oxford University Press, 1988).

Andrew Frank, *Creeks and Southerners: Biculturalism on the Early American Frontier* (Lincoln: University of Nebraska Press, 2005).

Tim Hashaw, *Children of Perdition: Meleungeons and the Struggle of Mixed America* (Macon: Mercer University Press, 2006).

Martha Hodes, ed., *Sex, Love, Race: Crossing Boundaries in North American History* (New York: New York University Press, 1999).

Thomas N. Ingersoll, *To Intermix with Our White Brothers: Indian Mixed-Bloods in the United States from Earliest Times to the Indian Removals* (Albuquerque: University of New Mexico Press, 2005).

Ilona Katzew, *Casta Painting: Images of Race in Eighteenth-Century Mexico* (New Haven: Yale University Press, 2004).

Daniel Mandell, *Behind the Frontier: Indians in Eighteenth-Century Eastern New England* (Lincoln: University of Nebraska Press, 1996).

Gary B. Nash, *Forbidden Love: The Hidden History of Mixed-Race America* (Los Angeles: National Center for History in the Schools, 2010).

Theda Purdue, *"Mixed Blood" Indians: Racial Construction in the Early South* (Athens: University of Georgia Press, 2003).

INDEX